EQS

Structural Equations

Program Manual

Peter M. Bentler
University of California, Los Angeles

Multivariate Software, Inc.
15720 Ventura Blvd., Suite 306
Encino, CA 91436-2989
Voice: (818) 906-0740 Fax (818) 906-8205
E-mail: sales@mvsoft.com

The correct bibliographic citation for this document is as follows:

Bentler, P. M. (1995). **EQS Structural Equations Program Manual**.
Encino, CA: Multivariate Software, Inc.

ISBN 1-885898-02-9

Version 3.0, May, 1989
Appendices, 1992, 1995

Printed in the United States of America
Printing Nos. 1-6 by BMDP Statistical Software, Inc.
Seventh Printing, May 1995

TABLE OF CONTENTS

PREFACE

Linear structural equation modeling has become a useful methodology for specifying, estimating, and testing hypothesized interrelationships among a set of substantively meaningful variables. Although the basic ideas of structural modeling are really very simple, as will be seen in Chapter 2, an arcane language tends to be used in the field that unnecessarily hides first principles and suggests the need for complicated specialized procedures to handle anything other than standard applications. The prepublication version of EQS (which can be pronounced like the letter "X") verified that it was possible to take many complications out of structural modeling by providing a simple, consistent, yet technically advanced and accurate approach to structural modeling (Brecht, Tanaka, & Bentler, 1986). The first public release of EQS through BMDP provided an extensive set of error messages to help novice modelers run even their first jobs successfully (Bentler, 1985), while an intermediate update provided several new methods for model improvement (Bentler, 1986a). This manual for EQS, EQS/PC, and EQS/EM, Version 3.0, aims to continue the growth of simplicity and generality in structural modeling while providing the user with the most current statistical methods. Although there are many new features to the program, the most important of these for the nontechnical user are again in the interface, especially the on-line help facility, in the ability to run mainframe-size jobs on a PC with EQS/EM, and in the statistics, especially the ability to handle multiple population models and models with structured means, including missing data models, in a very straightforward way. The technical user will appreciate new features such as statistics for least-squares estimation, robust standard errors that remain correct under distributional misspecification, the Satorra-Bentler scaled χ^2 statistic, the Lagrange Multiplier (LM) and Wald tests for distribution-free estimation, the ability to vary estimation methods across groups in multisample covariance structure analysis, the LM test to evaluate cross-group equality constraints, effect decomposition and standard errors for indirect effects, the new comparative fit index and Akaike's information criterion, a facility for conducting simulations including the bootstrap and jackknife, improved precision of estimation, the ability to write statistics to external files for further analysis, greater print control, and related improvements.

The theoretical statistics, algorithmic experiments, and applied data analysis that form a conceptual and experimental basis for EQS were developed in part with support by research grants DA00017 and DA01070 from the U. S. Public Health Service. Invaluable programming contributions to this research were made by J.-C. Wu, and, to a lesser extent, by S.-T. Wu, while the interface between statistics and computations was substantially improved through the efforts of C.-P. Chou. The advice on statistical, computational, human engineering, and a variety of other issues provided by various colleagues and students, especially A. Satorra, A. Mooijaart, G. Rudinger, S.-Y. Lee, W.-Y. Poon, M. Berkane, M. D. Newcomb, J. Stein, M. Jamshidian, J. Weng, S. West, S. Guy, and R. Olmstead is gratefully acknowledged. The staff at BMDP Statistical Software, especially K. Roberts, L. Kern, J. Row, T. Bennett, A. Bryan, K. F. Gold, M. A. Hill, and W. Dixon, provided generous encouragement and cooperation. J. Speckart provided excellent support in manuscript production.

Criticisms and suggestions for improvement of the program and its documentation are actively solicited. Ideas on enhancements to EQS should be communicated directly to Peter M. Bentler.

Note Added in 7th Printing: Earlier versions of this **Manual** were published by BMDP Statistical Software. With minor exceptions to describe recent program features, the content of this version is identical to the earlier printings. However, the typestyle and page format have been modified slightly, so that each printed page varies slightly from the earlier version. The Table of Contents and Index have been modified accordingly. In addition, minor corrections were made as needed, Appendixes IV and V were added, and the figures were replaced with path diagrams created with Diagrammer, a feature of EQS for Windows (Bentler, P. M., & Wu, E. J. C. 1995. **EQS for Windows User's Guide**. Encino, CA: Multivariate Software, Inc.) and EQS for Macintosh (Bentler, P. M., & Wu, E. J. C. 1995. **EQS for Macintosh User's Guide**. Encino, CA: Multivariate Software, Inc.).

The assistance of Brian Lorber of Multivariate Software and Elizabeth Houck in creating this updated version of the **Manual** is greatly appreciated.

1. OVERVIEW

The computer program EQS was developed to meet two major needs in statistical software. At the theoretical level, applied multivariate analysis based on methods that are more general than those stemming from multinormal distribution theory have not been available to statisticians and researchers for routine use. At the applied level, powerful and general methods have also required extensive knowledge of matrix algebra and related topics that are often not routinely available among researchers. EQS is meant to make advanced multivariable analysis methods accessible to the applied statistician and practicing data analyst. This document provides a brief overview of the steps required to run EQS. It is hoped that the reader is already familiar with the basic concepts of structural modeling, but a brief introduction to the topic is provided in the next chapter. This section outlines some features of the program to allow the knowledgeable reader to skip to Chapter 3 on program input. It also gives some references to the statistical literature relevant to EQS that may interest the technical reader. The casual reader can skim the more technical material, which is not required as a background to Chapter 2.

BACKGROUND

EQS implements a general mathematical and statistical approach to the analysis of linear structural equation systems. The mathematical model (Bentler & Weeks, 1979, 1980, 1982, 1985; Bentler, 1983a,b) subsumes a variety of covariance and mean structure models, including multiple regression, path analysis, simultaneous equations, first- and higher-order confirmatory factor analysis, as well as regression and structural relations among latent variables. The model can handle all the linear data structures of the Jöreskog-Keesling-Wiley (Jöreskog, 1973, 1977; Jöreskog & Sörbom, 1988; Wiley, 1973) and related models (e.g., Bentler, 1976; Kiiveri, 1987; McDonald, 1980; McArdle & McDonald, 1984), but the model has a particular simplicity and coherence that makes it easy to learn and apply to new modeling situations. An illustration of the generality of the Bentler-Weeks model and its implementation in EQS can be found in the application to specialized models that, at one time, were not thought to be amenable to linear structural analysis, such as generalized multimode latent variable models (Bentler, Poon, & Lee, 1988). The statistical theory (Browne, 1982, 1984; Chamberlain, 1982; Shapiro, 1983, 1986; Bentler, 1983a,b; Bentler & Dijkstra, 1985; Satorra, 1989) allows for the estimation of parameters and testing of models using traditional multivariate normal theory, but also enables the use of the more general elliptical and arbitrary distribution theories, based on a unified generalized least squares (GLS) or minimum chi-square (Berkson, 1980) approach. This unified approach loses nothing in generality (Shapiro, 1985a), while also providing for computation of more traditional statistics such as maximum likelihood (ML) based on the "normal theory" assumption that variables are multivariate normally distributed. In practice, normality is often an unreasonable assumption (Micceri, 1989). Elliptical theory (Browne, 1982, 1984; Bentler, 1983a; Bentler & Berkane, 1985; Berkane & Bentler, 1987a; Shapiro & Browne, 1987) is meant to loosen the strict normality requirement to permit a wider range of symmetrically distributed data to be analyzed. Arbitrary distribution theory permits modeling of data that has any distributional form.

The statistical theory is closely related to computational theory. Estimation can be classified by type of variable distribution assumed and weight matrix used during the computations. The function minimized is given by

$$Q = (s - \sigma(\theta))'W(s - \sigma(\theta)), \tag{1.1}$$

where s is the vector of data to be modeled — the variances and covariances of the observed variables, and possibly the means — and σ is a model for the data. The model vector σ is a function of more basic parameters θ that are to be estimated so as to minimize Q. The parameter vector θ is given by the elements of the parameter matrices of the Bentler-Weeks model. These are easily specified in EQS without the use of vectors or matrices, as will be seen in Chapter 2. The weight matrix W can be specialized in several ways to yield a number of different estimators that depend on the distribution assumed (normal, elliptical, arbitrary) and the computations invoked ($W = I$, W optimal and fixed, W optimal and reweighted). The following table of methods is thus generated:

Weight Matrix	Distribution Theory		
	Normal	**Elliptical**	**Arbitrary**
Identity	LS	ELS	ALS
Fixed	GLS	EGLS	AGLS
Reweighted	RLS=ML	ERLS	ARLS

In this table LS means least squares, and the qualifiers "E" (elliptical) and "A" (arbitrary) are used to designate the relevant nonnormal distributions. (Normal theory needs no qualifier.) In estimation with a fixed weight matrix, the matrix is chosen to be calculable once from the input data, subject to belonging to the class of optimal weights that yield minimum chi-square or best GLS estimates. In estimation with a reweighted (R) matrix, the weight matrix not only belongs to the class of optimal matrices, but also is updated iteratively. That is, W is considered to be expressible in terms of the parameters of the model $W = W(\theta)$, and, as the parameter estimates are improved, so is W. Ordinary normal theory RLS yields maximum likelihood estimates. The current version of the computer program does not yield ALS and ARLS estimates.

The elliptical and arbitrary distribution GLS and RLS estimators are available in two variants: fully iterated and linearized. The fully iterated estimators are based on optimizing Q iteratively until a convergence criterion is met. The linearized ("L") variants take one of the other iterated solutions as a starting point, e.g., normal theory GLS, and, based on a linearization of the structural model $\sigma(\theta)$, move one iterative step towards the fully iterated estimator. The resulting two-stage linearized estimator, e.g., LEGLS or LAGLS, has the same large sample statistical properties as the fully iterated estimator, but costs much less in computer time (Bentler & Dijkstra, 1985). In general, E and A estimators are obtained by default as linearized estimators in EQS. This default can be overridden. The user also can control the number of iterations and the convergence criterion. Estimation with fully iterated AGLS will tend to be most computer-intensive, and, because of the heavy computer demands, probably becomes impractical as the number of variables exceeds 20 or so.

Models with intercepts, called mean and covariance structure models, are in principle estimable by any of the methods in the above table. In Version 3.0 of EQS, however, only the ML method is available for such models. As will be seen in Chapter 8, specification of mean structures involves the use of a constant (called V999 in EQS) and is thus somewhat more involved than the basic procedures reviewed in Chapter 2. Multisample covariance structures, useful in evaluating the equivalence of models for several groups, are set up in EQS in the same simple way as models for a single group, though cross-group constraints typically are also specified. See Chapter 7. All of the estimation methods available for one group are available for multiple group models. In the current version of EQS, multisample analysis involving intercepts is restricted to ML estimation. See Chapter 9.

The statistical theory that forms the basis of the normal, elliptical, and arbitrary distribution estimators in EQS can be found in numerous sources, including the following. Jöreskog (1977), Browne (1974), Lee and Bentler (1980), and Lee and Poon (1985) describe multivariate normal theory estimation in structural models, for which Lee and Jennrich (1979) show that RLS estimation leads to ML estimators. Estimation with mean structures is given in Sörbom (1974, 1978, 1982) and Schoenberg (1982). Elliptical distribution theory is described in such sources as Cambanis, Huang, and Simons (1981), Muirhead (1982), Tyler (1983), Waternaux (1984), and Berkane and Bentler (1986, 1987a,b), and is applied to structural models by Browne (1982, 1984), Bentler (1983a), Bentler and Dijkstra (1985), and Shapiro and Browne (1987). Bentler and Dijkstra give the distribution of elliptical estimators under distributional misspecification. Elliptical theory allows symmetrically distributed variables to have either heavier or lighter tails than their normal theory counterparts, but the kurtoses of the variables are assumed to be equal. Normal distributions are obtained under the special case that all variables' kurtoses are not only equal, but also exactly zero. When the model is invariant under a constant scale factor, the LERLS estimator based on an initial ML estimator and the ERLS estimator yield Browne's elliptical estimator. No restrictions on skewness or kurtosis are assumed with arbitrarily distributed variables. Arbitrary distribution estimation theory is described in such sources as Browne (1982, 1984), Chamberlain (1982), Shapiro (1983, 1986), Bentler (1983a), Bentler and Dijkstra (1985), Dijkstra (1981), Van Praag, Dijkstra, and Van Velzen (1985), Van Praag, De Leeuw, and Kloek (1986), Wesselman (1987), Satorra (1989), and also generically by Berkson (1980). The fully iterated AGLS estimator is Browne's asymptotically distribution-free (ADF) estimator and Chamberlain's optimal minimum distance estimator. ARLS estimators are based on expressions for $W(\theta)$ (see Bentler, 1983a; Mooijaart & Bentler, 1985; Browne, 1987; Browne & Shapiro, 1988) which are not yet implemented in EQS. A partial implementation was done by Tanaka (1984). The theory of estimation via linearization is discussed by Ferguson (1958), Lehmann (1983), Pfanzagl (1982), and Bentler and Dijkstra (1985), and is applied to structural models by De Leeuw (1983) and Bentler (1983a,b). The statistical theory for multisample covariance structure analysis is given in Jöreskog (1971), Lee and Tsui (1982), and, more generally for arbitrarily distributed variables, by Bentler, Lee, and Weng (1987). Although a specialized statistical theory exists to cover problems stemming from missing data (Van Praag, Dijkstra, & Van Velzen, 1985; Lee, 1986), multisample analysis based on patterns of missing data (Allison, 1987; Muthén, Kaplan, & Hollis, 1987; Werts, Rock, & Grandy, 1979) is a practical method in many applications.

A major attempt has been made in EQS to provide the most up-to-date methods for the analysis of mean and covariance structures. As a result, statistics have been provided for the first time that have been available theoretically but were not included in public structural modeling programs, and in some cases these statistics were extended to new situations.

Examples include: χ^2 statistics for LS (Browne, 1982, 1984) extended to cover normally distributed (Satorra & Bentler, 1988, 1994) and elliptically distributed variables; robust standard errors for normal and elliptical theory methods that hold under violation of the distributional assumption (Bentler & Dijkstra, 1985); Lagrange Multiplier (LM) χ^2 tests (Lee & Bentler, 1980) for model modification, extended to distribution-free and linearized estimation (Bentler & Dijkstra, 1985), to cross-group equality constraints, to conditional tests, and to stepwise and a priori hierarchical implementation (Bentler & Chou, 1986; Bentler, 1986a; Satorra, 1989); calculation of the parameter change expected when a fixed parameter is suggested to be free by the LM test (Bentler & Chou, 1986; Bentler, 1986a; Saris, Satorra, & Sörbom, 1987; Satorra, 1989); Wald test for the necessity of free parameters (Lee, 1985a) extended to linearized estimation (Bentler & Dijkstra, 1985), various distributions, and stepwise and a priori hierarchical implementation (Bentler & Chou, 1986; Bentler, 1986a); standard errors for indirect effects (Sobel, 1982, 1986; Bollen, 1987a; Fox, 1985; Wolfle & Ethington, 1985) extended to nonnormal variables, linearized estimation and constrained estimation; distribution-free multiple group covariance structure analysis (Bentler, Lee, & Weng, 1987) specialized to permit varying distributions in different groups; Akaike's information criterion (Akaike, 1987) and a consistent variant (Bozdogan, 1987) extended to cover varying distributions and types of estimation; and extension of various fit indexes (Bentler & Bonett, 1980; Bentler, 1988a) to multiple group models, as well as extension of Bentler's (1983a) general fit index, popularized by Tanaka and Huba (1985) and now also used by Jöreskog and Sörbom (1988), to the multiple group case. The Satorra-Bentler (1988, 1994) scaled χ^2 statistic, designed to improve the distribution of standard test statistics under violation of assumptions, also has been provided even though the documents describing its development had an uncertain publication status at the time this manual was written. Inadequate knowledge about the empirical performance of some of the newer statistics, it would seem, is best remedied by making these statistics easily accessible, and hence amenable to further study. The simulation feature of EQS can be used to study the behavior of the statistics under various conditions.

Although EQS makes available a wide variety of statistics, including statistics too new to have been studied empirically, the correct application of these statistics must of necessity lie with the informed community of structural modeling researchers (Muthén, 1987). There are many pitfalls in applications, and only partial solutions (Bentler & Chou, 1987). As knowledge grows, more refined decisions about the relevance of these statistics to varying data situations are possible. For example, an energetic line of research has made it apparent that some statistics based on normal theory ML and GLS can be robust to violation of the normality assumption (Amemiya, 1985a; Amemiya & Anderson, 1985; Amemiya, Fuller, & Pantula, 1987; Anderson, 1986, 1990; Anderson & Amemiya, 1988; Browne, 1987; Browne & Shapiro, 1988; Mooijaart & Bentler, 1987, 1989; Satorra & Bentler, 1986; Shapiro, 1987) as indeed can be normal theory statistics based on LS (Satorra & Bentler, 1990). Such robustness has also been observed empirically (Harlow, 1985). While a few methods have been proposed to evaluate the plausibility of some possible conditions for robustness (e.g., Bentler, Chou, & Lee, 1987; Browne, 1987; Browne & Shapiro, 1988; Mooijaart & Bentler, 1989; Satorra & Bentler, 1986, 1990), not enough is known as yet regarding the practical relevance of these results to data analysis to suggest any routine computer evaluation in EQS. A test for the appropriateness of a normal distribution assumption is provided in EQS via Mardia's (1970) coefficient of multivariate kurtosis. A transformation of this coefficient (Browne, 1982, 1984; Bentler & Berkane, 1985, 1986; Berkane & Bentler, 1987a; Shapiro & Browne, 1987) provides the default value used by EQS to estimate the elliptical kurtosis parameter, although several other coefficients are computed and can be used instead. Elliptical theory appears to be quite unrobust as currently implemented (Harlow, 1985; Satorra & Bentler, 1988, 1994), even though it is a generalization of normal theory. Thus although it is available in EQS, it should not be misused, e.g., when skewness of variables or heterogeneous kurtoses (Berkane & Bentler, 1987b) makes the theory implausible. Similarly, though AGLS estimation and its variants were introduced to yield more optimal statistical properties (e.g., Browne, 1982, 1984; Chamberlain, 1982; Bentler, 1983a,b), it is not yet certain to what extent these properties are realized in smaller samples and large models (Harlow, 1985; Tanaka & Bentler, 1985; Muthén & Kaplan, 1985, 1992). Certainly the availability of any particular method in EQS is not intended to be a blanket endorsement of use. Research is still needed to determine conditions under which each of these methods, and newer methods such as the Satorra-Bentler (1988, 1994) scaled χ^2 statistic, out-perform each other in practice, i.e., under various degrees of violations of several assumptions. A new simulation section has been provided in EQS to make it easier to study the empirical behavior of modeling statistics under various conditions, such as variation in sample size or violation of distributional assumptions. Bootstrap and jackknife sampling methods have also been provided (see e.g., Boomsma, 1986).

The current release of EQS contains no feature to deal specifically with dependent categorical variables.[1] When the number of categories in a variable is large, this omission probably does not matter much (Atkinson, 1988; Babakus, Ferguson, & Jöreskog, 1987; Huba & Harlow, 1987; Johnson & Creech, 1983; Muthén & Kaplan, 1985). Where the number of categories in dependent variables is small, say $2-3$, and the variables are not symmetrically distributed, the linear model used in EQS is probably not optimal (see e.g., Olsson, 1979). Some latent variable methods exist for dealing with categorical data (Bartholomew, 1987; Bock, Gibbons, & Muraki, 1988; Bye, Gallicchio, & Dykacz, 1985; De Leeuw, 1983; Küsters, 1987; McFadden, 1984; Mislevy, 1986; Muthén, 1984; Olsson, Drasgow, & Dorans, 1982; Poon & Lee, 1987) and new ones are being developed (Lee, Poon, & Bentler, 1989, 1990a,b; Poon, Lee, Bentler, & Afifi, 1989). However, whether the violation of the assumption, typically made with categorical variable methods, of normality of the unmeasured continuous variables underlying the categorical variables, yields greater or lesser distortion than using AGLS with an inappropriate linear model has not been established. Although there is some evidence that distributional assumptions on latent variables may not matter much in simple models (Bartholomew, 1988), arguing for the use of categorical variable methodology, on the other hand there are some indications that the wrong linear model can lead to better results than the theoretically more correct categorical variable approach (Collins, Cliff, McCormick, & Zatkin, 1986). Methods for testing basic assumptions have only recently been developed (e.g., Muthén & Hofacker, 1988; Bentler, Poon, & Lee, 1989). Methods based on minimal assumptions are too new to have had any impact on practice (Lauritzen & Wermuth, 1989).

The statistical theory underlying EQS is based on the assumption that observations (cases, subjects) are independent. This is a standard assumption of multivariate analysis, but it may be false in some situations (e.g., time series). An appropriate theory to allow some types of dependence (e.g., Weng & Bentler, 1987) has not been implemented. Similarly, the statistical theory is asymptotic. Thus, in principle, relatively large sample sizes should be used to estimate and test models. This is also true in application, since computational problems during optimization are an inverse function of sample size. Empirical research regarding the relevance of asymptotic theory to practical data analysis to yield recommendations about sample sizes that might be appropriate under various circumstances is only now beginning to

---

[1] This feature was added since the original printing of this **Manual**. See Appendix IV.

appear (e.g., Anderson & Gerbing, 1984; Balderjahn, 1985; Bearden, Sharma, & Teel, 1982; Boomsma, 1983; Gallini & Mandeville, 1984; Geweke & Singleton, 1980; Harlow, 1985; Huba & Bentler, 1983; Muthén & Kaplan, 1985, 1992; Tanaka, 1984, 1987). An over-simplified guideline regarding the trustworthiness of solutions and parameter estimates might be the following. The ratio of sample size to number of free parameters to be estimated may be able to go as low as 5:1 under normal and elliptical theory. Although there is little experience on which to base a recommendation, a ratio of at least 10:1 may be more appropriate for arbitrary distributions. These ratios need to be larger to obtain trustworthy z-tests on the significance of parameters, and still larger to yield correct model evaluation chi-square probabilities.

Version 3.0 of EQS is limited to mean and covariance structure models. The higher-order moment structure modeling and estimation machinery described by Bentler (1983a) and others (Mooijaart, 1985; Van Montfort, 1989) has not yet been implemented. Although many apparently nonlinear models can be linearized (see e.g., Bentler, Poon, & Lee, 1988) and thus estimated and tested by EQS, nonlinear latent variable models (Bentler 1983a; Etezadi-Amoli & McDonald, 1983; Kenny & Judd, 1984; Mooijaart & Bentler, 1986) typically can make use of sample moments higher than only means and covariances, and therefore cannot be handled optimally. For numerical reasons, the EQS user is urged to scale variables by known constants so that variables' variances are approximately equal, but data-dependent scaling to yield correlational data is theoretically inappropriate here as it is in related computer programs when χ^2 tests and standard errors are to be relied upon. Appropriate modifications to handle standardized variables (Browne, 1982; Bentler & Lee, 1983; Cudeck, 1989; Lee, 1985b) have not yet been made in the program.

The parametric constraints available in EQS are quite general in that individual parameters may be fixed to specific numerical values, may be freely estimated, may be constrained equal to other free parameters, may be constrained with other parameters to satisfy a general linear equality, or may be constrained to lie between an upper and/or lower bound. Because of the frequent occurence of improper solutions and the uninterpretability of some associated parameters such as negative variance estimates (Boomsma, 1985; Dillon, Kumar, & Mulani, 1987; Gerbing & Anderson, 1987; Rindskopf, 1983, 1984a,b; Sato, 1987), the program automatically constrains variance estimates to be nonnegative, and correlations between variables having fixed variances as lying between +1 and − 1. These defaults can be user-modified. Possible corrections to test statistics due to population boundary values of parameters (Shapiro, 1985b) are not incorporated in the program. Nonlinear restrictions such as are relevant to correlation structure and related models are not yet available. However, some can be handled in EQS by reparameterization (Wong & Long, 1987).

EQS makes use of a simple and straightforward specification language to describe the model to be analyzed, and provides extensive syntax error checking in order to make the program as easy and error-free to use as possible. However, the program has no data-cleaning features such as procedures for handling missing data. The user must rely on other computer programs to be sure that complete and adequate raw or covariance input data are available for analysis. In view of the likely nonrobustness of structural modeling methods to outliers in the data (see, e.g., Berkane & Bentler, 1988; Bollen, 1987b; Comrey, 1985; Devlin, Gnanadesikan, & Kettenring, 1981; Gallini & Casteel, 1987; Rasmussen, 1988), a procedure is included to locate outliers by marking those cases that contribute maximally to Mardia's (1970) coefficient of multivariate kurtosis. It is also possible to specify that EQS should delete cases during computations if, for example, they are found to be outliers.

MODEL SPECIFICATION WITH EQS

Several major sections of input information are used in EQS, most of which are not required in simple problems. A brief description of each section is given below. More detailed information follows in Chapter 3 of this manual. Information on computer-specific control statements that might be needed in a mainframe environment (e.g., the JCL set-up to increase region or CPU time) are not described in this manual and must be obtained from the user's computer center.

Each section is begun by a slash and a keyword, capitalized below. Those sections which are not always needed are noted as optional.

/TITLE (Optional)

EQS permits the user to supply as much title information as desired to help identify the program output. All title information is reprinted once in the output. Subsequent output pages print only the first line.

/SPECIFICATIONS

This section describes the problem to be analyzed, including the number of cases (observations), the number of variables and type of input matrix, the method(s) of estimation desired, type of matrix to be analyzed, input datafile name, cases to be deleted, etc.

/LABELS (Optional)

Labels may be provided for measured latent variables and latent factors.

/EQUATIONS

This section describes the equations involved in the model under consideration. There is one equation for each dependent variable in the system. A dependent variable is one that is a structured regression function of other variables; it is recognized in a path diagram by having one or more arrows aiming at it. The /EQUATIONS section also provides information for the automatic selection of variables from the input matrix.

/VARIANCES

Every independent variable in the model must have a variance, which is specified in this section. The fixed constant V999 used in structured means models does not have a variance.

/COVARIANCES (Optional)

If independent variables are correlated, their covariances are specified in this section. In addition to the usual covariances, such as those between the residuals of observed variables or between independent latent variables, the covariances between any pair of independent variables may be estimated, subject only to the requirement that the model be identified.

/CONSTRAINTS (Optional)

Parameters that are constrained to be equal are indicated in this section. In addition, any parameter may be related to other parameters by a particular linear constraint. Cross-groups constraints in multisample analysis are specified here.

/INEQUALITIES (Optional)

An upper and/or lower bound for any free parameter to be estimated can be specified in this section.

/MATRIX (Optional)

The /MATRIX section signals the beginning of the input covariance or correlation matrix. When raw data is used, it will be read from another file.

/STANDARD DEVIATIONS (Optional)

If the input provided in /MATRIX is a correlation matrix, providing standard deviations will cue the program to transform the correlation matrix into a covariance matrix prior to estimation and testing.

/MEANS (Optional)

Models with intercepts structure the means of latent and observed variables. This section provides the sample means of the observed variables.

/TECHNICAL (Optional)

This section is used to override the program's default values for various technical constants, e.g., the convergence criterion and number of iterations. It also enables the use of arbitrary start values to override the program's defaults.

/DIAGRAM (Optional)[2]

The /DIAGRAM section is used to specify variables to be included in a path diagram, which is generated automatically from the user's model specification provided in previous input statements. (Not available in multisample analysis.)

/PRINT (Optional)

The results of an effect decomposition, the model-reproduced covariance and correlation matrices, including model-based estimates of means in structured means models, and the

---

[2] This feature has been completely overtaken with **Diagrammer**, as implemented in **EQS for Windows** and **EQS for Macintosh**.

correlations among parameter estimates are not printed unless the user specifies, in this section, that this output is desired.

/LMTEST (Optional)

Inadequacies in models can be evaluated by the /LMTEST. It can suggest fixed parameters to free (not available in multisample analysis), and constraints to release.

/WTEST (Optional)

Unnecessary free parameters can be evaluated by the /WTEST. It can suggest free parameters to fix to zero without much degradation in fit. (Not available for multisample analysis.)

/SIMULATION (Optional)

The empirical behavior of statistics produced by EQS can be determined by repeated sampling from a population or by bootstrapping or jackknifing. The design of such a study is specified in this section. (Not available for multisample analysis.)

/OUTPUT (Optional)

Technical output from EQS can be saved in a compact form and with greater precision, as specified in this section. This would usually be done in a simulation study. (Not available for multisample analysis.)

/END

This keyword marks the termination of the program input.

The output from EQS includes an echo of the input, giving the user a record of the job submitted. If the input contains information that the program finds problematic, error messages will be printed. If the errors appear to be trivial, the program will continue into the computational section, but if the errors are major the program will not proceed. The user will then have to correct such errors and resubmit the job.

Details on input and output are given in Chapters 3 and 4. Some examples are given in Chapter 5.

This introduction to EQS will have made it apparent that EQS is a powerful program that performs many types of structural modeling analyses. It will become clear in the next chapter that EQS is also extremely easy to use. Although there is great ease and flexibility in the program, the reader should be reminded that some critics of structural modeling have serious reservations about the appropriate role of structural modeling in data analysis (e.g., Cliff, 1983; Freedman, 1987), and that alternative approaches to causal inference in statistics have been proposed (e.g., Holland, 1986, 1988). For a more positive point of view about linear structural modeling, see, for example, Bentler (1987a, 1988b), Glymour, Scheines, Spirtes, and Kelly (1987), and Mulaik (1987). Users of EQS would be well-advised to become acquainted with the critical literature, to assure themselves that the methodology is appropriate for their particular application. Structural modeling has become an important tool in applied multivariate analysis for theory testing with nonexperimental data (Bentler, 1986b), but, like any tool, it must be used appropriately. An interesting discussion of the historical development and role of structural modeling with measured variables in economics is given by Epstein (1987).

Appropriate use of the statistical techniques made available in EQS does not necessarily imply that appropriate inferences will be drawn from the results of an analysis. Such inferences typically require additional assumptions about the context of a study and its data, especially when "causal" interpretations of the results are desired. The meaning and role of the philosophical concept of "causality" as applied to structural modeling is not discussed in this manual, although it is recognized that analyses are often undertaken in order to evaluate a causal hypothesis regarding the influences that may exist among the variables in a system. However admirable it may be to model a causal process, such a motivation does not provide adequate justification for uncritical use of causal language in describing some particular result or application of a linear statistical model. Mulaik (1987), Marini and Singer (1988), and other sources should be consulted for a discussion of this important concept. See also Leamer (1988).

ILLUSTRATIVE APPLICATIONS

Although this manual is self-contained, it cannot have enough illustrations to make structural modeling come alive in each of the research areas to which EQS might be applied. Readers are urged to study some applications of structural modeling in their own research area. Some illustrative recent applications of structural modeling to varied substantive topics (skewed, no doubt, by the author's personal research interests) that might be consulted are the following: *accident research* (Hansen, 1989); *alcohol effects* (Cooper, Russell, & George, 1988; Jaccard & Turrisi, 1987); *attitudes* (Bagozzi & Burnkrant, 1985; Bentler & Speckart, 1981; Dillon & Kumar, 1985; Fredricks & Dossett, 1983; Homer & Kahle, 1988; Reddy & LaBarbera, 1985; Speckart & Bentler, 1982); *attitudes toward guest workers* (Faulbaum, 1987; Jagodzinski & Kühnel, 1987; Saris & Van den Putte, 1988); *attribution theory* (Russell, McAuley, & Tarico, 1987); *behavior genetics* (Boomsma & Molenaar, 1986; McArdle, 1986; Neale & Stevenson, 1989; Rice, Fulker, & DeFries, 1986); *career choice and counseling* (Fassinger, 1985, 1987); *communication* (Finke & Monge, 1985); *consumer behavior* (Punj & Staelin, 1983); *crime and delinquency* (Kaplan, Johnson, & Bailey, 1987; McCarthy & Hoge, 1984; Piliavin, Thornton, Gartner & Matsueda, 1986; Silverman & Kennedy, 1985; Smith & Patterson, 1984); *decision making* (Wood & Bandura, 1989); *depression* (Cochran & Hammen, 1985; Harlow, Newcomb, & Bentler, 1986; Tanaka & Huba, 1987); *discrimination in salaries* (McFatter, 1987); *drug use* (Bentler, 1987b; Hays, Widaman, DiMatteo, & Stacy, 1987; Kaplan, Johnson, & Bailey, 1988; Martin & Robbins, 1985; Newcomb, 1988; Newcomb & Bentler, 1988; Stein, Newcomb, & Bentler, 1988; Windle, Barnes, & Welte, 1989); *education* (Ecob, 1987; Ethington & Wolfle, 1986; Miller, Kohn, & Schooler, 1985; Parkerson, Lomax, Schiller, & Walberg, 1984); *EEG* (Ten Houten, Walter, Hoppe, & Bogen, 1987); *evaluation and treatment research* (Bentler & Woodward, 1978; Judd & Kenny, 1981; Patterson & Chamberlain, 1988; Prochaska, Velicer, DiClemente, & Fava, 1988); *family processes* (Forgatch, Patterson, & Skinner, 1988; Patterson & Bank, 1989); *health beliefs* (Chen & Land, 1986; Newcomb & Bentler, 1987); *infant development* (Crano & Mendoza, 1987); *intelligence* (Bynner & Romney, 1986; O'Grady, 1989); *job characteristics and satisfaction* (Hogan & Martell, 1987; James & Tetrick, 1986; Williams & Hazer, 1986); *job involvement* (Lorence & Mortimer, 1985); *learning* (Hill, 1987); management science (Fritz, 1986); *marketing* (Anderson, 1985; Bagozzi, 1980); *mood states* (Herzog & Nesselroade, 1987); *mouse physiology* (Stanislaw & Brain, 1983); *neurotic syndromes* (Parkes, 1987);

nuclear anxiety (Newcomb, 1986, 1988); *organisational analysis* (Laumann, Knoke, & Kim, 1985); *personality* (Buhrmester, Furman, Wittenberg, & Reis, 1988; Marsh & Richards, 1988; Zautra, Guarnaccia, & Reich, 1988); *political attitudes* (Sidanius, 1988); *quality of life* (Abbey & Andrews, 1985; Allen, Bentler, & Gutek, 1985); *schizophrenia* (Tanaka & Bentler, 1983); *second language proficiency* (Clément & Kruidenier, 1985; Nelson, Lomax, & Perlman, 1984); *self-concept* (Byrne, 1988; Hoelter, 1983; Marsh & Hocevar, 1985); *sex-role attitudes* (Bielby & Bielby, 1984; Thornton, Alwin, & Camburn, 1983); *sexual behavior* (Newcomb & Bentler, 1983; Newcomb, Huba, & Bentler, 1986); *social support* (Catrona & Russell, 1987; Newcomb & Bentler, 1986; Newcomb & Chou, 1989); *socialization and achievement* (Anderson, 1987); *spatial vision* (Sekuler, Wilson, & Owsley, 1984); and *status attainment* (Hauser & Mossell, 1985; Hauser, Tsai, & Sewell, 1983). These publications are illustrative, rather than exhaustive, and no claim is made that the most significant works in each field have been provided.

FURTHER READINGS[3]

This manual provides a self-contained presentation of the basics of structural modeling and enough advanced topics to enable the reader to understand and use EQS in a meaningful fashion. It must be recognized, however, that this manual is not a self-contained text, since a course in structural equation modeling would need to cover in greater detail such topics as path analysis, confirmatory factor analysis, simultaneous equations, and various aspects of multivariate analysis. The concept of latent variable, and the related idea of errors of measurement, is a crucial aspect of structural modeling. Various levels of introductory and survey materials on latent variable models is given in the following sources, covering several disciplines.

Articles that provide a good survey of various aspects of structural modeling, from basic to advanced topics, include: Aigner, Hsiao, Kapteyn, and Wansbeek (1984), Anderson and Gerbing (1988), Bagozzi and Yi (1988), Bartholomew (1984), Bentler (1980, 1982, 1983b, 1986c, 1988c), Bentler and Bonett (1980), Bentler and Newcomb (1986), Bentler and Weeks (1982), Biddle and Marlin (1987), Bielby and Hauser (1977), Browne (1982), Carmines (1986), Cole (1987), Dijkstra (1983), Fassinger (1987), Finke and Monge (1986), Fornell (1983), Freedman (1987), Huba and Harlow (1987), Hughes, Price, and Marrs (1986), Irzik and Meyer (1987), Jackson and Chan (1980), Jöreskog (1969, 1978), Judd, Jessor, and Donovan (1986), Lomax (1983), Martin (1987), McGaw, Sörbom, and Cumming (1986), Reichardt and Gollob (1986), Rindskopf (1984c), and Tanaka, Panter, Winborne and Huba (1990).

Texts and monographs that are wholly or partially devoted to topics on latent variables and structural modeling include: Aigner and Goldberger (1977), Asher (1983), Bagozzi (1980), Berry (1984), Blalock (1985a, 1985b), Bohrnstedt and Borgatta (1981), Bollen (1989a), Cohen and Cohen (1983), Cuttance and Ecob (1987), Dillon and Goldstein (1984), Duncan (1975), Dwyer (1983), Everitt (1984), Fornell (1982), Fuller (1987), Goldberger and Duncan (1973), Gorsuch (1983), Heise (1975), Hayduk (1987), Jaech (1985), James, Mulaik, and Brett (1982), Jöreskog and Sörbom (1988), Jöreskog and Wold (1982), Kenny (1979), Kessler and

---

[3] Since this **Manual** was written, many excellent additional texts have been written. Two books that focus specifically on EQS are: Byrne, B. M. (1994). **Structural Equation Modeling with EQS and EQS/Windows.** Thousand Oaks, CA: Sage, and Dunn, G., Everitt, B., & Pickles, A. (1993). **Modelling Covariances and Latent Variables using EQS.** London: Chapman & Hall.

Greenberg (1981), Li (1975), Loehlin (1987), Long (1983a, 1983b), Lunneborg and Abbott (1983), McDonald (1985), Möbus and Schneider (1986), Pedhazur (1982), Pfeifer and Schmidt (1987), Plewis (1985), Saris and Stronkhurst (1984), and Sullivan and Feldman (1979). In addition, of course, the many fine texts in multivariate analysis, econometrics, sociometrics, and psychometrics are relevant to the mathematical models and statistical theory used in structural modeling (e.g., Gallant, 1987).

There are many areas of active research on methodological topics related to structural modeling. In addition to work cited above, e.g., on the robustness of normal theory statistics to violation of assumptions, there is work on such topics as: *factor analysis* (Bynner, 1988; Finke & Monge, 1986; Hattie & Fraser, 1988; Kano, 1989, 1990; Kano & Shapiro, 1987); *dynamic factor analysis* (Molenaar, 1985); *second-order factor analysis* (Rindskopf & Rose, 1988; Wothke & Browne, 1990); *unidimensional measurement* (Anderson, Gerbing, & Hunter, 1987; Kumar & Dillon, 1987); *measurement error models* (Amemiya, 1985b; Fuller, 1987; Heise, 1986; Raajmakers & Pieters, 1987); *multitrait-multimethod models and method variance* (Bank, Dishion, Skinner, & Patterson, 1990; Cudeck, 1988; Levin, 1988; Schmitt & Stults, 1986; Widaman, 1985); *multimode models* (Bentler, Poon, & Lee, 1988; Wothke & Browne, 1990); *nonstandard models* (Bentler, 1989; Newcomb & Bentler, 1988); *differential equation models* (Arminger, 1986; Dwyer, 1992); *equivalence of models* (Stelzl, 1986); *identification* (Bekker, 1986; Bollen & Jöreskog, 1985; Shapiro & Browne, 1983); *cross-validation* (Cudeck & Browne, 1983; Kroonenberg & Lewis, 1982); *missing data* (Allison, 1987; Muthén, Kaplan, & Hollis, 1987); *multisample analysis* (Cole & Maxwell, 1985; Faulbaum, 1987; Kühnel, 1988; Porst, Schmidt, & Zeifang, 1987); *optimal scaling* (De Leeuw, 1988a); *standardization* (Acock & Fuller, 1986; Bielby, 1986; Greenland, Schesselman, & Criqui, 1986; Henry, 1986; Sobel & Arminger, 1986; Williams & Thompson, 1986); *power of test procedures* (Matsueda & Bielby, 1986; Saris, den Ronden, & Satorra, 1987; Satorra & Saris, 1985); *assessment of fit* (Balderjahn, 1988; Bentler, 1988a; Bollen, 1986, 1989b; Botha, Shapiro, & Steiger, 1988; LaDu & Tanaka, 1989; Marsh, Balla, & McDonald, 1988; Sobel & Bohrnstedt, 1985; Tanaka & Huba, 1985; Wheaton, 1987); *model parsimoniousness* (Bentler & Mooijaart, 1989; Mulaik et al, 1989); *model selection* (Akaike, 1987; Bozdogan, 1987; Chou & Bentler, 1988; De Leeuw, 1988b); *detection of outliers* (Berkane & Bentler, 1988; Bollen, 1987b; Comrey, 1985; Gallini & Casteel, 1987; Rasmussen, 1988); *misspecification* (Arminger, 1987; Farley & Reddy, 1987; Kaplan, 1988, 1989); *methods for detecting misspecification* (Bentler, 1986a; Bentler & Chou, 1986; Chou & Bentler, 1988; Glymour, Scheines, & Spirtes, 1988; Glymour, Scheines, Spirtes, & Kelly, 1987; Lance, 1989; Saris, Satorra, & Sörbom, 1987); *performance of model modification procedures* (Chou & Bentler, 1977; Herting & Costner, 1985; Luijben, Boomsma, & Molenaar, 1988; MacCallum, 1986; Silvia & MacCallum, 1988); *limited information estimation* (Kaplan, 1988; Lance, Cornwell, & Mulaik, 1988); *human factors issues* (Brecht, Bentler, & Tanaka, 1986; Steiger, 1988); *program comparisons* (Brown, 1986; Spirtes, Scheines, & Glymour, 1990); *role of time in causal models* (Gollob & Reichardt, 1987); *issues in simulation research* (Acito & Anderson, 1984; Fornell & Larcker, 1984; Lewis & Orav, 1989); and *methodology of effect decomposition* (Bollen, 1987a; Chen, 1983; Fox, 1980, 1985; Graff & Schmidt, 1982; Sobel, 1982, 1986, 1987; Stone, 1985; Wolfe & Ethington, 1985). In the above listing, only the most recent references have been given. For example, effect decomposition goes back at least a decade to Alwin and Hauser (1975) and Greene (1977), while recent work covers new theory such as standard errors of indirect effects. However, this is a program manual, and not a comprehensive text. The references are intended primarily to provide the reader with an entry into the ever-growing literature.

2. INTRODUCTION TO STRUCTURAL EQUATION MODELS

A minimal set of key concepts are needed to translate a substantive theory into the form of a model that can be statistically estimated and tested. Models are specified in EQS using a specially developed language that is intended to be easy and straightforward to use. The language is concerned primarily with the unambiguous specification of the variables involved in a structural model. Since there are different types of variables in any model, the language must allow for these types of variables. The variables in the input data file to be analyzed are observed or measured variables; they are called Vs in EQS. Hypothetical constructs are unmeasured latent variables, as in factor analysis, and are called factors or Fs. Residual variation in measured variables is generated by errors or Es. The corresponding residuals in factors are called disturbances or Ds. Thus V, F, E, and D variables are introduced as needed in the examples below. In addition to specifying variables, a model must contain information on the hypothesized effects of variables on each other (shown in regression coefficients) and the specification of variables that are not explained by other variables (shown in their variances and covariances). This latter information is implemented in the program in accord with the representation system of Bentler and Weeks (1979, 1980). This chapter introduces the relevant and nonmathematical part of the Bentler-Weeks approach, and shows how to use the concepts and the EQS language to set up regression, path, factor, and general structural models. The reader is urged to study each setup and run the corresponding model, or some variant of it, with EQS, using the program's on-line HELP facility. *The experienced researcher or technical reader may skip this chapter.*

One empirical study will provide a concrete illustration of how the basic Bentler-Weeks concepts are implemented in EQS. The example is the well-known model of the stability of alienation taken from the work of Wheaton, Muthén, Alwin, and Summers (1977). In this study, 932 individuals' responses to a series of attitude items on several occasions were modeled in accord with a particular concept of what the items were measuring. An assumption (here untested) is that items could be meaningfully aggregated into scales of "anomie" and "powerlessness." The anomie and powerlessness variables were actually measured at several time points, given here for the years 1967 and 1971. A question of interest involved the stability of these measures across time. Since it is possible that the stability of these measures could be influenced by irrelevant sources of variance, especially socioeconomic status, two measures of such status, "education" and Duncan's occupational status index ("SEI"), were obtained as well.

The six variables (V) that are available for analysis are thus:

V1 = Anomie (1967)   V2 = Powerlessness (1967)
V3 = Anomie (1971)   V4 = Powerlessness (1971)
V5 = Education   V6 = Occupational status index, SEI.

The covariance matrix of these six variables in the sample of 932 respondents or cases is as follows (only the lower triangle is reported):

	V_1	V_2	V_3	V_4	V_5	V_6
V_1	11.834					
V_2	6.947	9.364				
V_3	6.819	5.091	12.532			
V_4	4.783	5.028	7.495	9.986		
V_5	− 3.839	− 3.889	− 3.841	− 3.625	9.610	
V_6	− 21.899	− 18.831	− 21.748	− 18.775	35.522	450.288

The 6(7)/2 = 21 elements of this matrix represent the data vector s given in equation (1.1) that is to be modeled according to a theory that proposes to explain how the data were generated. Before turning to a meaningful structural theory for these data, let us consider a model for these data associated with standard multivariate analysis. In the absence of a structural theory, the variances and covariances of the variables V1 − V6 are themselves parameters to be estimated. For example, they are parameters in the multivariate normal distribution that might be hypothesized to have generated the sample data. Thus the vector σ in (1.1) is simply the vector of population variances and covariances, which is not considered to be a further function of structural parameters θ. Rather obviously, (1.1) can thus be minimized for any nonnegative definite choice of W by setting the estimate $\hat{\sigma} = s$, since the function attains its lower bound of zero. But there are as many parameters in σ (here, 21) as there are data points (sample variances and covariances), so this unstructured or "saturated" model has no degrees of freedom and will always fit any set of data. As a consequence, unless a further hypothesis is imposed, the saturated model is very uninteresting. Traditional hypotheses in the absence of a structural theory might be that $\sigma_{13} = 0$, or that $\sigma_{24} = \sigma_{56}$. In that case, since $\hat{\sigma} \neq s$, Q would be nonzero, and a nonstructural but potentially interest
ing hypothesis would be testable.

The following is a path diagram of the saturated model:

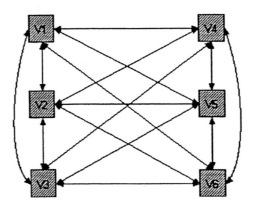

Figure 2.1

In this diagram, each measured variable is shown in a square, as is traditional. The variance of each of these variables is not shown, but it is a parameter of the model, so each square has been shaded as a reminder. Each variable's variance is a parameter here, but in subsequent models this will not be true and some variables will not be shaded. The covariances between variables are shown as two-way arrows, as is traditional. Each of these pairwise associations is a parameter in the model. There are thus six variances and 15 covariances in the model. The traditional hypothesis $\sigma_{13} = 0$ would be shown in the diagram by removing the two-way arrow that connects V1 and V3. Removing such a path would introduce a degree of freedom, and yield a testable hypothesis that may or may not be true. (Note: The number following a variable should be read as a subscript, but it is written here in the format required by EQS. Most computers cannot read subscripts.)

In the absence of a structural model, only a relatively limited range of hypotheses on σ or on functions of σ can be evaluated. In this particular study, where variables V1 and V3, as well as V2 and V4, are the same variables measured at two time points, one might consider a hypothesis such as $\sigma_1^2 = \sigma_3^2$, which can be tested by EQS if desired. The range of such hypotheses involving parametric restrictions on the variances and covariances is generally rather limited, so that a more generic approach to multivariate analysis would impose a structure on the measured variables based on fewer parameters (elements of θ) than data (elements of s). Ideally, the model should contain very few parameters, so that the difference between data points and number of parameters, the degrees of freedom, is quite large. Then, even the optimal choice of parameters $\hat{\theta}$ will yield a $\hat{\sigma} = \sigma(\hat{\theta})$ that may not exactly reproduce the data. Thus the residual $(s - \sigma(\hat{\theta}))$ will be nonzero, $\hat{Q}$ (= Q evaluated at $\hat{\theta}$) will be nonzero, and a major statistical question is whether $\hat{Q}$ is sufficiently small, given the sample size involved and the degrees of freedom associated with the model. If $\hat{Q}$ is statistically small, the model gives a good representation of the data.

This chapter will approach the problem of developing and testing a structural theory for the alienation data in stages, allowing a number of rather simple concepts to be introduced in turn. Several small models for these data, or subsets of the data, will be developed, and the problem of specifying the models in EQS will be described as a way of gaining familiarity with the program. The chapter will begin with a diagrammatic introduction to the familiar topic of multiple regression.

A SIMPLE REGRESSION MODEL

The ordinary multiple regression equation $Y = \beta_1 X_1 + \beta_2 X_2 + \cdots + \beta_p X_p + e$ serves as the basic building block of all linear structural models. In most single population covariance structure models, regression included, the intercept β_0 is typically not of interest and the variables are taken to be deviations from means (i.e., β_0 is not included in the equation, as above). See Chapter 8 for a discussion of models that involve means. As is well known, the parameters of the equation are the regression coefficients. These can be estimated by some method such as least squares when a sample of observations on the variables exist. It is somewhat less well known among data analysts that the variance of the residual σ^2 also is a parameter to be estimated, but this is usually considered to be a minor point because the estimate falls out readily via the standard approach to regression. From the structural modeling perspective, however, even this specification is incomplete. In particular, from the perspective of the Bentler-Weeks model:

The parameters of any linear structural model are the regression coefficients and the variances and covariances of the independent variables.

(Actually, the parameters may include the higher-order multivariate product-moments such as skewnesses and kurtoses of the independent variables, but this point will not be discussed here. See Chapter 10, and Bentler, 1983a. Models with means also will have means and intercepts as additional parameters. See Chapter 8.) Thus, the variances of the variables $X_1 - X_p$ and each of the pairwise covariances among these variables are also parameters of the model. These are typically considered to be known numbers when the regression model is based on the concept of fixed regressors X_i. In virtually all structural modeling applications, however, these variables are best considered to be random variables whose variances and covariances are not known a priori before sample data is obtained, and that must be estimated as well. Of course, in the regression model, the optimal estimates turn out to be the sample values of these variances and covariances, but this convenience should not obscure the point that they are parameters that need to be estimated.

The Bentler-Weeks concept of "independent" variables is broader than the typical one. Any variable that is not a dependent variable in any regression equation is an independent variable, including, in this case, the residual variable e. But in regression models the variables X_i are all taken to be orthogonal or uncorrelated with e, so that these zero covariances are not parameters of the model while the variance of e is a parameter. And, of course, "dependent" variable is any variable that is expressed as a structural regression function of other variables. In a single equation, as in this case, there is thus only one dependent variable. In models with many equations there are as many dependent variables as there are equations. Note in particular that a corollary of the Bentler-Weeks approach is that *dependent variables do not have variances or covariances with other variables as parameters of a structural model.* Such variances and covariances are to be explained by the parameters. Thus Y indeed has a variance, and Y covaries with X_i, but these numbers are a function of, i.e., generated by, the model parameters.

A simple regression problem with the previously given data can serve to fix ideas as well as to introduce the EQS language. Consider the stability of Powerlessness. One could index this by the regression of V4 on V2, that is, by the size of the coefficient β#in V4 = βV2 + E4. But if one suspects that stability is influenced by Education, it may be more desirable to consider the regression V4 = β_1V2 + β_2V5 + E4. The coefficient β_1, obtained when V5 (Education) is included in the equation, may differ from β. EQS uses the convention that measured variables are indexed sequentially V1, V2, ... as read in; all six variables of the example will be read (some can be discarded internally). Residuals in measured variables, or errors in variables, are denoted E and are followed by the number of the measured variable being predicted. A path diagram for the problem is as follows, using the usual convention that measured variables (Vs) are represented in squares while the unmeasured residual is not in a square. The independent V variables, V2 and V5, are shaded, while the dependent variable, V4, is not shaded. Thus the independent variables are the shaded variables and the residual:

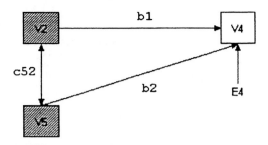

Figure 2.2

The independent variables are V2, V5, and E4. The dependent variable is V4. According to the Bentler-Weeks concepts, the parameters of the model are:

Regression coefficients: β_1 (=b1), β_2 (=b2), 1.0

Variances of independent variables: σ_{v2}^2, σ_{v5}^2, σ_{e4}^2

Covariances of independent variables: $\sigma_{v5,v2}$ (= σ_{52}=c52).

It will be apparent that the path diagram represents regression coefficients as unidirectional arrows, and covariances between independent variables as two-way arrows. Note also that the path from E4 to V4 is implicit; it is actually another regression coefficient, but it is known and fixed at 1.0 (because it is implicit in the equation V4 = β_1V2 + β_2V5 + 1.0E4). Virtually all path diagrams do not clearly show that the variances of the independent variables are also parameters. One could put this information in the diagram, but since it is typically absent the user who translates a diagram into equations must be quite careful. In principle, there is a one-to-one correspondence between a diagram and a model specified via equations, but lack of a standard convention makes this point obscure. Furthermore, just as diagrams typically do not tell the whole story of a model, neither do equations; the variances and covariances of independent variables are sometimes forgotten or presented as an afterthought in presentations of linear structures.

Structural models represented in diagram form must also be carefully scanned for what is *not* present in the model, as is true even in this simplest of all possible models. In this diagram, for example, we note two main points. Most obviously, no other variables are included in the model, hence such other variables should be eliminated from any program input. Less obviously, the model has imposed the typical — and almost always necessary — assumption that the predictor variables V2 and V5 are not correlated with E4, the residual error variable. If a correlation were to be specified, the diagram would have had a two-way arrow connecting these variables. The absence of a two-way arrow says "this covariance is fixed at zero." Similarly, the absence of a one-way arrow would say that a regression coefficient is known and fixed at zero.

A few more words need to be said about the fixed 1.0 path from E4 to V4, because a generic principle of identification is involved. Parameter, equation, and model identification is a complex topic that deals with the issue of whether a structural model has been specified so that the parameters of the model are unique. If the parameters are subject to any arbitrariness, it would be difficult to speak of them as true parameters that are to be estimated, since a wandering target would be involved. In the simple case of regression, we can always write the equation in two different but equivalent forms. The first involves fixing the path and then considering the variance of the residual as a free parameter, as was done above. But it would also be possible to write the equation as $V4 = \beta_1 V2 + \beta_2 V5 + \beta_3 E4$, considering β_3 as a free parameter to be estimated and the variance of E4 as fixed (say, at 1.0). While regression is rarely developed this way, it certainly could be since it is a trivial variation of the identical model. Note that it is *not* possible to free both parameters β_3 *and* the variance of E4, since the product ($\beta_3 E4$) must be a single and unique number given the other parameters (= $V4 - \beta_1 V2 - \beta_2 V5$). Similarly, it is *not* possible to fix both parameters (e.g., $\beta_3 = 1.0$, $\sigma_{e4}^2 = 1.0$) because that would imply that the residual variance is not to be minimized by optimal choice of β_1 and β_2. More generically, then, in all structural models including multiple equation models:

> *Every unmeasured variable in a structural model must have its scale determined. This can always be done by fixing a path from that variable to another variable at some known value (usually 1.0). An alternative method for determining the scale of an independent unmeasured variable is to fix its variance at some known value (usually 1.0).*

Note that the scale of a dependent unmeasured variable cannot be determined by fixing its variance, because dependent variables do not have variances as parameters. In the author's experience, the above simple rule will cover a large proportion of identification difficulties encountered by novice structural modelers.

As will be noted below, EQS allows variables to be denoted as V, F, E, and D types (V and E variables have already been defined). F variables are typically taken as factors or substantive latent variables, while D variables are residuals or disturbances in equations. Thus measured variables are always V variables, and all F, E, and D variables must have their scales fixed for a model to have a chance of being identified.

The simple regression model is intended to be compared to the second moment summary statistics, specifically, the variances and covariances of the measured variables. Thus the data vector s for the regression model consists of all of the variances and covariances of the measured variables. With p variables, there are p(p + 1)/2 such elements. Here p = 3, so there are 3(4)/2 = 6 data points (the sample variances of V2, V4, and V5, and their three pairwise covariances). The number of parameters to be estimated is the sum of the unknown regression coefficients (2), the variances of the independent variables (3), and their covariances (1). Thus, there are six parameters to be estimated, based on six data points. Evidently, the regression model has as many free parameters as data points, so it is basically an uninteresting model considered alone since there are no degrees of freedom to test any hypothesis in the model. If one of the parameters, most typically a regression coefficient, were fixed at a certain value, e.g., $\beta_2 = 0$, then there would be only five parameters and the model would have one degree of freedom that could be used to test the null hypothesis (that $\beta_2 = 0$).

The EQS program can be used to perform a regression analysis, although when the data are multivariate normal, programs specifically developed for regression are more appropriate because of the many special features they contain. However, there do not appear to be many programs to perform such estimation for variables that are elliptically or arbitrarily distributed. EQS can be used to implement the general theory of Van Praag, Dijkstra, and Van Velzen (1985) on least squares theory under various distributional assumptions. The regression problem discussed previously, considered in a simple normal theory least squares context, is submitted to EQS as shown on the left:

Input	Comments
/TITLE	Optional - can be omitted
STABILITY OF POWERLESSNESS	"
/SPECIFICATIONS	Necessary
CAS = 932; VAR = 6; ME = LS;	Number of cases and variables, and least squares estimation method
/EQUATIONS	Necessary
V4 = 1*V2 − 1*V5 + E4;	Free parameters shown by stars; +1, − 1 are initial guesses or estimates
/VARIANCES	Necessary for independent variables
V2 = 9*; V5 = 9*; E4 = 2*;	Arbitrary start values given
/COVARIANCES	Optional in general, but needed here to show covariance is a free parameter
V5,V2 = − 4*;	
/MATRIX	Not needed if data are in a computer file

						Comments
11.834						Data given in free format
6.947	9.364					VAR=6 requires the 6 × 6
6.819	5.091	12.532				matrix
4.783	5.028	7.495	9.986			Compare last row of input to
− 3.839	− 3.889	− 3.841	− 3.625	9.610		original matrix
− 2.1899	− 1.8831	− 2.1748	− 1.8775	3.5522	4.50288	No semicolons here
/END						Last input statement

The input to EQS evidently uses the Bentler-Weeks concept of independent and dependent variables, since as discussed above, variables V2, V5, and E4 are considered to be independent variables while V4 is a dependent variable. As the regression diagram shows, only one covariance is a parameter of the model since the other covariances among independent variables are fixed at known, zero values. In EQS, free parameters such as the regression coefficients β_i are not denoted by a Greek symbol; rather they are indicated by a star with an associated number that represents the researcher's guess as to the value of that parameter. Thus the input stream can be scanned for the number of stars, which represents the number of free parameters to be estimated by the program. In this example, there are evidently six parameters to be estimated, as was noted earlier.

It may seem peculiar to read an input MATRIX that is 6 by 6 corresponding to VAR=6 when the problem under consideration is only concerned with three variables. Actually, EQS has an automatic variable selection feature that performs the necessary reduction to the relevant variables internally: nothing needs to be explicitly stated. After all, the model is completely given by the EQUATIONS and VARIANCES sections; if a variable does not appear in these sections, it will not be included in the model. (Note that independent variables cannot have covariances without having variances. Thus, COV does not help to define which variables are to be selected.) The advantage of this automatic selection device is that a researcher may have dozens of models to evaluate on various parts of a given data set. In such a case it may be desirable to have the variable numbers of the large data set have a constant meaning even in subanalyses, and only critical changes need to be made from one run to the next. In particular, the input MATRIX can simply stay the same in all runs.

If the last row of the MATRIX section is compared to the matrix presented on p. 14, it will be apparent that the variance of V6 has been divided by 100 while the covariance of V6 with each other variable has been divided by 10. Such a change reflects a rescaling of the raw scores of the original variable by multiplying by .1; that is, Final V6 = .1 times Original V6. (Remember that if $x = kX$, then $var(x) = var(kX) = k^2var(X)$ and $cov(xY) = cov(kXY) = kcov(XY)$; here, $k = .1$.) This change was made to make the variances of the input variables more similar to each other. In the original data, the variance of V6 was on the order of 45 times as large as the variances of the other variables. In the modified matrix, the ratio of smallest to largest variance is more on the order of 1:3. It is known that the efficiency and accuracy with which programs like EQS can optimize a nonlinear function of many parameters, or solve a simple linear regression problem, depend on the condition number of the input matrix, which in turn is strongly affected by differences in scale of the input variables.

It is good practice, in general, to scale input variables so that they have similar variances. The scaling constants should, however, be numbers that do not depend on the particular sample of data under study. They should not be random variables such as would be chosen if one standardizes all variables to unit variance in the sample (transforms a covariance matrix into a correlation matrix). Such scaling "constants" would vary with the sample, which would complicate the statistical theory. The rather simple idea of moving a decimal place for some input variables (e.g., changing the format statement F3.0 to F3.1, indicating a field of 3 numbers should be interpreted as having one number to the right of the decimal, when reading raw score data) is a convenient way to deal with this problem. Of course, it must be remembered that the resulting parameter estimates and standard errors are based on the particular scales chosen. It will be obvious, of course, that rescaling V6 will not have any effect on the problem under consideration, which is the regression of V4 on V2 and V5. Thus the rescaling does not need to be done in this case, but it was done because the rescaled matrix will be used in subsequent analyses without further comment.

EQS generated the LS regression solution to this problem as follows: V4 = .457*V2 − .192*V5 + E4. It would thus appear that the main effect on powerlessness in 1971 (V4) is by the same variable measured in 1967 (V2), even though education has a slightly negative impact. As expected, the variances of the two independent Vs are estimated at the sample values, as is their covariance. The variance of the residual is estimated at 6.991.

It is apparent that regression equations for unstandardized variables may be quite difficult to interpret in the social sciences because of the typical absence of a meaningful scale for the variables. In order to alleviate this problem, EQS produces a completely standardized solution, one in which each and every variable in a model has been standardized to unit variance. In this case the standardized solution gives the ordinary standardized beta weights typically encountered in regression: V4 = .443*V2 − .189*V5 + .837E4. Note that the residual E4 is also standardized. Thus the standardized variance of the E4 is $.837^2 = .70$, so that the squared multiple correlation between the predictors and V4 is $1 − .7 = .30$. Evidently powerlessness is not very stable, while it is marginally negatively affected by education. The program also provides the correlations among the standardized independent variables; the V5, V2 correlation is $-.410$.

The above example used the covariance matrix of all six variables as input to EQS. This is not necessary when only a subset of three of the six variables is being analyzed. Thus, an alternative program input would be the following:

Input	Comments
/SPE	Can be abbreviated
CAS = 932; VAR = 3; ME = LS;	Only three variables
/EQU	Abbreviated
V2 = 1*V1 − 1*V3 + E2;	Note change in variable
	numbers
/VAR	Abbreviated
V1 = 9*; V3 = 9*; E2 = 2*;	Again note change in numbers
/COV	Abbreviated
V3,V1 = − 4*;	Changed numbers also
/MAT	Abbreviated
9.364	Much smaller three variable
5.028 9.986	matrix, selected from larger
− 3.889 − 3.625 9.610	matrix
/END	

Since EQS assumes that the input variables are numbered in sequence, and three variables are in the matrix, it assumes that the variables are numbered V1, V2, and V3. Thus the EQUations, VARiances, and COVariance sections must use a notation that corresponds to this sequence. If the equation had specified the model V4 = 1*V2 − 1*V5 + E4; as previously, the program would have searched for variables V4 and V5, not found them, and would have printed an error message and quit.

Input data, such as the covariances in the /MATRIX section above or raw score data that would reside in an external file, must be complete and have no missing elements or special missing data codes (such as 9's or other arbitrary numbers or symbols). The current release of EQS has no feature for handling or manipulating missing data.[1]

Another job setup equivalent to the above two variants of the regression problem is the following: a correlation matrix rather than a covariance matrix is used as input, and standard deviations are provided to transform the correlations into covariances.

---

[1] The more complete environments of **EQS for Windows** and **EQS for Macintosh** now do provide several features for evaluating and handling missing data. Nonetheless, a raw score data matrix that is to be used as input to a modeling run with EQS must be complete, i.e., contain no missing data or missing data codes.

Input	Comments
/SPE	
CAS = 932; VAR = 3; ME = LS;	As above
/EQU	
V2 = 1*V1 − 1*V3 + E2;	As above
/VAR	
V1 = 9*; V3 = 9*; E2 = 2*;	As above
/COV	
V3,V1 = − 4*;	As above
/MAT	
1.00	Correlation input
.52 1.00	
− .41 − .37 1.00	
/STANDARD DEVIATIONS	Required
3.06 3.16 3.1	No semicolon
/END	

EQS will create the covariance matrix from the correlations and standard deviations without any further instruction, and the analysis will be done on the covariance matrix. It follows that the parameter guesses provided in the input should be of a magnitude consistent with the scaling implied by the covariances, and not that of the correlations. The output estimates will be in the covariance metric. The use of an input correlation matrix with standard deviations, as above, integrates well with some statistical packages that easily provide such information but do not readily provide covariance matrices. EQS can also analyze the correlation matrix directly, but this practice is not recommended since the statistical estimates, e.g., standard errors and χ^2 statistics, may well be incorrect in this case (see Bentler & Lee, 1983; Cudeck, 1989).

A regression equation in the context of a causal model is called a structural equation, and the parameters, structural parameters. Structural parameters presumably represent relatively invariant parameters of a causal process, and are considered to have more theoretical meaning than ordinary predictive regression weights, especially when the regression equation is embedded in a series of simultaneous equations designed to implement a substantive theory. The variables that one uses in the equations must, of course, adequately operationalize critical substantive concepts, and the model design must be appropriate to the theoretical specification and should include relevant causal variables if at all possible (Pratt & Schlaifer, 1984). The theoretical meaning of the model parameters is also based on the invariance characteristics of the solution made possible by the design. Thus, for example, ordinary regression coefficients can be arbitrarily affected by the amount of measurement error in the variables, but similar coefficients for the regression among latent variables would not be so affected. Multiple equation models, which are necessary to implement latent variable modeling, are introduced next.

A TWO-EQUATION PATH MODEL

Structural equation models are virtually always multiple equation models, with multiple dependent as well as independent variables. The simplest extension of the regression model is the multivariate regression model, in which several dependent variables are regressed on several predictor variables. In the ordinary multivariate regression model, there are again as many parameters as data points, so that as a structural model, it can always be fit exactly for any set of data. The next example is a trivial variant of such a model in which there is one overidentifying restriction, leading to a model that is potentially rejectable. In particular, a consideration of the anomie and powerlessness variables measured on the two occasions leads to the standard cross-lagged panel design:

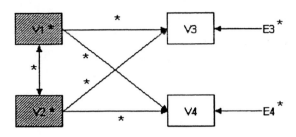

Figure 2.3

As before, measured variables are in squares, and independent measured variables are shaded. The arrows from the residuals E3 and E4, having no further designation, are assumed to represent fixed, known values of 1.0 (not shown in the diagram for simplicity). In addition, however, the diagram includes the nonstandard but practically valuable feature of having a star (asterisk) in every location where a free parameter exists in the model. A star next to a variable indicates that the variable has a variance that is to be estimated. Thus, it can be seen quickly that there are nine parameters in the model, which, for 4(5)/2 = 10 data points leaves one degree of freedom. The degree of freedom is associated with the question of whether the covariation between variables V3 and V4 can be totally accounted for by variables V1 and V2. Allowing the errors E3 and E4 to covary would lead to a saturated model with as many parameters as data points, i.e., a model with zero degrees of freedom (df).

The cross-lagged panel design is often also used to test more restrictive models regarding the relative influence of the crossed variables on each other. In this instance, where anomie and powerlessness are each measured on two occasions, one might be interested in whether initial feelings of anomie (V1) more strongly affect feelings of powerlessness at a later time point (V4), than initial feelings of powerlessness (V2) affect feelings of anomie (V3). Such questions involve null hypotheses regarding whether the V1 → V4 path is equal to the V2 → V3 path, or whether one or the other cannot be statistically differentiated from zero. These hypotheses will not be evaluated in this section. They are best evaluated in a design in which the key variables are latent rather than observed, as in the case. Such designs have been used in studies on the effects of attitude on behavior vs. the effect of behavior on attitude (see, e.g., Bentler & Speckart, 1981; Speckart & Bentler, 1982).

The path diagram will clearly indicate how many equations exist in this model. In such a diagram, dependent variables can be unambiguously recognized because they have unidirectional arrows aiming at them. The above diagram has two variables that have unidirectional arrows aiming at them: V3 and V4. Thus, the model consists of two equations since there are as many equations in a model as dependent variables. (A single dependent variable is not allowed to have more than one equation. If such a situation occurs, the model can generally be rewritten so as to avoid this problem.) An analysis of the path diagram also indicates, for each dependent variable, how many predictor plus residual variables there are that determine the variable. This number is, of course, also the number of terms on the right-hand side of an equation (when equations are written with the dependent variable on the left).

In this example the diagram shows that there are three unidirectional arrows aiming at V3; thus, the equation for V3 must have three terms in it. Similarly, three unidirectional arrows aim at V4, so the equation for V4 has three terms in it as well. The particular variables involved in the equation are simply determined by tracing back from the dependent variable to the originating variables, e.g., the equation for V3 must involve V1, V2, and E3. Furthermore, the free and fixed coefficients in the equation can also be read in the diagram since a free parameter is given by a star and a fixed parameter is without a star. If any such equation had to be represented symbolically, one could substitute a Greek label for each free parameter. As was seen above, the input to EQS does not use such a symbol but utilizes a guess as to the parameter value. The program output would provide the improved, optimal value.

Any complete job setup also requires knowledge of the independent variables in the model. Every variable in a diagram that does not have a unidirectional arrow aiming at it is thus an independent variable; these are the shaded variables and the residual Es. In the diagram, these are V1, V2, E3, and E4. Thus these variables must have variances as parameters, and only they are allowed to covary. In this case, there is only one covariance because, in general, residuals are taken to be uncorrelated with predictor variables. The job setup in EQS is as follows:

<u>Input</u>	<u>Comments</u>
/TITLE	
PATH ANALYSIS MODEL	
/SPECIFICATIONS	
CAS = 932; VAR = 6; ME = ML;	ML = maximum likelihood
/LABELS	Optional
V1 = ANOMIE67; V2 = POWRLS67;	8 characters maximum per label
V3 = ANOMIE71; V4 = POWRLS71;	
/EQUATIONS	
V3 = 1*V1 + 1*V2 + E3;	V3,V4 are dependent variables
V4 = 1*V1 + 1*V2 + E4;	V1,V2,E3,E4 are independent
/VARIANCES	
V1 TO V2 = 10*;	"TO" sets sequential parameters
E3 TO E4 = 2*;	in one statement
/COVARIANCES	
V2,V1 = 7*;	
/MATRIX	
(6 × 6, as on p. 19)	
/DIAGRAM	Specifies what to put in a path
V1 V3 E3;	diagram and where to put it
V2 V4 E4;	on the page
/END	

The output from EQS contains a test statistic that can be used to evaluate the adequacy of the model. The ML chi-square is 341.9, which is very large compared to 1 df; the probability value for the chi-square statistic is very small. That is, the model must be rejected. In fact, the model reproduces the observed covariances of all variables perfectly, except that the

V4,V3 covariance is not well reproduced: it has a residual $(s_{43} - \hat{\sigma}_{43})$ between data and model of 4.282. The statistical test verifies that this residual is significantly different from zero.

Corresponding to each free estimated parameter in the estimating equation — which, in the EQS output, is associated with a variable label when one is provided — the program reports its estimated standard error (S.E.) and prints that value immediately below the estimate. A simple univariate test of whether the estimate is consistent with a population coefficient of zero is made by dividing the estimate by S.E.; the result is printed below the S.E. In this instance,

$$
\begin{array}{llll}
\text{ANOMIE71} = \text{V3} = & .455\text{*V1} + & .206\text{*V2} + \text{E3} \\
 & .037 & .041 \\
 & 12.407 & 4.988 \\
\text{POWRLS71} = \text{V4} = & .158\text{*V1} + & .420\text{*V2} + \text{E4} \\
 & .034 & .038 \\
 & 4.658 & 11.042
\end{array}
$$

Since each of the test statistics exceeds the standard normal critical value of 1.96 associated with a normal z-test .05 probability level, the parameters appear to be significantly different from zero. However, these tests should be considered suggestive rather than conclusive because they are associated with a model that does not fit the data. As in ordinary regression, the values of the coefficients may be difficult to interpret when the variables have different and relatively arbitrary scales, and the standardized solution may be of interest:

$$
\begin{array}{lll}
\text{ANOMIE71} & = \text{V3} = 0.443\text{*V1} + 0.178\text{*V2} + 0.818\,\text{E3} \\
\text{POWRLS71} & = \text{V4} = 0.172\text{*V1} + 0.407\text{*V2} + 0.844\,\text{E4}
\end{array}
$$

It appears as if anomie is slightly more stable than powerlessness (.443 vs. .407). The cross-lagged effects are small and about equal in magnitude (.172 and .178).

The program produces a path diagram that is generated from the model specification and the diagram format provided by the user. In this case, the diagram is intended to reproduce Figure 2.3. Since it is printed on a line printer on which uni- and bidirectional arrows aiming in various directions are difficult to produce, some suggestions of Huba and Palisoc (1983) were followed to produce symbols that give the appropriate impression of directionality. For example, a line of "A"s is designed to represent an upwardly moving arrow, as shown on the next page. However, it might be noted that a true graphical publications-quality path diagram will be available in subsequent releases of EQS beginning in mid-1991.[2]

---

[2] The text in this section has been overtaken by new developments and is no longer relevant. As noted previously, **Diagrammer** is a tool available in **EQS for Windows** and **EQS for Macintosh** that not only permits drawing a publication-quality path diagram, but the diagram also serves as input and output to the model. That is, a model file is created automatically from the diagram, and the output from a computer run is automatically placed into the diagram. The figure on p. 26 shows the standardized solution from the output as it appears in **Diagrammer**.

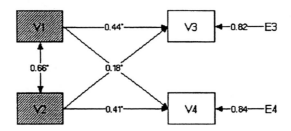

Note: This figure was produced as output from a run, using **Diagrammer**. The estimates are the standardized coefficients. In **Diagrammer**'s output, an asterisk next to a free parameter indicates that the corresponding unstandardized coefficient was statistically significant.

A FACTOR ANALYSIS MODEL

Although it was stated previously that a major application of structural modeling involves latent variables, the previous examples have not used any latent variables. It is true that the residuals in variables of the regression and path models are unmeasured variables, but in principle, once the coefficients in the equations are known (e.g., in the population), these residuals are simply linear combinations of observed variables. Such is not the case in true latent variable models, in which the latent variables cannot be expressed as a linear combination of measured variables. The reason for this is that the dimensionality of the space of latent variables exceeds the dimensionality of the space of measured variables (see Bentler, 1982). Note that in the regression example there were three measured variables and three independent variables; in the path analysis example there were four measured variables and four independent variables.

Factor analysis is one of the oldest latent variable models. In its early form it was used as an exploratory data analysis technique. More recently, it has been developed as a hypothesis-testing tool, primarily due to the work of Jöreskog (1969). In the exploratory factor analysis approach, the analysis is concerned with finding the smallest number of common factors to account for the correlations or covariances between variables. In the confirmatory approach, the analysis is concerned with implementing a theorist's hypothesis about how a domain of variables may be structured, and testing the adequacy of the hypothesis using statistical means. In practice, of course, structural theories are not perfectly clear-cut, and a variety of alternative model specifications may be evaluated. Although the structural modeling approach to factor analysis includes exploratory factor analysis, in practice specialized programs are superior in that domain because they are able to handle larger data sets and also include features such as orthogonal and oblique rotations that are typically not included in structural modeling programs. EQS is certainly best suited to confirmatory, not exploratory, analyses.

The sociologists who provided the data for the stability of alienation example proposed that anomie and powerlessness may both be indicators of the same underlying construct, say, "alienation." The implication of such a concept is that the observed variables are correlated only to the extent that they share this underlying construct. Diagrammatically, considering only the 1967 measurement point, this hypothesis can be represented as follows:

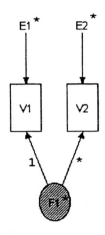

Figure 2.4

In this diagram, there are only two measured variables, V1 and V2. Notice from the direction of the arrows that both of these variables are dependent variables, i.e., they are a linear combination of the latent variables, and not the reverse. The variable F1, "alienation," is the common factor latent variable that generates any covariance between V1 and V2, while E1 and E2 are so-called unique factor variables. Factors such as F1 are usually shown in circles in a path diagram. The shaded variable F1 and the residual variables E1 and E2 are the independent variables in the model: there are three uncorrelated independent unmeasured variables, but fewer measured variables (only two), as is true by definition of a true latent variable model (Bentler, 1982).

In the diagram each of the latent variables has its scale fixed by fixing a path from the variable to another variable. As before, the error variables E1 and E2 are taken to have unit paths aiming at the measured variables, and their variances are taken to be free parameters to be estimated (thus the star next to the variable). The common factor F1 also has its scale fixed by such a device; one path emanating from F1 is fixed, the other is free to be estimated. It is arbitrary which choice is taken. When the path is fixed, the variance must be a free parameter as noted previously (hence the star next to F1). Thus the diagram implies that there are four free parameters. But a quick count as to the data involved, namely the two variances of V1 and V2, and their covariance, indicates that there are three data points. Thus the model has more parameters than data, and it cannot be uniquely estimated. It is underidentified.

The identification problem in this small factor model with one common factor could be resolved in several ways. Constraints could be placed on the parameters, so that there would be fewer than four effective parameters. For example, the residual variances of E1 and E2 could be set equal to each other, so that in this part of the model only one rather than two free parameters would be involved. A much better general solution is to have more indicators of the factor. For example, one could entertain the model in Figure 2.5, where as usual, the independent factor F1 is shaded. The measured variables V1 − V4 are not shaded, i.e., they are dependent variables.

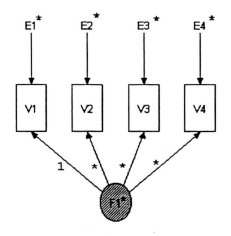

Figure 2.5

The single common factor F1 is presumed to generate the covariances of variables V1 – V4. In this model there are 4(5)/2 = 10 data points and only eight parameters, and it can be shown that the model is identified. In this instance, however, such a model may not make sense, since variables V1 and V2 represent data obtained in 1967, while V3 and V4 represent data obtained in 1971. While anomie and powerlessness may indeed represent indicators of alienation, the above model forces the construct of alienation (F1) to be identical in 1971 as 1967. Perhaps alienation is not this stable, and a more realistic model is of the form

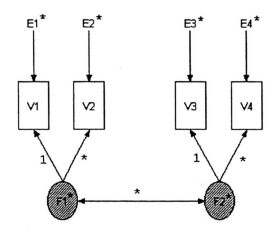

Figure 2.6

where the original model for the 1967 data (Figure 2.4) is essentially replicated for the 1971 data, with a single factor underlying each measurement occasion, and the factors are allowed to covary.

Although it appears that factors F1 and F2 have only two indicators as in Figure 2.4, and hence that the combined model should be underidentified because parts of the model are underidentified, the covariance between factors F1 and F2 acts like another indicator of each factor and serves to identify the model. This concept may not be obvious, but it might be noted that the covariance F2,F1 could be replaced by a unidirectional arrow from F1 to F2. Thus, F2 acts like V1 and V2 in identifying F1. However, a model such as is proposed above remains very fragile because if the covariance F2,F1 is in fact precisely zero — which is one of the values that such a covariance can take — the model again becomes underidentified because the left and right parts of Figure 2.6 suffer from the underidentification problem noted in Figure 2.4. This type of situation can arise in practice, when the researcher specifies a model such as Figure 2.6 and expects it to be identified because of the covariance F2,F1 term. But when estimated from the data, the covariance may turn out to be very close to zero, leading to a situation called "empirical" underidentification (Kenny, 1979; Rindskopf, 1984a). In such a case EQS will indicate that a parameter appears to be linearly dependent on others, i.e., that there is a problem in obtaining unique estimates for all the parameters in the model.

It should be clear by now that the two factor model can be reparameterized by using an alternative convention for fixing the scale of the unmeasured variables. In particular, factors F1 and F2 could have their variances fixed at 1.0 and the fixed path from each factor to its measured variable indicator could be set free to be estimated. In that case the covariance F2,F1 can be interpreted as a correlation. Thus the model of Figure 2.6 is equivalent to the following model.

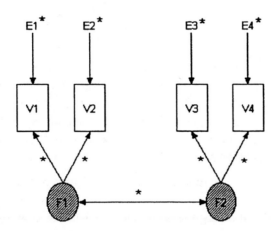

Figure 2.7

There is no star next to F1 and F2 because the variances of F1 and F2 are fixed at 1.0. This is the standard representation for a confirmatory factor analysis model, in which the common factors are usually standardized to have unit variance. This model can be estimated for the data by the following EQS setup:

Input	Comments
/TITLE	
FACTOR ANALYSIS MODEL	
/SPECS	
CAS = 932; VAR = 6; ME = GLS;	GLS = generalized LS
/EQU	
V1 = 2*F1 + E1;	
V2 = 2*F1 + E2;	
V3 = 2*F2 + E3;	
V4 = 2*F2 + E4;	
/VAR	
F1 TO F2 = 1.0;	Fixed at 1.0 (no star)
E1 TO E4 = 3*;	Four free parameters
/COV	
F2,F1 = .3*;	Dangerous near 0*
/MATRIX	
(6 × 6, as before)	
/DIAGRAM	Optional[3]
E1 E2 E3 E4;	Uses fixed four space/variable
V1 V2 V3 V4;	format, right justified
F1 F2;	
/END	

The program obtained a chi-square statistic of 55.612 with 1 df. The value of 55.6 evaluated in a χ_1^2 table yields a probability less than .001, indicating that if the model were correct in the population then sample data of the sort obtained in the study would be extremely unlikely to be observed. At this point, there is the option of concluding a) the model is correct, but the sample is a very unusual one or b) the model is incorrect. In the absence of a compelling reason to reject the sample, it is more prudent to reject the model.

It would be desirable to modify the model in some reasonable fashion to determine if an alternative model might not fit the data. Unfortunately, it is impossible to add parameters to the model without running out of degrees of freedom. Thus, for example, it would not be possible simply to add paths missing in the model, e.g., by allowing a complex rather than unifactorial factor structure. However, it is possible to add parameters to the model if, at the same time, constraints are added to the model to reduce the number of effective parameters.

Any study that measures the same variables on two or more occasions should consider the possibility of so-called "correlated errors." It was noted that the errors in a factor analytic model are really unique factors, that is, they may contain specific but reliable variance that happens not to be shared with other variables. This specificity may be similar in the same variable on various occasions, and the possibility thus exists that the residuals may, across time, be correlated. In particular, E1 and E3, as well as E2 and E4, may covary. The modified EQS specification is made in the covariance section.

---

[3] Note again that this way of dealing with diagrams has been completely superseded with **Diagrammer**. The setup, however, still describes the mainframe/DOS versions of EQS.

Input	Comments
/COV	Modified input section
F2,F1 = .3*;	As before
E3,E1 = .2*;	New free parameter
E4,E2 = .2*;	"

However, adding these two parameters yields -1 degrees of freedom; evidently, this model is underidentified and cannot be tested. Therefore, it is important to reflect further on the design of the study. In particular, since it is hoped that the same factor of alienation underlies the measures on both occasions of measurement, and the same variables are used as indicators of the factor, it may be hypothesized that the factor structure is actually the same on both occasions. The most restricted form of such factorial invariance would be to say that the relevant factor loadings are the same, that the relevant error variances are the same, and, perhaps the strongest hypothesis of all, that the covariances of errors are equal in magnitude (this is the strongest statement because the former hypotheses involve the same measured variable, but the latter involves different variables). These hypotheses would be specified as follows in EQS:

Input	Comments
/CONSTRAINTS	New program section
(V1,F1) = (V3,F2);	Two factor loadings
(V2,F1) = (V4,F2);	Other two factor loadings
(E1,E1) = (E3,E3);	Error variances
(E2,E2) = (E4,E4);	Other error variances
(E3,E1) = (E4,E2);	Covariances of errors

The program uses a convention that allows each parameter in any model to be uniquely identified by the double-label of the pairs of variables involved in the specification. The parameter in any equation can be simply found by the pair (dependent variable, predictor variable). For example, in the equation V1 = 2*F1 + E1, the parameter 2* is clearly identified by (V1,F1) because V1 defines the equation, and F1 the relevant part of the right-hand side; similarly, (V1,E1) would define the fixed 1.0 implicit in the equation. The parameter in the variances section can be identified by the variable involved, and considering it as the double-labeled diagonal element of a matrix. That is, for the E1 variable, (E1,E1) indicates its variance as a parameter. The parameter in any covariance section is already defined by its standard double-label name, e.g., (E3,E1) is the covariance between E3 and E1. The /CONSTRAINT section can impose constraints only on free parameters. After all, if one wants to specify that the parameter (E2,E2) = 3, say, this could be done directly in the variance section and there would be no need to add a /CONSTRAINT section. Finally, it may be noted that the parameters are placed in parentheses in this section.

This restricted model has 11 parameters but 5 constraints. The degrees of freedom are $10 - 11 + 5 = 4$. The GLS $\chi^2 = 2.958$, giving a probability value of .56. Evidently, the model fits the data very well. The estimated free parameters and standard errors (below the parameters) are:

Equations	Variances	Covariances
V1 = 2.937*F1 + E1	E1 = 3.520*	F2,F1 = .685*
.090	.267	.026
V2 = 2.446*F1 + E2	E2 = 3.644*	E3,E1 = .901*
.081	.206	.122
V3 = 2.937*F2 + E3	E3 = 3.520*	E4,E2 = .901*
.090	.267	.122
V4 = 2.446*F2 + E4	E4 = 3.644*	
.081	.206	

It will be noted that parameter estimates that are supposed to be equal, in fact *are* equal. Of course equality constrained estimates have the same standard error as well. The path diagram produced by the program is as follows. (Note: Using various menu options (on top) and diagramming tools (left side), **Diagrammer** lets you customize the diagram, add unstandardized or standardized estimates, add a statistical summary of the modeling run, etc.. This diagram replaces the line-drawing from the first printing of this **Manual**.)

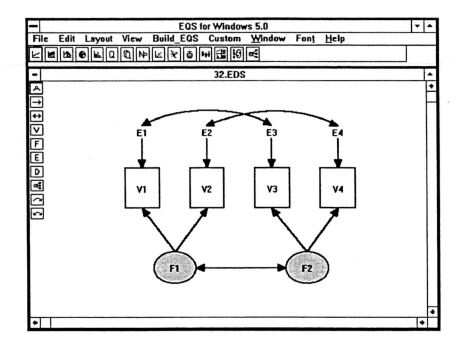

The factor correlation estimated by EQS is .685, with a very small S.E. of .026. Thus, it is unlikely that the true factor correlation between F1 and F2 is 1.0. In addition to doing a normal z test by dividing the estimate by the standard error and obtaining the highly significant value of 26.6, a model respecification can be done and the model reestimated under the restriction. The entire model, except for the covariance section, is kept intact. The modified covariance section that replaces the previous section is

/COV
 F2,F1 = 1.0;
 E3,E1 = .2*;
 E4,E2 = .2*;

in which the factor correlation is fixed at 1.0 rather than free to be estimated. The associated GLS χ^2 = 162.292 based on 5 df, which clearly does not fit the data. Thus, this very restricted model, having two factors that are perfectly correlated, must be rejected.

When two models are nested, that is, when two models are special cases of each other, chi-square difference tests can be used to evaluate the structural importance of the parametric constraints that differentiate two models. In the simplest and most typical application, two models would differ in that one model would contain extra parameters beyond those provided by the other model; all other parameters would be the same. In such a case, the chi-square difference test evaluates whether the added parameters, considered simultaneously, are necessary to the model. In the particular comparison given above, the two models are nested because the value of 1.0 for the factor intercorrelation is one special value that the parameter can take when it is simply a free parameter. Thus a chi-square difference test would evaluate whether the restricted value is a significantly poorer estimate for that parameter than the optimal freely estimated value. In this case this test of the restriction that differentiates the two models is given by 162.292 − 2.958 = 159.334, with degrees of freedom also given by the difference 5 − 4 = 1. Clearly, the hypothesis that (F2,F1) = 1.0 must be rejected. As noted above, chi-square difference tests are particularly useful when sets of parametric restrictions are tested simultaneously. In this case, where a single parameter is involved, such a test is simply equivalent to the square of a $\underline{z}$ test.

Parameters that differentiate two nested models also can be evaluated for significance by two other procedures called LM-tests and W-tests. These tests are described in Chapter 6.

Since the model comparison yielded the conclusion that the (F2,F1) correlation is not 1.0, it is apparent that alienation is not perfectly stable across the four years between measurement occasions. The estimated correlation of .685 suggests that $.685^2$ = .469 proportion of the variance of F2 is predictable from F1. However, this evaluation of the stability of alienation has not simultaneously considered the effects of SES. These effects are considered in the next section, in which a complete model for the data is evaluated.

A COMPLETE LATENT VARIABLE MODEL

Although factor analysis uses the concept of latent variables, it does not allow a regression structure on the latent variables. Factors either are correlated or not. The importance of allowing a simultaneous regression among factors was noted by Jöreskog (1973), Keesling, and Wiley (Wiley, 1973) when they joined the simultaneous equation and factor analytic models to yield a single model. The concept is straightforward: allow latent variables to be connected by unidirectional arrows rather than two-way arrows, with the directionality reflecting a hypothesis about the process or causal structure of the variables.

It is easy to see how the previous factor models would be modified to encompass a regression structure on the factors. Since F1 and F2 represent the construct of alienation at time points 1967 and 1971, it would make sense to replace the covariance between F1 and F2 by the structural equation F2 = *F1 + D2, where * is a free parameter and D2 is a $\underline{disturbance}$ in the factor. Then, F2 would be determined by F1 plus some residual, and * represents the extent of stability of the construct. If D2 were zero, F2 would be a constant times F1, and hence the construct would be totally stable. If * were zero, F2 would be an entirely new construct, unrelated to the prior F1 construct. Intermediate values of * would represent varying degrees of stability.

In the introductory section of this chapter it was noted that the stability of alienation might, however, be influenced by levels of education and SEI in the respondents. Whenever a theorist has reason to suspect that a structural relation might be impacted by other variables, it is important to try to include those variables in a simultaneous model of a phenomenon. In this case, biased estimates of the stability of alienation might be obtained if such stability were not evaluated in the context of socioeconomic status (SES). Since SES is a variable on which the respondents presumably have not varied substantially before 1967 (e.g., educational attainment expressed as years of school completed was probably virtually the same before the attitudes were measured), the SES variables were considered to influence alienation in 1967 as well as in 1971. Furthermore, the education and occupational status measures V5 and V6 could reasonably be interpreted as indicators of SES, leading to the following overall model:

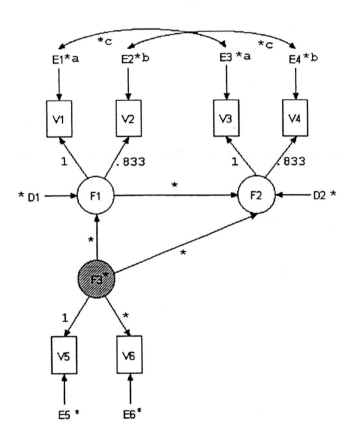

Figure 2.8
Note: Parameters Marked "a", "b", or "c" Are Equal

As can be seen, the upper part of the model is intended to be similar to the factor analytic models considered above, but the factor correlation is replaced by a unidirectional arrow representing the hypothesized across-time regression relation. In addition, the measured variables V5 and V6 are taken as indicators of the SES factor F3, which is hypothesized to affect alienation in 1967 (F1) as well as alienation in 1971 (F2). Whenever a variable such as F1 or F2 changes its status from an independent variable to a dependent variable, a residual is added on the assumption that the variable cannot be perfectly predicted. The disturbances are given in the diagram by D1 and D2.

As the diagram shows, the factor F3 has its scale fixed by the fixed unit path to V5; thus, the variance of the factor is taken to be a free parameter to be estimated. The factors F1 and F2, now dependent variables, cannot have their variances fixed, so the basic choice for fixing such factors is taken: let one path from the factor to a variable be fixed at 1.0. Each of the error variables has its scale fixed by a unit path from the error variable to the corresponding measured variable. The disturbances D1 and D2 similarly have a path fixed at 1.0, so their variances become parameters to be estimated.

The model of Figure 2.8 shares many features of standard latent-variable models. However, it also is intended to maintain most of the characteristics of the highly restricted factor analytic model considered in the previous section. In particular, the model constrains the error variances and covariances as before. These restrictions are shown in the diagram by the letters next to the stars; free parameters with the same letter are constrained to be equal. The model contains one additional restriction that will not be obvious: the paths F1 → V2 and F2 → V4 are fixed rather than free, and the parameters are set at the value .833. The very restricted hypothesis that these paths should equal the given value in this combined model was developed from the previous factor analytic results. In the factor analytic model these two paths were constrained equal, but they were free to be estimated. In that model, the estimated value of the F1 → V2 path was observed to be 2.446, while the F1 → V1 path was 2.937. Thus the F1 → V2 path was .833 as large as the value of the F1 → V1 path. In Figure 2.8, the F1 → V1 path is 1.0, and hence .833 times that value is .833. Thus, the model that is being tested includes the hypothesis that the ratio of factor loadings for the indicators of the F1 and F2 factors found in the four-variable factor analysis problem also holds in the larger problem including variables V5 and V6 and the associated factor and regression structure.

Although data-based model respecifications are widely practiced in structural modeling, the legitimacy of imposing a constraint in one model based on the outcome of an analysis of a previous model on the same data raises some interesting statistical questions that cannot be pursued here. What is important here is the idea that any structural model requires a careful analysis of the parameters of the model, as well as their status as fixed, free, or constrained parameters. If the rationale for a constraint or fixed value is appropriate, it can be implemented in EQS. *Typically, however, one would not want to fix factor loadings at a nonzero value as was illustrated above*, especially if the variables' scales or variances did not have a well-justified rationale. If the scales of the measured variables are in any way arbitrary, one should allow factor loadings to be freely estimated parameters, except for those factor loadings that are fixed for identification purposes. See Cudeck (1989) for a discussion. In any case, the reader is urged to ponder how one might respecify the current model so that the paths F1 → V1 = F2 → V3 = free and F1 → V2 = F2 → V4 = free, precisely as in the restricted factor analytic model considered previously. The model of Figure 2.8 is specified as follows:

Input	Comments
/SPE	
CAS = 932; VAR = 6; ME = ML;	Maximum likelihood
/EQU	
V1 = F1 + E1;	
V2 = .833 F1 + E2;	.833 is fixed — no star
V3 = F2 + E3;	
V4 = .833 F2 + E4;	
V5 = F3 + E5;	
V6 = .5* F3 + E6;	
F1 = − .5* F3 + D1;	
F2 = .5* F1 − .5*F3 + D2;	
/VAR	
D1 TO D2 = 4*;	
F3 = 6*;	
E1 TO E6 = 3*;	
/COV	
E3,E1 = .2*;	
E4,E2 = .2*;	
/CON	
(E1,E1) = (E3,E3);	"a" in Figure 2.8
(E2,E2) = (E4,E4);	"b" in Figure 2.8
(E3,E1) = (E4,E2);	"c" in Figure 2.8
/MAT	
(6 × 6 as before)	
/END	

It should be appreciated by now that the basic approach to setting up a model in EQS is the same regardless of whether path models, factor models, or more generic models are entertained. The basic requirement of any specification is information on the equations of the model and on the variances and covariances of independent variables. The definition of independent and dependent variables should be clear by now. Notice, for example, that F1 is on the right-hand side of some equations but on the left-hand side in one equation; since F1 is once on the left, it is a dependent variable and hence its variance is not a parameter to be specified. F3, in contrast, is never on the left-hand side and is thus an independent variable that must have a variance specification.

EQS adjusts the initial user-provided parameter estimates sequentially in the process of minimizing function Q in (1.1). The above input leads to the following iterative sequence, copied from the EQS output:

Iteration	Parameter Change	Function
1	.533222	.01597
2	.040300	.01448
3	.002334	.01448
4	.000134	.01448

The program took four iterations to converge to an optimal set of parameter estimates. The second column gives the average change in parameters from iteration to iteration. The average is based on the absolute differences between individual parameters from iteration to iteration. It can be seen that by the fourth iteration, the parameters were changing only in the fourth decimal place. The function value is decreasing systematically as it should if the process is converging well. In all methods of estimation except ML, the printed function is the GLS function Q in (1.1) as specialized appropriately. In the case of ML estimation, considered here, the function is a constant times the likelihood ratio statistic used for model evaluation. In all cases, the printed function times $(N - 1)$, where N is the sample size, yields a value that in large samples can be interpreted as a chi-square statistic. Thus, $\chi^2 = 931 \times .01448 = 13.48$, which, based on 9 df yields a probability value of .142. This value is larger than the standard .05 cutoff probability used for model rejection. The model can be considered to fit the data. (The program also prints the χ^2 based on Q, which is 13.27 and yields the same conclusion.)

Five of the eight equations of the model involve only fixed parameters, so their final values are the same as the initial values. The remaining equations and variance and covariance estimates and S.E.s are:

Equations	Variances	Covariances

V6 = .537*F3 + E6
   .043
	F3 = 6.616*
	      .639
		E3,E1 = E4,E2 =.906*
		      .122

F1 = − .630*F3 + D1
   .056
	E1 = E3 = 3.608*
	      .201	

F2 = .593*F1 −   .241*F3 + D2
   .047   .055
	E2 = E4 = 3.595*
	      .164	

	E5 = 2.994* .499	
	E6 = 2.596* .183	
	D1 = 5.671* .423	
	D2 = 4.515* .335	

It is apparent that all parameters are significantly different from zero by the $\underline{z}$ = estimate/S.E. test. SES (F3) more strongly affects F1 than F2, i.e., the contemporaneous effect is stronger than the lagged effect. These direct effects are more interpretable in the standardized solution

$$
\begin{aligned}
V1 &= .835F1 + .551E1\\
V2 &= .785F1 + .620E2\\
V3 &= .845F2 + .535E3\\
V4 &= .797F2 + .604E4\\
V5 &= .830F3 + .558E5\\
V6 &= .651*F3 + .759E6\\
F1 &= -.563*F3 + .827D1\\
F2 &= .569*F1 - .206*F3 + .708D2,
\end{aligned}
$$

with correlations E3,E1 = .251* and E4,E2 = .252*. The direct effect of SES on alienation remains most strongly negative contemporaneously ($-$ .563 vs. $-$ .206). As seen in the structural coefficient of .569, alienation remains quite stable even when SES is controlled. Since $.708^2 = .50$, however, only half of the variance in 1971 alienation is accounted for by 1967 alienation and SES. Substantial instability exists in this attitudinal construct. As compared to the factor model, only a trivial increase in variance explained in F2 was achieved by taking SES into account. Finally, it might be noted that parameters that are constrained to be equal in the statistical metric do not necessarily remain equal in the totally standardized metric. This can be seen, for example, in the standardized coefficients for the error variables E1 and E3.

In the above example, a specific rationale was given for proposing that the equations V2 = .833F1 + E2 and V4 = .833F2 + E4 should have a coefficient of .833 that is a fixed parameter. This rationale was based on the output from the factor analytic output on p. 32, regarding the loadings of V1 and V2 on F1, giving the ratio of 2.446/2.937. It can be argued that creating a specific fixed parametric constraint on the basis of fallible data is an unnecessarily restrictive procedure in general. An approach in the spirit of the constraint that is liable to be more broadly applicable in general would be to use the results of one analysis to suggest bounds on parameters rather than specific values. In particular, the standard errors of the factor analytic solution can also be used to provide something akin to a stochastic rather than fixed constraint. On p. 32, the value of 2.446 is associated with an estimated standard error of .081. Under the usual assumptions, 2.446 $\pm$ .081 is quite likely (with p $\cong$ .68) to contain the true parameter (or, one could use bounds of 2 or 3 S.E.s, depending on the certainty one might desire). Thus, the fixed value of 2.446 could be replaced by lower and upper bounds of 2.365 and 2.527. In that case, it may be desirable to bound the (V2,F1) and (V4,F2) parameters between the values 2.365/2.937 = .805 and 2.527/2.937 = .860 rather than fixing the parameters at .833 in the new, larger model. Such an effect can be implemented quite easily in EQS using the /INEQUALITIES section that permits the direct implementation of inequalities that are otherwise somewhat difficult to specify (McDonald, 1980; Rindskopf, 1983, 1984b). The input of p. 36 would be modified as follows:

	Comments
/EQUATIONS	Changes only shown
V2 = .833*F1 + E2;	.833 becomes a free parameter
V4 = .833*F2 + E4;	Same
/INEQUALITIES	New program section
(V2,F1) GE .805, LE .860;	GE = greater than or equal to .805
(V4,F2) GE .805, LE .860;	LE = less than or equal to .860

This model specification has two more free parameters than the previous one, so that there are 7 df rather than 9 df. EQS yielded $\chi^2 = 12.647$, p = .081, implying a statistically acceptable model. The above equations were estimated as

$$V2 = .860*F1 + E2; \qquad V4 = .855*F2 + E4.$$
$$\quad .027 \qquad\qquad\qquad\qquad .033$$

Only the (V2,F1) parameter was actually held to the boundary. The (V4,F2) parameter was inside the bounds and thus the value is not restricted. The rest of the solution is virtually identical to that previously described, so it is not presented.

A SECOND-ORDER FACTOR ANALYSIS MODEL

The literature discusses structural models in which factors are further decomposed into other factors (e.g., Bentler, 1976; Bentler & Weeks, 1980). In the ordinary factor model, there are a number of factors that are arbitrarily correlated, as in the model of Figure 2.7 where there are two factors F1 and F2; these factors are independent variables in the model. Such factors, which are only one unidirectional arrow away from measured variable indicators, are usually called "first-order" factors. It may be desired to further analyze the intercorrelations among these first-order factors so as to yield higher-order factors. The number of higher-order factors, and the levels of order that one could use, depend on the number of first-order factors. With two first-order factors, as in Figure 2.7, at most one higher-order factor could be obtained, and, even then, only with appropriate restrictions. (See the discussion surrounding Figure 2.4.) This higher-order factor is thus a second-order factor. It is two levels away from the measured variables. The following diagram presents a second-order model for the variables in Figure 2.7.

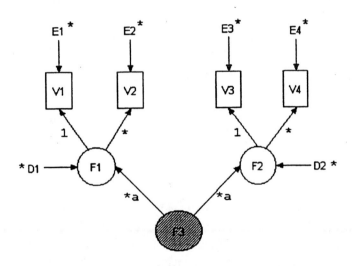

Figure 2.9
Note: Parameters Marked "a" Are Equal

The top part of the figure is a measurement model expressing the variables V1 — V4 in terms of factors F1 and F2, plus residual errors. In contrast to Figure 2.7, however, factors F1 and F2 are no longer correlated, and as dependent variables they are now not drawn shaded. The correlation is no longer a parameter of the model since F1 and F2 are now dependent variables, and such variables cannot have variances or covariance as parameters. Any correlation or covariance between F1 and F2 is explained by the second-order factor F3, which generates F1 and F2 (with imprecision, as indicated by the disturbances D1 and D2). The bottom part of the figure is really of the form of Figure 2.4, except that measured variables to be explained have been replaced by first-order factors to be explained. In order to identify the model, the two second-order factor loadings are constrained equal, as indicated by the letter "a". The variance of factor F3, an independent variable, is fixed at 1 for reasons of identification. The EQS setup for this model is as follows:

Input	Comments
/TITLE	
SECOND-ORDER FACTOR ANALYSIS MODEL	
/SPECIFICATION	
CAS = 932; VAR = 6; ME = GLS;	
/EQUATIONS	
V1 = F1 + E1;	F1 and F2 are 1st-order factors
V2 = 2*F1 + E2;	
V3 = F2 + E3;	
V4 = 2*F2 + E4;	
F1 = 1*F3 + D1;	F3 is the 2nd-order factor
F2 = 1*F3 + D2;	
/VARIANCES	
F3 = 1;	Fixed
D1 to D2 = 1*;	Free
E1 to E4 = 3*;	
/CONSTRAINTS	
(F1,F3) = (F2,F3);	Necessary!
/MATRIX	
(6 × 6 as before)	
/END	

In the factor model of Figure 2.7, F1 and F2 are never on the left side of any equation, while in this model they are. The equations for F1 and F2 specify how these factors are generated by a second-order factor F3 plus a residual. F1 and F2 serve as indicators of F3, in the same way that V's usually serve as indicators of F's. If there had been more than two indicators of F3, the constraint of equal loadings for F1 and F2 on F3 would not have been needed. A second-order factor is interpreted by its indicators in the same way that a first-order factor is interpreted via its indicators. In this example, F3 might be considered to be that part of "alienation" that is stable across the measurement span 1967 – 1971. D1 and D2 represent the part of alienation that is specific to a given time period. If V1 through V4 in Figure 2.9 were first-order factors rather than variables (with their variable indicators not shown), then F1 and F2 would be interpreted as second-order factors and F3 would be a third-order factor. Quite complex hierarchies of factors can be constructed with appropriate data.

The model of Figure 2.9 contains exactly the same number of degrees of freedom as the model of Figure 2.7. The second-order parameterization did not gain degrees of freedom as it usually would with a greater number of indicators. In this case, the two parameterizations are exactly equivalent, and the fit of the model is also the same. Thus, the GLS χ^2 for the above model is 55.612 with 1 df. A residual covariance between errors, along with some further constraints, would lead to a model that fits the data. Space limitations preclude giving more details.

It will be apparent by now that *the residual variables E and D are essentially always independent variables*, see, e.g., Figs. 2.8 and 2.9. Thus *EQS has been written so that E and D variables cannot be specified as dependent variables in an equation.* If a residual is intended to be predicted by other variables, that residual should be called an F variable.

The examples will have clarified that essentially any linear structural model can be specified by a series of equations with known and unknown coefficient parameters. In covariance structure models, the variances and covariances of the independent variables complete the specification. Thus, a single, unified approach to model specification based on the Bentler-Weeks (1980) concepts of dependent and independent variables is used in EQS, irrespective of the particular type of model being studied: whether measured-variable, latent-variable, higher-order, or any other model. The simple principles described above always remain applicable, and no special cases are needed. Given an adequate rationale for a model, and appropriate data against which to evaluate the model, the main difficulty in practice will be deciding whether the model is identified, so that it can be estimated and tested. A helpful device in this regard is to visually search a complex diagram for parts in which identification problems are understood, e.g., to see the bottom part of Figure 2.9 as a factor model with two indicators.

It will be apparent in Figure 2.9 that one can trace a path from F3 to the measured variables, e.g., F3 → F1 → V2. Thus, although F3 has no *direct* effect on V2 because there is no arrow emanating at F3 and ending at V2, F3 has an indirect effect on V2 through the mediation of F1. Direct effects are typically interpreted as causal effects, and are associated with parameters, as shown in the model setup and the output parameter estimates. In contrast, indirect effects are computed from the parameters of the model, and are obtained in EQS in the output stream by a specification in /PRINT. A more detailed discussion of the input options for EQS, and the resulting output, is given in the next two chapters. Chapter 5 provides some additional examples to illustrate structural modeling concepts and the EQS program. /LMTEST and /WTEST procedures for evaluating restrictions, and for guidance towards model improvement, are given in Chapter 6. The topics covered in Chapters 5 and 6 will be relevant to virtually all applications of structural modeling. More specialized topics are discussed in subsequent chapters. Methods for specifying and testing models in several samples simultaneously are given in Chapter 7. Models that involve intercepts are discussed in Chapter 8, while Chapter 9 discusses models that combine features of models in Chapter 7 and 8. Finally, a technical overview of the mathematics involved is given in Chapter 10.

3. PROGRAM INPUT

This chapter provides detailed information on how to set up a job to run EQS. It presumes that the reader has a basic understanding of structural modeling, in particular, the basic concepts of the Bentler-Weeks approach and the estimators that might be appropriate to the model and data under consideration. In the absence of such knowledge, the reader may wish to review the relevant sections of Chapter 2, and, possibly, study some technical material in Chapter 10.

In all the computing environments to which EQS has been ported to date, EQS runs as a stand-alone batch program. In all of these environments, the user must create a basic input file that contains all the key model information required to specify an EQS job. The information that is needed in this *model file* was illustrated in the last chapter, and is explained more fully in this chapter. This input file must be given a name in accord with the computer's operating conventions, say, INPUT.FIL for PCs. EQS is then run (executed) by using the computer's conventional name for the program, typically, by typing EQS (or EQSS). This command calls the program, which then prompts the user for the name of the INPUT.FIL. The user will also be prompted to provide the name of an output file, say, OUTPUT.FIL, into which the results of the run will be placed. If necessary, a file containing the raw data (scores for all cases on the variables, with no missing data or missing data codes) can also be specified; in most computing environments, this will be done in the INPUT.FIL as described below. Directories, subdirectories, and other path information required to specify where these files are located are allowed, using the computer's typical conventions.

An extensive Help Facility is available interactively on most computer systems to answer any questions the user may have when setting up a job for EQS. This library will appear to the user as a pop-up menu that can be invoked by pressing the system's typical Help Function Key (usually F1 or PF1; Alt-H on a PC, after the EQSHELP command has been issued). The help menu can be invoked from any editor, and will be especially useful when creating an INPUT.FIL if some information is needed about EQS conventions. Operation of the Help Facility is self-explanatory. In general, when the name of an input paragraph or keyword (e.g., TITLE) is chosen from a menu, a screen will appear that summarizes the relevant information described in this chapter. Thus the information given below is available, in summary form, through the interactive help facility. As a consequence, this chapter does not need to be explicitly studied. While it should be skimmed to provide a good general overview of the options available with EQS, it will frequently be most helpful as a reference source to provide clarifying information to expand upon the Help Facility's summary assistance.

In general, a structural modeling job is set up in EQS via an input model file containing several sections or paragraphs of material. Each of these sections or paragraphs is preceded by a slash and a keyword (e.g., /TITLE), where the keyword can be abbreviated to the first three characters. The keywords can be started in any column of an input line, but *the line that contains the keyword should contain no other input information*. Specific statements of information regarding the model and data must be provided within each paragraph. Such information is typically separated by a semicolon (;). The user is urged to develop a standard practice that makes it easy to review the program input, e.g., starting keywords in column 1, and beginning statements below the keyword, perhaps indented a few characters. Not all of the paragraphs are needed in any particular job.

In-line comments can be placed in any line of the input file by use of the exclamation mark (!). Any material to the right of the exclamation mark will be ignored by the program. This feature is helpful in documenting the ideas behind a run.

It is easy to be overwhelmed by the many possibilities in a program like EQS. Users new to structural modeling should make use of the simplest job specification possible, e.g., as shown in Chapter 2. Advanced options can be a source of confusion if not selected judiciously, building upon prior experience. This chapter also describes some options, such as /SIMULATION, that will only rarely be invoked by the data analyst, but that may be of special interest to the methodologist.

The input to EQS must be a plain file that contains no invisible control characters that may be generated by a terminal or editor but that may not be seen on a video display. Ordinary word processors use special characters and formats that must be avoided unless a plain text file can be created that strips the file of such special characters. Thus, if there is any chance that an editor will produce unseen characters when using functions such as tabs, these functions should be avoided, since they will usually affect the true (computer-read) input. The program expects the input to be specified with no more than 80 columns of information in each input line.

Covariance or correlation matrix data to be used in a model may reside in a separate data file. Raw data is always assumed to reside in a separate file. These data files may contain as many columns per line as the computer involved will allow. Specific instructions on how to integrate such files into EQS are given below.

In addition to providing input information, in a minicomputer/mainframe environment, the user may have to provide some computer hardware/software-dependent control statements relevant to implementing EQS on his/her computer system. These statements control such things as the available CPU time, memory, etc. Information on these matters should be obtained from the user's computer center. Such information is not needed in interactive or standalone environments, e.g., on a PC.

/TITLE (Optional)

This section is identified by specifying the keyword /TITLE in an input record. On the next line following the keyword /TITLE (abbreviated to /TIT is acceptable), one or more lines of job information can be entered.

An example of a typical /TITLE input might be the following:

```
/TITLE
          CONFIRMATORY FACTOR ANALYSIS RUN.
          PROBLEM BASED ON A RANDOMLY SELECTED SUBSET OF
          OBSERVATIONS FROM THE 1972 COHORT.
```

While the /TITLE section is optional, that is, is not needed to run EQS, it is a good idea to be liberal with title information since it is sometimes the major source of information to help you identify the purpose of the analysis at a later time. A familiar occurrence is that what was all too obvious at the time of job submission turns out to be totally mysterious a few months later. Liberal use of title information is especially urged when dozens of EQS runs are generated. In that case, carefully labeled title information along with the path diagram produced by EQS provides a quick review of the purpose of an analysis. EQS prints all /TITLE information once, and repeats the first line as a header on all output pages. (The reader might also consider making a photocopy of any critical notes, path diagrams, etc. associated with the run, and attaching this material to the printed output. In addition, a few notes marked in large colored writing on the face of the output are usually very helpful.)

/SPECIFICATIONS[1]

This section is identified by entering the keyword /SPECIFICATIONS (abbreviated /SPE) on a new line. It gives the number of cases, the number of input variables, and the method (or methods) of estimation desired, as well as a variety of information to guide the EQS run. The items that can be specified are shown in the table on the next page in three sections: 1) those that are required in any run; 2) those that need not be given if the defaults are acceptable, and 3) optional features that may only be involved in special circumstances.

The information in the /SPEC section can be placed in any order, but each separate type of information must be delineated by the semicolon (;). Information on numbers of cases and variables must always be provided.

CASES

"CASES" refers to the number of subjects, observations, entities, respondents, etc. that were used to generate the covariance matrix, or that are in the input data file (if raw data are to be read). This number should be the number of cases in the input file even if cases are to be deleted during computations (i.e., this number will not change with such deletions). With covariance matrix input, this number is required in order to be able to compute statistics such as chi-square values and standard errors. The program creates a default value when none is given; if the default is wrong, the statistics will be wrong as well. Example: CASES = 200;

A specific number of cases need not be provided when raw score data are used. EQS keeps a running tally of the number of cases of raw data read. It will continue to read data until the end of file is found. The actual number of case data that have been read will be used in the computations and statistics. If the user specifies more cases than can be found in the input data file, EQS uses its computed number in generating the chi-square statistic. A warning message will also be provided.

VARIABLES

This number represents the number of variables in the input raw data file to be read, or in the covariance matrix to be read. It may or may not represent the actual number of variables analyzed in the program (a maximum of < 100, or 200 on unix/mainframes), because EQS automatically uses the model specification to search out the subset of input variables needed to perform the analysis. That is, if the input contains ten variables, but the model requires only six, the relevant six variables will be selected automatically by the labeling V1, V4, etc. used in the /EQUATIONS and /VARIANCES section. The program assumes that variables are ordered in the input matrix as V1, V2, V3.... Example: VAR = 15; Abbreviations, defaults, and other options available under /SPEC are summarized in the following table.

---

[1] See Appendix IV on how to specify variables as categorical for modeling purposes.

/SPECIFICATIONS Keywords

OPERAND	ABBREVIATION	DEFAULT	MEANING
Required Information:			
CASES	CAS = n;	100	Number of cases
VARIABLES	VAR = n;		Number of input variables
Not Required If Defaults Are Acceptable:			
METHOD	ME =	ML	Estimation methods:
	= LS;		Least squares
	= GLS;		Generalized LS
	= ML;		Maximum likelihood
	= ELS;		Elliptical LS
	= EGLS;		Elliptical GLS
	= ERLS;		Elliptical reweighted LS
	= AGLS;		Arbitrary distribution GLS (<u>requires</u> MATRIX=RAW)
	= xx, ROBUST;		Robust statistics, xx is any method except AGLS
MATRIX	MA = COV;	COV	Covariance matrix input
	= RAW;		Raw data input
	= COR;		Correlation matrix input
ANALYSIS	AN =	COV	Type of matrix to be analyzed
	= COV;		Covariance is default
	= COR;		Correlation
	= MOM;		Means & covariances
GROUPS	GR = m;	1	# of input samples (m<10 / 100)
KAPPA	KA = x;	Eq. (10.30)	Elliptical kurtosis parameter to override default
Optional:			
DATA_FILE	DA='INPUT.FIL';		Name of external file where input data resides
DELETE	DEL = a,b,...,z;		Case numbers to be deleted
FIELDS	FI = n;		Max. entries in row of re-arranged covariance matrix
FORMAT	FO = '(....)';		FORTRAN format for input matrix e.g. '(1X,6F10.3)';
UNIT	UN = n;	UN = 9;	Input unit for raw data
		UN = 8;	Input unit for covariance matrix
CATEGORY	CAT = V7,V8;		List of categorical variables for method in Appendix IV
WEIGHT	WEI = 'FILE.NAM';		External file name for AGLS weight matrix (with elements 11, 21, 22, 31, 32, 33, ...)
WFORMAT	WFO = '(....)';		Format needed if WEIGHT is full sym., not lower triangle

METHOD

The program provides for estimation by any one of the methods listed above and described in more detail in Chapter 10 in this manual. If no method is specified, maximum likelihood (ML) is used. However, by the use of compound statements such as ME = ML, AGLS;, the program also allows the running of several estimation methods with one job submission. In actuality, several methods may be run in a single job submission even if only one method is specified.

The elliptical and arbitrary distribution methods are always preceded by a normal theory run, and all methods that are run are printed out. E methods are by default preceded by their normal theory counterpart (ELS by LS; EGLS by GLS; ERLS by ML), although the user can override this by specifying ME = LS, ERLS; for example. AGLS is by default preceded by LS. However, the user may specify any other prior method, by indicating xx, AGLS where xx is any valid normal or elliptical theory method.

The program can yield three or more computational methods in a single job submission, as the following examples clarify:

Method	Comments
ME = LS, GLS, ML;	are always computed in this order even if the methods are permuted;
ME = EGLS, LS;	gives LS, GLS, EGLS in sequence;
ME = AGLS;	gives LS, AGLS;
ME = ERLS, EGLS, ELS;	gives LS, ELS, GLS, EGLS, ML, ERLS.

In general, a maximum of two methods can be specified when AGLS is included, and a maximum of three methods otherwise.

Normal theory estimates are always obtained by an iterative process that starts at the input parameter values provided by the user, or the program's default values, even if two methods such as ME = LS, ML; are specified. Elliptical and arbitrary theory estimates are obtained by starting the iterative process with converged values based on the previous method. If a user desires a run of these methods with parameter estimates starting at the values provided in program input, this must be done by a statement in the /TECHNICAL section of the input. Elliptical and AGLS methods are 1-iteration linearized estimators (based on Bentler & Dijkstra, 1985; see Ch. 10, Eqs. (10.17) – (10.20)) unless their number of iterations is increased in /TECHNICAL.

ME = xx, ROBUST; provides robust statistics for any method specified in xx except AGLS. The robust statistics that are computed are the 1) Satorra-Bentler scaled test statistic (Satorra & Bentler, 1988, 1994) that is designed to have a distribution that is more closely approximated by χ^2 than the usual test statistic (see Ch. 10, Eq. (10.49)), and 2) robust standard errors (Bentler & Dijkstra, 1985, eq. 1.4.5; see Ch. 10, Eq. (10.13)) that are correct in large samples even if the distributional assumption regarding the variables is wrong. Robust statistics can only be computed if raw score data are provided on the input variables, and are not available for AN = MOM. Since xx can be any permitted method specification, if ME = LS, ERLS, ROBUST; the program will compute robust statistics on LS, ML, and ERLS. Robust statistics are computationally very demanding. However, they perform better than uncorrected statistics where the normal distribution assumption is false and better than AGLS in all but the largest samples (Chou, Bentler, & Satorra, 1991; Hu, Bentler, & Kano, 1992).

AGLS estimates cannot be computed without raw data input. Elliptical estimates also require the use of raw data unless a value of KAPPA is provided.

MATRIX

When a covariance matrix is input the user does not need to specify MA = COV;, since this will be assumed by default. The notation MA = COR; specifies a correlation matrix. Typically, when a correlation matrix is input, standard deviations must also be provided. MA = RAW; must be given when raw case scores are input. The words MATRIX, COVARIANCE, and CORRELATION may be spelled out in full.

The matrix to be read may be in the input or in a separate data file, with no missing data. While a covariance or correlation matrix may be in either location, the raw data matrix is always assumed to reside in an external file. The name of the file is usually specified with the DATA_FILE statement, see below. In mainframe systems, external files are located with reference to a unit number and a file name, see below.

ANALYSIS

In addition to specifying the type of matrix that is in the input file, or in the external data file, the user can specify the type of matrix to be analyzed. The program will transform the input data into the correct form for analysis, e.g., a correlation matrix can be transformed into a covariance matrix if standard deviations are also provided.

The default is ANAL = COV;, i.e., a covariance matrix will be analyzed. If this default is desired, the ANALYSIS statement is not needed. The program will automatically transform available input data into a covariance matrix for analysis, without a special instruction. The option ANAL = COR; for analyzing a correlation matrix is not generally recommended due to probable difficulties in statistical interpretation (see, e.g., Cudeck, 1989). However, at times this option may be useful. ANAL = MOM; must be specified if 1st and 2nd moments, i.e., means and covariances, are to be analyzed. This option is used with structured means models (see Chapter 8), in which equations contain the intercept V999, and raw score data and/or means for the variables are available. Robust statistics are not available with ANAL = MOM.

The keywords ANALYSIS, COVARIANCE, CORRELATION and MOMENT can be spelled out, or abbreviated.

GROUPS

This keyword can be omitted unless a multisample analysis (see Chapter 7) is undertaken. In multisample analysis, several datasets are analyzed simultaneously. GROUPS = m; informs EQS that data from m groups or samples are to be analyzed. GR = 2; is an example. A maximum of 9 groups (99 on unix or mainframe computers) can be analyzed together. GR = 1; is the default and need not be specified.

KAPPA

This coefficient is used when elliptical computations are requested. As a default, with raw data input, EQS computes the Mardia-based coefficient given in Chapter 10, Eq. (10.30) and uses it in the computations. However, if (10.30) does not fall within the appropriate range, EQS substitutes (10.34). If (10.34) also does not fall in the appropriate range, (10.35) is used instead. Thus, if these program defaults are acceptable, KAPPA does not need to be defined in the /SPE section. However, the user has the option of overriding the program's default values by specifying any given value. Whatever the value provided by the user, it will override any values computed in the program. Thus, the user could evaluate the alternate coefficients mentioned above, or the two coefficients (10.38) and (10.39) that are computed and printed out when AGLS estimation is used, and decide to use one of these coefficients in subsequent runs. The user must provide the actual numerical value of the coefficient that is to be used, e.g., KAPPA = .2;.

Specification of KAPPA also allows for the use of elliptical estimation when covariance matrix input (i.e., no raw data) is being used. Thus, if many elliptical runs with very large data sets will be done, kappa and the covariance matrix could be computed once and saved, to be used in subsequent runs.

DATA_FILE

This keyword can be used if: 1) the data to be analyzed is in an external file, i.e., it is *not* the covariance/correlation matrix given in the /MATRIX section; and 2) the user's computer system is interactive, e.g., an IBM/PC, VAX, or equivalent system. DA = 'INPUT.FIL'; uses single quotes to enclose the filename, which can be any name that is acceptable to the computer's operating system. The contents of the file can be raw data, or a correlation or covariance matrix. *Neither missing data or missing data codes are permitted; see p. 82 for more information.*

If the operating system is not interactive, it will have a procedure for specifying external file names. See UNIT, below. Please consult your computer center's staff for assistance.

DELETE

When raw data are read in, it is possible to eliminate the scores of certain cases from the computation using the DELETE statement. EQS reads input score vectors and labels them sequentially 1, 2, ... The DEL = 2, 17, 45; statement tells EQS to ignore the data from case numbers 2, 17, and 45. Obviously, each integer number given in the DEL statement cannot exceed the total number of cases in the input file. Up to 20 cases can be deleted with the DELETE statement. The numbers in the DEL statement can be in any order.

FIELDS

When a covariance or correlation matrix is read in, EQS assumes that the matrix is in lower triangular form with two exceptions. A full symmetric input matrix may also be used if a format statement is provided; this is discussed further under /MATRIX. The second exception involves the FIELDS statement. FIELDS permits a rearranged lower triangular input matrix to be read in. This type of rearranged matrix is available as output from standard statistical packages. Thus FIELDS would usually be used when a matrix created by such packages is used in the input stream or via an external data file. FIELDS is not relevant to raw data input.

It will be remembered that elements of a seven variable lower triangular input matrix are given, and computer-read, in the sequence

```
 1
 2  3
 4  5  6
 7  8  9  10
11 12 13 14 15
16 17 18 19 20 21
22 23 24 25 26 27 28
```

where elements 1, 3, 6, 10 ... are variances and the other elements are covariances. If such a matrix has very few fields of data in a given line, it is universally printed as shown. The above example has a maximum of seven fields, which is the number of separate data in the last row. The matrix in the input stream of p. 19 is a 6 × 6 lower triangular matrix, having six fields; the seventh element of that matrix is 4.783, and the fourteenth element is − 3.625. This way of printing output becomes difficult with a large number of variables. For example, if the matrix represents 50 variables, the last row would contain 50 covariances (including one variance). However, if each datum required four columns of space, these 50 numbers could not be printed in one row. Either the numbers must be printed sequentially using several lines for a single variable, in which case the matrix will no longer visually appear to be lower triangular, or the lower triangular matrix format must itself be modified. FIELDS describes the modified matrix.

    The standard modification to printing the lower triangular matrix is to cut off the matrix after a certain number of fields (usually 12 or so), and to move the entire section after that number of fields to a subsequent part of the output. This permits all covariances or correlations having a certain column (variable) designation to be printed sequentially. In the above example, suppose one sets FI = 3;. In that case, the program expects the input matrix to be in the form

```
 1
 2  3
 4  5  6
 7  8  9
11 12 13
16 17 18
22 23 24
10
14 15
19 20 21
25 26 27
28
```

When taken from some statistical packages, the matrix may also contain column variable designations, but EQS assumes, as in the example, that this extraneous information has been removed from the file. The FIELDS statement thus identifies the maximum number of input data in one row of a covariance matrix that has been rearranged as shown above. It can be used with a full symmetric matrix, provided a format statement is used. FI should not be used with an unmodified lower triangular matrix. *If a FORMAT statement is given, the number of fields in FO (e.g., 18F1.0) must be equal to the number of fields in FI.* FIELDS also directs EQS to reorganize the matrix into an ordinary lower triangular matrix prior to the computations. Verification of the program's actions can be found by looking at the printed output section labelled Matrix To Be Analyzed.

FORMAT

The format statement is optional and is not needed if 1) a lower triangular input covariance matrix is read in, as noted below, or 2) the user's computer system has a procedure for reading raw data in free format form, and the input raw data meet the conditions required by the system. If the user desires to read a lower triangular covariance matrix from either an input file or the body of the input with MA = COV;, the matrix is effectively read by EQS as being in free format. The optional format statement, such as F6.3, then merely informs the program as to where a decimal place is to be located.

The format statement is needed if a full symmetric covariance matrix is to be read in from a file. The format can not allow for the selection of variables; the entire full symmetric input matrix must be read in. (Variables will be automatically selected internally, later, via the user's model specification.) Of course, the format statement provides information on the location of decimals.

The format statement is also needed if a raw data file is to be read in, unless the user's computer system allows a free format. Raw data are assumed to be in a case (row) by variable (column) matrix. The format represents the scores for one case of raw data to be read. The CASES statement informs the computer how many such case scores are to be read.

The FORMAT statement should be embedded in a pair of apostrophes and parentheses, e.g., F0 = '(6F3.0)'; where, as usual, it must end with a semicolon. The format statement can wrap around to a new line, but cannot exceed a total of 240 characters, i.e., three lines of format is the maximum possible. Formats usually contain three possible parts. First, a statement like 5X, where X means columns to be ignored and not read; so, 8X means skip 8 columns. Second, statements like 3F7.2, indicating 1) to repeat the format F7.2 three times, 2) to read a field of 7 columns each of the 3 times, and 3) to place a decimal to the left of the last 2 columns each of the 3 times. Thus F7.2 transforms the number 1234567 to 12345.67, and 2F2.0 is equivalent to F2.0,F2.0. When a data value being read contains a decimal point, the decimal point in the data overrides the decimal point implied by the F-type format, e.g., 10.3 can be read using F4.1, F4.2, or F4.3. The space for minus signs must be counted. A third component of a format statement is the slash "/" which instructs the program to skip the remainder of the record and begin the next record. Slashes are used, e.g., when the raw scores of a case are recorded on more than one line. An example is F0 = '(3X,2F2.0,1X,5F3.2)'; giving instructions on how to read 23 columns of input information.

UNIT

The UNIT keyword is not needed in interactive systems like PCs. In mainframe and batch systems like IBM OS/MVS and IBM VM/CMS systems, if raw data are to be read, the location of the input data file must be given in integer form. The unit number is a Fortran logical unit which can be any number less than 99 (except 4, 6, 8, 11, 15, 20). If no value is specified, UN = 8; is assumed when MATRIX = COV; and UN = 9; is assumed when raw data (MA = RAW;) is to be read. Information on assigning unit numbers to files should be available at the user's computer center.

CATEGORICAL

This command specifies the categorical variables. It has the effect that ordinary correlations are replaced with polychoric and polyserial correlations. See Appendix IV.

WEIGHT and WFORMAT

An external weight matrix can be read in to replace the default matrix used in AGLS estimation; see p. 46. Elements must be arranged in sequence as described for the covariance and weight matrices on p. 82. It will be inverted within EQS to yield the W given in Eq. (1.1).

Examples

Examples of valid /SPECIFICATIONS section operands are:

/SPECIFICATION
    CAS = 348; VAR = 15; METHOD = ML;

/SPE
    ME = LS; VAR = 17; CAS = 200; DATA = 'INPUT.FIL';

/SPECS
    VARIABLES = 15; CASES = 257; MATRIX = COR; ANALYSIS = COV;

/SPEC
    CASES = 60; VARIABLES = 6; FIELDS = 5;
    MATRIX = COVARIANCE; METHOD = GLS;

/SPECIFICATIONS
    VAR = 6; MA = RAW;

/SPEC
    CAS = 112; VAR = 6; ME = ML,AGLS; UNIT = 9; MA = RA;
    FO = '(6X,3F5.1,10X,3F5.1)'; DEL = 24, 88;

/LABELS (Optional)

/LABELS (abbreviated /LAB) is a keyword that signals that identifying labels for the observed and/or latent variables are to be used. The use of V followed by a numerical value (such as V3) denotes that a label for the third measured variable follows. An F denotes a label for a latent variable.

Labels may be one to eight characters in length and may be assigned only to F or V type variables (see the "Types of Variables" section on the next page). Blanks will be suppressed in printing, so a blank should be replaced by an underscore or similar symbol.

As an example, the name V3 = MATH; defines the label for the third variable of the variance-covariance or raw data matrix as MATH. Similarly, F2 = VERB; attaches the label VERB to the second latent variable. Labels are not needed for variables that are not used in an analysis. Thus, if a covariance matrix of 20 variables is input in the MATRIX section, but only 13 variables are used, labels for the unused variables are superfluous. Fewer than 13 variables may be labeled if so desired.

As stated previously, the program automatically assigns V1 to the first variable, V2 to the second, and so forth. Thus, if the user does not give a label to a variable, this default numbering system will be used as labels. In a similar way, the latent variables will automatically be assigned the names F1, F2, F3, etc. If the user supplies names for some of the latent variables, these will override the default names.

The labels may be given in any order, but must be followed by a semicolon. Examples of information for the /LABELS section follow.

/LABELS
    V1 = SES1; V3 = SES2; V8 = VERB; V11 = PERFM;
    F1 = SES; F2 = IQ;

/LAB
    F1 = SEXRESPN; F2 = SEXEXPER;
    V1 = ORG_FREQ; V2 = ORG_INTS; V3 = NUMBDATS;
        V4 = NUMBPART; V5 = AGE;

/EQUATIONS

The /EQUATIONS keyword (abbreviated /EQU) signals that detailed information about the particular model under examination is to be input in the next paragraph. One and only one equation is required for each dependent variable. The dependent variables may be either observed or latent, and parameters within the equations may be specified as either fixed or free.

Types of Variables

EQS uses four types of variables. The measured variables and latent variables have already been referred to by the characters "V" and "F", respectively. Residuals of observed variables are denoted by "E", while residuals or disturbances of latent variables are denoted by "D". For reference, these codes are summarized here:

Code	Name	Meaning
V	Variable	Measured variable
F	Factor	Latent variable
E	Error	Residual of measured variable
D	Disturbance	Residual of latent variable

It is recommended that the user who is working with a path diagram label all the variables in the diagram in accord with these conventions. Information necessary for the /EQUATIONS section can then easily be read off the diagram. Following traditional usage in such diagrams, the observed variables (denoted by squares) will be labeled by V's, while the latent variables (diagrammed as circles) are labeled by F's.

Each variable having a V, F, E, or D designation can be followed by a one-, two-, or three-digit integer. Thus, the range of variable numbers within each variable type is from 1 to 999. Examples are V3, F6, D278. Note that leading zeros are suppressed. *A maximum of 100 Vs and 100 Fs (200 each on unix/mainframes) can be used in a model.*

Independent and Dependent Variables

Independent variables are defined in EQS as those measured variables or latent variables that are never structurally regressed on any other variables in the system. When working from a path diagram, independent variables are easily recognized; they are the variables that have no directional arrows aiming at them. Dependent variables are those that are structurally regressed on at least one other variable in a model. It is possible for a dependent variable to also be a predictor of other variables in a model. However, this does not mean it is an independent variable in the sense used by EQS. If a variable is ever structurally regressed on any other variable in the model, i.e., if it appears at least once on the left-hand side of one equation in the /EQU section, then it is a dependent variable, regardless of its relationships to other variables in the system. Dependent variables are also easily recognized in a path diagram; they are those variables with one or more unidirectional arrows aiming at them.

Only V and F variables can be dependent variables, i.e., on the left side of an equation. E and D variables must never be on the left side of an equation. As residuals, they are always independent variables.

Equations Format

Each dependent variable in the model must be given one and only one equation. Thus there are exactly as many equations as there are dependent variables in a model. For each parameter within an equation, an asterisk or star (*) after a numerical value specifies that the parameter is to be estimated, with the number to the left of the asterisk as a starting value. If no number is given next to *, the program will insert the start value. Numerical values not followed by an asterisk specify that the parameter is to be fixed to the numerical value.

As an example, consider the following two equations:

/EQUATIONS
   V2 = .6*F1 + E2;
   F3 = .78*F1 + .64*F2 + D3;

The first equation characterizes the information for the measured variable V2. It states that V2 is based upon a regression on F1 plus a residual term E2. The parameter for V2 on F1 is to be estimated, and a starting value of .6 is to be used. If the equation had been V2 = .6F1 + E2; then the value .6 would be interpreted as a fixed value, never changed by the program. Of course, the first equation is exactly the same as V2 = .6*F1 + 1.0E2; where 1.0 is a fixed parameter. It is possible to use the equation V2 = .6*F1 + 1.0*E2; where 1.0 is a free parameter, but this approach will almost always require fixing the variance of the E2 variable. The second equation describes the structural equation for the latent variable F3. It shows that F3 is a function of F1, F2, and the residual D3. Two parameters are to be estimated in this equation, with starting values of .78 and .64. Note that embedded blanks are permissible in the equations, as well as completely blank lines. Each equation must end with a semicolon.

A given variable can appear only once on the right-hand side of an equation. Thus, V1 = .2*F1 + .6*F1 + E1; is not permitted. If such a situation is encountered, EQS will ignore all but the last occurrence of the duplicated variable. This example would be interpreted as V1 = .6*F1 + E1;

Equations can be of any length and can span several lines if necessary. However, the unit of a parameter estimate and the associated variable designation (e.g., .5*F2) cannot be split and appear on two lines. An equation can be wrapped around to the next line, but, as usual, the equation must end with a semicolon.

The sequence of equations is arbitrary, so they can be put in any order. The user is urged, nonetheless, to group the measurement equations (equations for V variables) together, and similarly to group the construct equations (equations for F variables) together, as well as to sequence equations in a logical numerical ascension within each set. Equations organized in this way are more easily scanned for possible errors. Blanks can be inserted into equations so that they more visibly reflect the intended structure. Thus, V1 = .5*F1 + E1; and V2 = .3*F2 + E2; might be written as follows when embedded in a large number of equations

```
/EQU
      V1 = .5*F1      + E1;
      V2 =      .3*F2 + E2;
```

making the factor structure more visible. However, care must be taken to avoid unseen control characters such as those stemming from tabs. Finally, it is recommended that whenever possible, the numerical designation for V's and E's correspond in a given equation. Thus, while one could write V2 = .6*F1 + E13; where the number 13 is arbitrary, this practice is liable to lead to confusion. Similarly, it is suggested that the disturbances D be numbered in accord with the number of the dependent factor F.

Start Values

Start values are not needed for most jobs. That is, equations of the form V4 = *F1 + *F2 + E4; are acceptable, and the program will generate values for the * parameters that, in most cases, will allow the iterative procedure to find the optimal estimates. The typical default start value is 1.0*. However, it is probably good practice to provide start values because EQS's start values may be inadequate in some models and thus the program may not converge. More importantly, providing start values helps to clarify which coefficients are expected to be large positive or large negative. The final results then can be informative about one's expectations.

Because of the varying types of models that are run with EQS, it is difficult to give rules about the relative size of coefficients in equations. Actually, it is only necessary to have a reasonably good guess about the size and sign of a few key start values, since the relative size of others then tends not to matter much in the iterative calculations. Thus a few key factor loadings should always be on the large size. What is "large," of course, depends on the scale of the variables, how unmeasured variables are identified, and on the true model. (If necessary, a few runs with small models on parts of the data, or of a complete model, will quickly establish this information.) Coefficients for predictor and criterion variables of a similar designation (e.g., predicting a V from a V, or an F from an F) and conceptual nature (e.g., first-order factors) can usually be started at small values such as .1 or zero. Of course, if one knows that an effect, such as a factor loading, is strong, the start value should reflect this information. The better the start values, the quicker the iterative calculations will converge on a solution.

Selecting a Subset of Variables

The information in the /EQUATIONS paragraph can be used to select a subset of variables out of the original input covariance or data matrix. EQS scans the equations, and then selects only those variables from the input covariance or data matrix that are specified in the /EQUATIONS or in the /VARIANCES section. For example, if an input covariance matrix has fifteen variables, but the equations contain only V2, V6, V8, V9, and V10, then only those five variables will be selected as data to be analyzed. The remaining variables will be ignored unless the variable is mentioned in the VARIANCES section, in which case it will also be selected. The covariance matrix to be analyzed will be constructed with V2 as the first variable, V6 as the second, and so forth.

Editing Equations

Models that contain a large number of equations can be tedious to specify. The advanced features of many editors make it easy to generate equations with an editor, using e.g., a block copy command to duplicate a set of equations, and then modifying the duplicate blocks so that the equations are exactly as desired. Blocks can be as large or small as desired, even consisting of single equations. For example, the single equation V1 = .8*F1 + E1; could in many editors be easily duplicated, say 20 times. Then, a global search can be undertaken for all Vs, and V1 replaced by V2, V3, and so on in sequence, doing only a few keystrokes. Similar procedures would change the E numbers. Then the Fs can be changed using another editor feature, for example, F1 can be changed to F2 in some equations by doing a global search (for F1) and replace (with F2) within a section. Start values are easy to find by searching for "*".

/VARIANCES

The /VARIANCES paragraph (abbreviated to /VAR) specifies fixed and free values for the variances of the independent variables. In EQS, E and D variables are always independent variables. *Dependent variables are not allowed to have variances as parameters, whether fixed or free.* As in the /EQUATIONS section, numerical values followed by "*" denote a free parameter that is to be started at the number provided by the user. Numerical values not followed by "*" are considered fixed parameters. As always, each sentence or piece of information is terminated by a semicolon.

A sequence of variances can be started at the same value by using the "TO" convention. For example,

/VARIANCES
    E1 TO E6 = .67*; E7 TO E9 = .5*;
    F1 TO F2 = 1.0; D3 = 3.4*;

Here the variances of the two latent variables F1 and F2 are fixed parameters with values of 1.0, while the remaining variances are free to be estimated. The first six E1, E2,...,E6 are started at .67, while the variances of the residuals E7, E8, and E9, are started at .5. The latent variable residual D3 has its variance started at 3.4. As usual, the better the start value, the quicker the program will converge to a solution.

Variables also can be listed in sequence with a single start value. When some variables are in a sequence of variables generated by the TO convention, and then *subsequently* listed separately with particular start values, the subsequent start values *override* the start values given in the TO section. Thus,

/VAR
    F2,F4,V8 = 1;

E14 TO E20 = 0.5*; E15,E17,E19 = 0;

fixes the variance of F2, F4, and V8 at 1.0, while the second line is equivalent to E14=.5*;E16=.5*; E18=.5*; E20=.5*; since the fixed 0 values override the sequence specified by TO. Blanks are ignored.

As noted in Chapter 8, V999 is a special independent variable (a constant) that has variance that is fixed at zero. This need not be specified; it will be assumed.

As always, a logical ordering of information will make viewing the input and understanding its purpose much easier. It is possible to write multiple sentences of information on a single line, as long as a sentence is not split. *Each line must end with a semicolon.* The user is urged to group the variance information in a meaningful way across several lines whenever possible.

If a measured variable is specified in this section, it will also be selected in the creation of a subset covariance matrix to be analyzed. If a measured variable is not mentioned in either /EQUATIONS or /VARIANCES, it will not be used in the analysis.

Start Values

As usual, EQS will provide simple and typically adequate start values where none are given. Most variances are started at 1.0*, while E variables will have variances started at .9 times the variance of the associated V variables. Independent V's have their variances started at the input data values. Of course, user-specified values can be helpful in creating quicker convergence to a solution, though it can be difficult to get a feel for the appropriate size of a start value. In the case of variances, it is a good practice to make them quite large relative to the covariances that might be in a model. For example, the variance for an E term should be some substantial fraction of the variance of the corresponding measured variable. Overestimation of the variances of the independent variables only rarely creates computational difficulties. On the other hand, underestimation will frequently lead to singularities in the model matrix Σ, which may create iterative problems with several types of estimators. Variances started near zero are usually problematic.

/COVARIANCES (Optional)

The /COVARIANCES keyword (abbreviated /COV) begins the paragraph specifying the fixed and free covariances among independent variables. If a variable is involved in a covariance, its variance must also be specified in /VAR. A pair of variables whose covariance is to be estimated by EQS is specified by giving both variable names followed by a numerical value, and optionally, an asterisk or star if the parameter is to be estimated. If the "*" is deleted, the covariance will be fixed at the number. For example,

/COVARIANCES
    F2,F1 = .3*;

specifies that the covariance between variables F2 and F1 is a free parameter, started at the .3 value. As always, fields in the /COVARIANCES section must be delimited by semicolon. *Dependent variables cannot have covariances.*

Although the pair of variables involved in a covariance can be specified in any arbitrary sequence (e.g., the above example could be given as F1,F2 = .3*;), the user is urged to adopt a consistent way of specifying covariances, for example, by systematically listing the covariances as if taken from a lower or upper triangular matrix form. In the former case the subscript for the variable with the larger number is always written first e.g., F2,F1 = .4*; and rows of the lower triangular matrix are listed sequentially.

Covariances that are not specified in this section are assumed to be fixed zeros, so there is no need to specify fixed zero covariances. However, fixed nonzero covariances among independent variables also have to be specified. And, of course, all free covariance parameters must be included and provided an asterisk for identification.

The /COV paragraph also has a TO convention, which can be used to generate all possible lower triangular pairs among a set of variables of the same type. For example,

/COV
        E1 TO E4 = .2*;

is equivalent to the input

/COV
        E2,E1 = .2*;
        E3,E1 = .2*; E3,E2 = .2*;
        E4,E1 = .2*; E4,E2 = .2*; E4,E3 = .2*;

It is apparent that /COV excludes the diagonal elements of a covariance matrix, which must be specified in the /VAR section. Furthermore, TO cannot be used to connect different types of variables, e.g., E1 TO F3 = .3*; does not make any sense to the program.

When the TO convention is *followed* by specific covariances that are not consistent with the TO statement, the specifically designated covariances *override* the statements generated by "TO". For example,

/COV
        E1 TO E4 = .2*; E3,E2 = 0; E4,E3 = 0;

is equivalent to the statement

/COV
        E2,E1 = .2*;
        E3,E1 = .2*;
        E4,E1 = .2*; E4,E2 = .2*;

so that four rather than six free covariances are created.

As in the /VAR section, V999 is a special variable; it always has fixed zero covariances with other variables that need not be specified. Also, blanks in the input will be ignored, and *each line must end in a semicolon*. As before, the reader is urged to create a visual layout for the specifications that makes them easy to understand and review.

Start Values

Start values for covariances to be estimated should usually be small, compared to the size of the variances of the variables involved. In fact, unless the user has some knowledge that gives reason to predict a relatively large positive or negative covariance between a pair of variables, a start value of 0* is usually safe, as well as effective. In contrast, large values frequently lead to iterative problems. The default start value of a covariance is 0*, except for V variables whose covariance is started at the input value. Thus a statement like E2,E1 = *; will have the initial parameter estimate taken at zero.

/CONSTRAINTS (Optional)

EQS permits two types of constraints to be imposed on estimated parameters within a sample that are specified in the /CONSTRAINTS section (abbreviated /CON). The two types are equality constraints and general linear constraints. Only simple equalities are allowed for cross-group constraints; see below or Chapter 7.

Equality constraints are specified when two or more parameters are to be estimated with the same numerical value. For example, one may want $\theta_i = \theta_j$, where θ_i and θ_j are some parameters. Such a constraint can be specified in the straightforward way just given: $\theta_i = \theta_j$. However, as a lead into the more complicated general linear constraint, the program also gives the user the option of specifying the constraint such that a constant appears on the right of the equation. In this example, one has $\theta_i - \theta_j = 0$, where the constant is zero. If several parameters are to be set equal, this can be done directly by a statement of the form $\theta_i = \theta_j = \theta_k$. However, as an introduction to the general linear constraints, the user can also specify three equalities with two equations. That is, if $\theta_i = \theta_j = \theta_k$, two equations are needed, for example: $\theta_i - \theta_j = 0$ and $\theta_i - \theta_k = 0$, or else $\theta_i - \theta_j = 0$ and $\theta_j - \theta_k = 0$. Note that with m equalities, m − 1 equations are needed. That leaves m − (m − 1) = 1 free parameter to be estimated. It does not matter which m − 1 equations are used, as long as they are not redundant (linearly dependent). Thus $\theta_i - \theta_j = 0$ and $\theta_i - \theta_j = 0$ as two constraints would not be correct.

General linear equality constraints represent the constraint hypotheses that are found in most linear models. They allow the weighting of parameters in arbitrary fashion, as long as the weights w_i are known. Thus, one may believe that − or be interested in testing whether − one parameter is a linear combination of others. Thus, if $\theta_i = 5\theta_j + .3\theta_k + 1$, one would need to specify the constraint equation in a form with the constant on the right-hand side, as $\theta_i - 5\theta_j - .3\theta_k = 1$. In the general case, $w_i\theta_i + w_j\theta_j + \cdots + w_k\theta_k = c$. As in the case of simple linear equalities, it is necessary to assume that the constraint equations are not redundant. If the constraint equations are linearly dependent, the program will print an error message and will adjust the degrees of freedom. At a minimum, there should be fewer constraint equations than free parameters involved in these equations.

It is important to note that only free parameters can be involved in constraint equations. If a fixed parameter needs to be included in such an equation, the user must do the arithmetic that will absorb the fixed parameter into the constant on the right-hand side of the equation. Thus, if $w_i\theta_i + w_j\theta_j + w_k\theta_k = c$, but θ_k is a fixed or known number, the equation must be specified in the form $w_i\theta_i + w_j\theta_j = \bar{c}$ (= c − $w_k\theta_k$), where $\bar{c}$ is the new constant. The program will not do this arithmetic for the user.

Both types of constraints can be imposed on any of the free variances, covariances, and measurement or construct equation parameters. Such parameters must be associated with asterisks (*) to denote a value to be estimated. If a parameter defined in the /CONSTRAINTS section is not a free parameter, an error message will be printed and the program will terminate. It will not continue into the computational section. The error must be corrected, and the job resubmitted.

Double Label Convention

To implement equality and general linear constraints, a unique designation must be available for each parameter of a model. Since EQS does not use Greek symbols such as θ_i, a "double-label" convention based on the model specification language is used instead. Each parameter is defined by a {left parenthesis, variable name, comma, variable name, right parenthesis}, such as (V1,F1), for example, so two variable labels uniquely define a parameter. Since all parameters are either coefficients in equations, or variances or covariances, there are three cases to consider.

Equations. Regression coefficients appearing in equations are identified by the pair (dependent variable, independent variable). Thus in the equation V1 = 2*F1 + E1;, the parameter 2* is identified as (V1,F1) since V1 defines the unique equation involved, and F1 the relevant part of the right-hand side. Note that (V1,E1) defines the fixed 1.0 parameter; however, since only free parameters can be involved in constraints, the parameter (V1,E1) could not be used in a constraint specification. In the longer equation F1 = .6*F2 + .1*F3 − 2*F4 + D1;, the parameter − 2* is given by (F1,F4). The ordering of the labels is critical; (F4,F1) does not define any parameter in the equation since each of these parameters must be given by (F1,XX), where XX would be any of the three predictor variables F2, or F3, or F4.

Variances. The variance of an independent variable is uniquely defined by repeating the variable name. Thus, if V6 = .3*; was specified in the /VAR section, the parameter 3* would be given by (V6,V6). The mnemonic is, of course, the row and column designation for the diagonal element of a matrix. If /VAR contained F1 TO F4 = .8*; V1 = 1.0; E5 = .3*; etc., then (F2,F2) would define the relevant .8* free parameter, (V1,V1) could not be used in a constraint since it is a fixed, not free, parameter, etc.

Covariances. The covariances among independent variables are specified as in the /COV section, except that in the /CON section they are surrounded by parentheses. Thus, with /COV specifying E6,E3 = .3*; V1,F5 = − .2*; etc., these parameters are double-label identified as (E6,E3) and (V1,F5). To avoid confusion, the reader is urged to use the same double-labels in the /COV paragraph as in the /CON section, e.g., the E6,E3 = .3*; parameter should not be labeled (E3,E6).

Equality Constraints

After using the keyword for the /CON section, any free parameter can be set equal to one or a group of parameters — whether a regression coefficient, variance, or covariance — by a simple statement. Examples are:

	Comments
/CONSTRAINTS	Required
(E1,E1) = (E2,E2);	Simplest case
(V5,F1) = (V3,F2) = (V9,F3) = (V12,F1);	Cannot exceed 80 cols!

A maximum of eight to ten equalities can be specified in a single statement due to the 80 column limitation. Each equality statement must be terminated with a semicolon on each line — more than one statement per line is not permissible, i.e., *exactly one ";" per line must be given*. Of course, the parameters specified in an equality must 1) exist in the model, 2) be free, and 3) start at the same value. The latter point requires the user to assure that the start values provided for the free parameters meet the constraints to be imposed. If the start values do not meet the constraint, the program may not be able to impose the constraint during optimization. Note that no weighting constants can be used when simple equalities are specified. Thus, (E1,E1) = 2(E2,E2); is an illegal specification.

General Linear Constraints

As noted above, m equalities require m − 1 linear constraint equations. For example,

	Comments
/CON	
3(V4,V4) − (V8,V8) = 0;	No "*" permitted
.2(E1,E1) + .8(E2,E2) = 1;	One constraint per line

The first constraint sets the free parameter (V4,V4) at 1/3 the value of the free (V8,V8) parameter. The second says that the weighted sum of the (E1,E1) and (E2,E2) parameters equals 1.0.

Constraints must be used with a great deal of care in order to avoid problems. An example of an *inappropriate* job set up is the following.

/EQUATIONS
    V4 = .68*F3 + E4;
    V5 = 1.0 F3 + E5;
    V6 = .8* F4 + E6;

/CONSTRAINT
    (V6,F4) − (V5,F3) − .2(V4,F3) = 0;

Because the parameter (V5,F3) is a fixed parameter that takes on the value 1.0, the correct CONSTRAINT specification would be

/CON
    (V6,F4) − .2(V4,F3) = 1.0;

The above example, however, is not strictly correct due to one more requirement of the program. *The starting values of the free parameters should meet any constraints that are to be imposed.* In this instance, the constraint is not met by the given estimated parameters, because $.8 - .2(.68) \neq 1.0$. The constraint would be met if the /EQUATIONS were respecified as

    V4 = − 1.0*F3 + E4; V6 = .8*F4 + E6;

because now $.8 - .2(- 1.0) = 1.0$, as required. Note that such a radically different estimate of the (V4,F3) parameter, with its sign reversed, may not make sense substantively;

alternatively, the constraint may not make sense with the original, well-estimated, parameters. Imposing constraints on an otherwise sensible and well-fitting model may make a model fit badly, thus suggesting that a constraint is not reasonable. *Constraints should only be considered in the context of an otherwise plausible model.* Estimation difficulties can easily occur with implausible models, or implausible constraints. The appropriateness of a constraint can be evaluated directly by the /LMTEST. See Chapter 6.

Cross-group Constraints

The method of specifying constraints described above is applicable to models involving data from several samples, but the description is limited to the *within-sample* constraints only. That is, the /CON section is placed within the input stream of the model for a given sample, and each of the parameters involved in the constraint is a parameter in the model for that sample. When the data contains only one group, this is, of course, the only possibility, but when multisample analysis is undertaken, with GROUPS in /SPEC being specified as 2 or more, there are other possibilities. Multisample covariance structure analysis is described in Chapter 7. In multisample analysis, there are within-sample constraints, but also *cross-sample* or cross-group constraints.

When GROUPS = 2 or greater, there are as many input segments (with sections from /SPEC to /END) as there are groups in the analysis. A /CONSTRAINT section can be placed within each of these input segments, as usual, to describe the within-sample constraints. However, the /CONSTRAINTS section of the *last* group is modified to permit specifying, in addition, cross-group constraints.

Cross-group equality constraints must be specified in the last group, using a special format. The format is essentially the same as in the one-group case, except that a group number is now added as the first specification inside a parenthesis. In a 3-group example with only one parameter constrained to be equal across the three groups, one would have, symbolically: (1,P1) = (2,P1) = (3,P1); where 1, 2, and 3 are the group numbers and P1 is any free parameter, designated in practice by a specific double-label name such as F2,F1. Thus an actual example would be

```
/CONSTRAINTS
    (1,E1,E1)  = (2,E1,E1);
    (1,V3,F1)  = (2,V3,F1);
    (1,F2,F1)  = (2,F2,F1);
```

where there are two groups and three parameters constrained to be equal. In these examples, the same type of parameter such as an error variance (E1,E1) is being constrained equal across the two groups. However, any free parameter from one group can be specified to be equal to any other free parameter in any other designated group. As usual, all the parameters listed must be free parameters in the model, and their start values must be equal.

General linear constraints across groups involving constant multipliers or additive constants can also be used. These constraints must be written in the form .5(1,V1,F1) + 3(2,V1,F1) = 1; and the start values must meet the constraint.

The appropriateness of constraints can be evaluated by the /LMTEST as described in Chapter 6.

If there are many cross-group constraints, the block-copy and search features of a program editor should be used: A few lines of constraints are written out precisely; these lines are duplicated several times; and the duplicated lines are then edited to yield the correct specification.

/INEQUALITIES (Optional)

The /INEQUALITIES keyword (abbreviated /INE) permits an estimated free parameter to be constrained between an upper and/or lower bound. Note that fixed parameters cannot be constrained this way — they already are, by their nature, maximally constrained.

Only one parameter at a time can be specified as constrained. This is done by specifying a constraint on a single line of the input stream using one of two conventions. The basic convention uses capitalized FORTRAN-like greater than (GT), greater than or equal to (GE), less than (LT), and less than or equal to (LE) symbols. An alternative convention, described further below, uses a more mathematical notation.

For example, the inequality (V3,F1) GT 0, LE 1; specifies that the free parameter (V3,F1) is to be greater than zero and less than or equal to one. The inequality (V8,F4) GT 50; specifies that the parameter (V8,F4) is to be greater than fifty. The inequality can also specify only an upper bound, for example (E6,E4) LT 100; inequality constraints on variances must be denoted by a double identifier as in (V10,V10) LT 100;. As before, every parameter involved in an inequality is inside parentheses.

EQS does not allow negative variance estimates. *The program automatically imposes an inequality constraint of nonnegativity on each variance.* Since most programs do not impose this necessary constraint, the results obtained under such a constraint may not match results obtained without the constraint. It should be noted, however, that the constraints are necessary to statistically-based estimation methods such as maximum likelihood; a solution with a negative variance estimate is not a maximum likelihood solution. The user may, of course, override this feature by specifying that each variance be greater than or equal to a large negative number. This constraint replaces the current implicit constraint that a variance be GE 0. Thus (E4,E4) GT − 999999; would eliminate the existing implicit constraint.

The program automatically imposes an inequality constraint on a covariance such that the corresponding correlation is in the ± 1 range; this is done if and only if the relevant variances of the variables are set to fixed numbers. If F1 and F2 are factors whose variances have been specified to equal fixed 1.0, the covariance F2,F1 actually represents a correlation. This correlation is automatically forced to lie in the range between − 1 and +1. If the variances of F1 and F2 are fixed at 4 and 9, the free parameter covariance F2,F1 is forced to lie in the range ± 6, since the end points of the range correspond to correlations of ± 1. This program feature can be overridden by specifying an appropriate very small lower bound and very large upper bound for the covariance in question. Note that since these inequalities are not automatically imposed in most covariance structure programs, results from EQS may not match those from similar programs. If the variances of variables are free to be estimated, EQS will not impose any inequality on the associated covariances. Thus, after standardization as provided in the program output, the researcher may find in pathological cases that the correlation that is associated with a covariance is out of the ± 1 range. Considering the standard error associated with such a covariance estimate, this often implies that the variables are perfectly associated and the researcher may wish to respecify the model based on this knowledge.

The program cannot effectively distinguish between GE or GT, or between LE or LT. In practice, GE and LE are used in the program. So, if the user says (V3,V2) GT 0; one may obtain a value of 0.0. If one wants a value strictly greater than 0, one will have to decide how much larger is large enough, and make the appropriate specification. Thus, (V3,V2) GT 0.0001; will insure the value is greater than 0. But the program acts by implementing (V3,V2) GE 0.0001;.

When no /INEQUALITY constraint is imposed on a parameter, the program acts as if any number that can be carried in the computer is an appropriate estimate. Such an estimate may be very small or very large. This effect is achieved in practice by imposing inequalities such as GE − 9999999. and LE 9999999. When an /INEQUALITY is imposed, *the user must be sure that the start value for the parameter is inside the permissible range.* Thus, variances must be estimated initially as nonnegative and covariances must be such that the corresponding correlations are in the +1 to − 1 range when the defaults noted above are used.

It should be noted that when a parameter is estimated at a specific boundary (e.g., at 0 for a variance), that parameter may not have a standard error associated with the estimate.

An alternative convention can be used to specify /INEQUALITIES. In this convention, an inequality sign (> or <) replaces the GT (GE) or LT (LE) symbol. Furthermore, the statement itself requires the inequality to be written in a standard mathematical form. To illustrate,

/INEQUALITIES	Equivalent Convention
− 1.0 < (V4,V3) < 1.0;	(V4,V3) GT − 1.0, LT 1.0;
1.0 > (V5,V4) > − 1.0;	(V5,V4) LT 1.0, GT − 1.0;
(E1,E1) < .5;	(E1,E1) LT .5;
.2 < (D2,D2);	(D2,D2) GT .2;

Thus while the original FORTRAN-like convention requires every inequality to start with the double-label name of the free parameter involved, statements involving the inequality sign embed the parameter inside the appropriately directed signs. As noted above, the program cannot distinguish between > and ≥, or < and ≤, i.e., the program assumes that the meaning of ">" is really " ≥ ", and acts accordingly. If the user is concerned with creating a strict inequality, an appropriately modified constant will have to be used in the statement. For example, .201 < (D2,D2); will assure that (D2,D2) is not equal to .2. However, it must be recognized that the computational accuracy of the estimates sets a limit on such discriminations.

Inequalities for Convergence Control

/INEQUALITIES can sometimes effectively be used in difficult estimation problems as a means of obtaining convergence when nothing else seems to work. This is especially true if it appears as if one estimated parameter is going outside of a reasonable range. Imposing a constraint that forces the parameter to stay in an appropriate range during the iterations may make the process work, yielding a final solution that is interpretable and statistically valid. The trick is to impose an /INE that will help the program converge, but that will finally not need to be imposed. At convergence, ideally, the parameter is not held to the boundary. If the parameter *is* held to the boundary at the solution, then the trick did more than help convergence; it obtained a restricted solution. If such a solution is not desired, a wider bound may be needed.

There will be cases, of course, when the bound will always be necessary. For example, inequalities should not be expected to solve the problem of underidentified parameters.

/MATRIX (Optional)

This section is used for covariance and correlation matrix input only, i.e., it is not applicable to raw data input. The keyword /MATRIX (abbreviated /MAT) signals to the program that the input covariance (correlation) matrix follows, beginning on the next record. Do not use a /MAT section if the matrix resides in a separate data file. As a default, EQS uses a "free-field" input format, which requires that elements of the matrix be separated by at least one blank space. It is assumed that no extraneous information, e.g., labels or missing data codes, exists.

Three different formats can be used for this (covariance or correlation) matrix, whether the matrix follows in the input or resides in a separate data file. The formats are: lower triangular form, rearranged lower triangular form, and full symmetric form. When a small problem is to be analyzed, the lower triangular form is usually the format of choice. When a large problem is to be analyzed, and the matrix is imported from one of the standard statistical packages, the rearranged lower triangular form is frequently used. In certain circumstances, a full symmetric matrix may be available and it can be used without modification.

An example of the /MATRIX section in lower triangular free format form is

```
/MATRIX
    2.0
     .67        1.8
     .32       − .09       1.4
```

It will be noted that this is only one of three sections of the input where *no semicolon is used to mark the end of the input sentence*. The simple rule is that input consisting of data only do not use ";". Thus /MEANS and /STANDARD DEVIATIONS also do not end their data segments with a ";".

EQS reads a lower triangular matrix as follows: in the first line, it expects one datum, and it stops reading after that is encountered. In the second line, it expects two data, and it stops thereafter. It continues in this fashion until more data would need to be read than can fit in a single line: at this point, it expects the data to "wrap" into the next line and it continues to read until it has read just enough to finish that variable's input. Consequently, it is not possible to list all the data as more or less continuous input, in as few lines as possible. In the example above, it would not be possible to place 2.0 .67 1.8 − .09 1.4 into a single line of input. For p variables, at least p lines of input are needed, but in a big job, more than p will be needed because of the wrapping feature.

If a FORTRAN format is provided in the /SPEC paragraph, and a lower triangular form of input is used in the /MAT section, the format's sole function is to specify a decimal place in the input numbers when no such decimals are provided.

If a FIELDS statement exists in the /SPECIFICATION paragraph, directing EQS that a rearranged covariance matrix exists having a certain number of fields as the dividing point for the rearrangement, then the input matrix must be in the form discussed in detail in the FIELDS documentation. If the above data were to be used with a FIELDS = 1; specification (in practice this would never be done), the /MAT section would have to be followed on the next six lines with the numbers 2.0 .67 1.8 .32 − .09 1.4 − one number per line with no punctuation.

When a FORTRAN format statement is provided in the /SPEC section, the /MAT paragraph will also accept a full, symmetric input covariance matrix. For example, with the format FO = '(3F3.1)'; specified in /SPEC, the following input of 3 rows with 9 columns per row

/MATRIX

18	6	− 1
6	12	4
− 1	4	9

is equivalent to the free format stream

/MAT

1.8		
.6	1.2	
− .1	.4	.9

Two strategies are generally used with regard to the input covariance matrix. The covariance matrix may contain only the variables planned for a particular analysis. The variables that are used for an analysis may occur in any order in the input matrix − no special ordering is needed. Alternatively, a large matrix (up to VAR = 99) may be used, from which those variables needed in an analysis are then automatically selected. The latter, more general approach is useful for those problems that require different combinations of variables from among a large set. The automatic selection procedure has been discussed previously.

/STANDARD DEVIATIONS (Optional)

If the input matrix is a correlation matrix rather than a covariance matrix, the correlations should be transformed into covariances prior to analysis. In order to do this, it is necessary to provide the standard deviations of the variables. This is done by providing the keyword /STA or /STANDARD DEVIATIONS, and, on the subsequent line, listing the standard deviations. There must be exactly as many standard deviations as there are variables in the correlation matrix to be read. The standard deviations are expected to be in the same sequence as the variables in the input matrix.

The numbers are read in free format. Thus, there must be a blank space between two different numbers. More than one line can be used if necessary. *No semicolon is used to end this data input section.* Examples are the following:

/STANDARD DEVIATIONS
    1.345 6.336 1.22 9.4

/STA
    .87   4.334 .969 3.01 2.78 3.4
    1.116   .45

Note that blanks are permissible (between numbers, but not within one number), and wrapping to the next line is permitted (however, a number cannot be split across two lines). Since the program expects to read a certain quantity of numbers as given by the number of variables in the input matrix, the first example must have four input variables and the second must have eight.

When /STANDARD DEVIATIONS are used in input, EQS assumes the matrix to be analyzed is a correlation matrix. As a safety feature, EQS will check the diagonal elements of the input matrix. If any of these elements are greater than 1.01 or less than .99, an error message will be printed.

/MEANS (Optional)

Means are not relevant to typical covariance structure models, and hence they usually need not be included in the input stream. However, when structured means models are analyzed, as described in Chapter 8, the model will contain the intercept V999, and variable or factor intercepts and means become parameters of the model. As a consequence, the means of the input variables become data to be analyzed, and they must be available. If raw data are read in, of course, the program computes the variable means, and they need not be provided separately. However, if a correlation or covariance matrix is used as input, the /MEANS paragraph must be used. This information is used to create the covariance/mean partitioned matrix that will be analyzed.

There must be exactly as many means given under /MEANS as there are input variables in the matrix to be read in. The means are expected to be in the same sequence as the variables in the input matrix. The numbers are read in free format. Thus there must be a blank space between two different numbers. More than one line can be used if necessary. As data input, *no semicolon is used to end this input section.* Some examples are:

/MEANS
    1.012 1.123 .564 2.10

/MEA
    .87 4.334 .969 3.01 2.78 3.4
    1.116 .45

In the first example, there must be four variables in the input covariance matrix, since four numbers are given. The second example shows wrapping onto a second line, with means given for 8 variables. Note that no ";" is used to end the means information.

/LMTEST (Optional)[2]

The Lagrange Multiplier or /LMtest procedure is designed to test hypotheses on the statistical necessity of restrictions that exist in a model. The first type of restriction tested is whether the equality constraints that may have been imposed in a model are appropriate. If some of the constraints are inappropriate, i.e., not consistent with the data, the overall fit of the model might be improved substantially by releasing the constraint in a future EQS run. The second type of restriction tested is whether fixed parameters, such as "missing" paths or covariances that are set to zero in the model, in fact are nonzero in the population, and hence would be better treated as free parameters and estimated in a future run. Univariate and multivariate LM χ^2 statistics are produced to permit evaluation of the statistical necessity of these restrictions. The program also produces a parameter change statistic to estimate the value that would be obtained if a fixed parameter were freed in a future run. The statistics that are computed are given in mathematical form in Chapter 10.

The /LMTEST procedure has many options that are described fully in Chapter 6. The basic default test procedure can be invoked by simply placing the phrase:

/LMTEST

or /LMT on a separate line in the input file. This will produce tests on equality constraints and tests on certain standard types of fixed parameters. The univariate χ^2 statistics that are printed out are modification indexes that can be consulted for suggestions as to which fixed parameters might be set free. The corresponding multivariate test should also be consulted, since it takes into account correlations among the many univariate tests. However, the results should not be accepted blindly. In this process, substantive theory is very important, because the /LMtest can suggest model changes that are theoretically meaningless, for example, effects that operate backward in time.

The options that are available in the /LMTEST include keywords such as APRIORI, HAPRIORI, PROCESS, SET, PVAL, AND NOFREE. These options provide customized application of the test. The a priori application of the LM test to particular fixed parameters or the given equality constraints is the most defensible statistically, since the probability statements given by the test may be distorted when the test is blindly applied as it can be in the default mode. If particular subsets of matrices are to be scanned for fixed parameters to free, for example, "correlated errors," the SET keyword needs to be implemented. Further information on these options, and the printout produced by the test, is given in Chapter 6.

/WTEST (Optional)[3]

The parameters denoted by "*" are estimated optimally in EQS, and standard errors are provided so that a z-test can be constructed to evaluate whether a given parameter might be zero in the population. When sets of parameters are to be evaluated, another procedure is

---

[2] The LM test has been substantially augmented by the BLOCK features described in Appendix I. The results of an LM test also can be carried forward into a new model, using the RETEST feature as described in Appendix II.

[3] The results of the WTEST can be incorporated into a new model via the RETEST feature described in Appendix II. The Wald test also has been extended, as decribed in Appendix III.

needed. The /Wtest or Wald test is designed to determine whether sets of parameters that were treated as free in the model could in fact be simultaneously set to zero without substantial loss in model fit. The test is implemented by typing

/WTEST

or /WT on a separate line in the model input file. This will produce a default test based on taking the least significant parameter (smallest z-test value), and adding other parameters in such a way that the overall multivariate test yields a set of free parameters that with high probability can, simultaneously, be dropped from the model in future EQS runs without a significant degradation in model fit.

The /WTEST procedure also contains a number of keywords (such as APRIORI, HAPRIORI, PVAL, NOFIX) that permit customized application. These are described in Chapter 6, which also explains the relevant EQS output that is produced. The most important keyword provides a way of specifying specific parameters to be tested in an apriori way. The probability statements associated with W tests are most likely to be accurate when a priori tests are implemented. The mathematical basis for the Wald test is given in Chapter 10.

/TECHNICAL (Optional)

The /TECHNICAL section, which is optional, is identified by entering the keyword /TECHNICAL (abbreviated to /TEC) in an input record. The /TECHNICAL section allows the user to specify the maximum number of iterations for normal, elliptical, and arbitrary distribution theory computations, as well as the convergence criterion and tolerance. This section also provides an option for using arbitrary start values for elliptical and arbitrary distribution theory computations. The operands of the /TECHNICAL section must be separated by a semicolon.

The defaults of the operands and their meanings are as follows, where n refers to an integer number to be specified by the user, which must be in the range 0 — 500, and x refers to a decimal number. For use of n = 0, see below.

OPERAND	ABBREVIATION	DEFAULT	MEANING
ITR	ITR = n;	30	Max. no. of iterations for normal distribution theory (LS, GLS, ML) Max. no. of iterations allowed = 500
EITR	EITR = n;	1	Max. no. of iterations for elliptical distribution theory (ELS, EGLS, ERLS) Max. allowed = ITR $\leq$ 500
AITR	AITR = n;	1	Max. no. of iterations for arbitrary distribution theory Max. allowed = ITR $\leq$ 500
CONVERGENCE	CON = x;	.001	Convergence criterion, based on mean of absolute differences of parameter estimates between two iterations
START	ST = ELL;		Arbitrary start values for elliptical methods (sets EITR = 30)
	ST = AGLS;		Arbitrary start values for distribution-free methods (sets AITR = 30)
TOLERANCE	TOL = x;	.000001	Tolerance to control accuracy in solving linear equations

Examples of valid /TECHNICAL section operands are:

/TECHNICAL
    ITR = 50;   AITR = 10;   EITR = 20;
    CONV = .0001;   START = ELL,AGLS;

/TEC
    START = ELL;   EITR = 50;

Regarding the number of iterations, note that the default in elliptical and arbitrary theory estimation is one iteration. That is, two-stage linearized estimates (e.g., LERLS, LAGLS) will be obtained for these methods unless an override is created in the /TEC section. Such estimates are meaningless if the initial estimation method, usually based on normal theory, has not converged. The program will indicate when such a situation has occurred. One iteration of these methods would not make any sense if the estimation is carried out from arbitrary start values, as done via the /TEC section. Therefore, if the START = ELL; or S = AGL; specification is made, the program defaults the number of iterations to 30. These defaults can be overridden.

The convergence criterion can be loosened or tightened in accord with the needs and funds of the researcher. Small values of criteria will typically require more iterations, and thus such computer runs cost more. The precision of the user's computer limits the maximum accuracy possible.

Tolerance is a technical concept associated with pivoting operations in solving linear equations. It determines the point at which one variable can be considered to be linearly dependent on a set of other variables. See Frane (1977) or the BMDP Statistical Software Manual (Dixon, 1988) for further information. In general, users would not adjust the default value. In some special situations, a difficult convergence problem may be cleaned up by adjusting TOL. For example, when the program informs the user that many parameters have been found to be linearly dependent on other parameters during the iterations, and the problem does not stem from identification difficulties, sometimes increasing TOL to, say, .001, may create a cleanly converged solution and sometimes also a dramatic reduction in the chi-square statistic.

Zero Iterations

It is possible to set the number of iterations ITR, EITR, and/or AITR to zero. In this case, the program produces estimates based on initial starting values without updating parameter estimates, i.e., there is no iterative process. This can be helpful in various circumstances, e.g., in power calculations, for obtaining statistics at particular parameter values, in checking the adequacy of an a priori set of estimates, in comparing results to those obtained by others, and so on.

/DIAGRAM (Optional)[4]

EQS permits plotting a path diagram via the /DIAGRAM (abbreviated /DIA) segment of the input. The user designs the layout of all variables into a 12 × 12 grid. The program will search for directions between two variables defined in the /EQUATIONS and /COVARIANCES sections and plot this information as a path diagram on a line printer using the given grid. While there are no limitations on the number of equations or covariances that will be scanned by the program for the placement of unidirectional and bidirectional arrows, the grid layout of /DIA, and the qualities of a line printer, limit the aesthetic results.

Type and Format of Variables

The variables in /DIAGRAM should agree with those variables in the /EQUATIONS section. If a variable is not found in the /EQUATIONS paragraph, an error message will be reported. The variables as described throughout the program must be defined by a combination of one alphabetic and up to three numeric digits. No blanks are allowed between alphabetic and numeric characters in this section. *This is the only section of the program that requires a rigid input format.*

Following the keyword (/DIAGRAM), there are several path diagram input lines. Each line reports on one row of variables that make up one line in the 12 × 12 grid. The location of variables in this row must be precisely described as follows: for m or fewer variables in a single row of the diagram, the first 4m columns will provide information on where in the grid

---

[4] This section is correct for character-based line printers, but it is irrelevant for Windows and Macintosh environments. In those environments, **EQS for Windows** and **EQS for Macintosh** uses **Diagrammer** to not only provide a publication-quality path diagram, but to serve as input and output to the modeling run itself.

given variables will be placed. Four spaces have been reserved for each variable, and each variable *must* be aligned at the right-most of the four spaces. There is no space between variables. For example, letting — be a space,

1. Correct   — — V 1 — — F 1 — — V 4 ;
    Incorrect   V 1 — — F 1 — — — — V 4 ;

The incorrect example contains two errors: variable V1 is not right-justified, and F1 is not right-justified.

2. Correct   — — V 1 F 1 2 3 — — V 4 ;
    Incorrect   — — V 1 — F 1 2 3 — — V 4 ;

In this example, the program will assume the incorrect specification as variables $-\ -V1,\ -F12,3-\ -V,4-\ -\ -$. Three error messages will be reported.

    A semicolon must be placed to the right of the last variable in each line of input (except for the keyword).

Limitations

    Only 12 variables can be allowed in each line. Thus a maximum of $12 \times 4 = 48$ spaces plus one for the semicolon will be used per line. Up to 12 lines (not including the keyword) will be accepted for the path diagram. In other words, the maximum allowance for the path diagram is a 12×12 grid.

Arrangement of Variables

    The arrangement of variables should be made carefully to permit the path diagram to be as clean and clear as possible. Perhaps only key variables might be included in the diagram so as to keep it uncluttered. This program is capable of connecting any two variables in the 12×12 grid, no matter how the variables are placed. However, a careful arrangement of variables is suggested so that lines do not cross randomly, the direction of flow is easy to see, etc.

    Because the diagram is printed by a line printer, it will not look as beautiful as one obtained using special graphics software and hardware. However, a good diagram will help the user remember the model more easily, and will help to communicate it more easily to others. Since the page size in the horizontal direction is limited on a line printer, if more than six columns of variables are specified in a diagram, the diagram will be printed in two halves. Connecting points are provided for the user, so that the pages can be torn apart and then reconnected by tape to provide an overall diagram. (It may be desirable to use a photoreducing copier to yield a smaller diagram if it will be consulted frequently.)

/PRINT (Optional)[5]

    The /PRINT segment controls a variety of printed information that can help to make sense of a model and the quality of the estimates. The most important of this is the effect decomposition.

---

[5] Appendices III and V describe several additional print features that now exist in the program.

Effect Decomposition

The parameters of a structural model are the coefficients in the equations and the variances and covariances of independent variables, and, in a structured means model, the means of the independent variables and the intercepts of the dependent variables. These parameters are listed in the input stream with a "*", and so they are estimated directly in EQS. As a consequence, standard errors are also obtained and the significance of these effects can be determined. While these parameters of the model are also the "causal" parameters of a model, if it permits a causal intepretation, nonetheless they may not be the only aspect of the model of interest. In particular, indirect effects and total effects are also important interpretively (see, e.g., Alwin & Hauser, 1975; Bollen, 1987a; Fox, 1985; Graff & Schmidt, 1982; Sobel, 1987).

Suppose that the variables F1 – F4 are connected by paths as follows: F1 → F2 → F3 → F4. (Residual variables are not shown.) Then F1 has a direct effect on F2, F2 has a direct effect on F3, and F3 has a direct effect on F4. These direct effects are coefficients in equations. There is no direct effect of F1 on F4; there is no path, and consequently the equation structure would mirror this fact, and there would be no "*" parameter for an F1 → F4 coefficient. However, F1 does have an *indirect* effect on F4, namely, through the variables F2 and F3. A measure of this indirect effect is given by the product of the coefficients represented by the arrows. If there are many sequences by which a variable like F1 can influence F4, the total indirect effect is a number indicating the size of this effect. Total indirect effects summarize how one variable influences another regardless of the particular paths chosen to trace from one variable to the other. In the example, if there were another variable F5, with F1 → F5 → F4 in addition to the above paths, F1 can influence F4 through F5 as well. While such specific indirect effects are sometimes of interest, EQS computes only the total indirect effects. Total effects are defined as the sum of direct and indirect effects. These are also computed and printed in EQS. To obtain these effects, one must put

/PRINT
    EFFECT = YES;

into the input stream. The default is no, and need not be specified.

The typical effect decomposition provides effects defined for variables in their natural metric, i.e., the metric implicit in the equations and the input variables. In many circumstances the size of these unstandardized effects are difficult to interpret. Hence, EQS also computes an effect decomposition for the standardized solution, i.e., the solution in which all variables have been rescaled to have unit variance.

Since indirect effects are sample statistics, they have sampling variability. One way to judge an unstandardized effect is to determine whether it is significantly different from zero, using the standard error estimate to form a normal z-test. The work of Sobel (1982, 1986, 1987) on this topic was extended and modified to be applicable to the classes of models, estimators, and constraints available in EQS.

Model Matrices

The final solution given in the standard EQS output consists of optimal parameter estimates, standard errors, residuals between data and model, and so on. It is sometimes useful also to examine the model matrices based on the optimal parameter estimates. An important matrix is the reproduced covariance matrix $\hat{\Sigma}$ based on the final parameter estimates $\hat{\theta}$. In models with structured means, the reproduced mean vector $\hat{\mu}$ is also part of the partitioned covariance/mean matrix. This output is provided in the fitted moments based on measured, or V, variables, but it is automatically augmented by the reproduced or fitted moments of the factor, or F, variables. Thus the statement

/PRINT
       COVARIANCE = YES;

informs EQS to print the reproduced covariance/mean matrix of all V and F variables. A standardized version of this matrix is available with

/PRINT
       CORRELATION = YES;

This is the reproduced covariance matrix of (V,F) variables, transformed into a correlation matrix. One can also write COV = YES; and COR = YES; in shorthand notation.

Correlation of Parameter Estimates

The parameter estimates obtained in a model covary. For example $\hat{\theta}_i$ and $\hat{\theta}_j$ covary (of course, the parameters themselves, θ_i and θ_j, are fixed numbers that do not covary). In extreme cases, the covariance could be so high that the corresponding correlation could approach 1.0, in which case the parameter estimates become linearly dependent and there is an empirical, if not also theoretical, identification problem. Of course, a parameter estimate may be linearly dependent on others if it can be perfectly predicted (in a multiple correlation sense) from a set of other estimates, even though no single correlation seems to be approaching 1.0. In any case, it may be of interest to evaluate these relationships among estimates. In the usual output, only the standard error estimates for parameter estimates are printed. The entire covariance matrix of the estimator $\hat{\theta}$, e.g., the matrix in Eq. (10.14) of Chapter 10, is not printed. It is possible to request that the standardized covariance matrix, i.e., the correlation matrix of parameter estimates, be printed. This is done with the statement

/PRINT
       PARAMETER = YES;

or PAR = YES; The default is no, but it need not be specified.

The printed matrix has as many rows and columns as there are free parameters to be estimated in the problem. In large problems, this matrix takes up a substantial amount of space in an output file or on printed paper. As a consequence, this print option should be used with caution.

Digits

The number of digits that are printed after the decimal point in an EQS output file can be modified. The default is DIG = 3; but any number from 1 to 7 can be obtained. Printing with greater accuracy would imply specifying, say, DIG = 5; in the /PRINT paragraph.

/SIMULATION (Optional)

A data generation procedure has been built into EQS to permit simulation studies, which can be used to create artificial data to evaluate the empirical performance of various statistics under controlled conditions. A good overview of simulation methodology is given by Lewis and Orav (1989). A simulation in EQS requires (1) specification of the population, (2) a method of sampling, (3) an estimation run in every sample, (4) specification of the total number of samples, and (5) whether the output raw data files will be saved or what file names will be used. In addition, results from the EQS estimation in each sample may be saved in a file for further analysis using the appropriate /OUTPUT section options.

In EQS, the population is specified in the usual job file; the model in the input file, or the input matrix, defines the population. However, variables in the population may be normal or non-normal continuous variables, or even categorical transformations of normal variables, providing that category thresholds are given. EQS performs two types of sampling: simple random sampling from the population (the default), or resampling (input raw data are taken as the population). Characteristics of each sample, and its EQS estimation, are controlled by the usual statements in the /SPECIFICATIONS section (e.g., estimation method, number of cases). In general, the sample statistics obtained from each sample will vary probabilistically from the population parameters, and a simulation study seeks to describe the sampling results. Most details of the simulation are specified in the /SIMULATION paragraph, using keywords to create the particular study desired.

Population

This keyword states how the population model is to be generated. Basically, there are two choices:

POPULATION = MODEL; or POPULATION = MATRIX;

If POP=MOD; is specified, the model will be generated from the linear relationship of the variables defined in equations, and the variances and covariances of independent variables. The numbers next to * are taken as population parameters, and the fixed parameters are also taken as fixed population quantities. Consequently, random numbers are generated for all the independent variables (e.g., F, E, D and possibly V) before transforming them to measured Vs as input for EQS. POP = MOD; is the default, so if no POPULATION keyword is given in the /SIMULATION section, this option is assumed to be chosen. If POP=MAT; is specified, the matrix provided in the input file, typically a covariance matrix (specified in the /MATRIX paragraph), serves as the population matrix. In such a case any particular structural equation model may or may not be consistent with the matrix.

Replications

A simulation requires repeated sampling from the specified population, in which new sample data is obtained and analyzed in each replication. The number of samples to be obtained is specified with this keyword. Specifically,

REPLICATIONS = n;

states that n number of samples or replications from the population are to be obtained. The maximum number of replications permitted is 999. The default is 1. The abbreviation REP can be used. In principle, a large number of replications is recommended for a simulation, but in practice a smaller number (say, 100) is often used due to limitations of computer resources.

Seed

The random number generator requires the specification of a seed. The keyword is

SEED = n;

where n is a very large integer number. The program's default is n=123456789. Any integer can be chosen, but in EQS this number cannot exceed 2147483647.

Data_Prefix

This keyword tells EQS where the data file of output from each sample analysis will be stored. The first three characters of the character string enclosed by a pair of single quotes will be used as the prefix of the output file name. The program will then append the replication number to that prefix to compose an output file name. The format for this keyword is

DATA_PREFIX = 'character string';

where "character string" is a meaningful set of 5 or fewer characters, and DAT or DATA is an acceptable abbreviation of DATA_PREFIX. To illustrate, if REPLICATIONS=3; and DATA='EQS';, then three output files will be generated, namely, EQS001.DAT, EQS002.DAT, and EQS003.DAT, respectively. It must be recognized that with a large number of replications, these files will take up a lot of computer storage space.

Resampling

In the standard simulation setup, sampling from the population is done with ordinary simple random sampling. Once the population is set up, EQS samples repeatedly from that population. However, two other options are available. These options are based on sampling an existing data file to create a new sample, resampling again from this same data file, and so on. See, e.g., Efron (1982), or Boomsma (1986). The input data file that will be resampled has to be specified in the DATA command of the /SPECIFICATION section. Sampling from this file is done in accord with two options: bootstrap and jackknife. Several options in /SIMULATION will automatically be turned off when the BOOTSTRAP or JACKKNIFE keyword is elected. In particular, since the population is the data file given in /SPEC, POPULATION (see above) will be unavailable. In addition, CONTAMINATION, TRANSFORMATION, and CATEGORIZATION options (see below) are not usable.

Bootstrap. This keyword activates the bootstrap sampling method. Bootstrap sampling independently and repeatedly selects data from the existing data file until the given number of cases has been selected.

BOOTSTRAP = n;

is the statement needed to invoke the bootstrap, where n is an integer number. In practice, one often takes BOOT = n; where n is the number of cases in the data file being sampled.

Jackknife. Jackknife simulation is a type of resampling that analyzes the existing raw data file, but excludes one observation on each replication. It excludes observation 1 on replication one, observation 2 on replication two, and so on. Thus, the number of replications must be less than or equal to the sample size. If REP is not given, REP will default to the number of CASES. The method is implemented by simply stating the jackknife keyword, abbreviated as JACK. An example is

/SIMULATION
    REPLICATIONS = 20; JACKNIFE;

The generated jackknife data that is analyzed on a given replication will not be saved, that is, the SAVE command of the /SIMULATION section is not applicable. Furthermore, the DELETE command of the /SPEC section is not valid.

Contamination

The contaminated normal distribution is a member of the elliptical class of symmetric distributions governed by two parameters in addition to the standard parameters of a multivariate normal distribution. In essence, a contaminated normal distribution is made up of a large normal population with parameters μ and Σ, and a small normal population having the same μ but a covariance matrix that is $k\Sigma$, i.e., bigger than Σ by a positive multiple k. The smaller population is typically called the contaminated population, since the variances of the variables are increased by the factor k relative to the larger parent population. The scale factor k is one of the parameters of the distribution, and the second parameter can be thought of as the probability of selection from the smaller population. The contaminated normal distribution is often used in robustness studies, and it serves as a good model for studying the effects of outliers in multivariate analysis. Berkane and Bentler (1988) show how to estimate the parameters of this distribution, and study its relevance to the deletion of outliers in multivariate analysis. In the /SIMULATION paragraph, this distribution is used as the parent population when the keyword

CONTAMINATION = percentile, factor;

is invoked. Here, the two arguments are the parameters of the distribution that need specification. The first gives the probability of selection from the contaminated population. It is a number between 0.0 and 1.0, usually 0.1 or less. The second argument gives the scale factor k that is used to create the contaminated population. Typically, the scale factor is a number in the range 1.0 − 10.0. An example: CON=.05,3;

Transformation

Simulated data will be multivariate normal with zero means, skewness, and kurtosis unless the variables are transformed. All transformations are univariate. Data is generated based on Uniform and Normal distributions, where, except when a LOG transformation is requested, the normal distribution is a default. The variables in each of the distributions can be transformed in four ways. All four transformations are mutually exclusive. Once a transformation is done, data can be further adjusted by variance and mean, if the user has provided M, the mean. CATEGORIZATION (see below) will then be applied if necessary. A list of transformations that are permissible under each distribution is as follows:

	Uniform distribution	**Normal Distribution**
1	Uniform or Normal transformation	Normal transformation
2	Skew and/or kurtosis	Skew and/or kurtosis
3	Nonlinear transformation (LOG, EXP, and Power function)	Nonlinear transformation (EXP and Power function)
4	Contaminated normal	Contaminated normal

The simulated data that is generated depends on how POPULATION is specified in /SIM. When POPULATION = MATRIX;, only the measured variables (Vs) can be transformed. When POPULATION = MODEL;, only the independent variables (Vs, Fs, Es, and Ds) can be transformed. Dependent variables are obtained by the reduced form of the population structural model, see discussion above Eq. (10.3), Chapter 10.

The following keywords are used to specify the transformations desired:

U	uniform distribution on the interval $0 - 1$
S	followed by the desired value of skew (do not use with C)
K	followed by the desired value of kurtosis (do not use with C)
M	followed by the desired value of the mean
C	followed by the value of the contamination factor
EXP	exponentiation
LOG	logarithm (default to Uniform distribution)
**	followed by an integer, to denote power function

Transformations to create the desired values of Skew and Kurtosis are based on the procedure described by Vale and Maurelli (1983), using formulae based on Fleishman (1978). All transformations are implemented with the keyword TRANS and designations:

TRANSFORMATION = variable : univariate transformation formula & (or ;)

where the information to the right of the equal sign depends on the desired result for a particular variable. Transformations for a set of variables are created by repeating the material to the right of the equal sign, provided that the "&" sign is used to denote that more information is coming on the next line. As usual, the final transformation is terminated by the semicolon ";".

As an illustration of /SIMULATION with a nonnormal population, consider the following six variable, two factor model, in which certain characteristics are desired. The model with its TRANSFORMATION can be specified as:

```
/SIMULATION
       SEED  = 123456789;
       REPLICATIONS = 50;
       DATA = 'EQS';
       POPULATION = MODEL;
```

$$\text{TRANSFORMATION} = \begin{array}{l} \text{e1 to e3 : exp \&} \\ \text{e4 : m2.5, s} - 0.2, \text{k1.0 \&} \\ \text{e5 : m2.0, s} - 0.2, \text{k1.0 \&} \\ \text{e6 : m1.5, s} - 0.2, \text{k1.0 \&} \\ \text{f1 to f2 : log;} \end{array}$$

Categorization

Data generated by the simulation procedure is continuous unless the categorization option is chosen. Categorization (abbreviated CAT), if any, is carried out only after TRANSFORMATION has been implemented. Each variable or variable on a list can be categorized in accord with the instruction:

CATEGORIZATION = variable or variable list : category thresholds & (or ;)

where & refers to continuation, on subsequent lines, of information to the right of the equal sign. The semicolon ";" completes the specification. The "TO" convention can be used to specify variables in a sequence. The number of thresholds must be at least 1, but no more than 15, and thresholds must be ordered. The number of categories created is the number of thresholds plus one. An example is:

/SIMULATION
    CATEGORIZATION = e1 to e6 : $-2.5, -1.5, -0.5, 0.5, 1.5, 2.5;$

The effect is to categorize each of the six error variables E1 to E6 using the thresholds stated. With 6 thresholds, there will be 7 scores, namely, 1, 2, ..., 7. For example, the continuous scores $-.22$ and $.3$ for an error variable would, with the above instruction, create the same category score 4 for both these numbers.

Save

This keyword tells the program whether to save the generated raw data file. If SAVE is not specified, the data file will not be saved. If, however, the SAVE keyword is provided, the program must be told whether to save the data from each replication separately, or to combine the data end to end in a single file. The SAVE keyword is implemented as

SAVE = SEPARATE; or CONCATENATE;

where either SEP or CON, but not both, can be specified. The default is SEPARATE. The data will be saved in the file whose name was provided with the DATA_PREFIX statement.

/OUTPUT (Optional)

The output section is designed to create EQS technical output in compact form and with greater precision. In the absence of an /OUTPUT section, all ordinary EQS output will be placed end to end in the single file specified in the job submission command procedure. The size of this file will be unmanageable even with a small number of replications of a SIMULATION run, so /OUT should always be used with simulations. If /OUTPUT is requested, minimal output is put into the standard output file (an echo of the model, a guide to technical output that will be produced, and format of the technical output), while the specifically requested output is stored in an external file that can be easily accessed by other programs, for further analysis. The keywords that can be specified in /OUTPUT are DATA, LISTING, and a variety of specific information as given below.

Data

The file name where technical output will be stored is given in this statement, using the format

DATA = 'file name';

where file name is any appropriate name in the computer system. If no file name is given, EQSOUT.DAT will be used as a default. No format is needed; the output file will be in free format.

Listing

This option controls only the regular EQS output, and not the technical output requested in /OUTPUT. When this keyword is not given, the regular output will be turned off, and only an abbreviated output will be produced. When this keyword is given, the regular EQS output will also be produced. The format is simply to state the name LISTING. An example that includes some specific output items (see below) is:

/OUTPUT
    Listing; parameter estimates; standard errors;

Automatic Output Information

Some output information is produced automatically, and thus need not be specified. In particular, if /OUT is specified without any other commands, EQS will generate some basic model statistics. These statistics will be printed on the first line of output associated with each replication. The statistics include:

Estimation method (1=LS, 2=GLS, 3=ML, 4=ELS, 5=EGLS, 6=ERLS, 7=AGLS)
Condition code flag (0 means no condition code or estimation problems)
Convergence flag (0 means iterations have converged)
Independence model chi-square value
Model chi-square value
Model degrees of freedom
Probability level
Bentler-Bonett normed fit index
Bentler-Bonett non-normed fit index
Comparative fit index
Satorra-Bentler scaled chi-square (Robust method only)
Probability based on Satorra-Bentler scaled chi-square
AGLS fit index (AGLS only)
AGLS adjusted fit index (AGLS only)

Optional Output Information

Besides basic model statistics described, more information is available if it is specified as shown below. Each keyword can be spelled in full length (a space in between two words is permitted), or by use of the first two characters. Each keyword has to be separated by a semicolon ";". The following output information may be requested:

> DE rivatives;
> GR adients;
> IN verted information matrix;
> PA rameter Estimates;
> RE sidual matrix;
> CO variance matrix;
> ST andard errors; or SE;
> WE ight matrix;
> LM test;
> WT est;
> ALL; all of above information if it is applicable

For example, if one wants to have derivative and gradient elements, one writes:

/OUTPUT
> DE; GR; listing; data='myfile.rst';

All optional information is evaluated at $\hat{\theta}$, the final solution of the particular method of estimation applied. In this technical printout, the input data and model covariance (or, covariance/mean) matrices have been rearranged from their normal sequential input form so that dependent variables are given first, in ascending order, and independent variables subsequently, in ascending order. The residuals and weight matrices are printed to coordinate to this sequence of variables. Parameters are ordered sequentially as indicated by a labeling provided in the normal EQS output file, with free parameters in Φ, Γ, and B given in sequence. Symmetric matrices are printed in full symmetric form.

A short description of the technical output is as follows:

DErivatives are the elements of $\partial\sigma/\partial\hat{\theta}$ for the model and free parameters chosen. Each row of the matrix represents a parameter, and, for each parameter, the derivatives are given in the sequence of the rearranged lower triangular model matrix.

GRadient elements are $\partial Q/\partial\hat{\theta}$ for the particular function chosen. For ML, the elements are $\partial F/\partial\hat{\theta}$.

INverted information matrix is n times the covariance matrix of parameter estimates, as given in the matrix of Eq. (10.19), Chapter 10. In the case of LS and ELS estimation, it is the matrix given in (10.13) with $W = I$ and V_{ss} given by (10.41). When ME= xx, Robust; is used, two full matrices are printed: first, the matrix of (10.19), then (10.13) with V_{ss} given by (10.22).

PArameter estimates provides the vector $\hat{\theta}$ at the solution.

REsidual matrix is the matrix $(S - \hat{\Sigma})$, rearranged with dependent variables first, followed by independent variables. In structured means models, this is the augmented covariance/mean residual matrix.

COvariance matrix is the sample matrix used in the analysis, rearranged with dependent variables first, followed by independent variables. In structured means models, this is the augmented covariance/mean matrix. It describes the sample data after all transformations (if any) have been applied.

STandard errors give the estimated sampling variability of $\hat{\theta}$, based on the covariance matrix of parameter estimates as defined in "INverted information matrix", above. When ME = xx, Robust; is used, two sets of standard errors are provided.

WEight matrix refers to the AGLS weight matrix W, which is the inverse of the matrix whose elements are given in Eq. (10.22), Chapter 10. The rows and columns of this matrix correspond to the ordering of the rearranged covariance matrix.

LMtest refers to the multivariate statistic obtained for an APRIORI or HAPRIORI test as given in Chapter 10, Eq. (10.53).

WTest refers to the multivariate statistic obtained for an APRIORI or HAPRIORI test as given in Chapter 10, Eq. (10.62), except for LS and ELS estimation, and ROBUST estimation, where, with appropriately defined W and V_{ss} matrices, it refers to Eq. (10.61).

/END

This keyword signals the end of the input.

MISSING RAW SCORE DATA

The current version of EQS has no features to handle missing data.[6] EQS will operate on a case of raw score missing data by converting a missing value to zero, and treating a numerical code such as "9" for missing data as a number to be processed at face value. This is usually an undesirable approach, and, to avoid such a result, cases having missing data must be removed from the data file. Removing a small number of cases is usually an appropriate methodology when the missing data points are randomly distributed among cases. If the case numbers with missing data are known, the DELETE option (p. 49) can be invoked.

When data are missing in a pattern (such as for variables 6 through 9) repeated over cases, you can use the BMDP AM program to identify the pattern of missing data. Then you can use a data editor to gather into a group all cases with identical missing data patterns. At that point, if you have n groups, you can use EQS to develop an n-group structural model with equations only for the variables containing data. This advanced use of EQS is described fully in Chapter 9 under "Missing Data Models."

---

[6] **EQS for Windows** and **EQS for Macintosh**, however, have a variety of ways of visualizing and imputing missing data, selecting complete cases, and computing statistics on subsets of the data defined with regard to missingness.

4. PROGRAM OUTPUT

A run of EQS produces several major sections of output information in a standard titled and paginated output file, using the usual 132 column print format. This chapter provides a brief description of the major output sections. The main part of the chapter is devoted to describing the output of the typical single sample analysis. All but a few of the sections describe output to be found in any modeling run. Some output is given only under specialized circumstances, e.g., when a simulation is undertaken. The output from multisample analysis is basically the same within each sample, but modified slightly and extended, as is described at the end of the chapter. Listings of actual EQS runs are given in Chapters 5 − 9, see, e.g., pp. 106 − 111.

COMPUTER MEMORY PROBLEMS

Personal computer. On a personal computer, EQS allocates all memory available for the analysis. If the memory is sufficient, the program will run; if it is not, the execution will terminate. No particular error messages are provided, and the user will have to cut down the size of the data, model, number of parameters in the model, or the requirements of the estimation method (e.g., giving up AGLS in favor of ML estimation), or some combination thereof.

Minicomputers and mainframes. In these environments the amount of memory available is to some extent under the control of the user and the operating system supervisors. EQS produces some messages on these machines that may permit an unsuccessful run to be resubmitted with modified computer requirements and then run successfully. In such environments, EQS allocates memory dynamically in three stages, and it is possible for the program to abort at any of these stages without completing the computations required for the problem. If the allocation is insufficient at the first stage, a message will be printed prior to the printing of sample statistics as 1ST STAGE DYNAMIC STORAGE ALLOCATION REQUIRES 26124 WORDS. PROGRAM ALLOCATED 25000 WORDS. If the space required (here, 26124) is more than the amount allocated (here, 25000), EQS will be unable to perform its functions and the job will be aborted. The user will have to resubmit the job after increasing the dynamic storage in accord with the user's computer system job control language. However, the dynamic storage needed to run the entire job is not given by the "required words". EQS cannot anticipate how much storage will be needed at a later stage. As a rough guide, the memory required to run the entire job is given by doubling the amount printed (here, 26124 × 2 = 52248).

If the allocation is insufficient at the second stage, a similar message (2ND STAGE DYNAMIC ...) will be printed after the sample statistics. At this stage the user can estimate the storage required to run the entire job as 1.5 times the given required words. Finally, if the program successfully passes the first two stages of dynamic allocation, a similar message (3RD STAGE DYNAMIC ...) will be printed after the Bentler-Weeks structural representation has been computed and printed. If the amount required at this stage is less than the amount allocated, the program will not be hindered by any allocation problems in further computations. If the amount required is larger than the amount allocated, the program will again abort. The following message will also be printed: DYNAMIC STORAGE ALLOCATION MAY BE

INSUFFICIENT TO SUPPORT THIS PROGRAM. PLEASE INCREASE REQUIRED PROGRAM MEMORY AS IT WAS SHOWN ABOVE. PROGRAM ABORTED. In this case, the given printed required words are accurate and can be used as a basis for job resubmittal.

PROGRAM CONTROL INFORMATION

The first output page, after any computer system-generated message, echoes back a numbered sequence of the program input. At the end of the input echo, EQS prints xx RECORDS OF INPUT MODEL FILE WERE READ. The number of records or lines of input read should correspond with the actual input file. This input feedback is given to help locate any problems in the input, and also to provide a summary of the proposed analysis.

If the DELETE option was requested, the program also prints out CASE NUMBERS DELETED FROM RAW DATA ARE: and lists the cases that were deleted during computations. This information can be used to verify the accuracy of the specification.

If GROUPS is greater than one, the program prints out the input information from the first group first, then from the second group, and so on.

ERROR MESSAGES

Minor errors. A variety of syntax-checking error messages will be printed if the input contains specifications that the program finds problematical. If the errors are relatively minor, in the sense that the program can make an educated guess as to the intended specification, error messages will be provided within the Program Control Information listing. The given message will refer to a possible problem with the input listed in the previous line. Minor errors will not interrupt the job run, though the user should be sure that the program's corrective actions are appropriate.

If the errors are minor, or there are no errors, the program will continue with the computational phase. For example, if the user specifies a certain number of CASES, but fewer actually exist in the data file, the program will print ***WARNING*** USER SPECIFIED 100 INPUT CASES, BUT ONLY 80 CASES WERE FOUND IN DATA FILE. THE CASE NUMBER IN DATA FILE WILL BE USED TO COMPUTE CHI-SQUARES. (Of course, the specific numbers printed depend on the situation.)

Serious errors. If input errors cannot logically be corrected by the program, they are considered fatal, and the program will not proceed to the computational sections. In that case, the error messages will appear subsequent to the Program Control Information. The user will need to study these messages to locate the problem, and correct the errors in the input. The corrected input file will have to be resubmitted to an EQS run.

SIMULATION DEFINITIONS

This section of output is not used in the context of data analysis, and hence is not standardly printed. It does appear when a /SIMULATION is being run. The specifications of the simulation are summarized on this page of output, giving such information as the number of replications, how the sample was generated, the sample size, the normality or nonnormality of the data, contamination (if any), seed, and instructions on saving the data file. The univariate characteristics of the simulated data are summarized, and the population matrix used to generate the data is shown.

SAMPLE STATISTICS

When raw data are read in, a number of sample statistics are computed and printed out. These can be used descriptively in the usual manner. However, they also serve an important diagnostic purpose, namely, to permit evaluation of the adequacy of the input data and the appropriateness of the statistical assumptions underlying the estimation methods to be used in the analysis. Equations that define the given statistics are given in Chapter 10.

Univariate Statistics

Each variable's mean and coefficients of skewness and kurtosis are printed out. The mean is the usual summary statistic, while the formulas for the other statistics are based on the equations given in Chapter 10 as follows:

Skewness (G1):	Equation (10.83)
Kurtosis (G2):	Equation (10.33)

When a structured means model is requested with ANALYSIS = MOMENT, and the intercept V999 is included in the /EQUATIONS section, V999 is treated as just another variable in this section. That is, its mean, skewness and kurtosis are printed out. As a constant, its mean is 1.0, and it has 0 skewness and kurtosis (as well as zero variance, which is not printed here). Of course, V999 is a program-created variable for which actual input data is not provided.

Multivariate Kurtosis

Two variants of Mardia's (1970, 1974) coefficient are printed out.

Mardia's coefficient (G2,P):	Equation (10.31)
Normalized estimate:	Equation (10.32)

The normalized estimate is distributed, in very large samples from a multivariate normal population, as a unit normal variate so that large values indicate significant positive kurtosis and large negative values indicate significant negative kurtosis.

Elliptical Theory Kurtosis Estimates

A number of estimates of the elliptical kurtosis coefficient are computed and printed out. The following estimates are always printed:

Mardia-based kappa:	Equation (10.30)
Mean scaled univariate kurtosis:	Equation (10.34)

The following estimates are computed and printed only when AGLS estimation is   requested:

Multivariate L. S. kappa: Equation (10.39)
Multivariate mean kappa: Equation (10.38)

As noted in the discussion surrounding Eqs. (10.30) − (10.40), the Mardia-based kappa is used as a default in the elliptical theory computations, but if the coefficient is smaller than the permissible bound it is replaced by another coefficient. The first attempted substitute is the mean scaled univariate kurtosis estimate. If both the Mardia-based and mean scaled univariate kurtosis estimates are not in the permissible range, EQS will compute and print out the

Adjusted mean scaled univariate kurtosis: Equation (10.35)

which will then be used in the elliptical computations. The program prints out the name and value of the coefficient that is actually used.

Case Numbers with Largest Contribution To Normalized Multivariate Kurtosis

The five case numbers and the corresponding estimates of the case contri-   butions to the multivariate kurtosis normalized estimate are printed out. The normalized estimate, Eq. (10.32), is the mean of such estimates across all cases in the sample. Consequently, these estimates can be compared to the normalized estimate and a judgment can be made as to whether any of these five cases are very deviant from the entire sample. If one or two cases are extremely deviant, i.e., have extremely large estimates, their raw scores and other data about these cases might be studied in order to evaluate problems such as whether any gross errors in recording may have occurred or whether, for some reason, the cases may have been mistakenly included in the sample.

MATRIX TO BE ANALYZED

Covariance Matrix

The lower triangular section of the covariance matrix, including the diagonal, will be printed. If user-defined labels were specified, they will be printed along the rows and columns of the matrix. If labels were not specified, default labels will be printed. If the model specification is such that the user has selected only part of the data to be analyzed, then just the selected portion will be printed. The number of observations is also printed.

The matrix to be analyzed will differ from the input matrix if ANALYSIS and MATRIX of /SPECIFICATIONS do not match, for example, if a correlation matrix with standard deviations was used in the input and analysis is to be on the covariance matrix. The matrix to be used in the analysis will be printed, e.g., covariances will be computed from correlations and standard deviations as input, and the covariance matrix will be printed. In addition, if the input covariance matrix is in rearranged format, it will be scrambled into the lower triangular form used by EQS during the computations. In such a case, it is valuable to check the matrix to be sure that the rearrangement was accomplished correctly. Only the variables selected for analysis will be printed.

Covariance/Mean Matrix

When ANALYSIS = MOMENT is specified and the intercept V999 is included in the equations, and appropriate input data exists to create the matrix, a covariance/mean matrix will be analyzed and is printed. This matrix contains the covariance matrix of the selected variables in the upper triangle, and the means of these variables in the final row of the matrix. The row designation of this final row is V999, and the final entry in the row is the mean of this constant, which is 1.0.

BENTLER-WEEKS STRUCTURAL REPRESENTATION

The program input is decoded to generate a matrix specification consistent with the Bentler-Weeks designation of dependent and independent variables. The number of dependent variables is printed, and index numbers are given for all measured and latent variables in the sequence V, F, E, D, with all V variables listed first, F variables listed next, and so on. Then the number of independent variables is printed along with the index numbers for the variables, again in the sequence V, F, E, and D. This information can be used, if necessary, to determine whether the model was specified as intended.

SUMMARY OF TECHNICAL INFORMATION FOR /OUTPUT

This segment of output will not appear in a standard EQS run. It will appear only when /SIMULATION is active, and if the DATA statement of /OUTPUT gives a file name where the technical information from the simulation is to be stored. Titled FOLLOWING TECHNICAL INFORMATION HAS BEEN STORED IN XX.YY, the section gives a summary of what information can be found in the XX.YY file. It gives the parameter names that are associated with parameter estimates and standard errors, using the usual double label convention, and indicates what information will be in the file, for example, how many elements of model statistics and what they represent, how many standard error estimates, etc. It also provides the format of the output file, and the number of lines per set of information, so that the output file can be easily decoded for further analysis.

ESTIMATION SOLUTION

A line of information on the estimation method and the distributional theory used in the analysis is printed next. This printed information will head each page of output associated with the given method. When this information changes, a new solution method is being reported. When a two-stage linearized estimation method is used, the program will so indicate.

Immediately following the initial mention of the solution method, some critical information on the solution is printed, as discussed next.

PARAMETER CONDITION CODES

If estimates for all parameters seem to be technically acceptable, the program prints out the message: PARAMETER ESTIMATES APPEAR IN ORDER. NO SPECIAL PROB-

LEMS WERE ENCOUNTERED DURING OPTIMIZATION. *This is the ideal case, and this message should be located, prior to evaluating the meaning of any results.* If any of the parameter estimates have become linearly dependent on other parameters, or if an estimate is held at a boundary, the program will print out this information in the following format.

PARAMETER	CONDITION CODE
V5,F1	Linearly dependent on other parameters
E6,E6	Constrained at upper bound
E7,E7	Constrained at lower bound

The parameter designation is based on the standard double-label designation of the parameter discussed in the /CONSTRAINT section of Chapter 3. The condition code for a given parameter will represent one of the following: 1) *Linearly dependent on other parameters.* This code indicates that the covariance matrix of parameter estimates or its equivalent is singular, with the given parameter as estimated being a linear combination of other parameters. Such a situation can occur because the parameter is underidentified in an equation, or it can simply represent the effects of empirical underidentification, due to the data (and not the model per se). 2) *Constrained at upper bound.* This code indicates that the parameter estimate is not inside the boundaries specified by the user, rather, the parameter is being held at the upper boundary. 3) *Constrained at lower bound.* This code indicates that the parameter estimate is not inside the specified boundaries. The parameter is being held at the lower boundary specified for the problem.

The constraint of a parameter at an upper or lower boundary may be a cause for celebration or a reason for distress. If the bound is desired, the solution may be totally acceptable. If the bound is not desired, it implies a possible problem. If a parameter is held to a boundary, it may be that releasing the boundary constraint would lead to a substantial improvement in fit. However, when the boundary is natural, such as nonnegativity for a variance estimate, it may not make sense to release the constraint.

Linear dependence among parameters is a potentially serious problem, because the solution probably cannot be fully trusted. In addition to reflecting underidentification, in a properly identified model it may reflect computational problems stemming from the data, the start values, the default technical parameters, etc. For example, modifying (often, increasing) TOLERANCE may alleviate the problem and lead to a substantially improved solution. The EQS user is urged to trace down the source of the problem, experimenting if necessary with various attempts at eliminating the difficulty.

Another message may appear here. VARIANCE OF PARAMETER ESTIMATE IS SET TO ZERO indicates that the statistical variability of the parameter estimate cannot be accurately computed. Thus the standard error of the estimate will not, in later sections, be printed. Furthermore, the correlation of the estimate with other estimates is not determinate. Such messages typically accompany solutions having computational difficulties, in which a diagonal element of the covariance matrix of estimates is zero or even negative.

It should be noted that even though some error messages may occur that reflect a problem in some part of the output, it is still possible that other parts can be relied upon. For example, if a solution converged cleanly, it is quite likely that the parameter estimates are correct even if there is a problem with a standard error of an estimate.

If linear constraints among parameters were specified in the /CON paragraph, and the program was able to produce estimates that meet the constraint, the program will print ALL EQUALITY CONSTRAINTS WERE CORRECTLY IMPOSED. If this message is not printed, the program could not impose the constraints. One possible reason for such a result is that the start values provided by the user did not meet the constraint. This problem is simple to fix. Other reasons are more difficult to trace down, but are typically associated with general difficulties in finding a legitimate, converged solution. When the estimation method has not been able to converge to a minimum of the function, the difficulty of imposing an equality constraint may be either a cause of the problem, a consequence of it, or both. Then the main problem becomes one of tracing the origin of the convergence problem, e.g., due to poor start values, parameter underidentification, etc.

If the constraint equations in /CON appear to be linearly dependent or redundant, the program will correct the degrees of freedom to reflect the actual number of independent constraints involved. EQS will print the message: 2 (or some other number) CONSTRAINTS APPEAR TO BE LINEARLY DEPENDENT, AND DEGREES OF FREEDOM HAVE BEEN ADJUSTED.

CORRELATIONS OF PARAMETER ESTIMATES

If requested in the /PRINT section, the correlation matrix summarizing correlations among estimates of free parameters is printed out. The number of rows and columns of this matrix represents the number of free parameters in the model. The matrix gives the large sample correlation matrix of the parameter estimates obtained by standardizing the estimated covariance matrix of parameter estimates. The covariance matrix is given by the matrix in (10.14), specialized via the distribution assumed, weight matrix used, and current optimal parameter estimates. In some methods (e.g., ML) it is the standardized inverse of the information matrix. In the case of least squares solutions, and when ME = xx, ROBUST; is requested, the matrix is given in (10.13) for appropriate definitions of W and V_{ss}.

It may be worthwhile to print and scan this matrix if PARAMETER CONDITION CODES indicate that there was some problem in parameter estimation that cannot be corrected with alternative start values, model respecifications, and so on. Most likely there will be problems associated with this matrix, for example, some of the estimated correlations may be outside the range $\pm$ 1. Correlations greater than 1.0 in absolute value are easy to spot because the program prints the symbol # in each row that has such a value. The parameters having such a problem are identified by the double-label descriptions that are associated with each row and column of this matrix. The parameters that have such problems are prime candidates to be studied for possible model respecification.

If a parameter estimate has no standard error or variance, there will be a nonpositive diagonal element in the covariance matrix of estimates. This would make it impossible to standardize the row or column to yield a correlation matrix in a meaningful way. In that case the corresponding row and column of correlation matrix of estimates will be zeroed out, indicating a problem with the parameter estimate. The parameter may lie on the boundary of the permissible parameter space, i.e., equal to its lower or upper bound, there may be linear dependencies among parameter estimates, or the estimate may be so poor that if it is changed the value of the function may hardly be affected.

If a parameter estimate is linearly dependent on others and some of its correlations are outside the range -1 to $+1$, one should suspect that the computer program failed to reach an appropriate optimum point. More generally, such solutions should be considered suspect, even if other error indicators seem all right. Currently, the only solution to such a problem in EQS is to try other runs using quite different start values and different technical constants (e.g., TOL, CON). This type of problem can also occur when a parameter is held on the lower or upper boundary, in which case the boundary constraint may be imposed inappropriately or unnecessarily. If the boundary is reasonably imposed, these standardized values should be in the range -1 to $+1$ (or at least approximately so; very minor deviations will not matter much in practice).

If the parameter is involved in a linear equality constraint, as specified via the /CON paragraph, it will correlate 1.0 with the relevant other parameters that are involved in the constraint. Such a result is necessary and not a cause for concern. It also may be worthwhile to scan this matrix to determine whether there are any extremely high correlations among nonconstrained parameters, indicating near dependence of the parameter estimates. Such a situation might suggest potential problems in future runs even if no problems were encountered in a given run.

RESIDUAL COVARIANCE MATRIX

The residual covariance matrix $(S - \hat{\Sigma})$ is printed on a new page. Its values should be small and evenly distributed among variables if the model is a good representation of the data. Large residuals associated with specific variables indicate that the structural model explaining the variable is probably inadequate. The program also computes two averages of the residuals (ignoring signs) and points these out. One average is based on all the elements of the lower-triangular residual matrix, while the other average ignores the diagonal elements. Usually, the off-diagonal elements are more critical to the goodness-of-fit chi-square statistics.

Residual Covariance/Mean Matrix

If the analysis involves the constant V999, the matrix that is analyzed is the augmented covariance/mean matrix. In that case, the residual matrix that is printed contains the residual covariances in the upper triangle, and the residual means in the bottom row. The residual means is the vector $(\bar{z} - \hat{\mu})\prime$, with 0 as the last element for the residual of V999. It is possible for a model to fit well in means, but not covariances, and vice versa. A well-fitting model will have all residuals small.

STANDARDIZED RESIDUAL MATRIX

A standardization is performed on the Residual Covariance Matrix so that the elements are in a more similar range. The residual matrix $(S - \hat{\Sigma})$ is pre- and post-multiplied by the diagonal matrix of inverse elements of standard deviations of the variables, so that the resulting residual matrix can be interpreted in the metric of correlations among the input variables. The standardized residual matrix contains elements $r_{ij} - \hat{\sigma}_{ij}/s_i s_j$, where r_{ij} is the observed correlation between two variables, $\hat{\sigma}_{ij}$ is the reproduced model covariance, and s_i and s_j are standard deviations of the measured variables V_i and V_j. In addition to printing this matrix, the averages of the absolute standardized residuals are printed. One average includes the diagonal elements in its computations, the other does not.

When the augmented covariance/mean matrix is analyzed, the standardized residual matrix that is printed will include residuals for means as well as covariances. The standardized means are $(z_i - \hat{\mu}_i)/s_i$.

Problems with a model are more easily seen in the standardized residual matrix than in the residual covariance matrix. Large values of standardized residuals point to the variables that are not being well explained by the model.

LARGEST STANDARDIZED RESIDUALS

The elements from the Standardized Residual Matrix are ordered from large to small in absolute value, and the largest twenty of these are printed out along with a designation of which pairs of variables are involved. Even though with some estimation methods, under some models, variance elements such as V5,V5 may be large, large covariance residuals tend to be more influential in lack of model fit. If V8,V2 is the largest standardized residual, and the model does not fit the data, both variables V2 and V8 must be studied as to why they are not explained well by the model. In general, it will be necessary to modify the structural antecedents or correlates of these variables, rather than their consequences. If these variables are dependent variables, residuals associated with them are antecedents to the variables, and at times they might be allowed to correlate.

DISTRIBUTION OF STANDARDIZED RESIDUALS

A frequency distribution of the standardized residuals is presented next. Ideally, the distribution is symmetric and centered around zero. The legend for the figure describes how many residual elements are described by a single asterisk in the figure, and gives information on the specific frequencies and percentages that fall within a given range used in the figure. Note that the diagram is labeled 1, 2, ..., 9, A, B, C. Each of these numbers or letters refers to a given range of numbers that describes the size of the residuals. "1" corresponds to residuals smaller than − .5; "2" to those in the range − .4 to − .5; "A" to those in the range .3 to .4; etc.

MODEL COVARIANCE MATRIX FOR V AND F VARIABLES

If COVARIANCE = YES; was specified in /PRINT, at this point the program prints the model-induced, or reproduced, covariance matrix of the V and F variables. Under the title MODEL COVARIANCE MATRIX FOR MEASURED AND LATENT VARIABLES, the covariances of sets of V − V, F − V, and F − F variables is printed. The segment of the matrix concerned with V − V variables, of course, contains $\hat{\Sigma}$, the reproduced covariance matrix. The covariances of F − V and F − F variables may be of interest in interpretation, since these elements are not necessarily parameters of the model unless the pairs involved are independent variables.

When a structured means model is undertaken, with ANAL = MOM; this matrix will also contain the intercept V999. Entries in the row and column corresponding to V999 give the reproduced means $\hat{\mu}$ of the V and F variables based on the model. These entries may be intercepts or total effects, as well.

MODEL CORRELATION MATRIX FOR V AND F VARIABLES

If CORRELATION = YES; was specified in the /PRINT segment of input, the program will print the standardized version of the matrix described in the previous paragraph. This is the MODEL CORRELATION MATRIX FOR MEASURED AND LATENT VARIABLES. The reproduced model correlation matrix is often easier to interpret than the corresponding covariance matrix because of the standardized metric of the variables. The standardization also will affect the means that are part of a structured means model with the constant V999.

GOODNESS OF FIT SUMMARY[1]

Summary information on goodness of fit is printed next. The χ^2 associated with the model of independent or uncorrelated variables is presented first. This model is estimated and tested because, in small samples, it may fit as well as the model actually under consideration, and, if it does, serious questions can be raised about the explanatory meaningfulness of the hypothesized model. In large samples, the independence model is also a good baseline model against which other models can be evaluated for the gain in explanation that they achieve.

The values of Akaike's (1987) information criterion (AIC) are printed out next, first for the independence model and then for the model of interest. Bozdogan's (1987) consistent version of this statistic (CAIC) is also presented for these two models. These criteria, developed for ML estimation, are applied in EQS to all the estimation methods available. It has been argued that, when selecting a model from a large number of models, one should take into account both the statistical goodness of fit and the number of parameters that have to be estimated to achieve that degree of fit. AIC and CAIC are measures designed to balance these two aspects of model fit. The model that produces the minimum AIC or CAIC may be considered, in the absence of other substantive criteria, to be a potentially useful model.

Let d_i be the degrees of freedom of the independence model and d_k be the degrees of freedom of the model of interest. Then EQS prints out the following:

Independence AIC $=$ Independence model $\chi^2 - 2d_i$
Model AIC $=$ Model $\chi^2 - 2d_k$.

Independence CAIC $=$ Independence model $\chi^2 - (\ln N + 1)d_i$
Model CAIC $=$ Model $\chi^2 - (\ln N + 1)d_k$.

Next EQS prints out the χ^2 goodness of fit test for the model of interest. In general, the model χ^2 is based on $n\hat{Q}$, where Q is some variant of (10.10), the function being minimized, evaluated at the computed function minimum (see Iterative Summary below). The χ^2 statistic for LS and ELS is computed using Eqs. (10.44) and (10.45), while the ML χ^2 is based on $n\hat{F}$ based on (10.43) in covariance structure models, and on (10.82) for models with structured means. When ME = xx, ROBUST; has been specified, the Satorra-Bentler scaled χ^2 statistic (10.49) is computed and printed as well.

---

[1] Appendix V describes how to obtain additional fit indices besides those described in this section.

The given χ^2 statistic and tabled values of the $\chi^2_{(df)}$ distribution are used to determine the probability of obtaining a χ^2 value as large or larger than the value actually obtained, given that the model is correct. This is printed out as the probability value for the χ^2 statistic. When the null hypothesis is true, the model should fit the data well and this probability should exceed a standard cut-off in the χ^2 distribution (such as .05 or .01). Thus, in a very well fitting model, the probability will be large. In a poorly fitting model, the probability will be below the standard cut-off.

In addition to the statistical information, the Bentler-Bonett (1980) and Bentler (1988a) fit indices are printed out. These are based on the fit function used, as well as the null or baseline model of uncorrelated or independent variables. The Bentler-Bonett normed fit index is computed for any particular fitting function as

$$\text{NFI} = 1 - \hat{Q}_k / \hat{Q}_i,$$

where $\hat{Q}_k$ and $\hat{Q}_i$ are the values of the fitting functions obtained at $\hat{\theta}_k$ for the model of interest and the corresponding $\hat{\theta}_i$ for the independence model, respectively; and the functions refer to any of the specialized functions available in EQS, namely, Q in (10.10), Q_E in (10.27), Q_N in (10.42), or F in (10.43). It is apparent that better model fits (i.e., smaller $\hat{Q}_k$) and worse baseline model fits (i.e., larger $\hat{Q}_i$) yield better fit indices. Values of NFI greater than .9 are desirable. The non-normed fit index takes into account the degrees of freedom of the model. It is computed as

$$\text{NNFI} = (\text{f}_i - \hat{\text{f}}_k) / (\hat{\text{f}}_i - 1),$$

where $\hat{\text{f}}_i = n\hat{Q}_i / d_i$ and $\hat{\text{f}}_k = n\hat{Q}_k / d_k$ are χ^2 variates divided by the associated degrees of freedom for the null (d_i) and substantive models (d_k), respectively. The nonnormed index can exceed the normed index in magnitude, and can be outside the $0 - 1$ range.

The comparative fit index (Bentler, 1988a) has the advantage of the NNFI in reflecting fit relatively well at all sample sizes, especially, in avoiding the underestimation of fit sometimes found in true models with NFI. CFI is computed as

$$\text{CFI} = 1 - \hat{\tau}_k / \hat{\tau}_i,$$

where $\hat{\tau}_k = \max[(n\hat{Q}_k - d_k), 0]$ based on the model of interest and $\hat{\tau}_i = \max[(n\hat{Q}_i - d_i), (n\hat{Q}_k - d_k), 0]$. In large samples, NFI, CFI, and an index developed by Bollen (1989b) all measure the comparative reduction in noncentrality proposed as a population measure of fit by Bentler (1988a). NNFI estimates a somewhat different population index. The concepts behind these fit indexes are spelled out in more detail in Chapter 5, Eqs. (5.1) − (5.12). Bollen's (1989b) index, Eq. (5.5), can be computed from the output provided.

An additional set of fit indices is computed under arbitrary distribution theory. These indices are not based on the Bentler-Bonett concept of judging fit relative to a baseline model. Rather, these formulas, given by Eqs. (3.5) and (3.8) of Bentler (1983a), are based on the size of weighted residuals compared to size of the weighted input data. The formula is

$$\text{FIT} = 1 - \hat{Q}_k / s'Ws$$

where $\hat{Q}_k$ is based on the AGLS function for the model of interest. The adjusted fit index is

$$\text{ADJUSTED FIT} = 1 - (p^*/d_k)(1 - \text{FIT}),$$

where $p^* = p(p + 1)/2$ for p variables and d_k is the degrees of freedom of the model. These indexes are printed out in LISREL (Jöreskog & Sörbom, 1988, p. 43) as GFI and AGFI indexes.

The index FIT involves the sample size N_g in each group. With $n_g = (N_g - 1)$, in multisample covariance structure analysis

$$\text{FIT} = 1 - \frac{\sum_1^m n_g (s_g - \hat{\sigma}_g)' W_g (s_g - \hat{\sigma}_g)}{\sum_1^m n_g \, s_g' W_g \, s_g}$$

where s_g and $\hat{\sigma}_g$ are sample and estimated model covariances in each of the m groups. See Eqs. (10.65) − (10.66) of Chapter 10. The ADJUSTED FIT = 1 − (p*/d$_k$)(1 − FIT) as before, but p* is the total number of sample covariances across all groups and d_k is the degrees of freedom of the model.

ITERATIVE SUMMARY

The iterative summary contains information obtained from each iteration. First, the iteration number is presented. This is followed by the change in parameter estimate, alpha, and the function value for each iteration. The PARAMETER ABS CHANGE is the mean of the absolute values of the vector $d^{(k)}$ in Eq. (10.85). ALPHA is the smallest value of α used in that iteration where α is defined in the same Eq. (10.85). FUNCTION depends on the current value of $\hat{\Sigma}$, and represents the value of the function being minimized on a given iteration. During normal theory estimation the function is $\hat{Q}_N$ in Equation (10.42), with $W_2 = I$ under LS estimation and $W_2 = S^{-1}$ under GLS estimation, except in maximum likelihood estimation, where it represents $\hat{F}$ in Eq. (10.43) or the augmented function (except the N multiplier) given for structured means models in (10.81). With ML estimation, $n\hat{Q}_N$ under $W_2 = \hat{\Sigma}^{-1}$ at the minimum is also printed out above the fit indices as THE NORMAL THEORY RLS CHI-SQUARE FOR THIS ML SOLUTION. During elliptical theory estimation, the function is $\hat{Q}_E$ in Eq. (10.27), based on the $\hat{\kappa}$ estimate chosen, with $W_2 = I$ under ELS, $W_2 = S^{-1}$ under EGLS, and $W_2 = \hat{\Sigma}^{-1}$ under ERLS. During arbitrary distribution theory estimation, the function is $\hat{Q}$ in (10.10), based on Eqs. (10.22) − (10.23). The linearized estimation functions under elliptical and arbitrary distribution theories are computed as just noted, except that only one iteration is implemented and displayed. Typically the χ^2 statistic is given by $n = (N - 1)$ times the final function value, but a different formula is used for LS and ELS, as well as the Satorra-Bentler scaled χ^2 statistic. See above.

The iterative summary should be scanned prior to evaluating the meaning of any result. In fully iterated estimation, the iterative process fails if the average of absolute values of elements of the parameter change vector is larger than about .001 (or the current convergence criterion specified in /TECH). In such a situation, the output cannot be considered to have any optimal properties. It may be necessary to restart the program, possibly with the currently best parameter estimates, to obtain further iterations to a better function value. Note that the program uses a default maximum of 30 iterations, so if this number is reached the program will very likely not have converged. A message will be printed warning the user not to trust the output if convergence was not achieved. If subsequent estimation methods were requested in the input, these will be aborted since the user must evaluate the seriousness of the problem. If the problem is not theoretical (e.g., underidentification), it may be practical (e.g., poor start values), and modifications of program input, including technical constants, may improve performance. If a very large number of iterations without convergence has been obtained, it is typically unlikely that simple resubmission with a request for more iterations will clean up the difficulty.

Alphas other than 1.0 indicate that the program did step-halving. If done frequently, this indicates that optimization problems may have been occurring. Such difficulties do not matter if, at the final iteration, the average parameter change is very small and the function is at a minimum.

In the absence of a converged solution, the iterative summary may provide a hint as to problems that the program encountered. In general, the function value should decrease across iterations, and the same effect should be noted for the parameter changes. If this did not happen, an iterative difficulty was encountered. One basis for failure is a model covariance matrix $\hat{\Sigma}$ that is not positive definite. In this case the message IN ITERATION #n, MATRIX C_FUNCT MAY NOT BE POSITIVE DEFINITE will be printed out after the Bentler-Weeks structural representation. Iterative difficulties do not matter if a proper solution meeting the convergence criterion is obtained in the end. However, it may suggest that future EQS runs based on similar models should use better start values.

In linearized estimation, the parameters are updated only once with one iteration. In such a case, the absolute parameter change from the starting estimates may be quite substantial. This is usually not a cause for alarm, since the statistical theory guarantees that in large samples, under the model, linearized estimation will perform equivalently to fully iterated estimation. However, if the user does not trust the estimates, it may be worthwhile to obtain a fully-iterated estimator.

MEASUREMENT EQUATIONS

The input equations are rearranged in the output into two sections. The measurement equations that relate measured dependent variables (Vs) to other variables are printed first, while the construct equations that have dependent latent variables (Fs) are printed in a separate section. Within each section the equations are printed sequentially, and thus may also be reordered as compared to their input sequence. The equations of course now contain the updated parameter estimates rather than the starting values.

Each measurement equation with optimal estimates for free parameters is printed using a three-line format. The equation is printed on the first line, using the plus sign "+" to connect parts of the equation even if an estimate is negative., e.g., F4 = .4*F3 + − .143*F1 + D4. (The extra plus sign can, of course, be ignored.) The standard error is printed on the second line immediately below each estimate. The test statistic (estimate divided by standard error) is printed below the standard error. This same format is repeated for all measurement equations.

Within the context of an appropriate model, the test statistics are univariate large-sample normal z-tests of the null hypothesis that a given parameter is zero in the population. Large values (e.g., exceeding ± 1.96 for a .05 size test) indicate that the null hypothesis can be rejected, i.e., that the structural coefficient is not zero. The standard errors should be scanned to see whether they are abnormally small. If a standard error approaches zero, the test statistic cannot be defined. This may reflect an estimation problem rather than excellent precision: it may be that a parameter is almost linearly dependent on others. It may be best to rescan the messages preceding the residual covariance matrix for possible error flags. This same evaluation should be made in subsequent sections.

The coefficients of the measurement equations can be evaluated for significance using the $\underline{z}$ test, as just stated. In all cases, however, the researcher should note that conclusions drawn from a series of univariate tests on parameters may not yield the same conclusion drawn from a simultaneous test on the significance of a set of parameters. A multivariate test of hypotheses on several coefficients, or for that matter, any other parameters, including construct coefficients, variances, and covariances, would be highly desirable. This can be done in three ways: by the χ^2 difference test, the Wald test, and the Lagrange Multiplier test. See Chapter 6 for details. A simple Wald test can be conducted automatically by specifying /WTEST in the input stream. This test would be concerned with locating parameters that can be considered zero simultaneously. The χ^2 difference test can be done as follows. One would create a restricted model in which all of the free parameters to be tested are simultaneously set to zero. The fit of this more restricted model can be compared to the previous, more highly parameterized model by taking the difference in χ^2 values obtained from the two runs, as well as by calculating the corresponding difference in df. This test would evaluate the hypothesis that all of the model-differentiating parameters can simultaneously be set to zero. The /LMTEST can also be requested when the more restricted model is run. In some situations, several parameters may be marginally unnecessary to a model by the univariate $\underline{z}$ ratios, but the multivariate test may indicate that all cannot be dropped at the same time because doing so would create a significant decrement in fit. In that case, perhaps one but not another parameter can be dropped simultaneously with a set of parameters due to the differing correlations of their estimates.

Robust Statistics

When the job is run with METHOD = xx, ROBUST; robust standard errors and test statistics are also computed. These are based on Eq. (10.13), and are printed in parentheses immediately below the test statistic based on the xx method. Again, the standard error estimate is printed first, and the test statistic below that. Preliminary indications are that when the distributional assumption underlying the xx method is not met, the robust statistics are more trustworthy than the ordinary statistics (Chou, Bentler, & Satorra, 1991). Robust standard errors are, of course, computed for free parameters in construct equations, variances, and covariances as well as measurement equations.

CONSTRUCT EQUATIONS

Each equation for an F-variable or factor is printed using the same format as for the measurement equations. First, the equation is printed with its final estimate. Then, on the next line just below the estimate, its standard error is printed. Finally, on the line below the standard error, the test statistic is printed. This format is repeated for all F-type or construct equations.

VARIANCES OF INDEPENDENT VARIABLES

The output page is divided into four equal columns. The columns are labeled from left to right V, F, E, D, corresponding to measured variables, factors, errors, and disturbances. The general format within each column is the same. The variable name is given first, followed by the label. On the same line at the right side, one finds the parameter estimate of a free parameter, or its fixed value. A standard error for the free parameter is given just below the estimate. The test statistic for the estimate is printed on the next line, immediately below the standard error. This format is repeated for all independent variables in these respective categories. An arbitrarily large test statistic is replaced by a row of 9's.

Variances should always be scanned to determine whether any unusual numbers are being reported. In particular, it is necessary to evaluate whether there are any negative variance estimates, or zero estimates. Negative estimates should not occur unless the program's automatic nonnegativity constraint on these parameters was overridden by the user. Zero estimates are likely to be constrained estimates, most likely on the boundary set by the program. If so, there may be no standard error for the estimate.

Robust standard errors and test statistics are given below the standard ones, when they are requested.

COVARIANCES AMONG INDEPENDENT VARIABLES

The covariances are presented in a table that immediately follows the variances of independent variables. The same format and column headings are used as in the VARIANCES output. The labels for the pair of variables involved in a covariance are printed below each other.

EFFECT DECOMPOSITION

If the /PRINT input paragraph contained the statement EFFECT = YES; the program prints the effect decomposition at this point. It is printed in two segments. The DECOMPOSITION OF EFFECTS WITH NONSTANDARDIZED VALUES is first. Within this segment, total effects and (total) indirect effects are given, in sequence. Effects are printed in an equation-like format, with the affected consequent variable on the left of an equal sign, and the variables influencing this variable on the right-hand side. This format is nothing more than a convenient way to give each of the effects involved. Some total effects may be direct effects, and some direct effects will be associated with free parameters so that an asterisk "*" will appear. As in the equations, + signs may connect different effects, even though the effect itself may have a negative sign associated with it; the "+" can be ignored.

Indirect effects are printed in the same equation-like format. However, each indirect effect is associated with a standard error that is printed directly below the effect estimate. The z statistic for the hypothesis that the effect is zero in the population is printed immediately below.

The second segment of printout is the DECOMPOSITION OF EFFECTS WITH STANDARDIZED VALUES. The format for this printout is similar to that for the nonstandardized values, that is, total effects first, followed by indirect effects. These standardized effects are those that obtain when all V, F, E, and D *model* variables are transformed to unit variance, as in the standardized solution (see next section). Because the effect sizes in this solution are not arbitrary, they may in many instances be easier to interpret than the nonstandardized values. However, no standard errors or test statistics are provided for the indirect effects in this solution. Statistical significance is a quality reserved for the nonstandardized effects in the current printout.

STANDARDIZED SOLUTION

Each measurement and construct equation is printed out giving the standardized solution. This is a completely standardized path analysis type of solution, except that observed variables are not standardized: all V, F, E, and D *model* variables are rescaled to have unit variance. Standardization is done for all variables in the linear structural equation system, including errors and disturbances. Consequently, all coefficients in the equations have a similar interpretation, and the magnitude of these standardized coefficients may be easier to interpret than the magnitudes of the coefficients obtained from the covariance or raw data metric. It should be noted explicitly that the standardized solution produced by EQS is not the same solution as provided by Jöreskog and Sörbom (1988), who do not standardize measured variables, errors in variables, or disturbances in equations.

The standardized residual variance in an equation can be obtained as the square of the coefficient associated with the residual variable. In recursive models, this value, when subtracted from one, yields the squared multiple correlation coefficient associated with the equation. For example, the standardized equation F2 = .569*F1 − .206*F3 + .708D2 given on page 37 indicates that $R^2 = 1 - .708^2 = 1 - .501 = .499$, i.e., almost half the variance in F2 is accounted for by F1 and F3.

The standardized solution cannot be obtained when some variances have been estimated at negative values, since square roots of these values are needed for the standardization. Consequently, in such a case the solution is not printed.

One feature of the standardized solution is that previously fixed parameters will take on new values. Another feature is that certain parametric constraints that were met in the problem may no longer be met in the solution. A consequence of these changes is that the interpretation of a standardized solution may, at times, be problematic.

CORRELATIONS AMONG INDEPENDENT VARIABLES

These correlations accompany the standardized solution when it is computed. Since the variances of the independent variables in a standardized solution must be 1.0, these are not printed. However, covariances will now be correlations. These should be scanned to see whether they are in the necessary ± 1 range. If not, the solution has a problem that may imply theoretical or empirical underidentification. The problem is not necessarily a computational one, in the sense that other programs may also yield the same estimates. However, an out-of-range correlation is a theoretical problem that may imply an inadequacy in the model. Assuming that theoretical identification is not a problem, it is possible that a constrained solution could be attempted. Sometimes, one way to achieve the constraint is to reparameterize the model so that variables' variances are fixed (rather than free), and the related regression coefficients are estimated. The program then can force the relevant covariance estimate to be such that the corresponding correlation lies in the range ± 1. This is done automatically by the program, but the feature can be overridden in the /INE section. However, this approach cannot solve parameter underidentification.

END OF METHOD

This phrase delineates the end of output from a given estimation problem with a given method. If more than one estimation method is being computed, output for the subsequent method follows this message, using the output format described in the previous pages. If an /LMTEST or /WTEST was requested, it follows the last segment of output from the last method of estimation requested. If a path diagram was requested, it follows the last method's output stream and completes the run. If no further output is in order, this message marks the end of the modeling output from EQS.

WALD TEST

If a /WTEST was requested, it is printed at this point. The W test is a test for evaluating whether any free parameters can be restricted without significant loss of information. See Chapter 6 for more information on the purposes of the test, its method of specification, and its printed output.

LAGRANGE MULTIPLIER TEST

If an /LMTEST was requested in the input, it is computed for the last method requested and printed at this point. The LMtest may not run if too many parameters were requested to be evaluated, and the computer did not have enough memory to do the computations. The program prints out the message: LAGRANGE MULTIPLIER TEST REQUIRES xx WORDS OF MEMORY, PROGRAM ALLOCATES yy WORDS. If xx is less than yy, EQS can do the computations and will report a result. If xx is greater than yy, this segment of the program will be aborted. The user will have to respecify the LM test, typically, by reducing the potential fixed parameters that need to be evaluated, and then resubmit the job to be run.

The specific output from the LM test, and the interpretation thereof, is discussed in depth in Chapter 6, and will not be repeated here.

PATH DIAGRAM OF EQS[2]

The final substantive output from the program is the path diagram, if one was specified to be produced. The diagram generates the connections prescribed in the /EQU and /COV sections of the input. Special notations and characters are used to produce the impressions of arrow directionality required by the standard path diagram conventions. Covariances or correlations are typically shown by lines of the form +++, for example, while directional arrows are given by A's, V's, $< - < - <$, or $> - > - >$ printed sequentially across the page.

---

[2] This description is valid only for printing on old-fashioned line printers. Graphical versions of path diagrams that serve as both model input and output are available via **Diagrammer**.

MULTISAMPLE ANALYSIS

In multisample analysis, models from several groups are analyzed at the same time, typically, subject to cross-sample constraints. The output from a multiple group analysis is very similar to that described above for a single group. However, some additional features are present that bear discussion.

The program echoes back each group's input file under PROGRAM CONTROL INFORMATION. This permits evaluating whether the job was correctly submitted. As usual, errors, if found, will be identified, with minor errors corrected and fatal errors leading to program termination. Subsequently, the Matrix To Be Analyzed and Bentler-Weeks representation for Group 1 is given, followed by the same information for Group 2 and all subsequent groups. A complete section of output is then produced for Group 1, consisting of the information discussed above. Similar information is then printed for Group 2, followed by Group 3, and continuing to the final group being analyzed.

The crucial GOODNESS OF FIT SUMMARY is produced only once, at the end of all groups' output. As usual, this gives the χ^2 statistic, based on (10.66), the relevant fit indexes, as well as the ITERATIVE SUMMARY that should be consulted to determine whether the estimation procedure converged to an appropriate solution.

The goodness of fit indexes are computed in an identical way as in a one-group setup, though the statistics needed for their computation have been redefined in an obvious way. For the Bentler-Bonett NFI and NNFI indexes, and the Bentler (1988a) CFI index, a null or baseline model is defined and the current model is evaluated against this baseline. The baseline model in the multisample analysis is the model of within-group independence or uncorrelated variables (with means freely estimated if appropriate), with no cross-group constraints. The χ^2 statistic for this multisample independence model is reported, in the usual format. The χ^2 for the model of interest is based on the entire parametric specification across all groups, taking into account all within-group and cross-group constraints. These statistics, along with their degrees of freedom, provide the components needed for calculation of NFI, NNFI, and CFI, as well as the AIC and CAIC indexes, using the formulas provided above. In distribution-free estimation, the FIT and ADJUSTED FIT indexes are computed in the usual way, using information from all groups.

The LM test, if requested, is printed at the end of the output using the standard format. In multisample analysis, this test is available for evaluating cross-group equality constraints, as well as the more standard within-group constraints. Results from this test are printed in the usual way, except that a group identifier is present for each free parameter. This test can be invaluable in evaluating whether cross-group restrictions are consistent with the data.

EXECUTION SUMMARY

The final printout from the program is the execution summary, which indicates the time the job began, the time it was completed, and the elapsed time (on a PC) or the CPU time (on a mainframe). This information can be used for planning or reporting purposes.

Computer system and compiler messages, if any, may be printed after this point, but they are not under the control of the EQS program.

5. MODELS AND STATISTICS: THEORY AND PRACTICE

A number of illustrative models were presented in Chapter 2 as a way of introducing structural modeling as well as the EQS program. Chapters 3 and 4 provided specific instructions on program input and output. This chapter returns to the basic didactic material on structural modeling initiated in Chapter 2. In particular, a few issues in model specification and evaluation that often arise in practice are pursued, and some more examples are given to illustrate the workings of the program.

Although models involving path analysis, factor analysis, and a complete latent variable model were illustrated in Chapter 2, it is important to recognize that these standard types of models do not exhaust the kinds of models that can be studied in practice. In fact, it is important not to be "straitjacketed" in one's thinking about models by the few standard designs that tend to be used in practice, because creative reconceptualization of models makes it possible to implement models in EQS that, at first glance, might not appear amenable to the program. Some advanced illustrations of this point can be found in Bentler, Poon, and Lee (1988), and Wothke and Browne (1990). In this chapter we make this point in a less technical way, which is possible because any conceptually appealing model can be set up in EQS the same way. It is valuable to distinguish between the standard model and some nonstandard variants.

Models are often motivated by the attempt to capture, in the equation structure, some causal process that explains the data, especially the interrelations among the variables. Whether any particular model truly reflects a causal process is very hard to determine. In general, this cannot be done on the basis of empirical results, but hinges on placing a proposed model into a larger conceptual framework. At a minimum, key variables of relevance to the structural system must not have been omitted, error of measurement must have appropriately been taken into account by the use of latent variables, and conditions and times of measurement must have been correctly specified to permit obtaining the hypothesized effects (see, e.g., Gollob & Reichardt, 1987; Reichardt & Gollob, 1986; James, Mulaik, & Brett, 1982; Mulaik, 1987). These considerations have led to the use of some rather standard designs, often involving latent variable models with repeatedly measured constructs, with each construct having multiple indicators. Control for initial levels of the variables is thus done at the latent variable level, avoiding bias due to ignoring the error of measurement in the predictors. An example of such a design is given by the typical use of the standard model developed by Jöreskog, Keesling, and Wiley (Jöreskog, 1973; Wiley, 1973), and illustrated in Figure 2.8 of Chapter 2. It is quite probable, however, that the use of such a design will not guarantee that a "causal" interpretation may be appropriate. In fact, the standard design may overlook some very important effects. When logically necessary effects are omitted from a model, it will generally be misspecified, and the resulting parameter estimates will be biased.

FASEM MODELS

By its very nature, the model invented by Jöreskog, Keesling, and Wiley is a factor analytic measurement model superimposed on a simultaneous equation model that describes the relations between latent variables. The measurement model describes how the measured variables are generated by the latent variables. In EQS output, the measurement model can be seen in the Measurement Equations that relate V-variables to F-factors, usually with E-error residuals. This part of the model is typically considered less important interpretively than the inner simultaneous equation model. This inner model represents the effects of the more important constructs on each other, as shown in the Construct Equations of the EQS output. The name "FASEM" to describe the factor analytic simultaneous equation model has been proposed (Bentler, 1986b) as more accurate and descriptive than "LISREL," the name of a particular computer program (Jöreskog & Sörbom, 1988). An example of a standard FASEM or LISREL model was given in Figure 2.8 of Chapter 2. In such a model, various types of effects of interest, for example, direct paths or arrows between V variables, paths from residuals such as E variables to F factors, and so on are not permitted. While a standard model such as this answers an interesting question about general latent variable effects — the consequences of general constructs on each other — it does ignore potentially important specific effects.

NONSTANDARD MODELS

A design that permits evaluation of specific effects as well as general effects was illustrated by Bentler (1989) using the drugs and health domains. An important problem associated with the isolation of unique consequences of the use of specific drugs is that some of the effects may not best be conceptualized as effects of drug use latent variables. Such latent variables are usually rather general constructs that contain common variance among several indicators, in this case, of drug use. A specific effect, however, would be associated with the unique action of a drug (possibly mediated by various social and personal processes). Of course, the unique consequence of taking a given drug cannot be identified unless one also simultaneously identifies common actions stemming from use of a group of drugs. A series of nonstandard models evaluating the consequences of general and specific drug use in adolescence on psychological and social functioning in young adults was given by Newcomb and Bentler (1988). Here we present the ideas in the context of the hypothetical model given by Bentler (1989). Spirtes, Scheines, and Glymour (1990) provide other examples of nonstandard models.

An example of how drug consequences might be detected in a structural model is shown in Figure 5.1, which represents a hypothetical example involving nine measured variables (V1 − V9). Three latent common factors F1 − F3 are assumed to generate these variables, along with errors in variables E1 − E9. With all the paths shown, the model is not identified. Imagine first that the paths marked "a", "c", "d", and "e" are not in the diagram. Then this model would be a standard FASEM model that might represent, for example, data obtained at two time points, with V1 − V6 measured initially, and V7 − V9 measured some years subsequently. Consider next that F2 might represent initial general health status, and F3 might represent final health status. If F1 represents early general drug use, path "b" would represent the effect of early drug use on subsequent health, holding constant initial levels of health (because the F2 to F3 path, representing health stability, is also in the model). D3 is the latent variable regression residual. Such a model, without the paths "a", "c", "d", and "e", would represent a standard FASEM model for drug use consequences. Such models were considered in Chapter 2. Of course other important control variables would also be included in the model, but these are not shown in the figure to conserve space. Also not shown are the correlated errors between identically measured variables across time (e.g., E4 – E7), or comparable paths (e.g., E4 → V7), and the designation of free or fixed parameters.

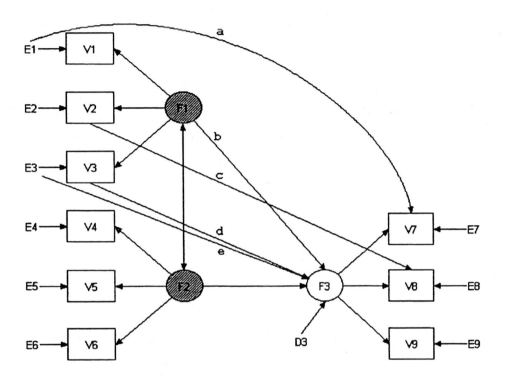

Figure 5.1

If V1 – V3 represent alcohol, marijuana, and hard drug use, respectively, F1 would be interpretable as a general drug use factor. With V4 – V6 and V7 – V9 representing, say, indices of hepatic (liver), pulmonary (lung), and cardiovascular functioning at the two time points, path "b" represents the effect of general drug use on general health. However, it is possible and, on the basis of prior knowledge, perhaps probable, that a cause-effect (drug use) → (poor health) sequence is much more specific. The figure shows four possible examples of specific effects that might be added to the general model first discussed, though in any application only one or another might be tested. Path "a" would represent the effect of alcohol use on hepatic functioning, in the context of the general model. Such a path might represent the idea that alcohol use has a particular effect on liver functioning. Since the path originates at E1, the effect shown in "a" is based on that part of alcohol use that is not in common with use of the other substances, i.e., it is a drug-specific effect. Path "c" would represent the effect of marijuana use on pulmonary functioning. This effect is specific, but more general than the previous effect: in this case general drug use (F1) also effects pulmonary functioning indirectly via V2 and path "c". (It already does so in the original model, via F3 to V8). Two very different types of effects are shown in paths "d" and "e". Both of these paths represent the effects of a specific drug, say, hard drug use, on general health (rather than on a specific aspect of health as noted above). The difference between these effects is that "d" also permits F1 to have an indirect effect on F3, while "e" does not permit such an indirect effect. Thus there are many potential nonstandard effects, and substantive knowledge must be used to choose the particular effects to evaluate in any given situation.

It is apparent from this example that the evaluation of drug use consequences may need to involve very careful theorizing and specialized model evaluation. It would not be desirable to utilize only standard designs to evaluate such effects, since these effects may be subtle and localized as illustrated above. If a model with specific effects such as is shown in Figure 5.1 represents the true nature of a causal process, then focusing only on the FASEM structure of these variables would misspecify the true model. Although the illustration dealt with the field of health, the idea that the structural model being investigated should mirror as well as possible the true causal process involved in the variables is applicable to all fields. While standard designs typically will help to focus on important model features, e.g., general influences in the context of control for errors of measurement, nonstandard designs should be considered whenever substantive theory so dictates. At times the substantive questions studied with nonstandard effects could, with the availability of a different set of measured variables, be studied with a standard model. For example, the specific part of an error-in-variable residual in one model can, with a different set of variables and measurement structure, become a common factor. The reader is urged to consider how this could be accomplished. More information on nonstandard models can be found in Bentler (1989) and Newcomb and Bentler (1988).

The typical application of nonstandard models is much less dramatic than considered above. In particular, a FASEM model may be desired in which several latent factors influence other latent factors, but it is recognized that one of the factors has only one indicator. Even though *a single measured variable cannot create a factor* unless external information is brought to bear on the problem, the literature shows many examples of a diagram and model setup in which a factor does appear to have been created from the single indicator: the diagram shows both a factor and its indicator, with a path such as F → V. However, careful study will show that the F and V actually are identical, and that a trick was used merely to allow the LISREL program to run. Such tricks are not necessary in EQS. In fact, they are not desirable because they obscure the model actually being tested. A simple example is shown next.

NONSTANDARD MODELS: EXAMPLE

Bagozzi (1980) reported a study on performance and satisfaction in an industrial sales force. Job satisfaction as a latent variable was predicted by an achievement motivation latent variable, a self-esteem latent variable, and two measured variables of performance and verbal IQ. A path diagram for this model is given in Figure 5.2.

An interesting feature of this model is that the measured and latent variables are used as both predictors and criteria. In the left part of the figure, factors F2 and F3 have the same status as variable V8: they are arbitrarily correlated independent variables. In the right side of the figure, V1 is a mediator of the effects of F3 and V8 on F1. From a substantive point of view, factors of need for achievement (F2) and self-esteem (F3), as well as verbal intelligence (V8), are hypothesized to explain the factor of job satisfaction (F1). The effects of self-esteem and verbal IQ on statisfaction are mediated by performance (V1).

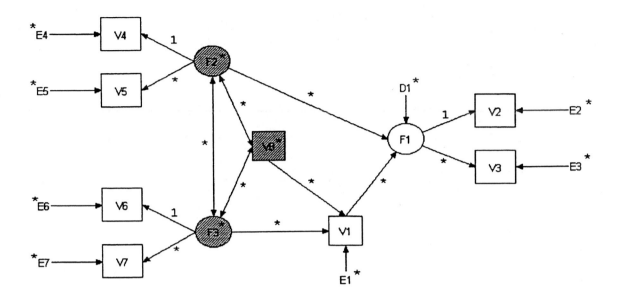

Figure 5.2

Figure 5.2 should be compared to the rather different diagrams for the same model given by Bagozzi (1980) and Dillon and Goldstein (1984), based on a LISREL representation. Since the basic LISREL or FASEM model does not allow Fs and Vs to correlate, dummy variables were used to create "latent variable" counterparts to measured variables V1 and V8, and the corresponding latent variables were then correlated and regressed. In fact, these so-called "latent" variables are in fact nothing other than measured variables. In Figure 5.2 there is no confusion that the V variables are just measured variables.

The following pages provide a condensed printout of the EQS output for this problem. Some comments have been added to the output to clarify the results. Material to the right of the exclamation mark "!" signifies a comment, added to the output file after the EQS run.

PROGRAM CONTROL INFORMATION

```
 1   /TITLE
 2   BAGOZZI (1980) EXAMPLE STUDIED BY DILLON & GOLDSTEIN (1984)
 3   PERFORMANCE AND JOB SATISFACTION IN AN INDUSTRIAL SALES FORCE
 4   CORRELATION MATRIX & STANDARD DEVIATIONS
 5   SCALE OF V1 HAS BEEN MODIFIED BY MOVING DECIMAL PLACE
 6   /SPECIFICATIONS
 7   CASES = 122; VARIABLES = 8; MATRIX=CORRELATION; ANALYSIS=COVARIANCE;
 8   /LABELS
 9   V1 = PERFORM;  V2 = SATISFC1;  V3 = SATISFC2;  V4 = ACHMOTV1;
10   V5 = ACHMOTV2;  V6 = SLFESTM1;  V7 = SLFESTM2;  V8 = VERBALIQ;
11   F1 = JOBSATSF;  F2 = N-ACHIEV;  F3 = ESTEEM;
12   /EQUATIONS
13   V1 =              1*F3 + .5*V8 + E1;  !NOTE THAT F AND V VARIABLES CAN BE
14   V2 =      F1              + E2;  !FREELY MIXED
15   V3 = 1*F1                 + E3;  !EQUATIONS ARRANGED SO THAT STRUCTURE OF
16   V4 =          F2          + E4;  !MODEL IS EASILY VISIBLE
17   V5 =        1*F2          + E5;
18   V6 =              F3      + E6;
19   V7 =            1*F3      + E7;
20   F1 =        1*F2   + .5*V1 + D1;
21   /VARIANCES
22   V8 = 10*;
23   F2 TO F3 = 1*;
24   E1 TO E7 = 5*;
25   D1 = 1*;
26   /COVARIANCES
27   F2,F3 = *;
28   F2,V8 = *;
29   F3,V8 = *;
30   /MATRIX
31   1.000
32    .418 1.000
33    .394  .627 1.000
34    .129  .202  .266 1.000
35    .189  .284  .208  .365 1.000
36    .544  .281  .324  .201  .161 1.000
37    .507  .225  .314  .172  .174  .546 1.000
38   -.357 -.156 -.038 -.199 -.277 -.294 -.174 1.000    !NO SEMICOLON TO END DATA
39   /STANDARD DEVIATIONS
40    2.09  3.43  2.81  1.95  2.08  2.16  2.06  3.65     !NO SEMICOLON TO END DATA
41   /print                                             !NOTE THAT UPPER OR LOWER CASE
42     effect=yes; covariance=yes; correlation=yes;     !CAN BE USED INTERCHANGEABLY
43   /LMTEST                                            !JUST THE DEFAULT TESTS
44   /WTEST                                             !ARE REQUESTED
45   /END
45 RECORDS OF INPUT MODEL FILE WERE READ
```

COVARIANCE MATRIX TO BE ANALYZED: 8 VARIABLES (SELECTED FROM 8 VARIABLES),
BASED ON 122 CASES.

	PERFORM	SATISFC1	SATISFC2	ACHMOTV1	ACHMOTV2	SLFESTM1	SLFESTM2	VERBALIQ
	V 1	V 2	V 3	V 4	V 5	V 6	V 7	V 8
PERFORM V 1	4.368							
SATISFC1 V 2	2.997	11.765						
SATISFC2 V 3	2.314	6.043	7.896					
ACHMOTV1 V 4	.526	1.351	1.458	3.803				
ACHMOTV2 V 5	.822	2.026	1.216	1.480	4.326			
SLFESTM1 V 6	2.456	2.082	1.967	.847	.723	4.666		
SLFESTM2 V 7	2.183	1.590	1.818	.691	.746	2.429	4.244	
VERBALIQ V 8	-2.723	-1.953	-.390	-1.416	-2.103	-2.318	-1.308	13.323

```
BENTLER-WEEKS STRUCTURAL REPRESENTATION:                !THIS IS USEFUL MAINLY TO
   NUMBER OF DEPENDENT VARIABLES = 8                     !CHECK FOR ERRORS IN THE
       DEPENDENT V'S :      1    2    3    4    5    6    7  !MODEL SETUP, IF THESE ARE
       DEPENDENT F'S :      1                            !NOT OBVIOUS FROM THE INPUT
   NUMBER OF INDEPENDENT VARIABLES = 11                  !FILE
       INDEPENDENT V'S :    8
       INDEPENDENT F'S :    2    3
       INDEPENDENT E'S :    1    2    3    4    5    6    7
       INDEPENDENT D'S :    1
```

DETERMINANT OF INPUT MATRIX IS   .21139D+06
MAXIMUM LIKELIHOOD SOLUTION (NORMAL DISTRIBUTION THEORY)

PARAMETER ESTIMATES APPEAR IN ORDER.
NO SPECIAL PROBLEMS WERE ENCOUNTERED DURING OPTIMIZATION. !IMPORTANT MESSAGE
!IF THIS IS NOT HERE, THERE WILL BE MESSAGES ON LINEAR DEPENDENCIES, ETC.

RESIDUAL COVARIANCE MATRIX (S-SIGMA) :

		PERFORM	SATISFC1	SATISFC2	ACHMOTV1	ACHMOTV2	SLFESTM1	SLFESTM2	VERBALIQ
		V 1	V 2	V 3	V 4	V 5	V 6	V 7	V 8
PERFORM	V 1	.000							
SATISFC1	V 2	-.049	-.039						
SATISFC2	V 3	-.011	-.030	-.023					
ACHMOTV1	V 4	-.165	-.137	.322	.000				
ACHMOTV2	V 5	-.030	.191	-.185	-.054	.000			
SLFESTM1	V 6	-.008	.090	.446	.148	-.137	.000		
SLFESTM2	V 7	.029	-.151	.489	.081	-.007	-.014	.000	
VERBALIQ	V 8	.000	.826	1.731	.007	-.348	-.331	.428	.000

                 AVERAGE ABSOLUTE COVARIANCE RESIDUALS = .1808   !LARGE? HARD TO TELL IN
AVERAGE OFF-DIAGONAL ABSOLUTE COVARIANCE RESIDUALS = .2303   !COVARIANCE METRIC

STANDARDIZED RESIDUAL MATRIX:

		PERFORM	SATISFC1	SATISFC2	ACHMOTV1	ACHMOTV2	SLFESTM1	SLFESTM2	VERBALIQ
		V 1	V 2	V 3	V 4	V 5	V 6	V 7	V 8
PERFORM	V 1	.000							
SATISFC1	V 2	-.007	-.003						
SATISFC2	V 3	-.002	-.003	-.003					
ACHMOTV1	V 4	-.041	-.021	.059	.000				
ACHMOTV2	V 5	-.007	.027	-.032	-.013	.000			
SLFESTM1	V 6	-.002	.012	.074	.035	-.031	.000		
SLFESTM2	V 7	.007	-.021	.085	.020	-.002	-.003	.000	
VERBALIQ	V 8	.000	.066	.169	.001	-.046	-.042	.057	.000

                 AVERAGE ABSOLUTE STANDARDIZED RESIDUALS = .0247 !MUCH EASIER TO INTERPRET
AVERAGE OFF-DIAGONAL ABSOLUTE STANDARDIZED RESIDUALS = .0315 !IN CORRELATION METRIC

LARGEST STANDARDIZED RESIDUALS: !MUCH EASIER TO ANALYZE THAN THE ABOVE MATRIX

V8,V3	V7,V3	V6,V3	V8,V2	V4,V3	V8,V7	V8,V5	V8,V6	V4,V1	V6,V4
.169	.085	.074	.066	.059	.057	-.046	-.042	-.041	.035
V5,V3	V6,V5	V5,V2	V7,V2	V4,V2	V7,V4	V5,V4	V6,V2	V5,V1	V2,V1
-.032	-.031	.027	-.021	-.021	.020	-.013	.012	-.007	-.007

DISTRIBUTION OF STANDARDIZED RESIDUALS

```
     --------------------------------------          !DISTRIBUTION SEEMS TO BE CLOSE TO
     !                                    !          !SYMMETRIC, AND CENTERED ON ZERO
     !                                    !
     !                                    !              RANGE        FREQ      PERCENT
  30-!                                    -
     !                                    !      1   -0.5  -  --        0        .00%
     !                                    !      2   -0.4  - -0.5       0        .00%
     !                                    !      3   -0.3  - -0.4       0        .00%
     !             *                      !      4   -0.2  - -0.3       0        .00%
  20-!             *                      -      5   -0.1  - -0.2       0        .00%
     !             *                      !      6    0.0  - -0.1      21      58.33%
     !             *                      !      7    0.1  -  0.0      14      38.89%
     !             *  *                   !      8    0.2  -  0.1       1       2.78%
     !             *  *                   !      9    0.3  -  0.2       0        .00%
  10-!             *  *                   -      A    0.4  -  0.3       0        .00%
     !             *  *                   !      B    0.5  -  0.4       0        .00%
     !             *  *                   !      C    ++   -  0.5       0        .00%
     !             *  *                   !        -----------------------------
     !             *  *  *                !             TOTAL          36     100.00%
     --------------------------------------
          1  2  3  4  5  6  7  8  9  A  B  C   NOTE: EACH "*" REPRESENTS 2 RESIDUAL(S)
```

MODEL COVARIANCE MATRIX FOR MEASURED AND LATENT VARIABLES

		PERFORM V 1	SATSFC1 V 2	SATSFC2 V 3	ACHMOT1 V 4	ACHMOT2 V 5	SLFEST1 V 6	SLFEST2 V 7	VERBLIQ V 8	JBSATSF F 1	N-ACHV F 2
PERFORM	V1	4.368									
SATISFC1	V2	3.046	11.804								
SATISFC2	V3	2.325	6.073	7.919							
ACHMOTV1	V4	.691	1.488	1.136	3.803						
ACHMOTV2	V5	.852	1.835	1.400	1.535	4.326					
SLFESTM1	V6	2.464	1.992	1.520	.698	.861	4.666				
SLFESTM2	V7	2.153	1.740	1.328	.610	.752	2.443	4.244			
VERBALIQ	V8	-2.723	-2.779	-2.121	-1.424	-1.755	-1.987	-1.736	13.323		
JOBSATSF	F1	3.046	7.957	6.073	1.488	1.835	1.992	1.740	-2.779	7.957	
N-ACHIEV	F2	.691	1.488	1.136	1.245	1.535	.698	.610	-1.424	1.488	1.245
ESTEEM	F3	2.464	1.992	1.520	.698	.861	2.796	2.443	-1.987	1.992	.698

		ESTEEM F 3
ESTEEM	F3	2.796

!THIS IS THE COVARIANCE MATRIX REPRODUCED FROM
!THE PARAMETERS OF THE MODEL. IT ALSO CONTAINS
!COVARIANCES OF V AND F VARIABLES, AND F-F COVARIANCES

MODEL CORRELATION MATRIX FOR MEASURED AND LATENT VARIABLES

		PERFORM V 1	SATSFC1 V 2	SATSFC2 V 3	ACHMOT1 V 4	ACHMOT2 V 5	SLFEST1 V 6	SLFEST2 V 7	VERBLIQ V 8	JBSATSF F 1	N-ACHV F 2
PERFORM	V1	1.000									
SATISFC1	V2	.424	1.000								
SATISFC2	V3	.395	.628	1.000							
ACHMOTV1	V4	.170	.222	.207	1.000						
ACHMOTV2	V5	.196	.257	.239	.378	1.000					
SLFESTM1	V6	.546	.268	.250	.166	.192	1.000				
SLFESTM2	V7	.500	.246	.229	.152	.176	.549	1.000			
VERBALIQ	V8	-.357	-.222	-.206	-.200	-.231	-.252	-.231	1.000		
JOBSATSF	F1	.517	.821	.765	.271	.313	.327	.300	-.270	1.000	
N-ACHIEV	F2	.296	.388	.362	.572	.661	.290	.265	-.350	.473	1.000
ESTEEM	F3	.705	.347	.323	.214	.248	.774	.709	-.326	.422	.374

		ESTEEM F 3
ESTEEM	F3	1.000

!THIS REPRODUCED CORRELATION MATRIX OF V AND F VARIABLES
!IS EASIER TO INTERPRET THAN THE COVARIANCE MATRIX

GOODNESS OF FIT SUMMARY

INDEPENDENCE MODEL CHI-SQUARE = 256.499,BASED ON 28 DEGREES OF FREEDOM !COMPUTED EVEN IF
                                                                       !NOT ASKED FOR

INDEPENDENCE AIC = 200.49879   INDEPENDENCE CAIC = 93.98620 !COMPUTED FOR THOSE WHO LIKE
       MODEL AIC = -14.60016   MODEL CAIC = -71.66048 !AKAIKE INFORMATION CRITERION

CHI-SQUARE = 15.400 BASED ON 15 DEGREES OF FREEDOM   !FIT IS GOOD BY CHI-SQUARE

PROBABILITY VALUE FOR THE CHI-SQUARE STATISTIC IS   .42302
THE NORMAL THEORY RLS CHI-SQUARE FOR THIS ML SOLUTION IS   15.418.

BENTLER-BONETT NORMED   FIT INDEX=   .940 !FIT INDEXES ARE VERY HIGH, INDICATING
VERY
BENTLER-BONETT NONNORMED FIT INDEX=   .997 !GOOD MODEL FIT
COMPARATIVE FIT INDEX   =   .998 !CFI IS PROBABLY THE PREFERRED INDEX

                ITERATIVE SUMMARY

	PARAMETER			
ITERATION	ABS CHANGE	ALPHA	FUNCTION	
1	1.398404	1.00000	1.14871	
2	.476569	1.00000	.70931	!FUNCTION WENT TO MINIMUM
3	.435321	1.00000	.23518	!QUITE SMOOTHLY AND PARAMETER
4	.178585	1.00000	.13277	!CHANGES BECAME SMALL SMOOTHLY
5	.041384	1.00000	.12742	!NO NEED TO DO STEP HALVING
6	.015907	1.00000	.12729	
7	.004635	1.00000	.12727	
8	.001867	1.00000	.12727	

MEASUREMENT EQUATIONS WITH STANDARD ERRORS AND TEST STATISTICS

```
PERFORM =V1  =     -.082*V8     +  .823*F3  + 1.000 E1 !(V1,V8)NOT SIGNIFICANT BY Z-TEST
                    .047            .147
                  -1.754           5.590

SATISFC1=V2  =    1.000 F1      + 1.000 E2

SATISFC2=V3  =     .763*F1      + 1.000 E3      !ALL OTHER PARAMETERS HAVE LARGE Z-VALUES
                   .132
                  5.784

ACHMOTV1=V4  =    1.000 F2      + 1.000 E4

ACHMOTV2=V5  =    1.233*F2      + 1.000 E5
                   .400
                  3.084

SLFESTM1=V6  =    1.000 F3      + 1.000 E6

SLFESTM2=V7  =     .874*F3      + 1.000 E7
                   .142
                  6.148
```

CONSTRUCT EQUATIONS WITH STANDARD ERRORS AND TEST STATISTICS

```
JOBSATSF=F1  =     .557*V1      +  .886*F2    + 1.000 D1
                   .139            .372
                  4.010           2.385
```

VARIANCES OF INDEPENDENT VARIABLES

V		F		E		D	
V8-VERBALIQ	13.323*I	F2-N-ACHIEV	1.245*I	E1-PERFORM	2.117*I	D1-JOBSATSF	
4.941*							
	1.713 I		.534 I		.382 I		1.382
	7.778 I		2.329 I		5.547 I		3.576
	I	F3-ESTEEM	2.796*I	E2-SATISFC1	3.848*I		
	I		.665 I		1.301 I		
	I		4.202 I		2.957 I		
	I				I		
	I			E3-SATISFC2	3.283*I		
	I				.818 I		
	I				4.012 I		
	I				I		
	I			E4-ACHMOTV1	2.558*I		
	I				.513 I		
	I				4.988 I		
	I				I		
	I			E5-ACHMOTV2	2.434*I		
	I				.668 I		
	I				3.643 I		
	I				I		
	I			E6-SLFESTM1	1.870*I		
	I				.445 I		
	I				4.198 I		
	I				I		
	I			E7-SLFESTM2	2.109*I		
	I				.396 I		
	I				5.330 I		

COVARIANCES AMONG INDEPENDENT VARIABLES

V		F		E		D	
F2-N-ACHIEV	-1.424*I	F3-ESTEEM	.698*I		I		
V8-VERBALIQ	.576 I	F2-N-ACHIEV	.303 I		I		
	-2.470 I		2.305 I		I		
	I		I		I		
F3-ESTEEM	-1.987*I		I		I		
V8-VERBALIQ	.693 I		I		I		
	-2.867 I		I		I		

DECOMPOSITION OF EFFECTS WITH NONSTANDARDIZED VALUES
PARAMETER TOTAL EFFECTS

```
PERFORM =V1  =   -.082*V8  +  .823*F3  + 1.000 E1
SATISFC1=V2  =    .557 V1  + 1.000 F1  + -.045 V8   +  .886 F2   +  .459 F3
             +    .557 E1  + 1.000 E2  + 1.000 D1
SATISFC2=V3  =    .425 V1  +  .763*F1  + -.035 V8   +  .676 F2   +  .350 F3
             +    .425 E1  +  .763 D1
ACHMOTV1=V4  =   1.000 F2  + 1.000 E4     !JUST IGNORE PLUS SIGN ABOVE
ACHMOTV2=V5  =   1.233*F2  + 1.000 E5     !THE MINUS SIGN OVERRIDES
SLFESTM1=V6  =   1.000 F3  + 1.000 E6
SLFESTM2=V7  =    .874*F3  + 1.000 E7
JOBSATSF=F1  =    .557*V1  + -.045 V8  +  .886*F2  +  .459 F3  +  .557 E1  + 1.000 D1
```

PARAMETER INDIRECT EFFECTS

```
SATISFC1=V2  =  .557 V1   + -.045 V8  +  .886 F2  +  .459 F3  +  .557 E1  + 1.000 D1
                .139         .026        .372        .082
               4.010       -1.754       2.385       5.590


SATISFC2=V3  =  .425 V1   + -.035 V8  +  .676 F2  +  .350 F3  +  .425 E1  +  .763 D1
                .111         .021        .288        .087        .074        .132
               3.840       -1.678       2.348       4.020       5.784       5.784


JOBSATSF=F1  = -.045 V8   +  .459 F3  +  .557 E1  !SOME INDIRECT EFFECTS ARE NOT
                .028         .137        .134      !SIGNIFICANT AND PROBABLY SHOULD NOT
              -1.610        3.360       4.145      !BE INTERPRETED
```

DECOMPOSITION OF EFFECTS WITH STANDARDIZED VALUES !STANDARDIZED EFFECTS ARE OFTEN
PARAMETER TOTAL EFFECTS   !EASIER TO INTERPRET THAN NONSTANDARDIZED EFFECTS

```
PERFORM =V1  =   -.143*V8  +  .659*F3  +  .696 E1
SATISFC1=V2  =    .339 V1  +  .821 F1  + -.048 V8  +  .288 F2  +  .223 F3
             +    .236 E1  +  .571 E2  +  .647 D1
SATISFC2=V3  =    .316 V1  +  .765*F1  + -.045 V8  +  .268 F2  +  .208 F3
             +    .220 E1  +  .644 E3  +  .603 D1
ACHMOTV1=V4  =    .572 F2  +  .820 E4
ACHMOTV2=V5  =    .661*F2  +  .750 E5
SLFESTM1=V6  =    .774 F3  +  .633 E6
SLFESTM2=V7  =    .709*F3  +  .705 E7
JOBSATSF=F1  =    .413*V1  + -.059 V8  +  .351*F2  +  .272 F3  +  .287 E1  +  .788 D1
```

PARAMETER INDIRECT EFFECTS

```
SATISFC1=V2  =    .339 V1  + -.048 V8  +  .288 F2  +  .223 F3  +  .236 E1  +  .647 D1
SATISFC2=V3  =    .316 V1  + -.045 V8  +  .268 F2  +  .208 F3  +  .220 E1  +  .603 D1
JOBSATSF=F1  =   -.059 V8  +  .272 F3  +  .287 E1
```

STANDARDIZED SOLUTION:

```
PERFORM =V1  =   -.143*V8  +  .659*F3  +  .696 E1 !HERE AND ABOVE, IN STANDARDIZED
SATISFC1=V2  =    .821 F1  +  .571 E2             !SOLUTION ALL VARIABLES HAVE BEEN
SATISFC2=V3  =    .765*F1  +  .644 E3             !TRANSFORMED TO HAVE UNIT VARIANCE
ACHMOTV1=V4  =    .572 F2  +  .820 E4             !THIS IS A WRIGHT-LIKE PATH ANALYSIS
ACHMOTV2=V5  =    .661*F2  +  .750 E5             !SOLUTION, OFTEN EASIER TO INTERPRET
SLFESTM1=V6  =    .774 F3  +  .633 E6             !THAN THE NONSTANDARDIZED SOLUTION
SLFESTM2=V7  =    .709*F3  +  .705 E7
JOBSATSF=F1  =    .413*V1  +  .351*F2  +  .788 D1
```

CORRELATIONS AMONG INDEPENDENT VARIABLES   !USEFUL TO CHECK FOR OUT OF RANGE VALUES

	V	F	E	D
	---	---	---	---
F2-N-ACHIEV	-.350*I	F3-ESTEEM .374*I	I	
V8-VERBALIQ	I	F2-N-ACHIEV I	I	
	I	I	I	
F3-ESTEEM	-.326*I	I	I	
V8-VERBALIQ	I	I	I	
	I	I	I	

```
-------------------------------------------------------------------------------
                      E N D   O F   M E T H O D
-------------------------------------------------------------------------------
```

!THE ABOVE MARKS THE END OF A STANDARD OUTPUT. IF OTHER METHODS WERE REQUESTED
!THEY COULD PRINT NEXT. WTEST AND LMTEST COME AT THE END OF THE OUTPUT

WALD TEST (FOR DROPPING PARAMETERS)

MULTIVARIATE WALD TEST BY SIMULTANEOUS PROCESS !DEFAULT TEST

		CUMULATIVE MULTIVARIATE STATISTICS			UNIVARIATE INCREMENT	
STEP	PARAMETER	CHI-SQUARE	D.F.	PROBABILITY	CHI-SQUARE	PROBABILITY
1	V1,V8	3.075	1	.079	3.075	.079

!THE TEST FOUND ONLY ONE PARAMETER THAT COULD BE DROPPED, SAME AS THE Z-TEST HERE

LAGRANGIAN MULTIPLIER TEST REQUIRES 5878 WORDS OF MEMORY, PROGRAM ALLOCATES 25000 WORDS
!IF THE MEMORY IS INSUFFICIENT, THE TEST WOULD HAVE TO BE CUT DOWN SOMEHOW

LAGRANGE MULTIPLIER TEST (FOR ADDING PARAMETERS)

ORDERED UNIVARIATE TEST STATISTICS:

NO	CODE		PARAMETER	CHI-SQUARE	PROBABILITY	PARAMETER CHANGE	
1	2	11	V3,V8	4.991	.025	.136	!ONLY THE FIRST FEW SEEM
2	2	15	F1,V8	3.749	.053	.159	!SIGNIFICANT, AND TO HAVE A
3	2	12	V3,F3	2.461	.117	.356	!GOOD-SIZED PARAMETER CHANGE
4	2	11	V5,V8	1.879	.170	-.109	
5	2	11	V6,V8	1.662	.197	-.077	
6	2	11	V7,V8	1.662	.197	.068	
7	2	12	V2,F3	.843	.359	-.251	!BIG PARAMETER CHANGE, BUT
8	2	20	V6,F1	.409	.522	.050	!NOT SIGNIFICANT
9	2	16	F1,F3	.347	.556	.180	
10	2	12	V5,F3	.276	.599	-.110	
11	2	12	V1,F2	.246	.620	-.109	
12	2	12	V6,F2	.127	.722	.082	
13	2	20	V4,F1	.106	.745	.041	
14	2	11	V2,V8	.103	.748	-.024	
15	2	20	V7,F1	.059	.808	.019	
16	2	20	V5,F1	.057	.811	.036	
17	2	12	V4,F3	.057	.812	.041	
18	2	20	V1,F1	.021	.885	-.017	
19	2	12	V2,F2	.019	.890	.068	
20	2	12	V3,F2	.019	.890	-.052	
21	2	12	V7,F2	.006	.936	.017	
22	2	11	V4,V8	.001	.982	.001	
23	2	0	V4,F2	.000	1.000	.000	
24	2	0	V2,F1	.000	1.000	.000	
25	2	0	V6,F3	.000	1.000	.000	

MULTIVARIATE LAGRANGE MULTIPLIER TEST BY SIMULTANEOUS PROCESS IN STAGE 1

!THIS IS THE DEFAULT PROCEDURE, MANY OTHER OPTIONS COULD HAVE BEEN CHOSEN

PARAMETER SETS (SUBMATRICES) ACTIVE AT THIS STAGE ARE:
   PVV PFV PFF PDD GVV GVF GFV GFF BVF BFF

!NOTE CORRELATED ERRORS, PEE, ARE NOT PART OF THE DEFAULT PROCEDURE

		CUMULATIVE MULTIVARIATE STATISTICS			UNIVARIATE INCREMENT	
STEP	PARAMETER	CHI-SQUARE	D.F.	PROBABILITY	CHI-SQUARE	PROBABILITY
1	V3,V8	4.991	1	.025	4.991	.025

!ONLY ONE PARAMETER SIGNIFICANT, OTHERS DON'T ADD ANY USEFUL INFORMATION

execution begins at 21:14:14.80   !THIS JOB WAS RUN ON AN IBM PS2
execution ends   at 21:14:41.44   !MODEL 70 -- AN ANCIENT MACHINE
elapsed time =   26.64 seconds !THIS IS THE END OF THE OUTPUT

STATISTICAL TESTS AND FIT INDEXES

A lot of emphasis is placed, in structural modeling, on the goodness of fit χ^2 statistic for evaluating model adequacy. This emphasis is quite appropriate when the assumptions underlying the test are met, and the model test represents a confirmatory test of an a priori hypothesis. In practice, these preconditions may not be met, and one may need to use adjuncts such as goodness of fit indexes to evaluate a model. The following discussion is taken from Bentler (1988a). Let us define T as the statistic that will be used to evaluate the model, using a reference χ^2 distribution for decision purposes. Typically, $T = n\hat{Q}$, where $\hat{Q}$ can be any of the functions minimized in EQS, e.g., (10.10), (10.17), (10.27), (10.42), (10.43), (10.65), (10.80). Similarly, T can be one of the statistics (10.44), (10.45), (10.49), or (10.49) that are presumed to have χ^2 distributions under the null hypothesis. Should T be relied upon for model evaluation?

Acceptance or rejection of the null hypothesis via a test based on T may be inappropriate or incomplete in model evaluation for several reasons: (1) some basic assumptions underlying T may be false, and the distribution of the statistic may not be robust to violation of these assumptions, (2) no specific model $\Sigma(\theta)$ may be assumed to exist in the population, and T is intended to provide a summary regarding closeness of the model $\hat{\Sigma}$ to S, the sample covariance matrix, but not necessarily a test of a specific hypothesized model $\Sigma = \Sigma(\theta)$, (3) in small samples T may not be χ^2 distributed, and hence the probability values used to evaluate the null hypothesis may not be correct, and (4) in large samples any a priori hypothesis $\Sigma = \Sigma(\theta)$, though only trivially false, may be rejected. As a consequence, the statistic T may not be clearly interpretable, and transformations of T designed to map it into a more interpretable $0 - 1$, or approximate $0 - 1$, range have been developed. Those indexes are usually called goodness-of-fit indexes (e.g., Jöreskog & Sörbom, 1988, p. 43; Bentler, 1983, p. 507). A related class of indexes, here called comparative goodness-of-fit indexes, assess T in relation to the fit of a more restrictive model. These comparative fit indexes, formalized by Bentler and Bonett (1980), are very widely used (Bentler & Bonett, 1987) and are thus discussed further below. Some alternative approaches to evaluating model adequacy are reviewed elsewhere (e.g., Bollen & Liang, 1988; Bozdogan, 1987; LaDu & Tanaka, 1989; Marsh, Balla, & McDonald, 1988; Wheaton, 1987). Historically, the existing indexes have been developed as purely descriptive fit indexes. Bentler (1988a) proposed a population index, which is estimated by the CFI index given in EQS. The rationale for model evaluation by fit indexes is the following.

Nested Models and Comparative Fit

In evaluating comparative model fit, it is helpful to focus on more than one pair of models. Typically, there will exist a series of nested models

$$M_i,...,M_j,...,M_k,...,M_s \qquad (5.1)$$

beginning with the most restricted model M_i that one might consider, and extending to the least restricted or saturated model M_s. The models are assumed to be nested so that a more restricted model is obtained by imposing constraints on a more general model. For example, M_j may be obtained from M_k by fixing a free parameter in M_k to some a priori value. That is, $M_i \subseteq M_j \subseteq M_k \subseteq M_s$. In covariance structure analysis, typically M_i is the baseline model corresponding to uncorrelated measured variables, or a model of modified uncorrelatedness that allows some independent variables to have known nonzero covariances. M_i is sometimes called a null model, indicating no mutual influences among variables. This is the baseline model used by default in EQS. If the measured variables that generate Σ are multivariate normally distributed, M_i is the independence or modified independence model. M_i is not necessarily the most restricted model that can be considered, but it is intended to be the most restricted one that would reasonably be considered in practice. Thus a model containing no free parameters would be still more restrictive than the independence model, but such a model would almost never describe data and is thus not considered seriously. At times it may also make sense to have M_i be a more general model than the uncorrelatedness model (Sobel & Bohrnstedt, 1985). At the other end of the continuum, M_s is the saturated model in which there are as many parameters in θ as there are nonredundant elements in Σ. In M_s there is no falsifiable structural hypothesis.

Corresponding to the sequence of nested models (5.1) is a sequence of goodness-of-fit test statistics

$$T_i,...,T_j,...,T_k,...,T_s \qquad\qquad (5.2)$$

and corresponding degrees of freedom $d_i,...,d_j,...,d_k,...,d_s$ obtained by optimizing a specific statistical fitting function such as mentioned above. Thus T_i is the "chi-square value" based on d_i degrees of freedom obtained by fitting model M_i to S; T_j and d_j are the corresponding values obtained for model M_j; T_k and d_k correspond to M_k; and T_s and d_s correspond to M_s. The saturated model M_s, not necessarily unique, has the characteristic that $T_s = 0$ and $d_s = 0$. When alternative models are compared with the same discrepancy function, $T_i \geq T_j \geq T_k \geq T_s = 0$, indicating that the independence model has the worst fit, intermediate models have intermediate degrees of fit, and the saturated model has a perfect fit. Similarly $d_i > d_j > d_k > d_s$. Corresponding to the models (5.1) and test statistics (5.2) are the parameter vectors $\theta_i,...,\theta_j,...,\theta_k,...,\theta_s$ and the corresponding model matrices $\Sigma_i = \Sigma(\theta_i),...,\Sigma_j,...,\Sigma_k,...,\Sigma_s$ as well as their estimated values $\hat{\Sigma}_i,...,\hat{\Sigma}_j,...,\hat{\Sigma}_k,...,\hat{\Sigma}_s$. In covariance structure analysis, under the model of uncorrelated variables, generally $\hat{\Sigma}_i = \text{diag}(S)$ and no covariances are accounted for by the model. Intermediate model matrices $\hat{\Sigma}_i$ and $\hat{\Sigma}_j$ account for the off-diagonal elements of S, the covariances, to varying degrees. And, at the other extreme, $\hat{\Sigma}_s = S$, so that the model perfectly reflects the data.

Comparative fit indexes evaluate the adequacy of a particular model M_k in relation to the end point models M_i and M_s on the continuum (5.1) of models. In practice this is done by evaluating where T_k falls in relation to T_i and T_s. If T_k is close to T_i, M_k is hardly an improvement over M_i and the fit index is close to zero. If T_k is close to T_s, M_k is almost as good as the saturated model, which corresponds to the data, and the fit index is close to one. Different fitting functions will, of course, yield somewhat different values of a fit index (LaDu & Tanaka, 1989).

Normed and Nonnormed Fit Indexes

Bentler and Bonett (1980) proposed to evaluate model M_k by comparing T_k to T_i via

$$\text{NFI} = \frac{T_i - T_k}{T_i}, \qquad\qquad (5.3)$$

which equals 0 when $T_i = T_k$, equals 1.0 when $T_k = 0$, and is in the $0 - 1$ range otherwise with higher values indicating better fit. Because of the $0 - 1$ range, this index was called the normed fit index. James, Mulaik and Brett (1982, p. 155) suggested multiplying (5.3) by d_k/d_i to yield an index to reflect model parsimony. For a discussion of the issue of parsimony, or degrees of freedom used in a model, see Mulaik, James, Van Alstine, Bennett, Lind, and Stillwell (1989) and Bentler and Mooijaart (1989). A disadvantage of NFI is that it is affected by sample size (Bearden, Sharma, & Teel, 1982). In small samples, it may not reach 1.0 when the model is correct. This can occur because the expected value of T_k may be greater than 0, for example, when T_k is a $\chi^2_{(d_k)}$ variate, $\mathcal{E}(T_k) = d_k$. This difficulty with range was resolved by the modified index

$$\text{NNFI} = \frac{T_i - d_i d_k^{-1} T_k}{T_i - d_i} \; , \tag{5.4}$$

called the nonnormed fit index. Bentler and Bonett (1980) built this index on one developed by Tucker and Lewis (1973) for evaluating the fit of exploratory factor analysis models estimated by maximum likelihood. The degrees of freedom adjustment in the index was designed to improve its performance near 1.0, not necessarily to permit the index to reflect other model features such as parsimony. When $T_k = \mathcal{E}(T_k) = d_k$, the NNFI = 1.0, thus obviating a major difficulty with NFI. However, NNFI can fall outside the $0 - 1$ range. It will be negative when $d_i d_k^{-1} T_k > T_i$, since usually $T_i \gg d_i$. It will exceed 1.0 when $T_k < d_k$. In fact, the index can be anomalously small, especially in small samples, implying a terrible fit when other indexes suggest an acceptable model fit (Anderson & Gerbing, 1984). As a consequence, the variance of NNFI is, in sampling studies, substantially larger than the variance of NFI. This is a negative feature.

The nonnormed fit index has the major advantage of reflecting model fit very well at all sample sizes (Anderson & Gerbing, 1984; Marsh et al., 1988; Wheaton, 1987). A modification relating to sample size was proposed by Bollen (1986), but it did not solve the major problem of variability in the index. This problem was addressed by Bollen (1989b). He defined the incremental fit index

$$\text{IFI} = \frac{T_i - T_k}{T_i - d_k} \tag{5.5}$$

and showed that it behaved like NNFI in a sampling study, but had a smaller sampling variance. Bentler (1988a) went one step further, to produce an index that would perform well but that, more importantly, also has a population rationale. This rationale is related to the noncentrality parameter of a χ^2 distribution, a concept that has not been considered in the literature on fit indexes.

Fit Indexes and Noncentrality

Suppose that the distribution of each of the test statistics T given in (5.2) can be approximated in large samples by the "noncentral" χ^2 distribution with a given degrees of freedom. This is a reasonable assumption for the true model and for small model misspecifications, i.e., if systematic errors due to discrepancy between the true population covariance matrix, say Σ^o, and the population model matrix, say $\Sigma(\theta^o)$, are not large relative to the sampling errors in the matrix S, see, e.g., Satorra (1989). Thus, the reference distribution for the statistic T_k is the noncentral $\chi^2_{(d_k)}$ distribution with parameter τ_k, called the noncentrality parameter. Asymptotically, i.e., as sample size $N \rightarrow \infty$, $\tau_k = T_k^o = nQ_k^o$, where T_k^o is the value of T_k obtained when Σ^o substitutes S in the discrepancy function Q utilized, and Q_k^o is the corresponding minimum of Q under M_k obtained when $\Sigma(\theta^o)$ is fitted to Σ^o. If M_k is the true model, $Q_k^o = 0$, and asymptotically T_k is distributed as a "central" $\chi^2_{(d_k)}$ variate with $\tau_k = 0$. Hence the size of τ_k can be taken as a measure of model misspecification in the population, with larger values of τ_k reflecting greater misspecification. The relative size of the noncentrality parameters associated with (5.2)

$$\tau_i \geq \tau_j \geq \tau_k \geq \tau_s = 0 \tag{5.6a}$$

will reflect the degree of model misspecification. In view of the fact that the models are nested, the standardized noncentrality parameters are also ordered

$$Q_i^o \geq Q_j^o \geq Q_k^o \geq Q_s^o = 0. \tag{5.6b}$$

The relations (5.6) were used by Bentler (1988a) to define a population measure of comparative model misspecification, i.e., a comparative fit index.

Let τ_k be the measure of misspecification of model M_k. The corresponding misspecification for model M_i is τ_i. In general, one hopes that τ_k is small, and expects that τ_i is large. The smaller the ratio τ_k/τ_i, the greater the information provided by model M_k as compared to M_i. Hence,

$$\Delta = 1 - \tau_k/\tau_i \tag{5.7a}$$

would equal 1.0 if τ_k is zero, and would be close to zero if $\tau_k \doteq \tau_i$. In view of (5.6), Δ is naturally a normed coefficient having a $0 - 1$ range. For a fixed null model misspecification τ_i, decreases in misspecification yield increasing values of Δ. Thus Δ is a measure of comparative fit. This index can equivalently be written as

$$\Delta = \frac{\tau_i - \tau_k}{\tau_i}, \tag{5.7b}$$

showing that the index Δ measures the relative improvement in noncentrality in going from model M_i to M_k.

It will be apparent that Δ is invariant to a rescaling of the noncentrality parameters by a nonzero constant, e.g., if for some c, $\tau_k \rightarrow c\tau_k$ and $\tau_i \rightarrow c\tau_i$, Δ is unchanged. This invariance is critical to the definition of comparative fit via noncentrality because the noncentrality parameters depend on sample size. The ordering (5.6a) only makes sense when all noncentrality parameters are based on the same sample size. As a consequence, it is assumed that all nested models and fit statistics (5.2) being compared are based on the same sample size, as in fact model comparisons essentially always are implemented. In the unusual situation that M_i is evaluated on a sample of size N_i and M_k on a sample of size N_k, for example, (5.7a) $-$ (5.7b) would need to be replaced by

$$\Delta = 1 - Q_k^o/Q_i^o, \tag{5.7c}$$

using the standardized noncentrality parameters (5.6b). Of course, asymptotically (5.7c) and (5.7a) are equal when N is equal for all models. Differential sample size would not affect (5.7c), while it could affect (5.7a).

The indexes (5.7) are population quantities. To implement them in practice, estimators of the noncentrality parameters (5.6) must be available. A variety of estimators can be obtained, but we concentrate on two. Let $\tilde{\tau}_k = T_k - d_k = n\tilde{Q}_k^o$, $\tilde{\tau}_i = T_i - d_i = n\tilde{Q}_i^o$, and correspondingly for other noncentrality parameters. Then

$$\tilde{\Delta} = \text{FI} = 1 - \tilde{\tau}_k/\tilde{\tau}_i = 1 - \tilde{Q}_k^o/\tilde{Q}_i^o \qquad (5.8)$$

is a natural index of comparative fit. FI is a linear function of NNFI having lower variance, but it can be outside the $0 - 1$ range (Bentler, 1988a). The alternative estimator

$$\hat{\Delta} = \text{CFI} = 1 - \hat{\tau}_k/\hat{\tau}_i \qquad (5.9)$$

based upon $\hat{\tau}_i = \max(\tilde{\tau}_i, \tilde{\tau}_k, 0)$ and $\hat{\tau}_k = \max(\tilde{\tau}_k, 0)$ is a normed comparative fit index. This is the CFI index computed in EQS. Since $\hat{\tau}_i \geq \hat{\tau}_k \geq 0$, (5.9) must lie in the 0 - 1 interval. Saxena and Alam (1982) note that $\hat{\tau}_k$ dominates the maximum likelihood estimator of τ_k with squared error as the loss function. In the unnatural situation that sample size is not constant for all models, $\tilde{Q}_k^o = (T_k - d_k)/n_k$ and $\tilde{Q}_i^o = (T_i - d_i)/n_i$ would be used in (5.8) and similarly applied to obtain (5.9).

The estimator FI is a consistent estimator of Δ. As $N \rightarrow \infty$, $\tilde{Q}_k^o = (T_k - d_k)/n$ and $\tilde{Q}_i^o = (T_i - d_i)/n$ converge in probability to the constants

$$\tilde{Q}_k^o \xrightarrow{p} Q_k^o \text{ and } \tilde{Q}_i^o \xrightarrow{p} Q_i^o. \qquad (5.10)$$

Assuming $Q_i^o > 0$, FI converges in probability to Δ. Similarly, CFI is a consistent estimator of Δ. In view of (5.10), (5.6b), and the definition of $\hat{\Delta}$, in the limit $\hat{\Delta}$ and $\tilde{\Delta}$ are equal, and equal to Δ. This means that FI behaves as a normed fit index asymptotically. Thus although FI can fall outside the $0 - 1$ range, such behavior would be a small sample effect. CFI, provided in EQS, is always in the $0 - 1$ range.

The large sample definitions of NFI, NNFI, and IFI, say NFI^o, NNFI^o, and IFI^o, are obtained similarly. Specifically, since T_k/n and T_i/n have the same probability limits as given in (5.10),

$$\text{NFI}^o = \text{IFI}^o = \Delta, \qquad (5.11)$$

so that these indexes have the same limit in very large samples. Thus asymptotically NFI and IFI also can be related to the comparative reduction in noncentrality. This explains why NFI is well-behaved in large samples. On the other hand,

$$\text{NNFI}^o = 1 - \frac{d_i Q_k^o}{d_k Q_i^o} = 1 - \frac{d_i \tau_k}{d_k \tau_i} \qquad (5.12)$$

does not have the same limiting definition as the other indexes. This result is consistent with Bollen's (1989) conclusions regarding the similar asymptotic limits of NFI and IFI, and their differences from NNFI and his (1986) index. NNFI does not have an interpretation as a comparative reduction in noncentrality, but it can be interpreted as a relative reduction in noncentrality per degree of freedom. Thus it does appear to have a parsimony rationale.

Bentler (1988a) provides a further analysis of these and related fit indexes; for example, he gives fit indexes based on Wald and Lagrange Multiplier tests. He also shows in a sampling study that CFI avoids the underestimation of fit sometimes noted for NFI in small samples, and that the sampling variability of CFI (and FI) is less than that of NNFI, i.e., these indexes are more precise in describing comparative model fit. At times, it may be important to use fit indexes such as those described above as adjuncts to the χ^2 statistic in evaluating model fit. This is especially true in large samples. But fit indexes may also be useful in small samples, as the following example on the effect of an outlier on structural modeling illustrates.

EFFECT OF AN OUTLIER

Raw scores of 50 cases on 6 variables were provided by Bentler (1985, p. 105). As artificial data, the case scores were created to conform to a two factor confirmatory factor analysis model, with the first 3 variables as indicators of one factor and the next 3 variables as indicators of the second factor. Factors were permitted to be freely correlated. Although sample size is small, ME = ML, ROBUST; was used, since it was considered likely that the variables might not be normally distributed. In fact, the data were normal except that scores for one case, subject number 50, were modified to be outlying. The EQS run yielded the following output, starting with an echo of the input file. The file has been edited to conserve space. Comments to the right of the exclamation mark "!" were added to the output file.

```
PROGRAM CONTROL INFORMATION

 1   /TITLE
 2     SIMULATED CONFIRMATORY FACTOR ANALYSIS EXAMPLE
 3     RAW SCORES IN BENTLER (1985, P. 105)
 4     DEFAULT START VALUES
 5   /SPECIFICATIONS                              !ORDINARY ML
 6     CASES = 50; VARIABLES = 6; ME = ML, ROBUST;  !AND ROBUST STATISTICS REQUESTED
 7     MA = RAW; FO='(1X,6F6.3)'; DATA='DATA67.DAT';!DATA ARE IN AN EXTERNAL FILE
 8   /EQUATIONS                                   !SPECIFIED HERE
 9     V1 = *F1     + E1;
10     V2 = *F1     + E2;                  !NO START VALUES GIVEN
11     V3 = *F1     + E3;                  !USE OWN START VALUES IF AT ALL POSSIBLE
12     V4 =      *F2 + E4;
13     V5 =      *F2 + E5;
14     V6 =      *F2 + E6;
15   /VARIANCES
16     F1 TO F2 = 1;                       !FIX FACTOR VARIANCES FOR IDENTIFICATION
17     E1 TO E6 = *;
18   /COVARIANCE
19     F1,F2 = *;
20   /END
20 RECORDS OF INPUT MODEL FILE WERE READ
```

```
SAMPLE STATISTICS
                    UNIVARIATE STATISTICS
VARIABLE        V1        V2        V3        V4        V5        V6
MEAN          .3053     .0958     .0722     .1834     .2035     .1220
SKEWNESS (G1) 3.1953    .3607     .2325     .8325     .4973    -.2391
KURTOSIS (G2) 15.0460  -.1832    -.8685    1.3213    1.2891    -.9145
!NOTE THE HIGH VALUE OF KURTOSIS FOR V1 -- NOT VERY NORMALLY DISTRIBUTED

                    MULTIVARIATE KURTOSIS
MARDIA'S COEFFICIENT (G2,P) = 18.9017  NORMALIZED ESTIMATE = 6.8206 !THIS IS HIGH ALSO

ELLIPTICAL THEORY KURTOSIS ESTIMATES
!KURTOSES NOT HOMOGENEOUS -- ELLIPTICAL THEORY INAPPROPRIATE

MARDIA-BASED KAPPA =              .3938 MEAN SCALED UNIVARIATE KURTOSIS =      .8717
MARDIA-BASED KAPPA IS USED IN COMPUTATION. KAPPA=            .3938

CASE NUMBERS WITH LARGEST CONTRIBUTION TO NORMALIZED MULTIVARIATE KURTOSIS:
CASE NUMBER      23          27          39          42          50
ESTIMATE       48.3404     19.6590     31.0902     41.3800     546.8184
          !CASE #50 HAS A VERY HIGH CONTRIBUTION TO KURTOSIS -- PROBABLY AN OUTLIER
```

COVARIANCE MATRIX TO BE ANALYZED: 6 VARIABLES (SELECTED FROM 6 VARIABLES),
                                    BASED ON 50 CASES.

		V1 V 1	V2 V 2	V3 V 3	V4 V 4	V5 V 5	V6 V 6
V1	V 1	2.845					
V2	V 2	.759	1.041				
V3	V 3	.227	.415	1.433			
V4	V 4	.760	.208	.006	1.051		
V5	V 5	.876	.198	.192	.576	1.073	
V6	V 6	-.162	-.100	.248	.084	.236	.810

BENTLER-WEEKS STRUCTURAL REPRESENTATION:
    NUMBER OF DEPENDENT VARIABLES = 6   !ALL V VARIABLES
        DEPENDENT V'S :   1   2   3   4   5   6   !ARE DEPENDENT VARIABLES
    NUMBER OF INDEPENDENT VARIABLES =   8
        INDEPENDENT F'S :   1   2
        INDEPENDENT E'S :   1   2   3   4   5   6

DETERMINANT OF INPUT MATRIX IS   .10649D+01

MAXIMUM LIKELIHOOD SOLUTION (NORMAL DISTRIBUTION THEORY)

PARAMETER ESTIMATES APPEAR IN ORDER.
NO SPECIAL PROBLEMS WERE ENCOUNTERED DURING OPTIMIZATION.

RESIDUAL COVARIANCE MATRIX   (S-SIGMA) :

		V1 V 1	V2 V 2	V3 V 3	V4 V 4	V5 V 5	V6 V 6
V1	V 1	.000					
V2	V 2	.003	.000				
V3	V 3	-.067	.323	.000			
V4	V 4	.096	.001	-.074	.000		
V5	V 5	.003	-.074	.086	-.013	.000	
V6	V 6	-.343	-.156	.227	-.038	.076	.000

              AVERAGE ABSOLUTE   COVARIANCE   RESIDUALS   =   .0752
      AVERAGE OFF-DIAGONAL ABSOLUTE   COVARIANCE   RESIDUALS   =   .1053

STANDARDIZED RESIDUAL MATRIX:

		V1 V 1	V2 V 2	V3 V 3	V4 V 4	V5 V 5	V6 V 6
V1	V 1	.000					
V2	V 2	.002	.000				
V3	V 3	-.033	.265	.000			
V4	V 4	.055	.001	-.061	.000		
V5	V 5	.001	-.070	.069	-.012	.000	
V6	V 6	-.226	-.170	.210	-.041	.082	.000

              AVERAGE ABSOLUTE STANDARDIZED RESIDUALS   =   .0618
      AVERAGE OFF-DIAGONAL ABSOLUTE STANDARDIZED RESIDUALS   =   .0866

!THERE ARE SOME FAIRLY LARGE RESIDUALS, WHEN CONSIDERED IN A CORRELATION METRIC
!THIS MIGHT IMPLY MODEL MISSPECIFICATION

LARGEST STANDARDIZED RESIDUALS:

V3,V2	V6,V1	V6,V3	V6,V2	V6,V5	V5,V2	V5,V3	V4,V3	V4,V1	V6,V4
.265	-.226	.210	-.170	.082	-.070	.069	-.061	.055	-.041
V3,V1	V5,V4	V2,V1	V5,V1	V4,V2	V1,V1	V2,V2	V3,V3	V6,V6	V5,V5
-.033	-.012	.002	.001	.001	.000	.000	.000	.000	.000

DISTRIBUTION OF STANDARDIZED RESIDUALS

```
       ------------------------------------------
    !                                           !
 20-!                                           -
    !                                           !
    !                                           !
    !                                           !
    !                                           !          RANGE        FREQ    PERCENT
 15-!                                           -
    !                                           !      1  -0.5  -  --      0      .00%
    !                                           !      2  -0.4  - -0.5     0      .00%
    !                                           !      3  -0.3  - -0.4     0      .00%
    !                *                          !      4  -0.2  - -0.3     1     4.76%
 10-!                *                          -      5  -0.1  - -0.2     1     4.76%
    !                *                          ! .    6   0.0  - -0.1    11    52.38%
    !                *                          !      7   0.1  -  0.0     6    28.57%
    !                *                          !      8   0.2  -  0.1     0      .00%
    !                *    *                     !      9   0.3  -  0.2     2     9.52%
  5-!                *    *                     -      A   0.4  -  0.3     0      .00%
    !                *    *                     !      B   0.5  -  0.4     0      .00%
    !                *    *                     !      C   ++   -  0.5     0      .00%
    !                *    *         *           !      -----------------------------------
    !           *  * *  *         *             !           TOTAL        21    100.00%
       ------------------------------------------
        1  2  3  4  5  6  7  8  9  A  B  C     NOTE: EACH "*" REPRESENTS  1 RESIDUAL(S)
```

!NOT A VERY SYMMETRIC PLOT, SUGGESTING POSSIBLE MISSPECIFICATION

GOODNESS OF FIT SUMMARY
INDEPENDENCE MODEL CHI-SQUARE = 63.248,BASED ON 15 DEGREES OF FREEDOM

INDEPENDENCE AIC =   33.24793   INDEPENDENCE CAIC =   -10.43242
        MODEL AIC =   .69169   MODEL CAIC =   -22.60449

CHI-SQUARE = 16.692 BASED ON 8 DEGREES OF FREEDOM   !MODEL SHOULD BE REJECTED
PROBABILITY VALUE FOR THE CHI-SQUARE STATISTIC IS .03348 !STATISTICALLY
THE NORMAL THEORY RLS CHI-SQUARE FOR THIS ML SOLUTION IS   15.458.

SATORRA-BENTLER SCALED CHI-SQUARE =   14.2030
!THE ROBUST CHI-SQUARE IMPLIES THE MODEL MAY BE ALL RIGHT

PROBABILITY VALUE FOR THE CHI-SQUARE STATISTIC IS .07663
!BUT PROBABILITY SHOULD BE HIGHER WITH SMALL SAMPLE SIZE

BENTLER-BONETT NORMED   FIT INDEX=   .736   !THESE ARE MUCH TOO LOW
BENTLER-BONETT NONNORMED FIT INDEX=   .662   !FOR A WELL-FITTING MODEL
COMPARATIVE FIT INDEX   =   .820   !SOMETHING IS WRONG

                    ITERATIVE SUMMARY

             PARAMETER
ITERATION   ABS CHANGE   ALPHA   FUNCTION
    1   .360627   1.00000   .60199   !DEFAULT START VALUES DIDN'T
    2   .256707   1.00000   .48133   !SEEM TO HARM THESE FIRST
    3   .090805   1.00000   .42627   !ITERATIONS
    4   .141212   1.00000   .38896
    5   .054784   1.00000   .35749
    6   .079526   1.00000   .34769
    7   .032769   1.00000   .34354
    8   .037659   1.00000   .34188
    9   .017680   1.00000   .34118
   10   .017888   1.00000   .34088   !CONVERGENCE IS PRETTY SLOW
   11   .009273   1.00000   .34075   !FROM HERE ON
   12   .008532   1.00000   .34069
   13   .004778   1.00000   .34067
   14   .004106   1.00000   .34066
   15   .002441   1.00000   .34065
   16   .001998   1.00000   .34065
   17   .001241   1.00000   .34065   !MINIMUM MAY NOT BE
   18   .000982   1.00000   .34065   !WELL-DEFINED

MEASUREMENT EQUATIONS WITH STANDARD ERRORS AND TEST STATISTICS
(ROBUST STATISTICS IN PARENTHESES)

```
V1   =V1 =  1.557*F1   +1.000 E1
                .355                       !STANDARD ERROR IS TWICE AS LARGE
               4.384                       !USING THE ROBUST FORMULA -- THIS
             (  .638)                      !IMPLIES DISTRIBUTIONAL ASSUMPTION
             ( 2.439)                      !UNDERLYING ML MAY BE WRONG
V2   =V2 =   .485*F1   +1.000 E2
                .167
               2.898
             (  .137)
             ( 3.532)
V3   =V3 =   .188*F1   +1.000 E3
                .185
               1.020
             (  .371)
             (  .507)
V4   =V4 =   .670*F2   +1.000 E4
                .158
               4.250
             (  .208)
             ( 3.218)
V5   =V5 =   .880*F2   +1.000 E5
                .166
               5.310
             (  .158)
             ( 5.586)
V6   =V6 =   .182*F2   +1.000 E6
                .143
               1.273
             (  .237)
             (  .766)
```

VARIANCES OF INDEPENDENT VARIABLES

V	F		E			D
I	F1 - F1	1.000 I	E1 -	V1	.420*I	
I		I			.953 I	
I		I			.441 I	
I		I			(1.126)I	
I		I			(.373)I	
I		I			I	
I	F2 - F2	1.000 I	E2 -	V2	.805*I	
I		I			.187 I	
I		I			4.295 I	
I		I			(.185)I	
I		I			(4.348)I	
I		I			I	
I		I	E3 -	V3	1.397*I	
I		I			.284 I	
I		I			4.927 I	
I		I			(.275)I	
I		I			(5.085)I	
I		I			I	
I		I	E4 -	V4	.602*I	
I		I			.171 I	
I		I			3.532 I	
I		I			(.152)I	
I		I			(3.955)I	
I		I			I	
I		I	E5 -	V5	.298*I	
I		I			.213 I	
I		I			1.396 I	
I		I			(.178)I	
I		I			(1.669)I	
I		I			I	
I		I	E6 -	V6	.777*I	
I		I			.159 I	
I		I			4.895 I	
I		I			(.157)I	
I		I			(4.952)I	

COVARIANCES AMONG INDEPENDENT VARIABLES

```
           V                      F                    E                    D

              I F2  -   F2       .637*I                      I
              I F1  -   F1       .171 I                      I
              I                 3.727 I                      I
              I                 (  .257)I                    I
              I                 ( 2.478)I                    I
              I                      I                       I
```

STANDARDIZED SOLUTION:

```
  V1   =V1  =    .923*F1   + .384 E1
  V2   =V2  =    .476*F1   + .880 E2
  V3   =V3  =    .157*F1   + .988 E3   !A PROBLEM WITH THIS LOW LOADING
  V4   =V4  =    .653*F2   + .757 E4
  V5   =V5  =    .850*F2   + .527 E5
  V6   =V6  =    .202*F2   + .979 E6   !ALSO WITH THIS ONE
```

CORRELATIONS AMONG INDEPENDENT VARIABLES

```
           V                      F                    E                    D

              I F2  -   F2       .637*I                      I
              I F1  -   F1            I                      I
              I                       I                      I
```

```
---------------------------------------------------------------------------
                       E N D   O F   M E T H O D
---------------------------------------------------------------------------
```

execution begins at 7:11:46.32   !LAST OUTPUT FROM EQS
execution ends   at 7:12:15.43   !INDICATING EXECUTION TIME
elapsed time =   29.11 seconds   !ON AN IBM PS2 MODEL 70

! IN ORDER TO DETERMINE WHETHER CASE 50 CREATED A PROBLEM FOR THE ANALYSIS, THE JOB
! IS RESUBMITTED WITH CASE 50 DELETED. OTHERWISE THE SETUP IS THE SAME. THE FOLLOWING
! IS THE INPUT, AND A MORE COMPLETELY EDITED OUTPUT FILE (NOT ALL OUTPUT IS SHOWN)

PROGRAM CONTROL INFORMATION

```
  1  /TITLE
  2   SIMULATED CONFIRMATORY FACTOR ANALYSIS EXAMPLE
  3   DELETE ONE CASE                           !SAME INPUT AS BEFORE
  4  /SPECIFICATIONS                            !EXCEPT THAT THIS RUN
  5   CASES = 50; VARIABLES = 6; ME = ML, ROBUST;   !DELETES ONE CASE WITH
  6   MA = RAW; FO='(1X,6F6.3)'; DATA='DATA67.DAT';  !THE DEL = 50; STATEMENT
  7   DEL = 50;                                 !MORE CASES COULD HAVE BEEN
  8  /EQUATIONS                                 !ELIMINATED THE SAME WAY
  9   V1 = *F1       + E1;
 10   V2 = *F1       + E2;
 11   V3 = *F1       + E3;
 12   V4 =       *F2 + E4;
 13   V5 =       *F2 + E5;
 14   V6 =       *F2 + E6;
 15  /VARIANCES
 16   F1 TO F2 = 1;
 17   E1 TO E6 = *;
 18  /COVARIANCE
 19   F1,F2 = *;
 20  /END
 20 RECORDS OF INPUT MODEL FILE WERE READ
```

CASE NUMBERS DELETED FROM RAW DATA ARE: 50   !EQS INFORMS ON THE ACTION IT TOOK

SAMPLE STATISTICS

UNIVARIATE STATISTICS

VARIABLE	V1	V2	V3	V4	V5	V6
MEAN	.1199	.0555	.1215	.1130	.1347	.1579
SKEWNESS (G1)	.4169	.3599	.3254	.3071	-.0813	-.2203
KURTOSIS (G2)	.2517	-.0403	-.9776	-.1634	.0902	-.9130

!NOW THE KURTOSIS OF VARIABLE 1 HAS BECOME VERY MUCH SMALLER --
!CASE 50 HAD A BIG IMPACT ON THAT VARIABLE

MULTIVARIATE KURTOSIS
MARDIA'S COEFFICIENT (G2,P) = -2.3786   NORMALIZED ESTIMATE = -.8497 !ALSO SMALL NOW

CASE NUMBERS WITH LARGEST CONTRIBUTION TO NORMALIZED MULTIVARIATE KURTOSIS:
CASE NUMBER   12   23   27   39   42
ESTIMATE   37.2676   46.7041   24.9805   62.8271   46.2463

!CASE CONTRIBUTIONS ARE NOW SIMILAR IN SIZE. NO INDICATION OF ANOTHER OUTLIER

COVARIANCE MATRIX TO BE ANALYZED: 6 VARS (SELECTED FROM 6 VARS), BASED ON 49 CASES.

			V1	V2	V3	V4	V5	V6
			V 1	V 2	V 3	V 4	V 5	V 6
V1	V	1	1.149		!VARIANCE OF THIS VARIABLE HAS BEEN CUT IN HALF			
V2	V	2	.393	.980	!JUST BY DELETING CASE 50			
V3	V	3	.698	.525	1.338			
V4	V	4	.110	.068	.183	.820		
V5	V	5	.243	.061	.369	.341	.854	
V6	V	6	.174	-.028	.163	.215	.367	.761

PARAMETER ESTIMATES IN ORDER.NO SPECIAL PROBLEMS WERE ENCOUNTERED DURING OPTIMIZATION.

RESIDUAL COVARIANCE MATRIX (S-SIGMA) :

			V1	V2	V3	V4	V5	V6
			V 1	V 2	V 3	V 4	V 5	V 6
V1	V	1	.000					
V2	V	2	.041	.000	!THE RESIDUALS ARE NOW HALF			
V3	V	3	-.010	.003	.000	!AS LARGE AS IN THE PREVIOUS RUN		
V4	V	4	-.012	-.022	.003	.000		
V5	V	5	.013	-.109	.028	-.004	.000	
V6	V	6	.044	-.123	-.029	.020	-.000	.000

          AVERAGE ABSOLUTE COVARIANCE RESIDUALS   =   .0220
     AVERAGE OFF-DIAGONAL ABSOLUTE COVARIANCE RESIDUALS   =   .0307

STANDARDIZED RESIDUAL MATRIX:

			V1	V2	V3	V4	V5	V6
			V 1	V 2	V 3	V 4	V 5	V 6
V1	V	1	.000					
V2	V	2	.039	.000				
V3	V	3	-.008	.003	.000			
V4	V	4	-.012	-.025	.003	.000		
V5	V	5	.013	-.119	.026	-.004	.000	
V6	V	6	.047	-.143	-.029	.025	-.000	.000

          AVERAGE ABSOLUTE STANDARDIZED RESIDUALS   =   .0236
     AVERAGE OFF-DIAGONAL ABSOLUTE STANDARDIZED RESIDUALS   =   .0331

DISTRIBUTION OF STANDARDIZED RESIDUALS

```
      -------------------------------------------
      !                                       !
      !                                       -        RANGE        FREQ    PERCENT
  15- !                                       -
      !                                       !    1  -0.5  -  --      0     .00%
      !                                       !    2  -0.4  - -0.5     0     .00%
      !                  *                    !    3  -0.3  - -0.4     0     .00%
      !                  *                    !    4  -0.2  - -0.3     0     .00%
  10- !                  *                    -    5  -0.1  - -0.2     2    9.52%
      !                  *                    !    6   0.0  - -0.1    12   57.14%
      !                  *                    !    7   0.1  -  0.0     7   33.33%
      !                  *  *                 !    8   0.2  -  0.1     0     .00%
      !                  *  *                 !    9   0.3  -  0.2     0     .00%
   5- !                  *  *                 -    A   0.4  -  0.3     0     .00%
      !                  *  *                 !    B   0.5  -  0.4     0     .00%
      !                  *  *                 !    C   ++   -  0.5     0     .00%
      !               *  *  *                 !        -----------------------------
      !               *  *  *                 !              TOTAL   21   100.00%
      -------------------------------------------
         1  2  3  4  5  6  7  8  9  A  B  C    NOTE:  EACH "*" REPRESENTS 1 RESIDUAL(S)
      !IMPROVED FROM PREVIOUS RUN, CLOSER TO SYMMETRIC AND CENTERED ON ZERO
```

GOODNESS OF FIT SUMMARY

INDEPENDENCE MODEL CHI-SQUARE = 59.395 ,BASED ON 15 DEGREES OF FREEDOM

INDEPENDENCE AIC =   29.39495   INDEPENDENCE CAIC =   -13.98235
        MODEL AIC =   -13.29875   MODEL CAIC =   -36.43331

CHI-SQUARE= 2.701 BASED ON 8 DEGREES OF FREEDOM !BIG IMPROVEMENT BY DROPPING ONE CASE

PROBABILITY VALUE FOR THE CHI-SQUARE STATISTIC IS   .95169
THE NORMAL THEORY RLS CHI-SQUARE FOR THIS ML SOLUTION IS   2.579.

SATORRA-BENTLER SCALED CHI-SQUARE = 3.1568   !GIVES THE SAME RESULT AS ML
PROBABILITY VALUE FOR THE CHI-SQUARE STATISTIC IS   .92414

BENTLER-BONETT NORMED   FIT INDEX= .955 !NOW THE FIT INDEXES ARE HIGH
BENTLER-BONETT NONNORMED FIT INDEX= 1.224 !THE NONNORMED INDEX CAN GO OUT OF 0-1 RANGE
COMPARATIVE FIT INDEX   = 1.000 !CAN'T DO BETTER THAN THIS

                    ITERATIVE SUMMARY

                 PARAMETER
ITERATION   ABS CHANGE   ALPHA   FUNCTION
    1   .293535   1.00000   .16997
    2   .077731   1.00000   .06464   !CONVERGENCE IS
    3   .031090   1.00000   .05680   !NOW MUCH QUICKER
    4   .008381   1.00000   .05632   !WITH THE SAME START VALUES
    5   .002404   1.00000   .05628
    6   .000690   1.00000   .05628

MEASUREMENT EQUATIONS WITH STANDARD ERRORS AND TEST STATISTICS
    (ROBUST STATISTICS IN PARENTHESES)

    V1   =V1 =   .692*F1   +1.000 E1
                 .166   !ORDINARY ML STANDARD ERRORS AND
                4.162   !ROBUST STANDARD ERRORS ARE NOW
               (.197)   !MUCH MORE SIMILAR
               (3.516)
    V2   =V2 =   .509*F1   +1.000 E2
                 .152
                3.353
               (.134)
               (3.806)
    V3   =V3 = 1.024*F1   +1.000 E3
                 .187
                5.464
               (.172)
               (5.941)
    V4   =V4 =   .427*F2   +1.000 E4
                 .148
                2.879
               (.126)
               (3.383)
    V5   =V5 =   .808*F2   +1.000 E5
                 .179
                4.517
               (.178)
               (4.550)
    V6   =V6 =   .455*F2   +1.000 E6
                 .145
                3.141
               (.130)
               (3.505)

VARIANCES OF INDEPENDENT VARIABLES

```
          V                    F                    E                    D
                    I F1  -   F1    1.000 I E1  -   V1      .670*I
                    I                     I                 .188 I
                    I                     I                3.565 I
                    I                     I               (  .213)I
                    I                     I               ( 3.139)I
                    I                     I                      I
                    I F2  -   F2    1.000 I E2  -   V2      .721*I
                    I                     I                 .165 I
                    I                     I                4.371 I
                    I                     I               (  .178)I
                    I                     I               ( 4.048)I
                    I                     I                      I
                    I                     I E3  -   V3      .289*I
                    I                     I                 .282 I
                    I                     I                1.024 I
                    I                     I               (  .285)I
                    I                     I               ( 1.016)I
                    I                     I                      I
                    I                     I E4  -   V4      .637*I
                    I                     I                 .148 I
                    I                     I                4.304 I
                    I                     I               (  .146)I
                    I                     I               ( 4.352)I
                    I                     I                      I
                    I                     I E5  -   V5      .201*I
                    I                     I                 .238 I
                    I                     I                 .847 I
                    I                     I               (  .221)I
                    I                     I               (  .910)I
                    I                     I                      I
                    I                     I E6  -   V6      .554*I
                    I                     I                 .137 I
                    I                     I                4.034 I
                    I                     I               (  .132)I
                    I                     I               ( 4.184)I
```

COVARIANCES AMONG INDEPENDENT VARIABLES

```
          V                    F                    E                    D
                    I F2  -   F2    .413*I                I
                    I F1  -   F1    .166 I                I
                    I             2.492 I                I
                    I            (  .159)I                I
                    I            ( 2.591)I                I
```

STANDARDIZED SOLUTION:

```
     V1   =V1  =   .646*F1   + .764 E1
     V2   =V2  =   .514*F1   + .858 E2
     V3   =V3  =   .885*F1   + .465 E3     !THIS LOADING IS NOW VERY HIGH
     V4   =V4  =   .472*F2   + .882 E4
     V5   =V5  =   .874*F2   + .485 E5
     V6   =V6  =   .522*F2   + .853 E6     !THIS ONE IMPROVED ALSO
```

CORRELATIONS AMONG INDEPENDENT VARIABLES

```
          V                    F                    E                    D
                    I F2  -   F2    .413*I                I
                    I F1  -   F1         I                I
                    I                    I                I
```

                    E N D   O F   M E T H O D
----
execution begins at 7:14:37.80   !AS USUAL, THIS CONCLUDES THE EQS OUTPUT
execution ends   at 7:14:59.27
elapsed time =   21.47 seconds   !SLOW ON THIS 1988 COMPUTER

6. LAGRANGE MULTIPLIER AND WALD TESTS

In addition to the general goodness of fit test that tests the adequacy of a given model, tests on the statistical necessity of sets of parameters that might be added to a model, or deleted from the model, are also frequently needed in structural equation and covariance structure modeling. The chi-square difference test (D test), based upon separate estimation of two nested models, and calculating the difference between the associated goodness-of-fit chi-square statistics and their degrees of freedom (df), historically has provided this information. However, there are two equivalent test procedures, known as Lagrange Multiplier (LM) and Wald (W) tests, that can be used as well. The LM test evaluates the effect of adding free parameters to a restricted model (i.e., reducing restrictions on the model). The W test evaluates the effect of dropping free parameters from a more complete model (i.e., adding restrictions to the model). This chapter provides a theoretical overview of these tests, and shows how they are implemented in EQS.[1] This material is an updated version of Bentler (1986a), using material summarized in Chapter 10.

There are several reasons for considering the use of LM and W tests in practice. First, statistical theory has verified that the D, LM, and W statistics are asymptotically equivalent chi-square tests (Bentler & Dijkstra, 1985; Engle, 1984; Lee, 1985; Lee & Bentler, 1980; Satorra, 1989). Thus, in large samples all three tests have the same size and power, so, from a technical point of view, they can be used interchangeably. This equivalence also means that an LM or W test statistic can be interpreted as if a D test had been carried out. In other words, the LM statistic can be interpreted as an approximate decrease in model goodness-of-fit chi-square resulting from freeing previously fixed parameters and from eliminating equality restrictions. Similarly, the W statistic can be interpreted as an approximate increase in model goodness-of-fit chi-square resulting from fixing previously free parameters. However, there is no need to actually estimate the alternative models to obtain statistics that can be used to form the D test: The actual difference between chi-squares obtained from estimating two models (i.e., the D statistic) is no more accurate or meaningful as a test on the model-differentiating parameters than are the LM or W tests.

A second practical reason for using LM and W tests is that these statistics can be obtained conveniently in a single computer run, which is not true of the D test where two runs need to be made, and the results compared. LM and W tests obtained from a single run, of course, do not provide information on exactly the same parameters: the LM test focuses on the effect of freeing parameters that are currently fixed in the given model, while the W test focuses on the effect of fixing parameters that are currently free in the given model. A second run with the more restricted model that fixes the specified previously-free parameters would provide the goodness-of-fit information for the D test which would be equivalent to the W test computed in the first run. A third run with the less restricted model that frees the specified previously-fixed parameters would provide the goodness of fit information for that D test which would be equivalent to the LM test computed in the first run. Thus, three computer runs would be needed to provide the difference tests that are equivalent to the LM and W tests obtained from a single run.

---

[1] The LM and W tests have been substantially improved in recent versions of the program. These improvements are described in Appendices I - III.

A third practical reason for considering the use of LM and W tests is that these tests can be relatively easily implemented in an exploratory mode, so that they may provide some guidance on how a model may be modified to yield improved fit of a model to data (Bentler, 1986a; Bentler & Chou, 1986). While D tests can be similarly used, because of the large number of computer runs needed, they do not lend themselves easily to model modification. Of course, when used in an exploratory fashion, the statistical theory associated with LM, W, and D tests is compromised, and the computed probability levels may not be accurate. When using these tests in an exploratory mode, cross-validation of results is highly recommended. Similar cautionary statements have been made regarding related univariate methods for model modification (e.g., Cliff, 1983; Luijben, Boomsma, & Molenaar, 1988; MacCallum, 1986; Silvia & MacCallum, 1988).

As will be seen below, the LM and W tests were implemented in EQS to give the user great control in the specification of hypotheses to test, in adding exploratory information to confirmatory tests, and in yielding guided exploratory results about the importance of parameters and constraints. As usual, there are a set of defaults that will cover many standard cases, but the tests will have their greatest value when specialized to the researcher's particular application.

The statistical theory for the LM test covers all estimation methods in EQS except least squares methods, but *the LM test is provided only on the last method of estimation requested.* Thus if both ML and ERLS estimators are computed, the LM test is provided only for the ERLS method. The W test is provided for every method in EQS. In multisample analysis, the LM test only evaluates the cross-group equality constraints. The W test is *not* available in multisample analysis.

A review of the ideas that form a basis of the LM and W tests is provided in the next sections. These sections explain the basis for computations used in EQS. The more technical parts of these sections can be skipped by the reader who is interested primarily in applications. A good introductory overview of LM, W, and D tests can be found in Buse (1982). A technical summary is given in Chapter 10, and a thorough statistical analysis can be found in Satorra (1989).

LM TEST: THEORY

If a structural model does not fit sample data adequately, theory may suggest that certain fixed parameters, or restrictions, be released. The LM test evaluates the statistical necessity of the restrictions, based on calculations that can be obtained on the restricted model alone. A test equivalent to the LM test in a maximum likelihood context, called the score test, was first introduced by Rao (1948). Aitchison and Silvey (1958) rationalized Rao's test by the use of Lagrange Multipliers. The LM principle is quite general, and it was adopted for normal theory GLS estimation in covariance structure models by Lee and Bentler (1980). Minor modifications of their approach make the theory applicable to elliptical and arbitrary distribution GLS estimation as well. As usual, the statistical theory continues to apply under iterative reweighting of the GLS weight matrix, as well as under linearization (Bentler & Dijkstra, 1985). Although developed in a single-group context, the abstract theory has been extended in EQS to cover multisample analysis. As a consequence, the following discussion emphasizes the common basis for all LM tests in EQS. The section covering Eqs. (10.50) − (10.58) in Chapter 10 provides greater technical detail.

It is helpful to think of all the restrictions involved in a model in a sequence, and to give a name to each restriction. The designation $c_1, c_2, ..., c_r$ will be used to describe the r restrictions in a model. Actually the number r is somewhat arbitrary — it includes all explicit equalities specified in the /CONSTRAINT section, plus a lot of additional restrictions that are implicit in the model and not listed in the input, such as "missing paths" or "fixed zero" parameters. The latter parameters are handled in the theory by first considering the parameters as "free", but then also subject to a constraint, e.g., θ_i is free, but also $\theta_i = 0$. (So of course it must be estimated at $\hat{\theta}_i = 0$.) Thus the ith constraint c_i states $\hat{\theta}_i = 0$.

Corresponding to each constraint c_i is a Lagrange Multiplier λ_i. In samples, λ_i is estimated as $\hat{\lambda}_i$. With r constraints, there is an $r \times 1$ vector $\hat{\lambda}$ of Lagrange Multipliers corresponding to the $r \times 1$ constraint vector $c(\theta)' = (c_1, ..., c_r)$. The LM test translates a test on the constraints c_i into a test on the significance of the Lagrange Multiplier $\hat{\lambda}_i$. The test is available in two versions, the multivariate version, which tests all r constraints simultaneously, and a univariate version, often called a modification index, which tests a single constraint. In particular, the multivariate LM statistic is distributed, in large samples, as a chi-square variate

$$LM \sim \chi^2_{(r)}$$

enabling the statistic to be used to evaluate the restrictions. For a specified single ith restriction, the univariate LM statistic is also an asymptotic chi-square variate

$$LM_i \sim \chi^2_{(1)}.$$

The univariate test, based on one df, provides an evaluation of the necessity of a given restriction. This test can be applied repeatedly to test a variety of single restrictions. However, results based on such univariate tests cannot be used to determine what the simultaneous effect of several restrictions may be. The reason is, of course, that the univariate LM_i statistics are correlated. Thus two restrictions may be, for all practical purposes, synonymous, and releasing one of the two restrictions may improve the fit of the model as much as releasing both restrictions, as could be seen by the multivariate test: The two-restriction LM statistic may be barely larger than one of the LM_i statistics. Thus, the multivariate test should be used whenever possible, since it is, of course, the more general one.

An innovation in the EQS program, based on the work of Bentler and Chou (1986), involves breaking down the multivariate test into a series of incremental univariate tests. That is, standard theory is used to partition the total chi-square statistic based on r df, into r separate 1 df components (see e.g., Satorra, 1989). Although there are many ways to accomplish such a partition, the "APRIORI" method used in EQS is based on forward stepwise inclusion, a standard procedure in regression analysis (see, e.g., Kennedy & Gentle, 1980). The starting point for this process is based on the restriction having the largest univariate LM statistic. Then, a fixed parameter is freed in turn, or a constraint released, by picking the associated largest univariate increment to cumulative chi-square. This process is repeated until all r constraints have been included, yielding the final multivariate LM statistic. The resulting partition of the multivariate LM statistic might show, for example, that the total chi-square is largely a function of only one or two restrictions. Consequently, releasing all of the hypothesized restrictions would have no greater impact on model fit than releasing only the few key restrictions. Thus the partition of chi-square can provide potentially useful, somewhat exploratory, information to an a priori confirmatory multivariate test. The total chi-square can also be decomposed by adding parameters (or, releasing restrictions) in a precise, a priori hierarchical order specified by the investigator. This "HAPRIORI" procedure, of course, also partitions the multivariate χ^2 statistic.

It is implicit in the LM test, as described above, that an investigator knows exactly which r restrictions should be subjected to statistical evaluation. In the early stages of model building, however, the model under investigation may be so highly restricted that it is extremely poor at describing the data being modeled; that is, the goodness-of-fit χ^2 may be very large compared to df. In such a case the researcher may not have precise enough knowledge to specify particular restrictions to evaluate, since typically there will exist a very large number of parameters that are erroneously fixed or omitted from the model, or are inappropriately constrained. For such applications, EQS provides an option that allows the investigator to specify sets of parameters in various matrices of the Bentler-Weeks model to be evaluated by LM test. While all of the relevant fixed parameters are evaluated by the univariate LM test, in this more exploratory context the multivariate LM test will contain only those parameters that provide significant univariate increments to the cumulative chi-square statistic.

Specific procedures for implementing the LM test are described in a subsequent section.

Parameter Change

The LM test is very useful for evaluating whether, from a statistical point of view, a model could be improved substantially by freeing a previously fixed parameter. Associated with each such LM test is an estimate of the value that the parameter might take if it were to be freely estimated rather than constrained. This estimate is called the Parameter Change, or expected parameter change. The estimate can be used to help determine whether a parameter, when freed, would be of such a magnitude that it is substantively important. It has been argued that even if an LM test does not suggest statistically that a fixed parameter should be freed, a large Parameter Change statistic implies that the model is badly misspecified and the parameter should be freed for that reason. This is the point of view taken by Saris, Satorra, and Sörbom (1987), who developed the concept. See also Kaplan (1989) and Luijben, Boomsma, and Molenaar (1988). However, the size of the Parameter Change can be affected by how variables and factors are scaled or identified, so the absolute size of this statistic is sometimes hard to interpret. (A standardized parameter change statistic has not yet been implemented in EQS.)

A technical development for the expected parameter change statistic is given in Chapter 10, Eqs. (10.56) – (10.58), and by Satorra (1989). The parameter change was developed independently for EQS by Bentler (1986a) and Bentler and Chou (1986).

W TEST: THEORY

It was pointed out above in the discussion of LM, W, and D tests that these tests are equivalent in large samples. Thus the W test could be used to test the same restrictions as discussed under the LM test above. If this were done, one would start with a different model as compared to the LM test, namely, the more complete model that contained the r restricted parameters as free parameters, in addition to the free parameters of the previously restricted model. The W test then can be used to evaluate whether the previously considered r restrictions are statistically significant. This can indeed be done in EQS, and, again, both univariate and multivariate tests are provided. In practice, however, the W test has better uses than simply evaluating the identical restrictions as the LM test. One would start with the given model — whatever that might be — and use the W test to evaluate whether some of the free parameters in the current model could be restricted. In contrast, the LM test would be used to evaluate whether some of the fixed parameters in the current model could be freed. When LM and W tests are both applied to the same model, they address different restrictions, and thus deal with different substantive questions.

The W test was developed by Wald (1943) many years ago. Since this test may be considered to be a multivariate generalization of the square of the normal $\underline{z}$-test, which tests the null hypothesis that a single free parameter is zero in the population, it is surprising to note that the W test was not used in structural modeling until recently (e.g., Bentler & Dijkstra, 1985; Lee, 1985). The W test has a natural application in evaluating whether a set of free parameters can be simultaneously constrained, usually, set to zero. This might be done, for example, to test an a priori hypothesis, to obtain a more simplified model for purposes of interpretation, or to improve model fit by gaining degrees of freedom at only minimal loss in overall goodness of fit. The theory of the W test is based on the following ideas. A more complete description is given in Chapter 10, Eqs. (10.59) − (10.64).

From a theoretical point of view (which would permit LM and W tests to evaluate the same restrictions), the W test differs from the LM test in that only the more complete, less restricted model is estimated to yield estimates $\hat{\theta}$ of the parameter vector θ. The hypothesis $c(\theta) = 0$, concerning r constraints, is evaluated on the basis of the distribution of $\hat{c} = c(\hat{\theta})$. Note that whether or not $c(\theta) = 0$, in general $\hat{c} \neq 0$ in the W test, because the restrictions are not imposed during the estimation. (This is in contrast to the LM test, where $c(\hat{\theta}) = 0$, since the restrictions are imposed.)

The multivariate W statistic is distributed asymptotically as a chi-square variate

$$W \sim \chi^2_{(r)}.$$

The test, which evaluates whether r nondependent restrictions can be imposed, has r df. For the specific single $\underline{i}$th free parameter, the univariate W test of the hypothesis $\theta_i = 0$ is

$$W_i \sim \chi^2_{(1)}.$$

As noted above, the univariate W test is the square of the (asymptotic) normal $\underline{z}$-test often used to evaluate the significance of a single parameter (LISREL's "t-value").

While the W test, as developed above, can be used to evaluate any restrictions, in structural modeling practice it would usually not be used to evaluate the same restrictions as the LM test. Thus, conceptually, it may be clearer to think of the LM test evaluating the restrictions $c_1(\hat{\theta})$ and the W test evaluating the restrictions $c_2(\hat{\theta})$. The restrictions c_1 are imposed during estimation (e.g., some parameters are fixed), and the restrictions c_2 are not imposed (e.g., some parameters are free). The LM test is concerned with the restrictions c_1 that may be harmful to model fit, while the W test is concerned with the restrictions c_2 that may be able to be added without also disturbing model fit. W test restrictions will typically be simple, namely, fixing to zero a previously free parameter.

In EQS, the multivariate W test is carried out in a novel stepwise fashion, again, by analogy to well-known procedures in the regression model. The stepping is backward, rather than forward as in the LM test. In backward stepping, the least significant parameter (potential restriction) is chosen first. This free parameter can be eliminated from the model without degradation of fit if the W test is not significant. Next, the parameter that provides the smallest univariate increment to the χ^2 gets added to create the 2 df W test. This process is repeated in sequence, where at each step the parameter adding minimally to the current cumulative χ^2 gets included in the current W test. Of course, parameters at the end of the sequence will have larger χ^2 increments than those at the beginning of the sequence. The process terminates when all r free parameters have been included, yielding the simultaneous multivariate W test on whether r restrictions can be imposed on the parameters, usually, whether r free parameters can be simultaneously set to zero. The value of the stepwise implementation of the simultaneous test is that it may indicate that only a few parameters carry all of the weight in the multivariate test. For example, a significant 10 df W test may indicate that 10 free parameters cannot simultaneously be set to zero. However, the stepwise W test may reveal that 8 of the 10 parameters could, in fact, be set to zero, since the 8 df W test based on those parameters may be nonsignificant. However, the final 2 parameters may be unable to be set to zero, since their increment to χ^2 may be very large. If the stepwise procedure is performed on a set of free parameters specified by the researcher, the procedure is called "APRIORI" in EQS. This procedure adds exploratory information to an otherwise completely a priori multivariate test. If the backward stepping is to be performed in the exact hierarchical sequence specified by the researcher, the procedure is called "HAPRIORI". The theory for these tests was developed by Bentler and Chou (1986; Bentler, 1986a). See Satorra (1989) for more technical detail.

A purely exploratory implementation of the W test has also been provided in EQS. In this approach, all free parameters automatically are candidates for inclusion in the W test to evaluate whether they could be simultaneously set to zero. Parameters are added to the W test (i.e., dropped from the model) as long as none of the univariate increments associated with inclusion of a given parameter in the test becomes significant, provided that the most current multivariate W test is nonsignificant. If the next parameter in the sequence were to lead to a significant univariate increment in chi-square, or to a significant multivariate statistic, the process stops and the new parameter is not included in the multivariate test, i.e., the free parameter is not fixed to zero. At this point, since the multivariate W test is nonsignificant, a set of parameters will have been located that can be simultaneously dropped from the model with only a trivial loss of fit.

/WTEST[2]

The W test is implemented if the keyword /WTEST (or /WTE) is included in the input section. If only the paragraph heading /WTEST is provided, with no further specification, the program will compute the sequential, backward-stepping, multivariate W test based on all free parameters currently in the model. Only those free parameters that are associated with a nonsignificant univariate increment to chi-square will be added to the W test, but a parameter may also not be added if the current multivariate test has become significant.

---

[2] Additional features have been built into the WTEST, as described in Appendices II and III. The procedure now permits testing against fixed nonzero constants, permits greater control of sequential tests with PRIORITY, and permits results to be brought forward into a new RETEST model file.

The user is urged initially simply to provide the specification:

/WTEST

in the input model file, which will provide for a default testing procedure. When this basic method is understood, additional features may become valuable as indicated next.

The W test can also be implemented under specified additional conditions given by the researcher. These conditions control the operation of the W test. They are as follows:

OPERAND	ABBREVIATION	DEFAULT	MEANING
PVAL	PVA = x	.05	Criterion probability value of statistic
NOFIX	NOF = (P,P);	None	List of parameters not to be dropped
APRIORI	APR = (P,P);	None	Parameters to be dropped first
HAPRIORI	HAPR = (P,P);	None	Parameters to be dropped in given sequence
PRIORITY	PRIOR = ZERO;	None	Sequences tests within APR

The information in the /WTEST section can be placed in any order, but each separate type of information must be delineated by the semicolon (;). Some additional information on each of the operands is given below.

PVAL

PVAL refers to the probability value to be used in evaluating the statistics computed in the W test. This value must be less than 1.0, and, by default, it is .05. Thus a parameter will be added to the W test (as a free parameter that can be fixed to zero) if the current univariate chi-square increment in the backward step has an associated probability which is larger than PVAL, or if the current multivariate test has a probability larger than PVAL. As a consequence, more parameters will be dropped (included in the W test) if PVAL is made smaller (say, to .01), and fewer parameters will be dropped if PVAL is made larger (say, to .10).

If an APRIORI or HAPRIORI W test is made, PVAL will be ignored in these computations, and all parameters specified by the user will be tested. Additional parameters, beyond those specified by the user, may also be included in the W test if they meet the PVAL criterion as noted above.

NOFIX

The stepwise multivariate W test is carried out on all free parameters unless the user specifies that certain free parameters are not to be considered in the test. This statement permits the user to specify up to 999 free parameters that should not be used in the W test. The specification is done by using the usual double-label convention to describe each parameter, enclosing each parameter in parentheses as is done in the /CONSTRAINT paragraph. Thus, if a researcher wants to have certain free parameters in the model whether or not they are needed by a statistical significance criterion, this can be assured by an NOF specification. Examples are the following:

        /WTEST
                NOFIX = (E1,E1), (V3,F2), (F3,F2);

        /WTEST
                PVAL = .10; NOF = (V1,V4),(V1,V5);

The first example specifies three free parameters that should be excluded from the W test, while the second forces two free parameters to be excluded from the test while also changing the criterion probability value used to make the test. Note that *only free parameters are allowed to be on the list* of NOF parameters. The list of parameters can extend across several lines, but care must be taken that a given parameter is on only one line, and that a "," is used as the last character of each line except the final line.

APRIORI

In the APRIORI procedure, the W test is carried out on the specific parameters designated by the user. An example is the following:

        /WTEST
                APRIORI = (V3,F2), (V5,F3), (V8,F1), (F2,F1);

which designates four free parameters to be used in the W test. Note that the usual double-label convention is used to specify the parameters, and that *all parameters must be free*. A maximum of 999 parameters can be included in such a list.

When the APR procedure is used, parameters are added into the W test using the backward selection procedure: the least significant parameter from the list is included first, then the next least significant parameter (as given by the univariate increment to chi-square) is added, etc. The complete multivariate a priori test is completed after all the designated parameters have been included in the test. PVAL is ignored in this procedure.

EQS does not necessarily stop dropping parameters when the a priori test is completed. It will search for additional free parameters − not specified by the user − to also drop, in addition to the ones specified in the APRIORI list. If these additional parameters meet the PVAL criterion, they will be included in the test. However, they are added subsequent to completion of the multivariate APRIORI test, so that each parameter added in this way must provide a nonsignificant increment to the APRIORI test. Of course, if the multivariate a priori test is significant to begin with, no further parameters will be added to the test.

HAPRIORI

The hierarchical a priori W test is specified in virtually the same way as the APRIORI test, except that the letter H is added as a prefix:

        /WTEST
                HAPR = (F2,F1), (F3,F1), (F4,F1);

The given free parameters (up to a maximum of 999 parameters) are all included in one W test. In this case, however, the parameters are added stepwise in the particular sequence given by the user. In the example, (F2,F1) is added first, (F3,F1) is added next, and (F4,F1) is added third. The given sequence is adhered to even if the first parameter is significantly different from zero, while the other two are not. (In contrast, the APRIORI procedure would have searched for the least significant parameter on the list to include first.) The HAPRIORI procedure is a completely confirmatory procedure, which, additionally, provides a partitioning of the total chi-square.

The HAPRIORI and APRIORI procedures *cannot* be used at the same time.

/LMTEST[3]

The LM test is specified in its own input paragraph, using the keyword /LMTEST (or /LMT). Initially, the user is urged simply to type the phrase:

/LMTEST

in the input file. This produces a default LM test. The default provides information on univariate LM tests for specific parameters fixed at zero, and for all parameters fixed at a nonzero value. It also provides for a forward stepwise procedure that, at any stage, selects as the next parameter to be added to the multivariate test that single fixed parameter that provides the largest contribution to the increment in current multivariate chi-square statistic. Another LM test may also be provided automatically. If the current model contains a /CONSTRAINT section specifying one or more equality constraints, a separate LM test is performed to evaluate the statistical necessity of each of the constraints. This test also is provided in a univariate version, and in a forward stepping multivariate version. After working with these basic tests for a while, the user may wish to modify the various program defaults in accord with the specifications discussed next.

Several characteristics of the test can be controlled by using similar operands as in the W test, but additional control is provided to permit detailed specification of the test when used in an exploratory mode. The following operands are applicable to the LM test.

---

[3] The LM test now has BLOCK and LAG features, as described in Appendix I. Appropriate use of these features can narrow the evaluation of potential misspecifications to parameters that are logical under the structure of the data. The results of an analysis can also be automatically brought forward with RETEST into a new model file, as described in Appendix II.

OPERAND	ABBREVIATION		DEFAULT	MEANING
PVAL	PVA	= x	.05	Criterion probability value of statistic
NOFREE	NOF	= (P,P);	None	List of parameters not to be included
APRIORI	APR	= (P,P);	None	Parameters to be included first
HAPRIORI	HAPR	= (P,P);	None	Parameters to be included in given sequence
PROCESS	PRO		SIM	Type of LM test be used (SEPARATE,
		= SEP;		SIMULTANEOUS, or
		= SIM;		SEQUENTIAL)
		= SEQ;		
SET	SET	= PFF,GVF;	#	Submatrices to be used
		= NO;		Use NO submatrices
BLOCK	BLOCK	= (V1,...),...,(V9,..);	None	Groups variables into sets
LAG	LAG	= 0, 1, ...;	None	Specifies time or block lag

Default for SET is PVV, PFV, PFF, PDD, GVV, GVF, GFV, GFF, BVF, BFF.

PVAL

PVAL is the probability value to be used as a criterion for inclusion of fixed parameters (or, constraints) in the LM test. It must be a number such that $0 < PVAL < 1.0$. The default is .05.

When the /LMTEST is implemented in a forward stepwise manner, the most significant parameter based on the univariate increment to chi-square will be added first. That parameter will have a low observed probability associated with the LM statistic, since the lower the probability value of the test, the more significant the parameter, and hence the more important it will be to a model. Parameters continue to be included in the test, or added to the test, if the associated univariate increment in chi-square at that step is significant when compared to PVAL. Thus, when the probability level for the univariate increment becomes greater than PVAL, the multivariate LM test will stop.

Changing PVA will generally alter the number of parameters added to the multivariate test. Lowering PVAL, to .01, say, will have the effect that fewer parameters will be added to the test. Increasing PVAL, to .10, say, will have the effect that a greater number of parameters will be added to the test.

NOFREE

Since the LM test can be implemented in a relatively blind manner, parameters could possibly be added to the test that, logically or on the basis of theory, should not be added. Stated differently, certain fixed parameters in a model should perhaps always remain fixed, no matter how the fit of the model might be improved if these parameters were free to be estimated. For example, it would be foolish to free a fixed parameter that corresponds to a causal action that operates backwards in time. NOF permits the user to specify parameters that should not be included in an LM test, using the usual double-label convention. An example is the following:

        /LMTEST
            NOF = (V1,V2), (V2,V3), (V3,V4);

In this example, the three fixed parameters given in the list are specified never to be included into the LM test. Even if one of them were to have a significant univariate LM statistic, or provide a significant univariate increment to the multivariate LM statistic, it would not be added. The NOF statement overrides the SET option, discussed below. *The NOFREE list may not contain any free parameters.* The list may extend across several lines of input, but each parameter should be stated on one line; and the last character should be a "," if the input continues to the next line.

APRIORI

The user may wish to obtain an LM test for certain fixed parameters to see whether freeing them simultaneously would significantly improve the fit of the model. This would imply that the given fixed parameters would be associated with a significant multivariate LM test. The test is specified by providing the list of parameters:

/LMTEST
        APR = (F1,F3), (F5,F4), (V2,V1);

In this example, the multivariate test is specified to be performed on the given three fixed parameters. *Each of the parameters in the list must be fixed (not free) in the basic model.* The maximum number of parameters in such a list is 999.

When an APRIORI LM test is specified, parameters are added to the test in a forward stepwise manner. The parameter having the largest univariate LM statistic is taken first. Succeeding parameters are added to the multivariate test one at a time, based on the size of the univariate increment to the then-current multivariate chi-square. PVAL is ignored in this process, which continues until all the parameters on the specified list have been included.

At the completion of the a priori testing procedure, the program checks to see whether additional parameters beyond those on the list could be usefully added to the LM test. Unless SET = NO, additional fixed parameters will be selected to add to the multivariate test if they are associated with a significant univariate increment in chi-square, using PVAL to evaluate significance. This procedure is implemented in a forward stepwise manner; it terminates when no fixed parameter can be found that is associated with a significant univariate increment in chi-square. If the phrase SET = NO is added to the specification:

/LMTEST
        APR = (D4,E5), (F2,F3); SET = NO;

then the LM test will be based only on the given parameters and no others. Otherwise, additional parameters on the list of matrices given by SET will be searched.

HAPRIORI

If HAPRIORI is specified, rather than APRIORI, the parameters on the list will be included in the multivariate LM test in the particular sequence described. Thus,

/LMTEST
        HAPR = (F2,F3), (F1,F2), (F3,F4);

will perform the forward stepwise inclusion of parameters in the order: F2,F3 first; F1,F2 second; F3,F4 third. As a consequence, the intermediate test statistics will generally not be the same as with APRIORI, but the final multivariate test will be the same as that obtained from APR. In all other respects, the HAPR procedure is the same as the APR procedure.

The following aspects of the LM test (SET and PROCESS) represent advanced features of the procedure. These features should be ignored until the user is familiar with the other features.

SET

Univariate LM test statistics can be determined for a very large potential set of parameters (subject to storage limitations of the program). The phrase SET determines which ones will be computed. In turn, this also specifies the potential parameters to be included in the multivariate forward stepwise procedure (in addition to those specified in an APR or HAPR statement). The specification of these parameters with SET requires utilizing some basic information from the Bentler-Weeks model that is used in the EQS program.

It will be remembered that all variables used in EQS are either *dependent* or *independent* variables. The designation of each variable as dependent or independent is needed to run the EQS program, since dependent variables have equations, and only independent variables may have variances and covariances. It is possible to specify that the LM test should be computed for certain types of structural regression coefficients, or for certain types of covariances. First we shall address the covariances.

The possible independent variables in any model are V, F, E, or D variables (e.g., V2, F3, E11, or D1). The possible variances and covariances are given as elements of the matrix PHI.

BLOCK and LAG

See Appendix I for a description of these commands.

<u>Covariance Matrix PHI of Independent Variables</u>

INDEPENDENT VARIABLES

		V	F	E	D
	V	VV			
INDEPENDENT	F	FV	FF		
VARIABLES	E	EV	EF	EE	
	D	DV	DF	DE	DD

DEFAULT: (VV,FV,FF,DD) OR PHI
SUBMATRIX NUMBERS: 1, 2, 3, ... , 9, 10

In any given application, there may not be any independent variables of a certain sort: for example, in factor analysis, all V variables will be dependent variables, so the row and column above associated with independent V variables will not exist.

Specific parts of PHI are addressed by the two letters shown. Thus, the EE part of PHI will contain potential correlated errors (actually, variances and covariances of error variables). The FF part of PHI will contain variances and covariances of factors. The DE submatrix will contain covariances among D and E variables (these usually represent quite nonstandard models). As noted above, the LM test will be applied as a default (unless otherwise specified) to the VV, FV, FF, and DD parts of PHI only. Thus LM tests on correlated errors would not be computed unless the user explicitly specifies these. Such specifications are based on adding the prefix P (for PHI) to the submatrix names, as in:

/LMTEST
    SET = PEE, PVV;

which would select only the EE and VV parts of PHI for the computation of LM tests. *Note that any specification of "SET" overrides all default matrices.* Thus covariances among factors, i.e., PFF, would not be tested in this example.

The program *output* will provide a submatrix number for each parameter considered (these numbers are not used in the input). This information can be helpful when uncertain about the meaning of a given parameter. The submatrices are numbered from 1 to 10 from upper left to lower right in the figure above. That is, VV is 1, FV is 2, FF is 3, EV is 4, ..., DE is 9, and DD is 10. Thus the default submatrices are 1, 2, 3, and 10.

Structural regression coefficients are similarly specified, using the GAMMA and BETA matrices. Regressions of dependent on independent variables are given in GAMMA, and dependent on other dependent variables, in BETA.

Regression Matrix GAMMA

INDEPENDENT VARIABLES

		V	F	E	D
DEPENDENT	V	VV	VF	VE	VD
VARIABLES	F	FV	FF	FE	FD

DEFAULT: (VV,VF,FV,FF) OR GAMMA

SUBMATRIX NUMBERS: 11, 12, ... , 17, 18

The letter G for GAMMA is used to specify particular submatrices above, such as GVV for the VV part of GAMMA, or GFV for the regression of dependent Fs on independent Vs. Note that only V and F variables can be dependent variables. If no subparts of GAMMA are specified, the defaulted parts noted above will be used in the LM test. The submatrices of GAMMA are numbered, in the *output* only, from 11 to 18, in the sequence 11 = VV, 12 = VF, 13 = VE, 14 = VD, 15 = FV, ... , and FD = 18. Thus the default submatrices that will be scanned in the LM test are 11, 12, 15, and 16.

The BETA matrix contains the coefficients for the structural regression of dependent on other dependent variables. The matrix is as follows.

Regression Matrix BETA

DEPENDENT VARIABLES

		V	F
DEPENDENT	V	VV	VF
VARIABLES	F	FV	FF

DEFAULT: (VF,FF) OR BETA

SUBMATRIX NUMBERS: 19, 20, 21, 22

This matrix contains only four submatrices, and two of them are used as a default in the LM test. The submatrices can be referred to with the letter B, as in BFF, which would compute LM tests for regressions of dependent factors on dependent factors. (In the *output*, VV = 19, VF = 20, FV = 21, and FF = 22.) An example of the use of SET with the LM test is the following.

```
/LMTEST
    SET = P, GVF, BETA;
```

It will be remembered that use of the word SET overrides all defaults, so only the specified matrices will be searched for fixed parameters to free. The letter "P" indicates the use of the default submatrices in PHI (namely, VV, FV, FF, and DD); GVF indicates use of the VF submatrix of GAMMA (which usually would represent factor loadings); BETA indicates use of the default submatrices of BETA (namely, VF and FF). Note that when only the default submatrices of a given matrix are to be specified, it is not necessary to use the three-letter code for the specific submatrices. Using either the full name (e.g., PHI) or the abbreviation (P) for the matrix will do the job.

There is a final feature of SET that works in cooperation with the PROCESS specification discussed next. This feature, based on parentheses, permits grouping of parameters from various submatrices into equivalent units or sets. Thus SET = PEE, BVF; creates two parameter sets. So does SET = (PDD,PFF),GFF; but here, PDD and PFF are in the same set, while GFF is in another set. The default (no SET specification) yields the 10 sets of parameters described previously. As another example,

/LMTEST
      PROC = SEP;
      SET = (P,PEE),(GFV,GFF),BFF;

groups the default matrices of PHI and PEE into one unit or set for analysis; groups the matrices GFV and GFF into another set for analysis; and keeps BFF as a third unit for analysis. Note that commas separate the various units or sets. The phrase PROC = SEP indicates that several LM tests are to be performed, as noted in the next section.

PROCESS

This statement controls the type of LM test to be performed and permits, in fact, several LM tests to be computed in a single run. When the statement is not included in the specification, the default method SIM or SIMULTANEOUS is used. The simultaneous LM test is a single test that uses all of the parameters from all matrices at once: all parameters specified in "SET" compete for simultaneous inclusion in the forward stepwise test. Thus, the most significant parameter may come from PFF, the next most significant from BVF, the next from GFF, etc., in accord with the forward stepping procedure described previously. (If SET is not specified, the default submatrices will be used.)

The statement PROC = SEP; noted above indicates that SEPARATE LM tests are to be performed for each set of parameters (as specified in SET). Thus each set of parameters has its own forward stepwise multivariate test. The above example with SET = (P,PEE),(GFV,GFF),BFF; in effect specifies that three multivariate LM tests are to be performed in a single run: one test based on the default matrices in P and PEE; another based on GFV and GFF; and a third based on BFF. Note that parameters from one set cannot compete for inclusion in the LM test for another set. Separate tests may be useful when attempting to clarify several different parts of a model, e.g., factor loadings or correlated errors, without letting these parts compete for importance in a single test. (As was noted above, EQS always automatically provides a separate LM test for equality constraints: this test does not need to be specified, and cannot be modified by the user.)

The statement PROC = SEQUENTIAL; (or SEQ) provides a way of adding a hierarchical, theory-based procedure to a single exploratory LM test. With this statement, sets of parameters are considered for inclusion in the multivariate LM test in accord with the grouping of matrices specified in the SET statement. In general, SET would thus be specified to reflect an a priori view of the importance of various types of parameters. Thus, the specification

/LMTEST
      PROC = SEQ; SET = PFF, (GVF, BVF), PEE;

indicates that any significant covariances among factors (PFF) are to be entered first in the LM test; that factor loadings for both independent (GVF) and dependent (BVF) factors are to be considered next, equally; that no factor loading is to be entered until all significant factor covariances are first entered; and that no correlated errors (PEE) are to be considered until all significant PFF, GVF, and BVF parameters have first been included. Thus, even if the largest univariate LM statistic were to be found in PEE, the corresponding error covariance or variance parameter would not be added to the stepwise LM test until all significant parameters in PFF, GVF and BVF were first included. It is, of course, entirely possible that the PEE parameter might then, when it is considered later in the sequence, no longer provide a significant increment to chi-square.

Output Code

The results of an EQS run will also contain, in the printout, a numbered CODE for each parameter representing information utilized during computation of the LM test. The CODE contains two numbers. The first number refers to whether the parameter is included in an *a priori* test (in which case it is 1), or which set of parameters it belongs to (2, 3, etc.). In a simultaneous test, all parameters will be labeled as belonging to set 2. The second number refers to the matrix number in which the parameter resides (01 to 22). However, if the parameter has been fixed at a nonzero value, its code is 0, and if the parameter is part of an *a priori* test, the code represents the parameter's sequence number in the *a priori* list.

ILLUSTRATIVE EXAMPLES

Constrained Latent Variable Model

The latent variable model reported on pp. 33 – 38 of this manual will be used to illustrate some features of the LM testing procedure. The input shown on p. 36 of the manual was modified in two ways: 1) The equality constraint (F1,F3) = (F2,F3); was added to the constraint section, and 2) the statement /LMTEST was added. As a consequence, only the default LM procedures are implemented. This model was submitted to EQS.

The EQS run was uneventful, yielding no condition codes and appropriately meeting the constraint at the solution. The resulting model had a chi-square of 48.565 with 10 df, p < .001. Apparently, adding this one additional constraint changed the model from adequate to inadequate. It would be interesting to see if /LMTEST could locate the problems with the resulting model.

As was noted above, when constraints exist in a model, EQS produces univariate tests and a multivariate test for all of the constraints. The original model contained three constraints, so the current model contains four. EQS first provides a title on its actions, then echos back information on the constraints and numbers them:

CONSTRAINTS TO BE RELEASED ARE:

CONSTR:1 (E1,E1) − (E3,E3)=0;
CONSTR:2 (E2,E2) − (E4,E4)=0;
CONSTR:3 (E3,E1) − (E4,E2)=0;
CONSTR:4 (F1,F3) − (F2,F3)=0;

Notice that constraint #4 is the new constraint added to the model. Next, EQS prints out the statistics for each of the separate constraints:

UNIVARIATE TEST STATISTICS:

NO	CONSTRAINT	CHI-SQUARE	PROBABILITY
1	CONSTR:1	0.151	0.698
2	CONSTR:2	0.548	0.459
3	CONSTR:3	1.526	0.217
4	CONSTR:4	32.650	0.000

Based on these results, we can conclude that only constraint #4 is associated with a significant LM test ($p < .001$). Apparently, constraints #1 − #3 are reasonable constraints, but #4 is not consistent with the data: the null hypothesis that #4 is zero in the population must be rejected. However, to be sure of our conclusions, we should look at the multivariate test, which is printed next:

	CUMULATIVE MULTIVARIATE STATISTICS				UNIVARIATE INCREMENT	
STEP	PARAMETER	CHI-SQUARE	D.F.	PROBABILITY	CHI-SQUARE	PROBABILITY
1	CONSTR:4	32.650	1	0.000	32.650	0.000
2	CONSTR:3	33.732	2	0.000	1.082	0.298
3	CONSTR:2	34.097	3	0.000	0.365	0.546
4	CONSTR:1	34.098	4	0.000	0.001	0.977

The multivariate test is a forward stepwise procedure. Since there are four constraints, there were four steps. The constraint with the largest univariate chi-square is entered first. It yields the same statistic as before. Next, the constraint adding the most to the current value (32.650) of chi-square is added to the test. This is #3, which yielded an increment of 1.083 chi-square points for a total 2 df multivariate test of 33.732. Two more forward steps are taken, with constraints #2 and then #1 added in sequence. In this particular case, the sequence for adding constraints to the LM test was the same as the relative size of the univariate statistics, but this will not generally be the case.

It will be noted that the final multivariate test, based on 4 df, is statistically significant. Thus, keeping all four constraints simultaneously implies a degraded model fit. However, from the multivariate test (and also in this instance, the univariate tests) we see that constraint #4 accounts for virtually all of the 34.098 value of the statistic. Clearly, only constraint #4 is unreasonable. In fact, none of the univariate increments to the multivariate chi-square, beyond the first, was significant. For example, the increment in step 2, for constraint #3, had $p = .298$, which is not significant at the .05 level, showing that the constraint is acceptable, i.e., cannot be rejected.

Next, the default procedure provides a series of tests on the fixed parameters of the model, starting with univariate LM statistics. The program prints these in order of size, starting with the largest:

LAGRANGE MULTIPLIER TEST (FOR ADDING PARAMETERS)

ORDERED UNIVARIATE TEST STATISTICS:

NO	CODE	PARAMETER	CHI-SQUARE	PROBABILITY	PARAMETER CHANGE
1	2 10	D 2,D 1	32.650	0.000	4.611
2	2 22	F 1,F 2	32.650	0.000	0.341
3	2 20	V 5,F 2	23.776	0.000	0.779
4	2 12	V 2,F 3	14.362	0.000	− 0.125
5	2 20	V 6,F 2	12.487	0.000	0.394
6	2 20	V 5,F 1	12.047	0.001	− 0.211
7	2 12	V 3,F 3	8.028	0.005	0.112
8	2 20	V 2,F 2	5.222	0.022	0.063
9	2 20	V 1,F 2	2.234	0.135	0.047
10	2 12	V 1,F 3	1.853	0.173	− 0.050
11	2 0	V 2,F 1	1.520	0.218	0.045
12	2 0	V 3,F 2	1.398	0.237	− 0.045
13	2 12	V 4,F 3	0.597	0.440	0.027
14	2 0	V 1,F 1	0.436	0.509	0.029
15	2 20	V 6,F 1	0.359	0.549	− 0.024
16	2 20	V 3,F 1	0.228	0.633	− 0.015
17	2 20	V 4,F 1	0.228	0.633	0.018
18	2 0	V 4,F 2	0.213	0.645	− 0.015
19	2 0	V 5,F 3	0.000	1.000	0.000

There were 19 fixed parameters evaluated by the univariate LM statistic. These parameters come from the fixed elements of the 10 default submatrices of PHI, GAMMA, and BETA as noted above (and also printed out, below). In each of the 19 rows of printout, we have the following information. First, the sequence number of the test, starting with the parameter having the largest value. Second, two items labeled CODE. The first of these indicates that the parameters all belong to set number "2", that is, they will be considered all together in the multivariate test. The next two numbers indicate the matrix from which the fixed parameter is taken. For example, the parameter D2,D1 comes from matrix 10, namely, PDD. The only exception to this numbering is when matrix 00 is indicated: *fixed nonzero parameters are not indicated by matrix number, but by the code 0*. Thus, for example, the 11th parameter, V2,F1, is a fixed nonzero parameter in the model: its actual location in the submatrices is not shown. Third, the parameter is given its usual double-label name, as was just noted. Fourth, the column labeled CHI-SQUARE gives the univariate LM statistic for testing the null hypothesis that the restriction on that particular parameter is true in the population. Fifth, the corresponding probability is printed out. Small values indicate high significance, i.e., that the restriction is unreasonable and perhaps the parameter should be freed. The final column, PARAMETER CHANGE, provides a projection of the change in parameter value that would occur when releasing the constraint. For example, D2,D1 is estimated to take on the value of 4.611. The parameter V4,F2, which was fixed at .833, is expected to be smaller by .015 if estimated freely. These values can be used as start values in subsequent runs, if they are needed. The parameter change statistic is based on Equation (10.58) of Chapter 10.

In the example, 8 of 19 univariate LM tests are significant (p < .05). Thus, one might be tempted to release all eight constraints. However, the multivariate test tells a different story.

MULTIVARIATE LAGRANGE MULTIPLIER TEST BY SIMULTANEOUS PROCESS IN STAGE 1

PARAMETER SETS (SUBMATRICES) ACTIVE AT THIS STAGE ARE:

PVV PFV PFF PDD GVV GVF GFV GFF BVF BFF

		CUMULATIVE MULTIVARIATE STATISTICS			UNIVARIATE INCREMENT	
STEP	PARAMETER	CHI-SQUARE	D.F.	PROBABILITY	CHI-SQUARE	PROBABILITY
1	D 2,D 1	32.650	1	0.000	32.650	0.000

The simultaneous process evaluates the contributions to the multivariate LM test of individual restrictions, using a forward stepwise procedure. The parameter having the largest univariate LM statistic is entered first, and then, parameters are added sequentially providing that they make a significant univariate increment to the multivariate test. In this case, the univariate LM statistics are highly misleading, since only one parameter is needed (i.e., one restriction needs to be released). The remaining 7 restrictions that are significant by univariate test are evidently so highly correlated with the D2,D1 restriction that they become nonsignificant when D2,D1 is entered first. This is why there is no second step to the multivariate test.

To conclude this example, one might now be tempted to reestimate the model with the two changes noted by the LM tests: 1) Release constraint #4, the artificial equality constraint that we added to the model on p. 36 of the manual, and 2) release the constraint that the covariance of D2,D1 is zero, i.e., let D2,D1 be a free covariance. There is a problem, however. We did not perform a simultaneous test on these two restrictions, and it is possible that these constraints are also redundant. Unfortunately, in the current EQS program, *there is no way of simultaneously testing equality constraints and fixed parameters with a single LM test.* We could now use either theory or practice to evaluate the situation. Theoretically, it can be shown that if we eliminate constraint #4, the inner part of the model describing relations among the three factors is saturated. Then additionally permitting D2,D1 to be a free covariance would produce an underidentified model. In practice, if we make the two changes, EQS will indicate that the parameters in the new model are linearly dependent, and it will point to parameter D2,D1 as creating the problem. Thus, in this case, the program would show us how to avoid making a mistake.

Factor Analysis Model

The factor analysis model given in the example of Chapter 5 on eliminating an outlier was modified slightly to illustrate both the W and LM tests. In particular, the model was modified as follows: 1) Two factor loadings (V5,F1 and V6,F1) were added to the model, 2) /WTEST was added as a section, with an APR = (V5,F1),(V6,F1); specification, 3) /LMTEST was added as a section, with SET = PEE; added to specify this test further, and 4) the estimation method was changed to maximum likelihood (ML). Since the original model fit the data quite well, we would expect that the W test would show that the two added parameters are not needed, and furthermore, we would expect that no correlated errors would help to improve the fit.

The new model obtained an ML chi-square of 2.55, which, based on 6 df, indicated excellent fit or even overfitting (p = .86). The W test section yielded the following result. Note that the title indicates that the test is a priori.

WALD TEST (FOR DROPPING PARAMETERS)

MULTIVARIATE WALD TEST BY APRIORI PROCESS

		CUMULATIVE MULTIVARIATE STATISTICS			UNIVARIATE INCREMENT	
STEP	PARAMETER	CHI-SQUARE	D.F.	PROBABILITY	CHI-SQUARE	PROBABILITY
1	V 6,F 1	0.028	1	0.867	0.028	0.867
2	V 5,F 1	0.169	2	0.919	0.141	0.707

The two parameters that were added to the model turn out to be unnecessary. Each univariate increment to chi-square is not significant (p > .05), and the simultaneous 2 df test is also nonsignificant (p = .919). The W test next proceeds to a second stage, called stage 1 below, in which an attempt is made to find additional free parameters that may not be needed in the model. The PROCESS is SIMULTANEOUS by default, that is, all free parameters will be considered.

MULTIVARIATE WALD TEST BY SIMULTANEOUS PROCESS

		CUMULATIVE MULTIVARIATE STATISTICS			UNIVARIATE INCREMENT	
STEP	PARAMETER	CHI-SQUARE	D.F.	PROBABILITY	CHI-SQUARE	PROBABILITY
1	E 3,E 3	1.146	3	0.766	0.977	0.323
2	E 5,E 5	2.870	4	0.580	1.724	0.189
3	F 2,F 1	6.387	5	0.270	3.516	0.061

Three parameters are added to the previously considered two free parameters, so the multivariate test has 3, 4, and 5 degrees of freedom successively as each parameter is added. Each parameter adds a low univariate increment to the current cumulative chi-square statistic, low enough not to be significant (each p > .05). The final 5 df test is not significant so that, from a statistical point of view, one could also drop the two error variances (of E3 and E5), and the factor correlation F2,F1, that is, fix them to zero. However, in a latent variable model it will not make sense to fix error variances to zero. Since the factor correlation is close to significant, it may be desirable to check this parameter again after dropping the unnecessary factor loadings. Next, the program provides LM test information on the correlated errors.

LAGRANGE MULTIPLIER TEST (FOR ADDING PARAMETERS)

ORDERED UNIVARIATE TEST STATISTICS:

NO	CODE	PARAMETER	CHI-SQUARE	PROBABILITY	PARAMETER CHANGE
1	2 6	E 3,E 1	1.329	0.249	− 0.546
2	2 6	E 5,E 2	0.660	0.417	− 0.080
3	2 6	E 2,E 1	0.566	0.452	0.131
4	2 6	E 6,E 1	0.565	0.452	0.074
5	2 6	E 5,E 3	0.505	0.477	0.098
6	2 6	E 6,E 2	0.463	0.496	− 0.067
7	2 6	E 4,E 2	0.095	0.758	0.032
8	2 6	E 4,E 1	0.044	0.834	− 0.022
9	2 6	E 6,E 3	0.044	0.835	− 0.026
10	2 6	E 5,E 1	0.027	0.870	− 0.017
11	2 6	E 3,E 2	0.013	0.908	0.033
12	2 6	E 4,E 3	0.000	0.987	− 0.002
13	2 0	F 2,F 2	0.000	1.000	0.000
14	2 0	F 1,F 1	0.000	1.000	0.000
15	2 6	E 5,E 4	0.000	1.000	0.000
16	2 6	E 6,E 4	0.000	1.000	0.000
17	2 6	E 6,E 5	0.000	1.000	0.000

As shown in the above column titled CODE, most of the parameters come from the 6th submatrix PEE. However, some parameters have the code 00. This indicates that EQS also computed statistics for the fixed nonzero parameters of the model, in this case, the variances of F1 and F2. Since these two parameters were fixed for identification purposes, one would expect the corresponding univariate LM tests to be zero, and they are. Since none of the univariate LM statistics is significant, the program prints the messages:

***** NONE OF THE UNIVARIATE LAGRANGE MULTIPLIERS IS SIGNIFICANT,

***** THE MULTIVARIATE TEST PROCEDURE WILL NOT BE EXECUTED.

and stops. If some parameters had been significant, the forward stepwise procedure would have been implemented.

Nonstandard Model

The nonstandard model given in Chapter 5 will provide the final example. The program input was modified in several ways: 1) Three free parameters (see APR next) were eliminated from the model, 2) an APR = (V1,V8), (F1,V1), (F3,V8); statement was added under an /LMTEST, and 3) a /WTEST statement was added. If all of the parameters of the original model are needed, the a priori LM test should verify that the three parameters should be added to the model. However, some of the other existing free parameters may also not be needed. The results yielded a model with an ML chi-square of 47.3 with 18 df (p < .001). The W test yielded:

MULTIVARIATE WALD TEST BY SIMULTANEOUS PROCESS

		CUMULATIVE MULTIVARIATE STATISTICS			UNIVARIATE INCREMENT	
STEP	PARAMETER	CHI-SQUARE	D.F.	PROBABILITY	CHI-SQUARE	PROBABILITY
1	F 2,V 8	2.486	1	0.115	2.486	0.115
2	F 2,F 2	5.251	2	0.072	2.766	0.096

indicating that two of the original free parameters could potentially be dropped from the model. However, the F2,F2 parameter represents the variance of a factor, and it may not be desirable to eliminate this parameter since this would have the effect of wiping out the factor by creating a factor with no variance.

The univariate LM test results were as follows.

LAGRANGE MULTIPLIER TEST (FOR ADDING PARAMETERS)

ORDERED UNIVARIATE TEST STATISTICS:

NO	CODE	PARAMETER	CHI-SQUARE	PROBABILITY	PARAMETER CHANGE
1	1 3	F 3,V 8	13.534	0.000	− 2.260
2	1 2	F 1,V 1	12.778	0.000	0.615
3	2 16	F 1,F 3	10.498	0.001	1.164
4	2 20	V 1,F 1	7.011	0.008	0.201
5	1 1	V 1,V 8	6.995	0.008	− 0.109
6	2 11	V 3,V 8	4.368	0.037	0.120
7	2 12	V 3,F 3	4.214	0.040	0.438
8	2 12	V 5,F 3	3.626	0.057	− 0.417
9	2 15	F 1,V 8	3.150	0.076	0.155
10	2 12	V 1,F 2	2.905	0.088	0.543

plus another 18 lines of output corresponding to less significant constraints. The a priori multivariate LM test showed:

MULTIVARIATE LAGRANGE MULTIPLIER TEST BY APRIORI PROCESS IN STAGE 0

		CUMULATIVE MULTIVARIATE STATISTICS			UNIVARIATE INCREMENT	
STEP	PARAMETER	CHI-SQUARE	D.F.	PROBABILITY	CHI-SQUARE	PROBABILITY
1	F 3,V 8	13.534	1	0.000	13.534	0.000
2	F 1,V 1	26.312	2	0.000	12.778	0.000
3	V 1,V 8	28.819	3	0.000	2.507	0.113

indicating that only two of the three parameters that had been dropped from the model are actually needed. The V1,V8 parameter does not provide a significant increment in chi-square, indicating that freeing this parameter will not improve the fit of the model. (In this case, this could have been seen on the normal z test for that parameter in the original model.) The program next searches the default list of fixed parameters to determine whether freeing any of these would help improve the fit. As can be seen, no other such parameter yields a significant improvement to the current 3 df multivariate chi-square. This effect occurs in spite of the fact that seven parameters were significant ($p < .05$) by the univariate test, as shown above.

MULTIVARIATE LAGRANGE MULTIPLIER TEST BY SIMULTANEOUS PROCESS IN STAGE 1

PARAMETER SETS (SUBMATRICES) ACTIVE AT THIS STAGE ARE:

PVV PFV PFF PDD GVV GVF GFV GFF BVF BFF

STEP	PARAMETER	CHI-SQUARE	D.F.	PROBABILITY	CHI-SQUARE	PROBABILITY

****

NONE OF THE PARAMETERS IN THIS SECTION IS SIGNIFICANT, THIS STAGE IS SKIPPED.

The size of the parameter change statistics was not emphasized in the above discussions. As noted earlier, these statistics show the value that the parameter is estimated to take, when subsequently freed. This information can be helpful as start values in a modified model. It may also be helpful in model modification, with larger values for fixed values of χ^2 indicating greater model misspecification.

MULTISAMPLE LM TEST

The LM test is available to test cross-group equality constraints in a multisample analysis, when specified as /LMTEST in the final group's input stream. This test is printed out after the Goodness of Fit Summary, which appears near the end of the output stream.

The constraint test is essentially the same in the multiple-group context as in its single-group version, see, e.g., under the section Illustrative Examples, Constrained Latent Variable Model. First the title LAGRANGE MULTIPLIER TEST (FOR RELEASING CONSTRAINTS) is printed, and the specific equality constraints to be tested are listed. The parameters involved in these constraints have a group identification number; see /CONSTRAINTS, Cross-group Constraints, Chapter 3. Thereafter, the UNIVARIATE TEST STATISTICS are printed, followed by the CUMULATIVE MULTIVARIATE STATISTICS and the associated UNIVARIATE INCREMENT. Interpretation of the χ^2 statistics is handled in the same way in multisample analysis as in any single group. Thus, no example is provided here.

This concludes the overview of the features of the LM and W tests.

7. MULTISAMPLE COVARIANCE STRUCTURES

In the typical application of structural modeling it is presumed that all the individuals whose data are being analyzed represent a random sample of observations from a single population. This assumption implies that, as far as the structural model is concerned, data from various individuals provide comparable information about a hypothesized process as operationalized in the model. This assumption will not always be reasonable. For example, data are frequently gathered from individuals who can be identified as belonging to certain groups, such as males and females, age cohorts, ethnic communities, geographical regions such as cities, states, or nations, and so on. In such cases it may be appropriate to inquire whether there are multiple populations rather than a single population, and multiple structural models rather than a single model. Hypotheses on multiple populations can be evaluated when data on the same variables exist in several samples. This chapter addresses covariance structure models, that is, structural models that do not involve means. Models that also involve means or intercepts are discussed in Chapter 9.

Multiple sample analysis can best be understood by first considering two extremes. At the one end, suppose that the populations are completely different as far as the measured variables are concerned. Then one would expect the covariance matrices in the various samples or groups to be different. For example, the correlation between a pair of variables in one sample would be different in magnitude and perhaps in sign as compared to another sample. Or, the variances of a variable may differ substantially across samples. Structural models that generate the corresponding covariance matrices would then also be completely different. In such a case there is not much reason for doing a multisample analysis: one may as well analyze each sample separately using the appropriate model for each sample. At the opposite extreme, suppose that the populations are actually indistinguishable as far as the measured variables are concerned. In that case, the same population covariance matrix would describe all populations, and different sample covariance matrices obtained from the various samples would simply be estimates of the same single population covariance matrix. Hence, structural models evaluated on data from the different samples should be describing the same population, and hence the models should be identical except perhaps for chance variations. In that case one would like to verify that there exists a single model that accurately describes each of the populations, as well as to obtain a single set of parameter estimates for the model. Finding this one model would be difficult if one analyzed the data from each sample separately, since optimal parameter estimates from each sample would surely not be precisely identical across samples even though the corresponding population parameters are the same. A multisample analysis analyzes data from all samples simultaneously and, in this case, ought to verify that a model, identical in all groups, reproduces the sample data of each group to within sampling accuracy. The goodness-of-fit χ^2 test can be used to describe the adequacy of the model.

Symbolically, assume that there are m populations. Each one has a population covariance matrix, say, $\Sigma_1, \Sigma_2, \ldots, \Sigma_m$. If all of the populations are identical, $\Sigma_1 = \Sigma_2 = \ldots = \Sigma_m$. If the populations differ, a covariance matrix from at least one group, say, the gth group, Σ_g, will be different from the others. Other covariance matrices may be the same. In the extreme, none of the covariance matrices may be the same. It is the task of multisample analysis to evaluate such similarities and differences, using the sample covariance matrices S_1, $S_2, \ldots, S_m$ based on samples of size $N_1, \ldots, N_m$ as data. As in the case of a single population, only the lower-triangular (nonredundant) elements of Σ_g, assembled into the vector σ_g, and of S_g, assembled into the vector s_g, are relevant to the analysis.

In EQS, of course, interest centers on the covariance matrices that are generated by linear structural models. The parameters of any such model are the coefficient matrices β and γ of the matrix equation $\eta = \beta\eta + \gamma\xi$ and the covariance matrix Φ of the independent variables. To simplify notation, all of the parameters from β, γ, and Φ are placed into the vector θ. The parameters θ of a model in a single population give rise to the vector σ of non-redundant elements of Σ via the general form $\sigma = \sigma(\theta)$. When there are m populations, there will be m linear structural models. The gth model is given by the equation $\eta_g = \beta_g\eta_g + \gamma_g\xi_g$ and the covariance matrix Φ_g. Since there are m such models, there are m vectors of parameters θ_1, θ_2, ... , θ_m which may or may not be the same; hence the corresponding covariances $\sigma_1 = \sigma(\theta_1)$, $\sigma_2 = \sigma(\theta_2)$, ... , $\sigma_m = \sigma(\theta_m)$ may or may not be the same. The statistical problem is one of estimating the various parameters in each sample and evaluating whether or not the model with these parameters adequately accounts for the sample covariances in each of the samples. Formally, the simultaneous hypothesis to be tested is that

$$\sigma_1 = \sigma(\theta_1),\ \sigma_2 = \sigma(\theta_2),\ \dots\ ,\ \sigma_m = \sigma(\theta_m). \tag{7.1}$$

Of course, substantively, one is concerned with the extent to which the parameters θ_1, θ_2, ... , θ_m are the same; thus different applications of (7.1) will contain different constraints on the parameters θ_g of the gth group. Thus, a more complete statement of the model includes sets of specifications of the form

$$\theta_{1(i)} = \theta_{2(j)} = \dots = \theta_{m(k)}, \tag{7.2}$$

giving the constraints of certain parameters across groups, specifically, the equality of the ith parameter in the first group with the jth parameter in the second group, and so on. The joint hypothesis $(7.1) - (7.2)$ is evaluated by the χ^2 goodness-of-fit statistic.

In practice, multiple sample analysis is done by fitting an ordinary EQS model in each sample, but doing this in a single run simultaneously for all groups, taking into account that some parameters are the same in each of the samples (using equality constraints across groups) while others are allowed to be different. Thus there are m models rather than one model, but there is a single goodness-of-fit χ^2 test to evaluate the joint hypothesis given in (7.1) under the particular cross-group (cross-sample) constraints (7.2). The hypothesis $(7.1) - (7.2)$ has the same form whether all of the parameters of a given group, θ_g, are the same in all groups, or whether certain parameters in θ_1, θ_2, etc. are different for the various groups; the χ^2 test evaluates the particular hypothesis that is implemented in the analysis. If a model having identical parameters in all groups can fit acceptably, the resulting model covariance matrices are identical (since all of the free parameters in a given group are constrained to take on the same values in the other groups), and the samples can be treated as arising from the same population. If the models of the various groups have parameters that are different, the resulting model covariance matrices will be different and the various samples must be treated as arising from different populations. One can then conclude that there is an interaction between population membership and structural model.

HYPOTHESES IN MULTISAMPLE ANALYSIS

The general models $(7.1) - (7.2)$ are used in practice to evaluate several popular hypotheses about multiple populations. These hypotheses concern the invariance of key parameters across populations (Alwin & Jackson, 1981; Jöreskog, 1971; Werts, Rock, Linn, & Jöreskog, 1976, 1977). While logically any free parameter, or any set of free parameters, can be evaluated for invariance or equality across populations, certain types of parameters tend to be evaluated together.

Equality of Sets of Parameters of a Linear Structural Model

(1). **Equal factor loadings (F → V paths).** If the observed variables are measuring the same factors in each of the groups, the regression of the variables on these factors, the factor loadings, ought to be the same. Equality of loadings can occur for some factors, but perhaps not others. Additionally, cross-group equality in loadings can exist even when the factors have different variances or covariances in the various groups, and when unique or error variances are not the same.

(2). **Equal factor variances and covariances (F ⟷ F variances and covariances).** If these are equal across groups while factor loadings are also equal, the factors are more specifically similar in the various groups. It is unlikely that the factor variances and covariances will be equal across groups when the factor loadings are unequal; and, if such a result were found, it would be difficult to interpret since it would be hard to argue that the factors are the same. Equality of factor variances may hold for the independent factors, while the covariances may not be equal. Furthermore, variances of the residuals (Ds) of dependent factors may remain unequal.

(3). **Equal factor regression coefficients (F → F paths).** If path coefficients among latent factors are the same across groups, the latent causal process being modeled is similar across groups. Such equality can occur even if variances or covariances of latent residual factors are not equal.

(4). **Equal factor residual variances and covariances (D ⟷ D variances and covariances).** In a model with latent dependent factors, the equality of these variances and covariances across groups is a still less important hypothesis to evaluate. Of course, in a standard factor analytic simultaneous equation (FASEM) model, if all factor variances and covariances, factor regressions, and factor residual variances and covariances are equal, all reproduced model factor variances and covariances will be equal as well.

(5). **Equal unique or error variances and covariances (E ⟷ E variances and covariances).** Except in special models, equality of error variances or covariances is probably the least important hypothesis to test. Typically, it is also the last hypothesis to test in a sequence of tests on nested hypotheses. Following upon a sequence of tests as outlined in $(1) - (5)$, acceptance of the hypothesis would imply, in a standard model, that all of the parameters of the model are equal across groups. Such a test is, of course, possible directly in all models, even in unusual or nonstandard models.

Equality of All Parameters of a Model

This hypothesis is very restrictive and implies not only that all covariance matrices Σ_g are equal, but also that the linear structural model that generates these matrices is identical in all respects across populations. It is unlikely to be strictly true except in very special circumstances. For example, models may be essentially equivalent, but a few nuisance parameters may differ trivially across samples.

Equality of Covariance Matrices

The hypothesis that covariance matrices Σ_g are identical may be true even when the underlying structural model is unknown. For example, the covariance matrices may be equal but no factor analysis model may be found to model these matrices. Exact equality of all Σ_g is hard to verify in large samples.

Equality of Correlation Matrices

This hypothesis allows covariance matrices Σ_g to differ between groups, as long as the underlying correlation matrices of the measured variables are the same. Then the covariance matrices are unequal only because variables need not have the same variances in all the groups.

Tests of equality of correlation matrices require the use of a device to set up the models correctly in EQS, since the statistical theory is based on covariance and not correlation matrices. This can be done as follows, using a two-group example. Let y_1 be the vector of observed (V) variables in the first group, and let the population covariance be $\mathcal{E}(y_1 - \mu_1)(y_1 - \mu_1)' = \Sigma_1$. The population correlation matrix is P_1, and hence $\Sigma_1 = D_1 P_1 D_1$, where D_1 is the diagonal matrix of standard deviations of the variables. Thus if we take $y_1 = D_1 x_1$, it is apparent that the covariance matrix of x_1 is P_1. This translation of the model can be analyzed in EQS by taking the y_1 variables as V variables, and the x_1 variables as F variables. Thus for the first V, there is an equation of the form V1 = *F1; without any error term, and there will be as many such equations as variables. The free parameter * in each equation is, in fact, just the standard deviation of the V variable involved, i.e., an element of D_1. Each of these standard deviations will be a free parameter since its value is unknown in the sample. The covariance matrix of the F variables is given by P_1, but since this is a correlation matrix, the variance of each F variable needs to be fixed at one. The covariances of all F variables are free parameters, and, corresponding to the off-diagonal elements of P_1, they are correlations between the measured variables. The same type of analysis and setup is done in the second group, where $\Sigma_2 = D_2 P_2 D_2$. To evaluate the hypothesis that $P_1 = P_2$, i.e., that the correlation matrices are equal, cross-group constraints will have to be made on the covariances of the F variables (which are in fact correlations because of the variance constraint). The diagonal matrices D_1 and D_2, i.e., the regression coefficients V ← F, are not constrained to be equal across groups. If this constraint were also made, the covariance matrices Σ_1 and Σ_2 would be forced to be equal as well. Thus a stronger hypothesis would be tested.

STATISTICAL CONSIDERATIONS

Historically, the statistical theory for multiple population covariance structure analysis was based on the assumption that the observed variables are multivariate normally distributed in all groups (Jöreskog, 1971; Lee & Tsui, 1982). This is a very restrictive assumption.

Populations may differ not only in terms of the structural models that generate their covariance matrices, but also because the distribution of the variables in the models, and hence the distribution of the measured variables, differ across populations. As a consequence, EQS implements a very general theory that allows different populations to have different distributions of variables (Bentler, Lee, & Weng, 1987). One population may be normal, another elliptical, and still another arbitrarily distributed. All may be taken to be normal, or all may be taken to be arbitrary in distribution. The theory has been extended in EQS to permit the use of any of the asymptotically equivalent fitting functions regularly available. Thus one normal population may involve estimation by GLS, while another normal population may involve estimation by ML, and a third population may be estimated by AGLS. Also, linearized estimation is available for elliptical and distribution-free methods. The overall χ^2 test takes into account the appropriate function and distributional theory for each group.

The multisample χ^2 test is most easily understood in the context of generalized least squares estimation. In a single group, say the gth, the function

$$Q_g = (s_g - \sigma_g)' W_g (s_g - \sigma_g),$$
(7.3)

is to be minimized with respect to θ in the model $\sigma_g = \sigma(\theta_g)$. At the minimum, the estimator $\hat{\theta}$ yields the function $n_g \hat{Q}_g = n_g (s_g - \hat{\sigma}_g)' W (s_g - \hat{\sigma}_g)$ which is distributed, in large samples, as a χ^2 variate with $p^* - q + r$ degrees of freedom, where p^* is the number of sample variances and covariances, q is the number of free parameters to be estimated, r is the number of equality restrictions, and $N_g = (n_g + 1)$ is the sample size. When there are m samples to be analyzed, there are m functions such as (7.3) that must be minimized simultaneously. The χ^2 statistic is given by

$$n_1 \hat{Q}_1 + n_2 \hat{Q}_2 + \ldots + n_m \hat{Q}_m,$$
(7.4)

which has $p^* - q + r$ degrees of freedom as before, but now p^* is the number of sample variances and covariances in all groups (usually, m times the number in a single group), q is the total number of free parameters in all groups, and r is the total number of within-group and between-group equality restrictions. A further discussion of the statistics in multisample analysis can be found in Chapter 10.

For a given lack of fit $\hat{Q}_g$ in a single group, it is apparent from (7.4) that larger samples influence the overall χ^2 more than smaller samples. It is also apparent that if $n_g \hat{Q}_g$ is especially large in any one sample, it is quite likely that the goodness-of-fit statistic (7.4) would be large overall, and the null hypothesis (7.1) − (7.2) most likely would be rejected. It will also be clear that multiple group models are hard to fit. That is, even minor model misspecifications translate into large values of χ^2, especially in larger samples. In one sense, this is desirable as it implies that the test has power to detect model misspecification. Given how hard it can be to fit a model in a single group, since multiple group analysis consists of several such models as well as additional cross-group constraints that make model-fitting harder yet, this difficulty should come as no surprise.

Standard errors for free parameters are computed similarly to single-group analysis. In particular, the basic formula for the covariance matrix of the estimator $\hat{\theta}$ has a divisor n_g in it. Since different groups may have different sample sizes, the standard error estimates will be smaller in larger samples in the usual way. However, a parameter estimate that is constrained to be equal across groups will have a standard error estimate that is the same in all groups.

The function Q_g in (7.3) is written in a general form. W_g is a weight matrix appropriate to the particular group and estimation method. The weight matrix that gives AGLS, the arbitrary distribution estimators, makes the fewest assumptions about the distribution of variables. In practice, of course, it becomes very difficult to implement the distribution-free theory when the number of variables, parameters, or groups gets large. Due to computer limitations, doing AGLS estimation in a single group is difficult enough. Doing AGLS estimation in many groups simultaneously is almost impossible in today's computing environment. The single-group compromise, ME = ML, ROBUST; has not been implemented in a multiple group version in the current release of EQS. Thus the Satorra-Bentler scaled χ^2 statistic and the robust standard errors are not available.

The goodness-of-fit indexes typically available in a single sample have been generalized to cover multisample analysis. Fit indexes such as the Bentler-Bonett (1980) NFI and NNFI indexes and Bentler's (1988a) CFI index rely on a null or baseline model. The null model used in multisample analysis is the same one in all groups, namely, that of uncorrelated variables. No cross-group restrictions are imposed in this baseline model.

Since multisample covariance structure analysis involves parameter estimation methods within a group that are standardly available in the one-group context, the principles associated with estimation in a single group carry over directly to the multiple group case. Thus sample covariance matrices (computable from raw scores) are the data to be analyzed. The considerations discussed in the first two chapters regarding scaling of the variables to achieve approximately similar variances are equally appropriate in this context, though, of course, the same scalings must be used in all the samples if cross-sample constraints are to be meaningful. Correlation matrices are not appropriate for analysis since the statistical theory used in EQS is based on the distribution of covariances and not correlations. See, e.g., Cudeck (1989). However, in practice, for most models it is permissible for the variables in one sample to be rescaled so that the resulting covariance matrix is close to (or, cheating somewhat, identical to) a correlation matrix, providing that the variables in all other samples are rescaled by the scaling constants from the reference sample. Such rescaling must be done prior to analysis with EQS.

LAGRANGE MULTIPLIER TEST

The Lagrange Multiplier test, or LM test, is a valuable test for evaluating whether restrictions on a model are appropriate or not. Chapter 6 provided an overview of the LM test, but in that context the emphasis was on applications to single-sample analysis. The LM test is also implemented in a limited way in multisample analysis, in particular, to provide assistance in evaluating simple cross-group constraints on the equality of parameters. A univariate LM test is provided for each of the cross-group equality constraints in the model. Each test provides evidence on the null hypothesis that the constraint is true in the populations involved. If the probability value of the LM statistic for such a constraint is low, this is a good indication that the constraint is unreasonable. As a consequence, one might consider another analysis in which the constraint is released. If the LM statistic yields a probability value for a cross-group constraint that is high, the null hypothesis of the equality of some parameters across populations cannot be rejected. In that case it makes sense to maintain the constraint in further analyses.

The forward-stepping multivariate LM test is produced automatically and printed out. The multivariate test is important to scan since the univariate tests will in general not be independent, and actions regarding one constraint can influence another.

PRACTICAL CONSIDERATIONS

Associated with the fact that multiple group models often have large χ^2 values is the corollary that they are hard to estimate. Good start values are critical to obtaining good convergence behavior during iterations, and depend upon having adequate single-group models. The greater the number of samples, the more difficult it will be to find an acceptable fit to the data from all groups simultaneously.

It is unrealistic to expect a multisample analysis to work well when one of the constituent models for a particular sample is very inadequate. Assuming that the sample size is not too small, lack of fit in one sample would almost surely lead to lack of fit of the multiple population model since, as seen in Eq. (7.4), the lack of fit in any sample contributes to the overall χ^2 test. In virtually all applications of multisample analysis, the model that would be run in just one sample is a less restricted version of the model that is run in several samples, since multisample analysis implies cross-group constraints and a greater number of constraints imply a worse fit. As a consequence, *if the model without the cross-group constraints fits very badly in a one-group analysis, it is quite likely that the model will not fit when part of a larger multisample analysis.* Of course, if the lack of fit is minimal in one sample, the added cross-group constraints could help to yield a multiple population model that is statistically acceptable due to the degrees of freedom that are gained and because one sample's excellent fit can offset, to some extent, a relatively bad fit in another sample.

EQS JOB SETUP

The basic idea of multisample analysis is simple. When analyzing a model for a single group, there is an input file that specifies the analysis to be performed. In a multisample analysis, there will be as many such input files as there are groups. The input file for any one group is, with a few critical exceptions to be explained shortly, identical to the file that would be created in a one-group analysis. However, all of these files are stacked end to end into a single file for job submission. A maximum of 10 groups can be analyzed simultaneously, subject to computer limitations. For clarity, the process of creating the job setup will be described in two parts.

The Unmodified Multiple Group File

One master file that contains all of the information typically present in a single-group job, stacked end to end for all the groups, should be created first. This file, without the special information needed to specify a multiple group run, looks as follows:

/TITLE

... } Typical input file for group 1

```
/END
/TITLE
...          ⎫
             ⎬  Typical input file for group 2
/END          ⎭
...
...
/TITLE
...          ⎫
             ⎬  Typical input file for group m
/END          ⎭
```

Within each group input file, information is provided with the same content and format as in a one-group analysis: the covariance matrix can be within the file or residing elsewhere, within-group equality and inequality constraints can be specified, the method of estimation to be used in that sample is given, and so on. This information may, of course, be different in the various groups. For example, in the standard application, the same method of estimation will be used in all groups, but in specialized applications, different methods may be used in some groups. In that case the ME = xx; statement in /SPEC of the relevant group must be altered appropriately.

An important practical point is the following. Creating this stacked input file can require a lot of typing. The solution is to use a good program (ASCII) editor that permits blocks of material to be copied. Thus one can create the input file for the first group; then duplicate or copy the input stream just created as many times as there are groups; and finally, modify the records of these subsequent groups in critical places in accord with the true specification (i.e., where parameters differ, the input /MATRIX, constraints, etc.). Since multisample models typically contain submodels that are very similar, this approach only requires typing the changes between groups. Also, start values for parameters that will be constrained across groups will be automatically equal, as they must be.

When this stacked input file is created by block copying with an editor, it is important to remember that each group's input file must reflect the characteristics of that particular group. Thus some modifications to the block-copied file are inevitable, especially with regard to the number of CASES in the sample (specified in /SPEC of each group), as well as the location of any external data file. If the data (raw data, covariance, or correlation matrix) for each group resides in a separate external file, this file is specified in the /SPECIFICATION section of each sample's input file. Since different data sets are being analysed for the various groups, each group's DATA = 'INPUT.FIL'; statement must reflect the appropriate location of that group's data. In typical mainframe environments, all of the data from all groups must be stacked sequentially, end to end, in a single external file. (This can be done also in a PC environment, in which case the filename must be given in the first group's /SPEC paragraph, and other groups must have no filename given in their /SPEC section. But this is an awkward procedure that is best avoided.)

Modifications for Multisample Analysis

1.   **GROUPS of the first group.** The number of samples to be analysed must be specified in the /SPECIFICATION section of the first group. Specifically, the following statement must be added in /SPEC of the input file of the first sample:

GROUPS = n;

where n is an integer between 2 and 10. (Without this statement, the program assumes n = 1, namely, that a single group analysis is being undertaken. Thus GROUPS = 1; can be used in a one-sample analysis without any effect.) The GROUPS (or GR) statement should not be included in the input files of subsequent groups.

2. **/CONSTRAINTS of the <u>last</u> group.** Cross-group equality constraints must be specified in the last group, using a special format. The format is essentially the same as in the one-group case, except that group numbers are now added as the first specification inside a parenthesis. In a three-group example with two parameters one might have, symbolically:

(1,P1) = (2,P1) = (3,P1);
(1,P2) = (2,P2) = (3,P2);

where 1, 2, and 3 are the group numbers and P1 and P2 are parameter names that must be replaced by specific double-label parameter names (e.g., F2,F1). Thus an actual example would be

(1,E1,E1) = (2,E1,E1);
(1,V3,F1) = (2,V3,F1);
(1,F2,F1) = (2,F2,F1);

where there are two groups and only three parameters being constrained to be equal. As usual, all the parameters listed must be free parameters in the model, and their start values must be equal.

General linear constraints across groups involving constant multipliers or additive constants are also available. These constraints must be written in the form .5(1,V1,F1) + 3(2,V1,F1) = 1; and the start values must meet the equality.

Within-group constraints are not affected by this procedure. Such constraints are stated within each group in the standard way. Within-group constraints for the last group can also be stated in the usual way within the same /CON paragraph that specifies cross-group constraints.

If there are many cross-group constraints, the block-copy feature of a program editor should be used: A few lines of constraints are written out precisely; these lines are duplicated several times; and the duplicated lines are then edited to yield the correct specification.

3. **/LMTEST in <u>last</u> group.** The only LM test available in multisample analysis deals with the appropriateness of the cross-group equality constraints. An evaluation of these constraints is highly recommended in all applications, and thus the test should be specified in the last group's input file.

EQS OUTPUT

Multisample output is basically identical to the standard output. However, just as there are several sets of input files stacked end-to-end, there are several sets of output files stacked end-to-end. The output file for each group contains the standard output from a single-group analysis, with one major exception. There is no iterative summary and no χ^2 test for each group. The iterative summary and the goodness-of-fit χ^2 test are presented at the end of the output stack, after the end of the output from the last group, in a section titled Statistics for Multiple Population Analysis. This section should also contain a statement on whether all cross-group equality constraints were correctly imposed (information on within-group constraints is printed within each group's output file, as usual).

EXAMPLE: EQUALITY OF FACTORS

Werts, Rock, Linn, and Jöreskog (1976) presented covariance matrices on four variables (a 40-item verbal aptitude score; a separately timed 50-item verbal aptitude score; a 35-item math aptitude score; and a separately timed 25-item math aptitude score) from two random samples of individuals who took the Scholastic Aptitude Test. Since the first two variables were designed to reflect verbal aptitude, and the other two, mathematical aptitude, a two-factor hypothesis with correlated factors for these variables is rather obvious. Further, since the data were obtained from two random samples, presumably from the same population, it is reasonable to expect that the factor loadings and factor variances and covariances (or, depending on the method of identifying the scale of factors, the factor correlations) are equal in the two samples. It is also possible that the unique or error variables have equal variances across the two samples; this hypothesis is not tested initially, but will be evaluated later. A highly edited version of the EQS output file is shown below.

```
 1   /TITLE
 2   2 GROUP EXAMPLE FROM WERTS ET AL 1976 - GROUP 1
 3   1 FACTOR MODEL WITH UNEQUAL FACTOR CORRELATIONS
 4   /SPECIFICATIONS
 5   CASES = 865; VARIABLES = 4; GROUPS = 2;
 6   /EQUATIONS
 7   V1=5*F1+E1;              !TWO FACTOR MODEL
 8   V2=5*F1+E2;              !FREE FACTOR LOADINGS
 9   V3=5*F2+E3;
10   V4=5*F2+E4;
11   /VARIANCES
12   F1 TO F2 = 1;           !FACTOR VARIANCES FIXED FOR IDENTIFICATION
13   E1 TO E4 = 50*;
14   /COVARIANCES
15   F2,F1=.5*;
16   /MATRIX
17   63.382
18   70.984 110.237
19   41.710   52.747 60.584
20   30.218   37.489 36.392 32.295
21   /END

21 CUMULATED RECORDS OF INPUT MODEL FILE WERE READ (GROUP    1)

22   /TITLE
23   2 GROUP EXAMPLE FROM WERTS ET AL 1976  - GROUP 2
24   /SPECIFICATIONS
25   CASES = 900; VARIABLES = 4;              !DIFFERENT SAMPLE SIZE
26   /EQUATIONS
27   V1=5*F1+E1;              !SAME SETUP AS IN GROUP 1
28   V2=5*F1+E2;              !REMEMBER TO USE SAME START VALUES
29   V3=5*F2+E3;              !IF CROSS-GROUP EQUALITIES WILL BE IMPOSED
30   V4=5*F2+E4;
```

```
31   /VARIANCES
32   F1 TO F2 = 1;              !SAME SETUP AS IN GROUP 1
33   E1 TO E4 = 50*;
34   /COVARIANCES
35   F2,F1=.5*;
36   /MATRIX
37   67.898
38   72.301 107.330
39   40.549   55.347 63.203
40   28.976   38.896 39.261 35.403
41   /CONSTRAINTS              !THESE ARE ALL CROSS-GROUP CONSTRAINTS
42   (1,V1,F1)=(2,V1,F1);      !1ST FACTOR LOADING EQUAL ACROSS GROUPS
43   (1,V2,F1)=(2,V2,F1);      !2ND FACTOR LOADING EQUAL
44   (1,V3,F2)=(2,V3,F2);      !3RD FACTOR LOADING EQUAL
45   (1,V4,F2)=(2,V4,F2);      !4TH FACTOR LOADING EQUAL
46   (1,F2,F1)=(2,F2,F1);      !FACTOR CORRELATION EQUAL
47   /LMTEST                   !EVALUATES CROSS-GROUP EQUALITY CONSTRAINTS
48 /END
```

48 CUMULATED RECORDS OF INPUT MODEL FILE WERE READ (GROUP   2)

  MULTIPLE POPULATION ANALYSIS, INFORMATION IN GROUP   1
  MAXIMUM LIKELIHOOD SOLUTION (NORMAL DISTRIBUTION THEORY)
  PARAMETER ESTIMATES APPEAR IN ORDER.   NO SPECIAL PROBLEMS WERE
ENCOUNTERED DURING OPTIMIZATION.

              AVERAGE ABSOLUTE STANDARDIZED RESIDUALS   =   .0193
AVERAGE OFF-DIAGONAL ABSOLUTE STANDARDIZED RESIDUALS   =   .0159

  MEASUREMENT EQUATIONS WITH STANDARD ERRORS AND TEST STATISTICS

```
  V1 = V1  = 7.443*F1 + 1.000 E1 !BE SURE TO COMPARE TO VALUES
              .156                !IN GROUP 2 IF EQUALITIES ARE IMPOSED
            47.854
  V2 = V2  = 9.682*F1 + 1.000 E2
              .199
            48.596
  V3 = V3  = 7.287*F2 + 1.000 E3
              .152
            47.976
  V4 = V4  = 5.195*F2 + 1.000 E4
              .114
            45.481
```

VARIANCES OF INDEPENDENT VARIABLES

V	F		E		D
	F1 - F1	1.000	E1 - V1	7.599*	
				1.025	
				7.413	
	F2 - F2	1.000	E2 - V2	19.740*	
				1.887	
				10.463	
			E3 - V3	9.581*	
				1.099	
				8.717	
			E4 - V4	6.191*	
				.590	
				10.489	

COVARIANCES AMONG INDEPENDENT VARIABLES

V	F		E	D
	F2 - F2	.767*		
	F1 - F1	.012		
		62.148		

MULTIPLE POPULATION ANALYSIS, INFORMATION IN GROUP 2
MAXIMUM LIKELIHOOD SOLUTION (NORMAL DISTRIBUTION THEORY)
 PARAMETER ESTIMATES APPEAR IN ORDER.   NO SPECIAL PROBLEMS WERE
ENCOUNTERED DURING OPTIMIZATION.

AVERAGE ABSOLUTE STANDARDIZED RESIDUALS	=	.0172
AVERAGE OFF-DIAGONAL ABSOLUTE STANDARDIZED RESIDUALS	=	.0138

MEASUREMENT EQUATIONS WITH STANDARD ERRORS AND TEST STATISTICS

$$V1 = V1 = 7.443*F1 + 1.000\ E1$$
$$.156$$
$$47.854$$
$$V2 = V2 = 9.682*F1 + 1.000\ E2$$
$$.199$$
$$48.596$$
$$V3 = V3 = 7.287*F2 + 1.000\ E3$$
$$.152$$
$$47.976$$
$$V4 = V4 = 5.195*F2 + 1.000\ E4$$
$$.114$$
$$45.481$$

VARIANCES OF INDEPENDENT VARIABLES

V	F		E		D
	F1 - F1	1.000	E1 - V1	13.507*	
				1.156	
				11.683	
	F2 - F2	1.000	E2 - V2	11.479*	
				1.705	
				6.731	
			E3 - V3	8.190*	
				1.067	
				7.674	
			E4 - V4	7.521*	
				.622	
				12.083	

COVARIANCES AMONG INDEPENDENT VARIABLES

V	F		E	D
	F2 - F2	.767*		
	F1 - F1	.012		
		62.148		

STATISTICS FOR MULTIPLE POPULATION ANALYSIS   !THE OVERALL STATISTICS
                                               !COME AT THE END
ALL EQUALITY CONSTRAINTS WERE CORRECTLY IMPOSED   !IMPORTANT MESSAGE

GOODNESS OF FIT SUMMARY
INDEPENDENCE MODEL CHI-SQUARE = 5472.640, BASED ON 12 DEGREES OF FREEDOM
  CHI-SQUARE =   10.870 BASED ON   7 DEGREES OF FREEDOM
  PROBABILITY VALUE FOR THE CHI-SQUARE STATISTIC IS .14440 !GOOD MODEL

  BENTLER-BONETT NORMED   FIT INDEX   = .998   !GOOD MODEL
  BENTLER-BONETT NONNORMED FIT INDEX   = .999   !BY ALL
  COMPARATIVE FIT INDEX   = .999   !FIT INDEXES

            ITERATIVE SUMMARY

                    PARAMETER
ITERATION   ABS CHANGE   ALPHA   FUNCTION

    1   18.038680   .50000   1.13517   !CONVERGENCE
    2   9.774520   1.00000   .00922   !WAS CLEAN
    3   .269461   1.00000   .00617   !AND FAST
    4   .014450   1.00000   .00617
    5   .001565   1.00000   .00617
    6   .000126   1.00000   .00617

LAGRANGE MULTIPLIER TEST (FOR RELEASING CONSTRAINTS) !THIS IS AN IMPORTANT
                                                     !TEST

CONSTRAINTS TO BE RELEASED ARE:

            CONSTR: 1   (1,V1,F1)-(2,V1,F1)=0;   !TESTS ON EACH CROSS-
            CONSTR: 2   (1,V2,F1)-(2,V2,F1)=0;   !GROUP CONSTRAINT
            CONSTR: 3   (1,V3,F2)-(2,V3,F2)=0;
            CONSTR: 4   (1,V4,F2)-(2,V4,F2)=0;
            CONSTR: 5   (1,F2,F1)-(2,F2,F1)=0;

          UNIVARIATE TEST STATISTICS:
  NO   CONSTRAINT   CHI-SQUARE   PROBABILITY

    1   CONSTR: 1   2.520   .112 !ALL OF THE UNIVARIATE
    2   CONSTR: 2   3.160   .075 !TESTS SUGGEST THAT
    3   CONSTR: 3   1.168   .280 !THE RESTRICTIONS ARE
    4   CONSTR: 4   .205   .651 !REASONABLE
    5   CONSTR: 5   3.242   .072

      CUMULATIVE MULTIVARIATE STATISTICS   UNIVARIATE INCREMENT
  STEP   PARAMETER   CHI-SQUARE   D.F.   PROBABILITY   CHI-SQUARE   PROBABILITY

    1   CONSTR: 5   3.242   1   .072   3.242   .072
    2   CONSTR: 1   6.732   2   .035   3.490   .062
    3   CONSTR: 2   7.370   3   .061   .638   .425
    4   CONSTR: 3   8.194   4   .085   .824   .364
    5   CONSTR: 4   8.631   5   .125   .437   .508

!ALL INCREMENTS ARE NOT SIGNIFICANT SO THE MULTIVARIATE TEST COMES TO THE
!SAME CONCLUSION

The LM tests generally provide very valuable information on the adequacy of constraints in a multisample model. In this case, the tests verify that the cross-group equality constraints on factor loadings and the factor correlation are all reasonable. If the model had not been statistically acceptable, i.e., the χ^2 goodness-of-fit test implied rejection of the model, lack of overall fit could possibly be due to an inappropriate cross-group constraint. The LM test is set up to detect such problems, as shown next.

Equal Error Variances Evaluated by /LMTEST

The model of equality of factor loadings and correlations, evaluated above, proved to be acceptable. Thus one might consider the more restricted hypothesis that adds to the above model the further constraints that each of the variable's error variance is equal between groups. This modification was made, and the job was run with the following result. Only the last segment of output is shown, consisting of the model fit and LM test.

```
STATISTICS FOR MULTIPLE POPULATION ANALYSIS
ALL EQUALITY CONSTRAINTS WERE CORRECTLY IMPOSED

GOODNESS OF FIT SUMMARY    !MODEL MUST BE REJECTED AS TOO RESTRICTED
CHI-SQUARE =        34.895 BASED ON     11 DEGREES OF FREEDOM
PROBABILITY VALUE FOR THE CHI-SQUARE STATISTIC IS LESS THAN 0.001

LAGRANGE MULTIPLIER TEST (FOR RELEASING CONSTRAINTS)
CONSTRAINTS TO BE RELEASED ARE:

        CONSTR:  1   (1,V1,F1)-(2,V1,F1)=0;
        CONSTR:  2   (1,V2,F1)-(2,V2,F1)=0;
        CONSTR:  3   (1,V3,F2)-(2,V3,F2)=0;
        CONSTR:  4   (1,V4,F2)-(2,V4,F2)=0;
        CONSTR:  5   (1,F2,F1)-(2,F2,F1)=0;
        CONSTR:  6   (1,E1,E1)-(2,E1,E1)=0;
        CONSTR:  7   (1,E2,E2)-(2,E2,E2)=0;
        CONSTR:  8   (1,E3,E3)-(2,E3,E3)=0;
        CONSTR:  9   (1,E4,E4)-(2,E4,E4)=0;

        UNIVARIATE  TEST STATISTICS:
NO   CONSTRAINT    CHI-SQUARE       PROBABILITY

1     CONSTR:  1   1.972           .160
2     CONSTR:  2   1.554           .213
3     CONSTR:  3    .000           .997
4     CONSTR:  4   1.630           .202
5     CONSTR:  5   2.522           .112
6     CONSTR:  6   7.403           .007 !PROBLEMATIC CONSTRAINT
7     CONSTR:  7   2.855           .091 !MULTIVARIATE TEST BELOW
8     CONSTR:  8    .041           .840 !DOESN'T LIKE THIS
9     CONSTR:  9   1.723           .189

        CUMULATIVE MULTIVARIATE STATISTICS        UNIVARIATE INCREMENT
STEP PARAMETER  CHI-SQUARE  D.F.  PROBABILITY CHI-SQUARE PROBABILITY

1   CONSTR:  6     7.403    1    .007      7.403  .007
2   CONSTR:  7    20.747    2    .000     13.345  .000  !SIGNIFICANT
3   CONSTR:  2    23.746    3    .000      2.999  .083  !INCREMENT
4   CONSTR:  5    26.064    4    .000      2.317  .128
5   CONSTR:  4    27.691    5    .000      1.627  .202
6   CONSTR:  1    28.789    6    .000      1.098  .295
7   CONSTR:  9    29.604    7    .000       .816  .366
8   CONSTR:  8    30.423    8    .000       .819  .366
9   CONSTR:  3    31.549    9    .000      1.126  .289
```

The analysis had added constraints #6 − #9 concerned with equal error variances, and the results indicate that constraints #6 and #7, concerned with equal variances across groups of

(E1,E1) and (E2,E2), were statistically unlikely to be true in the population. The equality across groups of the variance (E3,E3) and the variance (E4,E4) could not be rejected. Thus the model was resubmitted by removing the cross-group constraint of equal error variances for E1 and E2, with the following result. Again, only the final part of the printout is shown.

```
STATISTICS FOR MULTIPLE POPULATION ANALYSIS
ALL EQUALITY CONSTRAINTS WERE CORRECTLY IMPOSED

GOODNESS OF FIT SUMMARY   !NOW THE MODEL FITS FINE
CHI-SQUARE =         13.863 BASED ON      9 DEGREES OF FREEDOM
PROBABILITY VALUE FOR THE CHI-SQUARE STATISTIC IS       .12729

LAGRANGE MULTIPLIER TEST (FOR RELEASING CONSTRAINTS)
CONSTRAINTS TO BE RELEASED ARE:

          CONSTR:   1   (1,V1,F1)-(2,V1,F1)=0;
          CONSTR:   2   (1,V2,F1)-(2,V2,F1)=0;
          CONSTR:   3   (1,V3,F2)-(2,V3,F2)=0;
          CONSTR:   4   (1,V4,F2)-(2,V4,F2)=0;
          CONSTR:   5   (1,F2,F1)-(2,F2,F1)=0;
          CONSTR:   6   (1,E3,E3)-(2,E3,E3)=0;
          CONSTR:   7   (1,E4,E4)-(2,E4,E4)=0;

          UNIVARIATE TEST STATISTICS!NONE SIGNIFICANT
   NO   CONSTRAINT CHI-SQUARE      PROBABILITY

    1   CONSTR:   1   2.407         .121
    2   CONSTR:   2   3.046         .081
    3   CONSTR:   3    .001         .981
    4   CONSTR:   4   1.595         .207
    5   CONSTR:   5   2.981         .084
    6   CONSTR:   6    .067         .795
    7   CONSTR:   7   1.907         .167

          CUMULATIVE MULTIVARIATE STATISTICS        UNIVARIATE INCREMENT
   STEP  PARAMETER    CHI-SQUARE D.F. PROBABILITY CHI-SQUARE PROBABILITY

    1   CONSTR:   2     3.046    1     .081       3.046    .081   !NONE IS
    2   CONSTR:   5     5.406    2     .067       2.360    .125   !SIGNIFICANT
    3   CONSTR:   7     7.007    3     .072       1.601    .206
    4   CONSTR:   6     8.567    4     .073       1.560    .212
    5   CONSTR:   1    10.166    5     .071       1.599    .206
    6   CONSTR:   3    10.992    6     .089        .827    .363
    7   CONSTR:   4    11.429    7     .121        .437    .509
```

This final model is now acceptable, and there are no further indications of inappropriateness of cross-group constraints.

Since multiple group models are only minor extensions, conceptually, of single-group models, additional examples showing multisample analysis in action are not presented.

8. MEAN AND COVARIANCE STRUCTURES

In the typical application, the parameters of a structural equation model are the regression coefficients as well as the variances and covariances of independent variables. In such applications, the means of the measured variables are not decomposed into more basic parameters. As a consequence, the covariance structure of the variables carries the critical parametric information, and the model can be estimated and tested via the sample covariance matrix S. This approach does not work when the population mean vector μ is also expressed in terms of parameters. Then the sample mean vector $\bar{z}$ also carries statistical information and both S and $\bar{z}$ must be analyzed simultaneously. In addition, the model must be specified in a somewhat different form.

Consider the simple bivariate regression model $y = \beta x + \epsilon$, which has one dependent variable and two independent variables (in the sense of Bentler/Weeks). In covariance structure analysis, the means of y and x are irrelevant, and, since x and ϵ are assumed to be uncorrelated, the coefficient β in the equation and the variances σ_x^2 of x and σ_ϵ^2 of ϵ are sufficient to describe the model. Implicitly it is assumed that all variables have zero means. Now suppose that the means are not zero. Then we might consider writing

$$y = \alpha + \beta x + \epsilon, \qquad (8.1)$$

where α is an intercept parameter. *The intercept helps to define the mean of y, but it is not, in general, equal to the mean.* Taking expectations of both sides, and assuming that the mean of ϵ is zero, we have

$$\mu_y = \alpha + \beta \mu_x, \qquad (8.2)$$

where μ_y is the mean of y and μ_x is the mean of x. Thus μ_y can be expressed in terms of the model parameters α, β, and μ_x. This decomposition of the mean of the dependent variable provides an illustration of the nomenclature "structured means" as a way to designate a model in which the means of dependent variables are expressable or structured in terms of structural coefficients and the means of independent variables. As usual, moments of dependent variables (here, the mean μ_y) are not parameters, but moments of independent variables (here, μ_x) are. Thus incorporating a *mean structure* into the model (8.1) introduces the new parameters α and μ_x into the model. This illustration shows that models with means extend a basic idea used in covariance structure analysis.

> *The parameters of any linear structural model with structured means are the regression coefficients, the variances and covariances of the independent variables, the intercepts of the dependent variables, and the means of the independent variables.*

Intercepts of dependent variables are parameters because, as will be seen next, they are basically regression coefficients associated with a constant "variable" that is in fact an independent variable in the sense of Bentler-Weeks. This extension of the Bentler-Weeks model was given by Bentler (1983a,b) and is used in EQS. The ideas can also be extended to provide a structure for higher-order moments such as skewnesses and kurtoses (Bentler, 1983a), but such generality is not needed here.

In addition to introducing new parameters, mean and covariance structure analysis also requires rethinking the system of linear equations that describe a model. In (8.1), there is just one equation. As usual, the equation represents a structural equation for the dependent variable. While it contains an intercept term, this intercept is nothing more than a regression coefficient on a constant "variable." That is, (8.1) can also be written as

$$y = \alpha 1 + \beta x + \epsilon, \tag{8.1a}$$

where 1 is an independent variable that takes on the same value 1.0 for all observations and hence has no variance. As a consequence, intercepts are associated with an independent variable. Thus we have the following key idea, which will be useful in all types of models with constants.

The coefficient for regression on a constant is an intercept.

This simple fact permits introducing structured means into a model by adding a constant "variable" into a path diagram. In EQS, the constant is called V999. In principle V999 could literally be a column of 1.0s in the input stream, i.e., it is a measured variable, but in practice this input is not needed since the program creates the constant by default. The designation V999 was chosen so that the constant will always be in the same position, the last, relative to the measured variables in the input file.

A standard structural equation, even with an intercept as in (8.1), is insufficient to fully describe a structured means model. It is apparent that (8.1) does not contain information on the mean of the independent variable x. One solution would be to amend standard structural modeling procedures by incorporating a new type of equation into the system, such as (8.2), that does not describe relations between *variables*, but rather describes relations between *means*. This approach is feasible. However, another approach permits using standard EQS techniques, including the use of equations to describe relations among variables only.

> *In a structured means model, each independent variable can be decomposed into two new variables: the mean, and a deviation-from-mean variable. As a consequence, the variable becomes a dependent variable in a new equation, in which the intercept is the mean of the variable.*

As a result the model will be set up in such a way that *all measured and latent variables having nonzero means will be dependent variables*. In the example, we may write

$$x = \mu_x + x_d, \tag{8.3}$$

where x_d is the deviation-from-mean variable whose mean is zero. As before, (8.3) can be written equivalently as

$$x = \mu_x 1 + x_d, \tag{8.3a}$$

where 1 is the constant, and μ_x is the coefficient for the regression of x on the constant variable 1. Since x is a dependent variable in (8.3) or (8.3a), it has no variance as a parameter. Both 1 and x_d are independent variables, with 1 having no variance; while the variance σ_d^2 of x_d is actually the variance of x (i.e., $\sigma_x^2 = \sigma_d^2$). Of course, since 1 is a constant, it will have zero covariance with other independent variables, and x_d will have x's covariances with other variables.

> *The constant 1 (V999 in EQS) is an independent "variable" that has no variance and no covariances with other variables in a model.*

To conclude this example, if one now considers the complete model to consist of Eqs. (8.1) and (8.3), or (8.1a) and (8.3a), as well as the usual variances and covariances of the independent variables (here only σ_d^2 and σ_ϵ^2), it is apparent that all of the parameters associated with the original model $(8.1) - (8.2)$ are captured correctly. A diagrammatic representation is given in Figure 8.1.

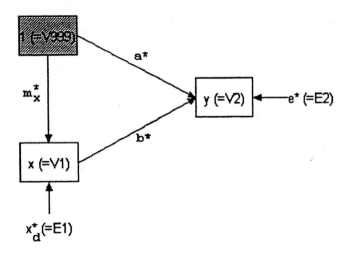

Figure 8.1

Figure 8.1 shows the model of Eqs. $(8.1) - (8.3)$ or $(8.1a) - (8.3a)$ in both the original notation and the parallel EQS notation. In the EQS notation, V999 replaces the constant 1.0, V2 replaces y, E2 (= e) replaces ϵ, V1 replaces x, and E1 replaces x_d. As usual, regression coefficients μ_x (= m_x in the figure[1]), α (= a), β (=b) have "*" attached to show they are free parameters, and independent variables have variances as parameters. The diagram follows the convention adopted in this manual of showing independent Vs (and Fs, but there are none here) in shading, and dependent Vs (and Fs, again, none here) without shading, to remind one to consider the variances of independent variables as parameters. What is new in the diagrammatic representation of a structured means model is that (1) the constant V999 does *not* have a variance as a parameter, more exactly, it has a variance that is fixed at zero; (2) coefficients for regressions on the constant, V999, are interpreted as intercepts; and (3) the *residual* of a variable that is a dependent variable solely by virtue of being regressed on the constant V999 carries the variance and covariance information of such a variable. Here, x_d (or E1), carries the variance of x (or V1). If x in (8.1) had covaried with other independent

---

[1] The figure substitutes Latin letters for the Greek letters α, β, and μ of the equation structure only because Diagrammer does not currently support printing Greek characters.

variables in a larger model, those covariances would now be given as covariances with this residual. This is natural, because *the residual is the deviation variable, and covariances or variances are always defined on deviation variables*.

EQS JOB SETUP

Once the diagrammatic representation of a structured means model has been created, the model is set up in EQS in the usual way. However, because the constant V999 is not in an input data file, the program must be informed to create the constant. In addition, the means of the measured variables must be available for analysis, and the program must be informed that the means, as well as the variances and covariances, are to be analyzed.

In the /SPECIFICATION section, the keyword ANALYSIS = MOMENT; (or MOM, or MOMENTS) tells EQS to analyze the 1st moments of the data, namely the means, as well as the 2nd moments of the data about the means, namely the variances and covariances. In principle, higher-order moments could also be analyzed (Bentler, 1983a), but EQS has not implemented such a procedure. The data to be analyzed are the sample means and covariances. These can be input to EQS as: 1) raw score data, using MA = RAW; in /SPEC, in which case the program will compute the summary statistics, 2) means and covariances using /MEANS to give the means and MA = COV; to give the covariance matrix, or 3) means using /MEANS, and MA = COR; to specify the correlation matrix as input, with /STANDARD DEVIATIONS to give the standard deviations, so that EQS will compute the covariances from the correlations and standard deviations. As usual, raw score data must be in an external file, while covariances and correlations may be so. The file can be specified using the DATA_FILE statement of /SPEC (except possibly in some mainframe environments, where other methods must be used).

Whenever ANALYSIS=MOMENT; is specified, EQS requires the constant variable V999 to be included in the /EQUATIONS section of the model file. V999 will be an independent variable having zero variance. Also, *ME=ML; must be used*, as noted below.

INTERPRETATION AND OUTPUT

Since structured means models are basically variants of standard linear structural models, all of the general information found in other chapters of this manual related to EQS input and output is relevant to these models. Special attention should, however, be addressed to the means in these models.

The intercepts of the dependent variables are parameters of the model, and hence the estimated values of these parameters are available in the standard EQS output. The means of the dependent variables, however, are not parameters, and hence these estimated means must be computed separately. One way is by computing total effects using EFFECT = YES; in /PRINT.

In the example of Eqs. (8.1) − (8.2), the estimated model means must obey $\hat{\mu}_y = \hat{\alpha} + \hat{\beta}\hat{\mu}_x$, i.e., the estimated mean of the dependent variable y is obtained as a sum of the intercept $\hat{\alpha}$ and the product $(\hat{\beta}\hat{\mu}_x)$. It is hoped that the estimated mean $\hat{\mu}_y$ is close to $\overline{y}$, the sample mean. In Figure 8.1, $\hat{\alpha}$ is given by the path V999 → V2, i.e., it is a direct effect whose value can be found in the output equations. The product $(\hat{\beta}\hat{\mu}_x)$ is not a single path, rather, it is the product of the coefficients in the path traced from V999 → V1 → V2. Thus it is an *indirect effect*. EQS computes such nonstandardized indirect effects, and prints out their values, as well as their estimated standard errors. As usual, the ratio of estimate/(standard error) provides a <u>z</u>-test to evaluate whether an indirect effect is significant. This is printed out as well. EQS also computes standardized indirect effects that can be interpretively more useful when the scales of the variables are arbitrary.

A *total effect* is the sum of direct and indirect effects. The mean $\hat{\mu}_y$ corresponding to Eq. (8.2) is thus $\hat{\alpha} + (\hat{\beta}\hat{\mu}_x)$ as can be seen from Fig. 8.1. This is printed out under nonstandardized total effects. The following important principle summarizes these ideas.

> *An intercept of a variable is its mean whenever there are no indirect effects of the constant (V999) on the variable. When there are such indirect effects, the total effect is the mean.*

The mean of an independent variable is a parameter of the model. In EQS, however, all independent variables have been transformed into dependent variables by the addition of new equations, see, e.g. Eq. (8.3). The means of such "independent, but set-up as dependent" variables remain as parameters of the model, specifically, they are intercepts that are found in the equations as coefficients on V999 variables, see, e.g., the V999 → V1 path in Figure 8.1. Since these variables are not affected indirectly by V999, the intercepts are the means. Thus they appear in the standard EQS output.

The model-based reproduced means of V and F variables — whether dependent or independent variables — can also be obtained by the COVARIANCE = YES; statement of the /PRINT paragraph. The covariance/mean model matrix

$$
\begin{array}{c c c}
 & V & F \\
V & \hat{\Sigma}_{VV} & \hat{\Sigma}_{VF} \\
F & \hat{\Sigma}_{FV} & \hat{\Sigma}_{FF}
\end{array}
$$

is obtained by this specification. This matrix contains variances and covariances, printed in matrix form. Additionally, if the constant V999 is in the model (as it will be for structured means models), the corresponding row and column contains means and not covariances. Specifically, in this output $\hat{\Sigma}_{VV}$ is the reproduced covariance/mean matrix of all V variables, $\hat{\Sigma}_{FF}$ is the reproduced covariance matrix of all F variables, and $\hat{\Sigma}_{FV}$ is the reproduced cross-covariance/mean matrix of F and V variables. Within each segment of V and F variables, the variables are ordered sequentially by number, so reproduced model values for the intercept V999 are given in the last row of $\hat{\Sigma}_{VV}$. These values represent $\hat{\mu}'$, the vector of means for all the V variables. Since $\hat{\Sigma}_{VF}$ and $\hat{\Sigma}_{FV}$ contain the same information, only $\hat{\Sigma}_{FV}$ is printed. The final column of $\hat{\Sigma}_{FV}$ contains $\hat{\mu}_F$, the vector of means for all the F variables.

A simpler way can be used to interpret the reproduced model matrix. The general rule for interpreting elements of the matrix is straightforward: Any single element in the reproduced model matrix indexes a pair of variables, say (V999, V7), (V3, F2), etc. If one of the pair of variables is V999, the corresponding element is the mean of the other variable. Thus the entry corresponding to (V999, V7) is the mean of V7, and the entry corresponding to (F3, V999) is the mean of F3. If the double label does not contain V999, the entry is a variance or covariance in accord with the usual convention: (F6, F6) is the variance of F6, (F1,V17) is the covariance of F1 and V17. Of course, if V999 is not included in the model, the reproduced model matrix is just a variance-covariance matrix. A standardized model matrix, a reproduced correlation matrix, is also available via /PRINT, but this matrix is not of special relevance here.

A SIMPLE REGRESSION EXAMPLE

Consider the following data on intellectual performance at four age points.

V1	V2
6.066	21.074
6.946	25.819
8.800	35.267
10.788	46.569

Variable V1 represents the four ages, and V2 represents four scores from an intelligence test. We are interested in the regression of intelligence on age, and want to include the means as part of the analysis. The conceptual model is that given in Eqs. (8.1) − (8.2), as represented in Figure 8.1 and set up in EQS using Eqs. (8.1) and (8.3). It is apparent from the figure that there are 5 parameters to be estimated. As data to be modeled, there are the two means of V1 and V2, and the two variances of V1 and V2 and their covariance. Thus there are 5 data points to be modeled. The number of degrees of freedom is $5 - 5 = 0$, i.e., the model is saturated and one should expect that the model will perfectly fit the data. It can also be calculated that the sample correlation between V1 and V2 across the 4 observations is .9995, so that the variables are almost perfectly linearly related, and thus one might expect some computational problems to arise due to near-multicollinearity of these variables. The source of these data is given at the end of this chapter.

The output from an EQS run, heavily edited, is as follows.

```
 1  /TITLE
 2  REGRESSION WITH MEAN
 3  /SPECIFICATIONS
 4  CASES = 4; VARIABLES = 2; MATRIX = RAW;
 5  DATA = 'AGE.DAT';      !THIS IS WHERE THE RAW DATA RESIDES
 6  ANALYSIS = MOMENT;     !SPECIFIES MEAN AND COVARIANCE STRUCTURE
 7  /EQUATIONS
 8  V1 =      8*V999 + E1; !EXCEPT FOR CONSTANT, V1=E1
 9  V2 = -10*V999 + 5*V1 + E2;
10  /VARIANCES
11  E1 = 5*; E2 = 1*;
12  /PRINT
13  EFFECT = YES;          !ONE WAY TO COMPUTE MEAN OF V2
14  COVARIANCE = YES;      !ANOTHER WAY TO COMPUTE MEAN OF V2
15  /END
```

```
SAMPLE STATISTICS
                         UNIVARIATE STATISTICS
VARIABLE              V1          V2          V999
MEAN               8.1500     32.1823       1.0000   !THE MEAN OF THE CONSTANT
SKEWNESS (G1)       .3278       .3717        .0000   !IS 1.0
KURTOSIS (G2)     -1.3966     -1.3469        .0000
```

MATRIX CONTAINS SPECIAL VARIABLE V999, THE UNIT CONSTANT
COVARIANCE MATRIX IS IN UPPER TRIANGLE; MEANS ARE IN BOTTOM ROW OF MATRIX
COVARIANCE/MEAN MATRIX TO BE ANALYZED: 2 VARIABLES
(SELECTED FROM 2 VARIABLES) BASED ON 4 CASES.

```
                V1          V2          V999
                V 1         V 2         V999
     V1       4.391                            !THE USUAL COVARIANCE
     V2      23.589      126.793               !MATRIX IN 1ST 2 ROWS
     V999     8.150       32.182      1.000     !SAMPLE MEANS (SEE SAMPLE STATISTICS)
```

MAXIMUM LIKELIHOOD SOLUTION (NORMAL DISTRIBUTION THEORY)
PARAMETER ESTIMATES APPEAR IN ORDER. NO SPECIAL PROBLEMS WERE ENCOUNTERED
DURING OPTIMIZATION.   !LUCKY, IN VIEW OF HIGH CORRELATION OF V1 AND V2

RESIDUAL COVARIANCE/MEAN MATRIX (S-SIGMA):

```
                V1          V2          V999
                V 1         V 2         V999
     V1        .000                             !BOTH THE COVARIANCES
     V2        .000        .000                 !AND THE MEANS ARE REPRODUCED
     V999      .000        .000        .000     !PERFECTLY WITH NO ERROR
```

MODEL COVARIANCE MATRIX FOR MEASURED AND LATENT VARIABLES

```
                V1          V2          V999      !THE MODEL COVARIANCES
                V 1         V 2         V999      !AND THE MODEL MEANS
     V1       4.391                               !PERFECTLY REPRODUCE THE
     V2      23.589      126.793                  !SAMPLE COVARIANCE/MEAN MATRIX
     V999     8.150       32.182      1.000
                 !V999,V2 IS THE PREDICTED MEAN OF V2
```

CHI-SQUARE =   .000 BASED ON 0 DEGREES OF FREEDOM !SATURATED MODEL

MEASUREMENT EQUATIONS WITH STANDARD ERRORS AND TEST STATISTICS

```
  V1 = V1 =     8.150*V999   + 1.000 E1 !INTERPRETED THE USUAL WAY, EXCEPT
                1.210                    !THAT THE COEFFICIENT NEXT TO V999
                6.736                    !IS AN INTERCEPT
  V2 = V2 =     5.372*V1  -11.597*V999 + 1.000 E2
                 .076        .643        !THE INTERCEPTS ARE STATISTICALLY
               70.323     -18.042        !SIGNIFICANT, I.E., NONZERO
```

VARIANCES OF INDEPENDENT VARIABLES !NO VARIANCE FOR V999, THE INTERCEPT

```
        V                 F                 E                    D
                          |                 | E1 - V1    4.391* |
                          |                 |            3.586  |
                          |                 |            1.225  |
                          |                 |                   |
                          |                 | E2 - V2     .077* |
                          |                 |             .063  |
                          |                 |            1.225  |
                          |                 |                   |
```

```
DECOMPOSITION OF EFFECTS WITH NONSTANDARDIZED VALUES
PARAMETER TOTAL EFFECTS

  V1 = V1 = 8.150*V999  + 1.000 E1
  V2 = V2 = 5.372*V1    + 32.182*V999 + 5.372 E1   + 1.000 E2
!EQUATION-LIKE FORMAT IS FOR SUMMARY PURPOSES
!V2,V999 ENTRY IS THE REPRODUCED MEAN OF V2, CALCULATED AS THE SUM OF
!DIRECT (-11.597) AND INDIRECT (43.780, SEE BELOW) EFFECTS

PARAMETER INDIRECT EFFECTS

  V2 = V2 =    43.780*V999    + 5.372E1
                6.529            .076
                6.706          70.323
!INDIRECT EFFECT OF V999 ON V2 IS SIGNIFICANT

STANDARDIZED SOLUTION:

  V1 = V1 =  .000*V999  + 1.000 E1
  V2 = V2 = 1.000*V1    + .000*V999 + .025 E2
!INTERCEPTS ARE ZERO IN A STANDARDIZED SOLUTION
!V2 IS ESSENTIALLY PERFECTLY PREDICTED FROM V1, I.E., R SQUARED IS CLOSE TO
1.0
```

This concludes the simple regression example. Next, the statistical ideas underlying structured means models will be summarized.

STATISTICAL BASIS

The general model $\sigma = \sigma(\theta)$ and corresponding data vector s that are used in EQS must be reconceptualized when both means and covariances are being analyzed. Since the data that are being modeled include means and covariances, both data and model vectors must take this into account. (The word "covariances" is used here to represent both variances and covariances, since a variance is a special case of a covariance.) In particular, the vector of parameters σ cannot be considered as containing only the population covariances; rather it must contain both the means and covariances. Suppose we use the designation $\sigma_1 = \mu$ for the 1st-order moments, the means, and σ_2 for the 2nd-order moments about the means, the covariances. Then $\sigma(\theta)$ really contains two parts, $\sigma_1(\theta)$ and $\sigma_2(\theta)$. That is, both population means and covariances depend on some parameter vector θ, whose elements in EQS are the elements of the matrices β, γ, and Φ of the Bentler-Weeks model, or, more precisely, Bentler's (1983a, 1983b) extension of this model. The corresponding sample vectors are $s_1 = \bar{z}$, the vector of sample means, and s_2, the vector of nonredundant sample covariances from the covariance matrix S.

In principle, any of the estimation methods available in EQS could be used to analyze mean and covariance structure models, see Chapter 10, Eqs. (10.67) − (10.82). The generalized least squares function $Q(\theta) = (s - \sigma(\theta))'W(s - \sigma(\theta))$ makes clear that overall goodness of fit will depend on a weighted function of the degree of fit of the mean structure and the covariance structure. Of course, the function will specialize under specific choices of distributional theory assumed for the observed variables. However, only the normal theory maximum likelihood method (ME = ML;) is currently available in EQS for structured means models, and a related function is thus optimized.

It is important to know that the ML function in structured means models reflects how closely the sample mean vector $\bar{z}$ is reproduced by the estimated model mean vector $\hat{\mu}$, as well as how closely the sample covariance matrix S is reproduced by the estimated model covariance matrix $\hat{\Sigma}$. As a result, a model may fit badly if the means are modeled poorly, or if the covariances are modeled poorly, or both. For the reader who is technically minded, the function that is optimized, Eq. (10.81) in Chapter 10, is obtained by considering the fit obtainable by maximizing, aside from a constant, the log-likelihood of the N observations

$$L = -N\{\ln|\Sigma| + trS\Sigma^{-1} + (\bar{z} - \mu)'\Sigma^{-1}(\bar{z} - \mu)\}/2 \tag{8.4}$$

under choice of $\hat{\mu} = \mu(\hat{\theta})$ and $\hat{\Sigma} = \Sigma(\hat{\theta})$, as well as the corresponding log-likelihood of the saturated model that obtains when the estimates $\bar{z}$ of μ and S of Σ are placed in (8.4):

$$\hat{L}_s = -N\{\ln|S| + p\}/2. \tag{8.5}$$

The statistic $2n(\hat{L}_s - \hat{L})/N$, evaluated at $\hat{\theta}$, is given by

$$n\{\ln|\hat{\Sigma}| + trS\hat{\Sigma}^{-1} - \ln|S| - p + (\bar{z} - \hat{\mu})'\hat{\Sigma}^{-1}(\bar{z} - \hat{\mu})\}, \tag{8.6}$$

which is the large sample likelihood ratio χ^2 statistic computed by EQS for structured means models. The function minimized by EQS is given in the braces in (8.6), i.e., it is (8.6) except for the constant multiplier n. It is the same function as in ordinary covariance structure ML estimation except for the added weighted sum of squares resulting from the discrepancy between $\bar{z}$ and $\hat{\mu}$, see (Eq. 10.43), Chapter 10. As usual, $n = (N - 1)$ times the function value at the minimum (i.e., at $\hat{\theta}$), gives the goodness-of-fit statistic. (The rationale for using n rather than N as the multiplier in (8.6) is discussed in Chapter 10. It has to do with the use of the unbiased sample covariance matrix S rather than the biased matrix more standardly applied in ML estimation. Researchers who use the biased sample covariance matrix in analysis can replace n with N in (8.6), but any such modification vanishes as N gets large.) The degrees of freedom is given by the number of sample means plus the number of nonredundant sample variances and covariances, minus the number of free parameters estimated, plus the number of equality restrictions imposed during the estimation. See Eq. (10.82), Chapter 10.

A check on normality of variables to be analyzed can be made by the usual EQS diagnostics, e.g., univariate skewnesses and kurtoses, and Mardia's normalized multivariate kurtosis coefficient.

When structured means models are used with latent variables, some care must be taken that the model is identified. In general, the part of the model excluding V999 that is an ordinary latent variable model should be identified using the usual criteria for covariance structure analysis. In addition, care must be taken that the number of intercepts being estimated is less than the number of sample means. It is possible, of course, to set up a model in which the number of intercepts and sample means is equal, where V999 imposes no special restrictions on the model. In that case, the model means will be estimated at the sample means, and the covariances can be modeled separately. Then there is not much point to doing a structured means analysis.

EXAMPLE: GROWTH IN WISC SCORES

An interesting application of a model with structure on the means as well as the covariances was given by McArdle and Epstein (1987), using data from R. T. Osborne and collaborators on the Wechsler Intelligence Scale for Children administered to 204 children at four times from about age 6 to 11. McArdle and Epstein rescored the WISC variables into a maximum percent format, so that each variable mean is interpretable as the percent of items answered correctly on the average. Summary means, correlations, and standard deviations were presented by McArdle and Epstein in their Table 1. These were transformed by them into a "cross-products moment matrix" for analysis. They developed several models for these data, none of which was statistically acceptable. A different model is developed below for the same means and covariances.

A one-factor model for these four variables may not be adequate. A two-factor model was hypothesized, with scores from the test at the earliest two ages as indicators of the first factor (F1), and scores at the latest two ages serving as indicators of the second factor (F2). Of course, F2 can be expected to be strongly influenced by F1, but a one-factor model implies that F1 and F2 are identical, which may not be true at these ages. The hypothesized measurement model is a standard covariance structure model, as shown in the upper part of the following figure.

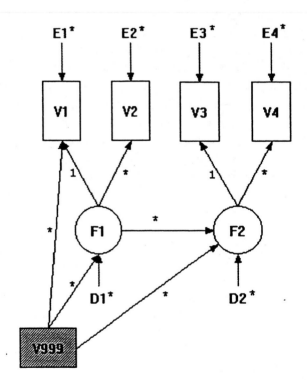

Figure 8.2

In addition to the factor structure of the measured variables, the means of the factors and variables are of interest. The bottom part of the figure shows V999, the constant, affecting V1 and the factors F1 and F2. As usual, V999 is an independent variable, but it has zero variance. The paths from V999 are intercepts, since a regression on a constant is an intercept. Without V999, F1 would be an independent variable, hence the intercept path from V999 is also the mean of the factor F1. The other variables influenced directly by V999, namely V1 and F2, are dependent variables even without V999, so the intercepts for these variables are not sufficient to define these variables' means. The means will be given as the sum of the direct effects and indirect effects, namely nonstandardized total effects. They are also obtainable in the reproduced model matrix.

The EQS setup follows the diagram exactly. No new principles are involved. Every variable that has a one-way arrow aiming at it is a dependent variable in an equation. The remaining variables are independent variables and may have variances and covariances. All independent variables will have variances, except V999, which is a constant, and hence has no variance. There are no covariances (two-way paths) in the figure. The EQS setup is shown in the first part of the edited output below. The "cross-products moment matrix" required by McArdle and Epstein (1987, Table 1C) in their use of the LISREL program is irrelevant to the setup of this model in EQS, or to the interpretation of any results. (Their matrix is not the simple covariance/mean matrix analyzed in EQS when ANAL = MOM; is specified.)

```
 1  /TITLE
 2  GROWTH IN WISC SCORES
 3  OSBORNE DATA (MCARDLE & EPSTEIN, 1987, P. 113)
 4  /SPECIFICATIONS
 5  CASES = 204; VAR = 4; ANALYSIS = MOMENT; MATRIX = CORRELATIONS;
 6  /EQUATIONS
 7  V1 =      F1      + E1 — 3*V999;
 8  V2 = 1*F1         + E2;
 9  V3 =          F2  + E3;
10  V4 =      1*F2  + E4;
11  F1 =                  21*V999 + D1;
12  F2 = 1*F1     +        8*V999  + D2;
13  /VARIANCES
14  D1 = 30*; D2 = 3*;
15  E1 TO E3 = 8*; E4 = 16*;
16  /PRINT
17  EFFECT = YES;
18  /MEANS
19  18.034 25.819 35.255 46.593
20  /STANDARD DEVIATIONS
21  6.374 7.319 7.796 10.386
22  /MATRIX
23  1
24  .809 1
25  .806 .850 1
26  .765 .831 .867 1
27  /END
```

MATRIX CONTAINS SPECIAL VARIABLE V999, THE UNIT CONSTANT
COVARIANCE MATRIX IS IN UPPER TRIANGLE; MEANS ARE IN BOTTOM ROW OF MATRIX
COVARIANCE/MEAN MATRIX TO BE ANALYZED: 4 VARIABLES (SELECTED FROM 4
VARIABLES), BASED ON 204 CASES.

	V1 V 1	V2 V 2	V3 V 3	V4 V 4	V999 V999	
V1	40.628					!THE MATRIX IS CREATED
V2	37.741	53.568				!FROM INPUT CORRELATIONS
V3	40.052	48.500	60.778			!AND STAND. DEVIATIONS
V4	50.643	63.169	70.200	107.869		
V999	18.034	25.819	35.255	46.593	1.000	!THE USUAL MEANS

MAXIMUM LIKELIHOOD SOLUTION (NORMAL DISTRIBUTION THEORY)
PARAMETER ESTIMATES APPEAR IN ORDER.   NO SPECIAL PROBLEMS WERE ENCOUNTERED
DURING OPTIMIZATION.

RESIDUAL COVARIANCE/MEAN MATRIX (S-SIGMA):

	V1 V 1	V2 V 2	V3 V 3	V4 V 4	V999 V999	
V1	.000					
V2	.000	.000				!RESIDUALS LOOK
V3	.682	.266	.858			!VERY SMALL IN
V4	-1.343	-.523	-.279	-2.233		!COVARIANCES AND
V999	.000	.000	-.012	.024	.000	!MEANS

STANDARDIZED RESIDUAL MATRIX:

	V1 V 1	V2 V 2	V3 V 3	V4 V 4	V999 V999	
V1	.000					
V2	.000	.000				!IN THIS METRIC, THE
V3	.014	.005	.014			!RESIDUALS ARE QUITE
V4	-.020	-.007	-.003	-.021		!SMALL BOTH FOR
V999	.000	.000	-.002	.002	.000	!CORRELATIONS AND THE !STANDARDIZED MEANS

GOODNESS OF FIT SUMMARY
INDEPENDENCE MODEL CHI-SQUARE =   820.575, BASED ON   6 DEGREES OF FREEDOM

CHI-SQUARE =   1.465 BASED ON   2 DEGREES OF FREEDOM
PROBABILITY VALUE FOR THE CHI-SQUARE STATISTIC IS   .48075

THE NORMAL THEORY RLS CHI-SQUARE FOR THIS ML SOLUTION IS   1.460.

BENTLER-BONETT NORMED FIT INDEX   = .998   !GOOD FIT BY ALL
BENTLER-BONETT NONNORMED FIT INDEX   = 1.002   !CRITERIA
COMPARATIVE FIT INDEX   = 1.000

              ITERATIVE SUMMARY

	PARAMETER		
ITERATION	ABS CHANGE	ALPHA	FUNCTION
1	.31079E+02	1.00000	.71170E+17 !THE START VALUES
2	110.113700	1.00000	8.77774 !WERE QUITE BAD, SEE
3	89.704370	1.00000	2.10110 !THE INITIAL FUNCTION
4	8.904931	1.00000	.57244 !VALUE, BUT IT DID
5	1.992430	1.00000	.12305 !CONVERGE ALL RIGHT
6	1.694196	1.00000	.03293
7	.179428	1.00000	.00751
8	.073296	1.00000	.00722
9	.002777	1.00000	.00722
10	.000284	1.00000	.00722

MEASUREMENT EQUATIONS WITH STANDARD ERRORS AND TEST STATISTICS

$$V1 = V1 = \quad 1.000\ F1 \quad + \quad -3.040*V999 \quad + 1.000\ E1$$
$$1.123$$
$$-2.706$$

$$V2 = V2 = \quad 1.225*F1 \quad + \quad 1.000\ E2$$
$$.063$$
$$19.325$$

$$V3 = V3 = \quad 1.000\ F2 \quad + \quad 1.000\ E3$$

$$V4 = V4 = \quad 1.320*F2 \quad + \quad 1.000\ E4$$
$$.010$$
$$126.650$$

CONSTRUCT EQUATIONS WITH STANDARD ERRORS AND TEST STATISTICS

$$F1 = F1 = 21.074*V999+ \quad 1.000\ D1$$
$$1.168$$
$$18.037$$

$$F2 = F2 = \quad 1.278*F1 \quad + \quad 8.334*V999+ \quad 1.000\ D2$$
$$.065 1.214$$
$$19.532 6.862$$

!THERE IS A SIGNIFICANT GAIN IN THE MEAN OF F2,
!SINCE THE INTERCEPT IS SIGNIFICANT

VARIANCES OF INDEPENDENT VARIABLES

V	F	E		D	
		E1 - V1	9.823*	D1 - F1	
30.805*			1.223		3.982
			8.030		7.736
		E2 - V2	7.329*	D2 - F2	
3.058*			1.326		1.458
			5.526		2.098
		E3 - V3	6.546*		
			1.172		
			5.584		
		E4 - V4	17.037*		
			2.399		
			7.103		

DECOMPOSITION OF EFFECTS WITH NONSTANDARDIZED VALUES

PARAMETER TOTAL EFFECTS !HERE'S WHERE TO FIND THE PREDICTED MEANS

```
V1 = V1 =   1.000 F1  +  18.034*V999+   1.000 E1   +  1.000 D1
V2 = V2 =  1.225*F1   +  25.819 V999+   1.000 E2   +  1.225 D1
V3 = V3 =  1.278 F1   +   1.000 F2  +  35.267 V999  +  1.000 E3+ 1.278 D1+ 1.000 D2
V4 = V4 =  1.688 F1   +  1.320*F2   +  46.569 V999  +  1.000 E4+ 1.688 D1+ 1.320 D2
F1 = F1 = 21.074*V999+ 1.000 D1  !THE MEAN OF F1, WHICH IS IN THE METRIC OF V1
F2 = F2 =  1.278*F1   +  35.267*V999+   1.278 D1   +  1.000 D2
```

PARAMETER INDIRECT EFFECTS

```
V1 = V1 =  21.074*V999+   1.000 D1
            1.168
           18.037
```

```
V2 = V2 =  25.819 V999+   1.225 D1
             .514           .063
           50.262          19.325
```

```
V3 = V3 =   1.278 F1  +  35.267 V999+   1.278 D1   +      1.000 D2
             .065         1.476
           19.532        23.902
```

```
V4 = V4 =   1.688 F1  +  46.569 V999+   1.688 D1   +      1.320 D2
             .087         1.976          .013             .010
           19.486        23.564        126.650          126.650
```

```
F2 = F2 =  26.933*V999+   1.278 D1
            1.359           .067
           19.813         19.162
```

STANDARDIZED SOLUTION:

```
V1 = V1 =   .871 F1  +   .000*V999+   .492 E1
V2 = V2 =  .929*F1   +   .370 E2
V3 = V3 =   .944 F2  +   .331 E3
V4 = V4 =  .919*F2   +   .393 E4
F1 = F1 =   .000*V999+  1.000 D1            !F1 = D1 WITHOUT V999
F2 = F2 =  .971*F1   +   .000*V999+   .239 D2
```
!F2 IS HIGHLY PREDICTED BY F1

The growth in WISC intelligence scores across these four ages is successfully described by the two-factor model in Figure 8.2. In contrast to the models considered by McArdle and Epstein, this model fits the data well by statitical criteria and fit indexes. The results show that the variables can be well described by the simple two factor model shown, with a substantial stability to the factors across time (a coefficient of .971 in the standardized solution, associated with an R^2 of .94). Furthermore, the means of the factors shift significantly over time. The factor mean for F2 is significantly greater than the mean of F1, i.e., there was substantial intellectual growth in the time period indicated. The means of all V variables can be expressed in terms of the means of the factors, as indirect effects. However, V1 acts differently from the other variables in this regard, needing an additional direct component not explainable by the factors in the model. Evidently the V1 mean of the WISC scores contains a specific component not mediated by the intellectual factor F1.

Although the output indicated that there were no problems during the optimization, in fact less optimal start values for this problem created substantial difficulty for the iterative procedure. Such a result ought perhaps to be expected since there are only two indicators for each of the factors. However, structured means models often have greater difficulty in reaching a stable optimimum as compared to covariance structure models. This is no doubt one reason for their relative unpopularity. The reader is urged to experiment with the difficulties that nonoptimal start values can have with the model of Figure 8.2 applied to these data. As usual, scaling of input variables (here, moving a decimal place in the means and standard deviations) so that the covariance/mean input matrix has diagonal entries that are similar, can help convergence.

To conclude this chapter, it may be interesting to consider the variable means that are implied by the factors in the model. For all variables, this is given by the indirect effects of V999 operating through the factors on the variable in question. These indirect effects are given in the printout above, but they can also be obtained by path tracing rules, for example, for V1, this is the product 21.074×1, tracing the paths $V999 \rightarrow F1 \rightarrow V1$. For the other variables V2 — V4, the result gives 25.819, 35.267, and 46.569. These were the values taken as the four scores on V2 in the simple regression example discussed earlier in this chapter. In fact, that example was constructed to predict the factor-based IQ scores, obtained from the model associated with Figure 8.2, from the means of the ages of the children. Those age means, taken from McArdle and Epstein (1987, p. 113), were given as V1 in the first example of this chapter. Remembering the result of the simple regression, it is apparent that in this data set there is an almost perfect linear prediction of factor-based mean intellectual performance from mean age.

9. MULTISAMPLE
MEAN AND COVARIANCE STRUCTURES

Models with structured means, applied in two or more samples simultaneously, basically require applying the procedures that were described in Chapters 7 and 8. However, such models do introduce some new ideas that are worth discussing and illustrating. First, a structured means model that is not identified in one group may become identified when analyzed in two groups simultaneously and subject to cross-group constraints. Second, structured means models in several groups that involve latent factors require a new concept of factor identification. Third, as shown at the end of this chapter, these models can be useful in some missing data situations.

A structured means model in one group will serve to illustrate the first point. This is a model with 6 variables and two factors, as shown below.

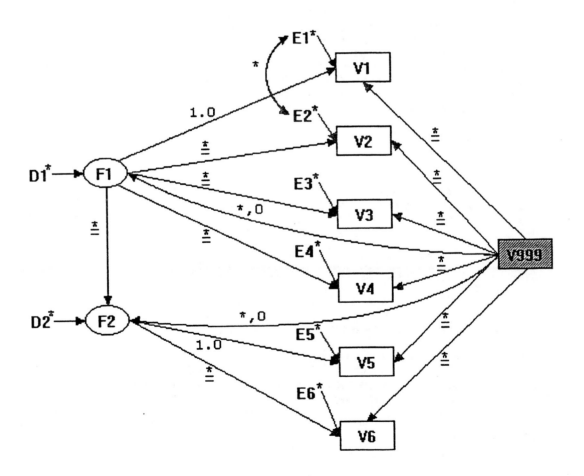

Figure 9.1

The left part of the figure shows two factors, with the factor regression F1 → F2. The measured variables are in the middle of the figure. Variables 1 − 4 are indicators of F1, while V5 − V6 are indicators of F2. Each variable has an error residual, with E1 and E2 being correlated. This is a standard factor analysis type of model, except that the constant V999, shown in the right part of the figure, transforms the model from a covariance structure model into a mean/covariance structure model. In this model, intercepts are hypothesized for all variables V1 − V6, as well as for both factors, F1 and F2. As usual, parameters that have a "*" are considered free parameters. At this point, the "=" and "0" next to "*" ought to be ignored. A highly edited version of the output file is as follows.

```
 1    /TITLE
 2         HEAD START ONE GROUP MODEL
 3    /SPECIFICATIONS
 4         CASES=148; VARIABLES=6; ANALYSIS=MOMENT; MATRIX=CORRELATION;
 5         METHOD=ML;
 6    /EQUATIONS              !AN INTERCEPT FOR EVERY DEPENDENT VARIABLE
 7    V1  =     3.9*V999 +      F1+ E1;
 8    V2  =     3.3*V999 + 0.85*F1+ E2;
 9    V3  =     2.6*V999 + 1.21*F1+ E3;
10    V4  =     6.4*V999 + 2.16*F1+ E4;
11    V5  =    20.3*V999 +      F2+ E5;
12    V6  =    10.1*V999 + 0.85*F2+ E6;
13    F2  =        *V999 + 2.10*F1+ D2;
14    F1  =    -0.4*V999 +  D1;
15    /VARIANCES
16         E1 TO E6 = 1.5*;
17         D1 TO D2 = 0.3*;
18    /COVARIANCES
19         E2,E1=*;
20    /PRINT
21         EFFECT = YES;
22    /MATRIX
23       1.000
24       0.441  1.000
25       0.220  0.203  1.000
26       0.304  0.182  0.377  1.000
27       0.274  0.265  0.208  0.084  1.000
28       0.270  0.122  0.251  0.198  0.664  1.000
29    /STANDARD DEVIATIONS
30       1.332  1.281  1.075  2.648  3.764  2.677
31    /MEANS
32       3.520  3.081  2.088  5.358 19.672  9.562
33    /END
         33 RECORDS OF INPUT MODEL FILE WERE READ
```

MATRIX CONTAINS SPECIAL VARIABLE V999, THE UNIT CONSTANT
COVARIANCE MATRIX IS IN UPPER TRIANGLE; MEANS ARE IN BOTTOM ROW OF MATRIX
COVARIANCE/MEAN MATRIX TO BE ANALYZED: 6 VARIABLES (SELECTED FROM   6 VARIABLES), BASED ON   148 CASES.

		V1	V2	V3	V4	V5	V6	V999
		V 1	V 2	V 3	V 4	V 5	V 6	V999
V1	V 1	1.774						
V2	V 2	.752	1.641					
V3	V 3	.315	.280	1.156				
V4	V 4	1.072	.617	1.073	7.012			
V5	V 5	1.374	1.278	.842	.837	14.168		
V6	V 6	.963	.418	.722	1.404	6.691	7.166	
V999	V999	3.520	3.081	2.088	5.358	19.672	9.562	1.000

```
PARAMETER          CONDITION CODE
   V5,V999         LINEARLY DEPENDENT ON OTHER PARAMETERS
   F1,V999         LINEARLY DEPENDENT ON OTHER PARAMETERS

CHI-SQUARE =        15.655 BASED ON      5 DEGREES OF FREEDOM
PROBABILITY VALUE FOR THE CHI-SQUARE STATISTIC IS       .00790
```

Although the program finds a minimum of the function, and computes a χ^2 statistic, there are two condition codes indicating linear dependencies among parameters. Such a message is a sign of theoretical or empirical underidentification. In fact, both linear dependencies involve V999, the intercept, suggesting that a careful theoretical analysis of the part of the model dealing with V999 should be made. In Chapter 7 it was noted that the number of intercepts must be less than or equal to the number of measured variables. In this case, there are 6 Vs, but 8 intercepts. Evidently, the intercepts for the V variables are already accounting for the means of these variables, so there is no need for the additional intercepts for the F variables. The job is modified slightly to delete as free parameters (or set to fixed zero) the intercepts for F1 and F2, given in lines 13 − 14 of the above output as *V999. Removing V999 from lines 13 − 14, and resubmitting the job, yields the following essential result.

```
PARAMETER ESTIMATES APPEAR IN ORDER.   NO SPECIAL PROBLEMS WERE ENCOUNTERED
DURING OPTIMIZATION.

CHI-SQUARE =        15.655 BASED ON      7 DEGREES OF FREEDOM
PROBABILITY VALUE FOR THE CHI-SQUARE STATISTIC IS       .02846
```

Now there is no sign of linear dependencies among parameters. The same function value, and χ^2 statistic, are obtained, but the probability changes because the degrees of freedom have increased by two. An analysis of the parameter estimates, not shown here, reveals that the intercepts have been estimated precisely at the observed sample means. This result should not be surprising. There is exactly one intercept for each measured variable, and, since there are no indirect paths from V999 to any of V1 − V6, the intercepts are the means. Thus the means are reproduced exactly.

Next we evaluate what happens to the model of Figure 9.1 when two groups are considered simultaneously.

MULTISAMPLE PATH DIAGRAM AND FACTOR MEANS

The model of Figure 9.1 is actually a representation of a two group model studied by Sörbom (1982) and summarized in Jöreskog and Sörbom (1988). It deals with two samples of children. One sample had been given a Head Start educational program; the other sample was a matched Control group. V1 − V4 represent mother's education, father's education, father's occupation, and family income. These variables were taken as indicators of F1, a latent socioeconomic status or SES factor. They were background variables, essentially to be controlled. The more important variables are V5 − V6, namely, scores on the Metropolitan Readiness Test and the Illinois Test of Psycholinguistic Abilities. These were taken by Bentler and Woodward (1978) as indicators of a construct of cognitive ability, shown in the figure by F2. It is presumed that SES (F1) will affect ability (F2), but the real interest is whether the mean in F2 is higher in the Head Start group as compared to the Control group, taking into account the SES background of the children. As shown in the figure, all Vs and Fs are presumed to have intercepts as parameters to be estimated. Next, Figure 9.1 is studied in greater detail, both for its specific meaning in this particular model, and for some principles for setting up multisample structured means models.

The figure, which is not a conventional path diagram, attempts to show the two models of the Head Start and Control samples simultaneously. A key to distinguishing the two groups is as follows:

*   Denotes a parameter that is free in both groups

$\overset{*}{=}$ Denotes a parameter that is free in both groups, but constrained to be equal in the two groups

*,0   Denotes a parameter that is free in one group (Head Start), and zero in the other (Control) group.

Thus the path diagram makes clear that:

- The variances of E and D variables are free parameters in each group, and not constrained to be equal across groups.
- The covariance of E1 and E2 is a free parameter in each group, and not constrained to be equal across groups.
- The free factor loadings of all variables (F → V paths) are free parameters in each group, but each loading is constrained to be equal in the two groups.
- The fixed 1.0 factor loadings are fixed for identification at 1.0 in both groups.
- The factor regression (F1 → F2) is a free parameter in each group, but the value is constrained to be equal across the two groups.
- The intercepts of the measured (V) variables are free parameters in each group, but each intercept is constrained to be equal in the two groups.
- The intercepts of the factors (Fs) are free parameters in the Head Start group, but set to a fixed zero value in the Control group.

Some of these points require further discussion.

Regarding the left part of the figure, if the same factor model holds for both samples, then it is helpful to have the factor loadings and factor regressions be equal across groups. Thus they are so specified. Equality of residual variances and covariances is not so important, and is not imposed.

Regarding the right part of the figure, *the paths from V999 to the Vs, each of which is held to be equal across groups, represent a kind of baseline level for the variables. Differences in means of the variables across groups, if they exist, must arise from other sources.* In the diagram, these sources can be traced back to the intercepts of F1 and F2. For example, the path V999 → F1 → V4 makes clear that the intercept of F1 will affect V4, and the path V999 → F1 → F2 → V6 shows that it will also affect V6. (The final means of the V variables, are, of course, total effects, or model moments, that can be obtained with /PRINT). The paths V999 → F1 and V999 → F2, the intercepts for F1 and F2, reflect coefficients that are free to be estimated in one group, but are held to zero in the other group. Consequently, if the freely estimated coefficients are not zero and large, the differences in factor intercepts will be reflected in mean differences of the observed variables across groups. In this model, the Head Start factor intercepts are estimated, but the Control intercepts are set to zero.

The rationale for parameters that are free to be estimated in one group, but fixed in another group, arises as follows:

> *In multisample latent variable models having measured variables with intercepts that are constrained equal across groups, the intercepts of the latent factors have an arbitrary origin. A standard way to fix this origin is to set the factor intercepts of one group to zero.*

When there are two groups, as here, each F intercept of one group is set to zero, and the other is freely estimated. As a consequence, these intercepts are interpretable only in a relative sense. If the Head Start intercept for F1 is significantly higher than 0, which is the value of the intercept in the Control sample, then the Head Start sample has more of whatever F1 is measuring. If the intercept is significantly negative, then the Head Start sample has less of whatever F1 is measuring. (That which F1 represents, and the meaning of "more" or "less", is not an issue that is new with these types of models; the simplest way to determine this is by studying the meaning and direction of scoring of the measured variables that are indicators of the factor. In this example, F1 measures SES, with higher numbers indicating higher status.) It is arbitrary as to which group has an intercept set to zero, but the estimated intercept of another group is always interpreted relative to this value of 0.0 used in some reference group. (Actually, the value 0.0 is also chosen arbitrarily.) In theory, different factors could have their zero intercepts set in different groups, but this is not a practical suggestion. Let the sample that has all factor intercepts set at zero be called the *reference* sample. There is a consequence of fixed zero factor intercepts.

> *In the reference sample, the coefficient for regression of a measured variable on a constant (V999) is the expected (model-reproduced) mean of the measured variable. Thus the mean is a direct effect of the constant (V999).*

How this works in the reference sample, but differs in other samples, can be seen by path-tracing in Figure 9.1. The expected mean of a measured variable in all non-reference groups is represented by a total effect, since as shown above and can be seen in the figure, there will be various indirect ways for V999 to affect a final V. Since the expected means in the reference group should be close to the observed sample means if the model is correct, the observed means in the reference sample provide a good set of start values for the cross-group constrained intercepts of the V variables.

EXAMPLE: EFFECTS OF HEAD START

The quasi-experimental Head Start study addressed whether children who received a special Head Start educational program subsequently perform better on cognitive tasks than Control children who did not receive this extra training. The study did not succeed in randomly assigning children to treatment conditions, and, as might be expected from the goals of a social intervention, the Head Start program was given to children who were relatively more disadvantaged (lower SES) than the Controls. The means of the variables, shown for the Head Start children above and shown for the Controls below, are not encouraging: the Controls actually have the higher means on V5 and V6, the cognitive ability measures. (Compare line 32 of program output above with line 68 of output below.) However, as just noted and as is clear from the sample means, it is also the case that the Head Start children are from lower SES families. Possibly the higher SES of the controls can explain their higher cognitive performance ability. So it is worthwhile to see whether the Head Start children might be higher than the controls on F2, the cognitive ability factor, if SES has been controlled as a factor (F1).

The job setup for the multisample structured means model is given in the next section, which represents an edited version of the EQS output. The first 9 lines serve as a reminder that, with the exception of some title information and specification that a 2 group model is being analyzed, the setup is identical to that shown previously for the Head Start sample; so, not all of this setup is duplicated again. Subsequently, the model setup is given for the Control group.

```
 1   /TITLE
 2       MULTIPLE GROUPS AND STRUCTURED MEANS -- GROUP 1
 3       HEAD START DATA -- LISREL 7 MANUAL, P. 254
 4       HEAD START GROUP
 5   /SPECIFICATIONS
 6       CASES=148; VARIABLES=6; ANALYSIS=MOMENT; MATRIX=CORRELATION;
 7       METHOD=ML; GROUPS=2;                        !GROUPS=2; ADDED HERE
 8   /EQUATIONS
 9       V1 =  3.9*V999 +        F1 + E1;

         (SAME AS PREVIOUS FILE GIVEN ABOVE)

35   /END
36   /TITLE
37       MULTIPLE GROUPS AND STRUCTURED MEANS -- GROUP 2
38       CONTROL GROUP
39   /SPECIFICATIONS
40       CASES=155; VARIABLES=6; ANALYSIS=MOMENT; MATRIX=CORRELATION;
41       METHOD=ML;
42   /EQUATIONS
43   V1=     3.9*V999 +        F1+ E1;
44   V2=     3.3*V999 +  0.85*F1+ E2;
45   V3=     2.6*V999 +  1.21*F1+ E3;
46   V4=     6.4*V999 +  2.16*F1+ E4;
47   V5=    20.3*V999 +        F2+ E5;
48   V6=    10.1*V999 +  0.85*F2+ E6;
49   F2=     2.10*F1  +  D2;          !NO V999 HERE
50   F1=         0V999 +  D1;          !FIXED 0 IS EQUIVALENT TO NO V999
51   /VARIANCES
52       E1 TO E6 = 1.5*;
53       D1 TO D2 = 0.3*;
54   /COVARIANCES
55       E2,E1=*;
56   /PRINT
57       EFFECT=YES;
58   /MATRIX
59       1.000
60       0.484  1.000
61       0.224  0.342  1.000
62       0.268  0.215  0.387  1.000
63       0.230  0.215  0.196  0.115  1.000
64       0.265  0.297  0.234  0.162  0.635  1.000
65   /STANDARD DEVIATIONS
66       1.360  1.195  1.193  3.239  3.900  2.719
```

```
67   /MEANS
68       3.839   3.290   2.600  6.435 20.415 10.070
         !COMPARE TO HEAD START GROUP -- ALL VARIABLES HAVE HIGHER MEANS
         !HIGHER SES, HIGHER COGNITIVE ABILITY
69   /CONSTRAINTS
70       (1,V1,V999)=(2,V1,V999);          !EQUALITY OF BASIC LEVEL
71       (1,V2,V999)=(2,V2,V999);          !OF EACH VARIABLE ACROSS
72       (1,V3,V999)=(2,V3,V999);          !THE GROUPS
73       (1,V4,V999)=(2,V4,V999);
74       (1,V5,V999)=(2,V5,V999);
75       (1,V6,V999)=(2,V6,V999);
76       (1,V2,F1)=(2,V2,F1);              !EQUALITY OF FACTOR LOADINGS
77       (1,V3,F1)=(2,V3,F1);              !ACROSS GROUPS
78       (1,V4,F1)=(2,V4,F1);
79       (1,V6,F2)=(2,V6,F2);
80       (1,F2,F1)=(2,F2,F1);              !EQUAL FACTOR REGRESSION
81   /LMTEST                               !TO CHECK ADEQUACY OF CONSTRAINTS
82   /END
```

COVARIANCE/MEAN MATRIX TO BE ANALYZED: 6 VARIABLES (SELECTED FROM   6
VARIABLES), BASED ON   155 CASES.   !GROUP 2 MATRIX TO BE ANALYZED

		V1 V 1	V2 V 2	V3 V 3	V4 V 4	V5 V 5	V6 V 6	V999 V999
V1	V 1	1.850						
V2	V 2	.787	1.428					
V3	V 3	.363	.488	1.423				
V4	V 4	1.181	.832	1.495	10.491			
V5	V 5	1.220	1.002	.912	1.453	15.210		
V6	V 6	.980	.965	.759	1.427	6.734	7.393	
V999	V999	3.839	3.290	2.600	6.435	20.415	10.070	1.000

MULTIPLE POPULATION ANALYSIS, INFORMATION IN GROUP 1
PARAMETER ESTIMATES APPEAR IN ORDER. NO SPECIAL PROBLEMS WERE ENCOUNTERED
DURING OPTIMIZATION.

MEASUREMENT EQUATIONS WITH STANDARD ERRORS AND TEST STATISTICS

```
V1 = V1 =    1.000 F1  +    3.869*V999+    1.000 E1
                                .094
                             41.084
V2 = V2 =     .851*F1  +    3.339*V999+    1.000 E2    !ALL INTERCEPTS ARE
              .144             .083                    ! SIGNIFICANT
             5.924           40.314
V3 = V3 =    1.207*F1  +    2.573*V999+    1.000 E3    !FACTOR LOADINGS ALSO
              .222             .090
             5.430           28.643
V4 = V4 =    2.758*F1  +    6.421*V999+    1.000 E4
              .517             .229
             5.334           28.095
V5 = V5 =    1.000 F2  +   20.357*V999+    1.000 E5
                              .287
                             70.885
V6 = V6 =     .850*F2  +   10.085*V999+    1.000 E6
              .141             .217
             6.018           46.442
```

```
CONSTRUCT EQUATIONS WITH STANDARD ERRORS AND TEST STATISTICS

F1 = F1 =    -.382*V999+    1.000 D1        !HEAD START GROUP SIGNIFICANTLY
             .104                           !LOWER IN SES
            -3.685
F2 = F2 =    2.137*F1  +    .184*V999+    1.000 D2
             .551           .378
            3.876           .487
!HEAD START GROUP HIGHER THAN CONTROLS ON ABILITY, GIVEN THAT SES IS
!CONTROLLED, BUT EFFECT IS NOT SIGNIFICANT
```

The regression of F2 on F1, ability on SES, is significant (and equal in both groups, see below). Higher SES children do better than lower SES children. Also, Head Start children were lower in SES to begin with, when $-.382$ is compared to the Control's value of fixed 0. Note that the experimental Head Start program produced a positive impact (.184) on ability, though the effect is not significant by z-test. This positive impact stands in contrast to the raw variable means (see input data of both groups), where the Controls had the higher means on the ability indicators V5 and V6, and to the total effects of V999 on V5 and V6, shown below, which also verify that the Controls have the higher expected variable means in the model.

The estimates of variances of the E and D variables are not shown below for either group to conserve space. These variances were not constrained to be equal across groups, though a more restricted model that imposes such a constraint could also have been considered. Similarly, the estimated covariance of E1 and E2 is not shown for either group.

```
DECOMPOSITION OF EFFECTS WITH NONSTANDARDIZED VALUES

PARAMETER TOTAL EFFECTS
 V1 = V1 =    1.000 F1   +    3.487*V999+    1.000 E1    +  1.000 D1 !V999 COEFFICIENTS
 V2 = V2 =    .851*F1    +    3.014*V999+    1.000 E2    +   .851 D1 !ARE REPRODUCED
 V3 = V3 =    1.207*F1   +    2.112*V999+    1.000 E3    +  1.207 D1 !MEANS OF VARIABLES
 V4 = V4 =    2.758*F1   +    5.367*V999+    1.000 E4    +  2.758 D1
 V5 = V5 =    2.137 F1   +    1.000 F2   +  19.724*V999  +  1.000 E5  +  2.137 D1 +1.000 D2
 V6 = V6 =    1.817 F1   +    .850*F2    +   9.548*V999  +  1.000 E6  +  1.817 D1 + .850 D2
 F1 = F1 =   -.382*V999+    1.000 D1        !* V999 GIVES THE MODEL FACTOR MEANS
 F2 = F2 =    2.137*F1   +    -.632*V999+    2.137 D1    +  1.000 D2

!THE ESTIMATED MEAN FOR THE ABILITY FACTOR F2 UNDER THE MODEL IS -.632
!LOWER FOR HEAD START CHILDREN COMPARED TO CONTROLS, BUT THIS IS BASICALLY
!DUE TO THE DIFFERENTIAL SES OF THE CHILDREN, I.E., THE INDIRECT EFFECT OF
!V999 ON F2, WHICH IS -.817, SIGNIFICANT WITH Z = -2.33 (PRINTOUT NOT
!SHOWN).
```

MULTIPLE POPULATION ANALYSIS, INFORMATION IN GROUP 2
  PARAMETER ESTIMATES APPEAR IN ORDER. NO SPECIAL PROBLEMS WERE
ENCOUNTERED DURING OPTIMIZATION.
  ALL EQUALITY CONSTRAINTS WERE CORRECTLY IMPOSED

  MEASUREMENT EQUATIONS WITH STANDARD ERRORS AND TEST STATISTICS

  V1 = V1 =   1.000 F1 +   3.869*V999+   1.000 E1
                               .094
                             41.084

!ADDITIONAL EQUATIONS NOT SHOWN SINCE ALL MEASUREMENT EQUATIONS HAVE
!IDENTICAL ESTIMATES AND STANDARD ERRORS IN GROUP 2 AS IN GROUP 1

  CONSTRUCT EQUATIONS WITH STANDARD ERRORS AND TEST STATISTICS

  F1 = F1 =   1.000 D1
  F2 = F2 =   2.137*F1 +   1.000 D2 !COEFFICIENT IS THE SAME IN BOTH GROUPS
               .551
              3.876

DECOMPOSITION OF EFFECTS WITH NONSTANDARDIZED VALUES

PARAMETER TOTAL EFFECTS

  V1 = V1 =   1.000 F1 +   3.869*V999+   1.000 E1   + 1.000 D1 !MODEL PREDICTS
  V2 = V2 =   .851*F1 +   3.339*V999+   1.000 E2   + .851 D1 !HIGHER MEANS ON
  V3 = V3 =   1.207*F1 +   2.573*V999+   1.000 E3   + 1.207 D1 !ALL Vs FOR
  V4 = V4 =   2.758*F1 +   6.421*V999+   1.000 E4   + 2.758 D1 !CONTROLS
  V5 = V5 =   2.137 F1 +   1.000 F2 + 20.357*V999 + 1.000 E5 + 2.137 D1+ 1.000 D2
  V6 = V6 =   1.817 F1 +   .850*F2 + 10.085*V999 + 1.000 E6 + 1.817 D1+ .850 D2
  F1 = F1 =   1.000 D1
  F2 = F2 =   2.137*F1 +   2.137 D1 +   1.000 D2

!BECAUSE GROUP 2 IS THE REFERENCE GROUP, THE TOTAL EFFECTS OF V999 ON Vs
!ARE THE DIRECT EFFECTS. SEE MEASUREMENT EQUATIONS ABOVE. THEY ALSO
!SHOULD REPRODUCE GROUP 2'S SAMPLE MEANS WELL.

  STATISTICS FOR MULTIPLE POPULATION ANALYSIS
  ALL EQUALITY CONSTRAINTS WERE CORRECTLY IMPOSED   !ALWAYS NICE TO SEE

GOODNESS OF FIT SUMMARY
CHI-SQUARE =   27.451 BASED ON   23 DEGREES OF FREEDOM   !GOOD FIT
PROBABILITY VALUE FOR THE CHI-SQUARE STATISTIC IS   .23726

BENTLER-BONETT NORMED   FIT INDEX   = .928 !FIT INDEXES ARE O.K. ALSO
BENTLER-BONETT NONNORMED FIT INDEX   = .984
COMPARATIVE FIT INDEX   = .987

            ITERATIVE SUMMARY

              PARAMETER
ITERATION   ABS CHANGE   ALPHA   FUNCTION
    1   1.110013   1.00000   .22246
    2   .536829   1.00000   .26116
    3   .680950   1.00000   .18950
    4   .332339   1.00000   .10795
    5   .087454   1.00000   .09126
    6   .008574   1.00000   .09120
    7   .001932   1.00000   .09120
    8   .000750   1.00000   .09120   !FUNCTION CONVERGED O.K.

```
LAGRANGE MULTIPLIER TEST (FOR RELEASING CONSTRAINTS)

CONSTRAINTS TO BE RELEASED ARE:
!THE 11 CONSTRAINTS IN LINES 70-80 OF THE INPUT ECHO, NOT DUPLICATED HERE
!TO SAVE SPACE

           UNIVARIATE TEST STATISTICS:

     NO     CONSTRAINT CHI-SQUARE     PROBABILITY

      1      CONSTR:  1   .035          .851       !NONE OF THE CONSTRAINTS
      2      CONSTR:  2   .784          .376       !IS SIGNIFICANT, I.E.,
      3      CONSTR:  3   .597          .440       !THE CONSTRAINTS ARE
      4      CONSTR:  4   .012          .912       !ALL ACCEPTABLE
      5      CONSTR:  5   .197          .658
      6      CONSTR:  6   .197          .658
      7      CONSTR:  7  1.700          .192
      8      CONSTR:  8   .019          .891
      9      CONSTR:  9   .008          .927
     10      CONSTR: 10   .001          .971
     11      CONSTR: 11   .108          .742
```

The multivariate test verified the univariate LM test results. This concludes the 2-group structured mean Head Start/Controls example.

An issue raised in the beginning of the chapter was that a model that may not be identified in one group can become identified when several groups are considered simultaneously and cross-group equality constraints are imposed. The Head Start (only) analysis with V999 failed as a model because there were more intercept parameters to be estimated than there were means to be modeled. Of course this fact is not changed when the 2-group model is considered. However, both groups provided 12 sample means. Parameters involving V999 that were estimated in both groups included the 12 free parameters for the common level of the variables, which, with 6 equalities, implies $12 - 6 = 6$ effective free parameters; and the two intercepts for F1 and F2 in the Head Start sample; for a total of 8 free parameters. Thus there are $12 - 8 = 4$ effective degrees of freedom for the part of the model concerned with the means. Of course, having fewer parameters in a model than there are data points is a necessary, but not sufficient, condition for model identification.

PRACTICAL AND STATISTICAL ASPECTS

Multisample structured means models obviously combine techniques relevant to multisample analysis and structured means models. It was noted in both Chapters 7 and 8 that these models can be difficult to estimate and test. Structured means models may be adequate for reproducing sample means, or covariances, but perhaps not both. Multisample models may be adequate in one sample, but inadequate in another sample. As a consequence, the type of models discussed in this chapter can also be difficult to apply in practice, especially when many variables and parameters are involved.

The most serious difficulty is probably the multisample aspect of an analysis. Since a model must be at least marginal to adequate in all of the samples, a model that fits very poorly in one sample, especially a large sample, can have an inordinate influence on the overall fitting function value in the multisample version of the same model. Of course, a model that fits marginally in one sample may be good enough in a multisample context because its poor fit is offset by a countervailing especially well-fitting model in the other samples, and because there may be a significant gain in degrees of freedom (df). The Head Start data illustrated these phenomena, since, when the model of Figure 9.1 was considered only in the Head Start sample, the model with 7 df yielded a fit probability of .028, which is below the standard .05 cutoff for model acceptance. Yet the same model in a 2-sample context yielded an acceptable overall probability of .237 based on 23 df.

Convergence difficulties will tend to occur when theoretical or empirical underidentification exists in a model. A clue to such underidentification is given by the error messages the program provides, especially, that one or more parameter estimates may be linearly dependent on others. But the more serious problem occurs if the model is extremely inadequate at describing the data, or if extremely bad starting values are used for an otherwise potentially acceptable model, for the iterations may not converge at all. Then it may be best to evaluate the models in their separate groups before attempting a combined multisample analysis. After all, the multisample analysis will, in general, impose additional restrictions on the models as compared to a single-sample analysis. If these restrictions are extremely inappropriate, even an otherwise acceptable model will become statistically inadequate. The /LMTEST that evaluates the cross-sample constraints can be extremely helpful in locating inappropriate constraints. If it makes sense to do so, such constraints should then be released in future runs.

Multisample models can be used in nonstandard ways to tackle a variety of interesting questions. For example, if the number of variables to be analyzed, or the number of factors, is intended to be different in the different groups, it is possible to introduce pseudo-Vs or pseudo-Fs so as to make the number of such variables equal in the job set-up (Jöreskog, 1971). This type of procedure has been used in recent approaches to dealing with missing data (Allison, 1987; Muthén, Kaplan, & Hollis, 1987). EQS uses a simpler procedure as will be seen in the last part of this chapter.

Multiple group structured means models were, historically, estimated in LISREL using a cross-products sample and model matrix sometimes called a moment matrix (not to be confused with EQS' use of the term "ANALYSIS = MOMENTS;" referring to the analysis of means, 1st moments, and covariances, 2nd moments about the means). See, e.g., the various versions of the LISREL manual (e.g., Jöreskog & Sörbom, 1988, p. 261). Hayduk (1987, Appendix D) summarizes the relevance of this matrix to LISREL's procedures. This matrix is irrelevant to either model specification or the statistical theory in EQS. Only standard ML statistical theory based on means and covariances is used in EQS; see Chapter 10. Other methods of estimation for multisample structured means models will be available in the next major release of the program.

The statistical theory used in EQS assumes that sample covariances and means are being analyzed in all groups, i.e., that the variables have not been standardized. Additionally, scales of the latent variables should be fixed in each group by fixing an $F \rightarrow V$ path for the same variable, to assure that the factor is on a common scale across all groups. For reasons outlined by Cudeck (1989), EQS does not provide a scaling in which the solution is standardized to a common metric across groups.

EXAMPLE: EXPERIMENTAL DATA

Sörbom (1978) reported on an experiment by Olsson on the effects of training on abilities to perform verbal tasks. In a pre-test, 11-year old children were assessed for their verbal ability with two kinds of verbal material, synonyms and opposites (presumably antonyms). Thereafter, they were randomly assigned to experimental and control conditions. The experimental group received training on similar materials, while the control group did not. Both groups were then retested, yielding post-test data. The pre-test and post-test data are to be analyzed.

Sörbom studied several models for these data. A path diagram for his final model is given in Figure 9.2, where V1 and V2 represent the pre-test scores on synonyms and opposites tasks, respectively, and V3 and V4 represent synonyms and opposites task performance after the experimental intervention. As seen in the left part of the diagram, it is hypothesized that synonyms and opposites, at each time point, can be conceived as indicators of a latent factor, say, verbal ability. Ability at post-test, F2, is expected to be a function of ability at the pre-test, F1. In addition, the residual in opposites at the two time points, E2 and E4, are expected to be correlated from pre-test to post-test.

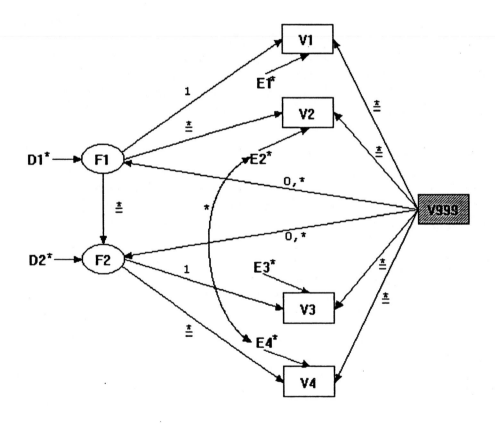

Figure 9.2

The right part of the figure gives the constant V999. This is presumed to affect each of the variables V1 − V4, reflecting their intercept, a general level for these variables. V999 also directly affects the factors F1 and F2, representing an intercept for these factors. The figure maintains the convention of Figure 9.1 that "*" represents a parameter that is free to be estimated in each group, without constraints; that "$\pm$" represents a parameter that is freely estimated in each group, but constrained to be equal in both groups; and that "0,*" represents a parameter that is fixed at 0 in the first group, the Control group, and is free to be estimated in the second group, the Experimental group. Thus, factor loadings, factor regressions, and variable intercepts are constrained to be equal across groups. Factor intercepts are fixed at 0 for identification in the Control group, and are free to be estimated in the Experimental group. All residual variances and the covariance of E2 and E4 are free to be estimated in each group, without any constraints.

Consider the model in one group only, say, the Controls. In this group, the factor intercepts (V999 → F1, V999 → F2) are set to zero. Then, counting parameters, there are 4 intercept parameters and 10 additional parameters. With 4 input variables, there are 4 means and 10 variances and covariances. It is apparent that the model is just identified for both the means and the covariances. Thus, running this model in the Control group alone would lead to a perfect fit, with zero residuals, zero χ^2, and zero degrees of freedom. Running the same model in the Experimental group would have the same effect; while including the factor intercept paths will lead to an underidentified model. These identification problems disappear when both groups are considered simultaneously. The cross-group restrictions serve to make the model estimable and testable. An abbreviated EQS output for the 2-group run is given below.

```
1   /TITLE
2    OLSSON'S DATA (SORBOM, 1978), CONTROL GROUP
3   /SPECIFICATION
4    VARIABLES = 4; CASES = 105; ANALYSIS = MOMENT; GROUPS = 2;
5   /LABELS
6    V1 = SYNONYM1; V2 = OPPOSIT1; V3 = SYNONYM2; V4 = OPPOSIT2;
7    F1 = ABILITY1; F2 = ABILITY2;
8   /EQUATIONS
9  V1 = 20*V999 +     F1 + E1;
10 V2 = 20*V999 + .9*F1 + E2;
11 V3 = 20*V999 +     F2 + E3;
12 V4 = 20*V999 + .9*F2 + E4;
13 F1 =     0V999        + D1;
14 F2 =     0V999 + .9*F1 + D2;
15  /VARIANCES
16   D1 = 30*; D2 = 5*;
17   E1 TO E4 = 10*;
18  /COVARIANCES
19   E2,E4 = 5*;
20  /MATRIX
21   37.626                !LOW VARIANCES WHEN COMPARED TO EXPERIMENTALS
22   24.933   34.680
23   26.639   24.236   32.013
24   23.649   27.760   23.565   33.443
25  /MEANS
26   18.381 20.229 20.400 21.343
     !LOW MEAN ON V1 COMPARED TO EXPERIMENTALS
27  /END
28  /TITLE
29   OLSSON'S DATA (SORBOM, 1978), EXPERIMENTAL GROUP
30  /SPECIFICATION
31   VARIABLES = 4; CASES = 108; ANALYSIS = MOMENT;
32  /LABELS
33   V1 = SYNONYM1; V2 = OPPOSIT1; V3 = SYNONYM2; V4 = OPPOSIT2;
34   F1 = ABILITY1; F2 = ABILITY2;
```

```
35   /EQUATIONS
36 V1  =  20*V999 +        F1+ E1;
37 V2  =  20*V999 + .9*F1 + E2;
38 V3  =  20*V999 +        F2- E3;
39 V4  =  20*V999 + .9*F2 + E4;
40 F1  =   2*V999          + D1;
41 F2  =   2*V999 + .9*F1 + D2;
42   /VARIANCES
43    D1 = 30*; D2 = 5*;
44    E1 TO E4 = 10*;
45   /COVARIANCES
46    E2,E4 = 5*;
47   /MATRIX
48    50.084
49    42.373   49.872
50    40.760   36.094   51.237
51    37.343   40.396   39.890   53.641
52   /MEANS
53    20.556 21.241 25.667 25.870   !HIGHER POST-TEST MEANS VS. CONTROLS
54   /CONSTRAINTS
55    (1,V1,V999) = (2,V1,V999);
56    (1,V2,V999) = (2,V2,V999);
57    (1,V3,V999) = (2,V3,V999);
58    (1,V4,V999) = (2,V4,V999);
59    (1,V2,F1) = (2,V2,F1);
60    (1,V4,F2) = (2,V4,F2);
61    (1,F2,F1) = (2,F2,F1);
62   /LMTEST
63   /END
```

Before examining the output, some comments on the data are in order. There would seem to be some question in these data as to whether the two groups in fact were randomly assigned to conditions, or, if so, whether randomization may have failed. In particular, one would expect the pretest means and variances and covariances for the two groups to be equal, but this does not appear to be so. In fact such a hypothesis can be tested by another structural model, but this will not be done here because, in the end, a complete model of all the data must be obtained. The results of Sörbom's model are presented below.

```
MEASUREMENT EQUATIONS WITH STANDARD ERRORS AND TEST STATISTICS !CONTROLS

SYNONYM1   = V1 =   1.000 F1  +  18.619*V999 +  1.000 E1
                                     .597
                                   31.205
OPPOSIT1   = V2 =    .878*F1  +  19.910*V999 +  1.000 E2
                     .051            .544
                   17.286          36.603
SYNONYM2   = V3 =   1.000 F2  +  20.383*V999 +  1.000 E3
                                     .538
                                   37.882
OPPOSIT2   = V4 =    .907*F2  +  21.203*V999 +  1.000 E4
                     .053            .534
                   17.301          39.719
```

The factor loadings look good, and the intercepts for the Vs are about the magnitude of the means in the Control group.

```
CONSTRUCT EQUATIONS WITH STANDARD ERRORS AND TEST STATISTICS  !CONTROLS

ABILITY1   = F1 =   1.000 D1
```

```
ABILITY2    = F2 =     .895*F1    +    1.000 D2
                       .052
                     17.145
```

The factor is quite stable from pre-test to post-test. The variances and covariances are not presented to save space, though it should be noted that the variances for D1 and D2 are substantially higher in the Experimental as compared to Control group. In the Experimental group, the following Construct Equations are obtained (Measurement Equations are the same as for Controls).

```
CONSTRUCT EQUATIONS WITH STANDARD ERRORS AND TEST STATISTICS
!EXPERIMENTALS

ABILITY1    = F1 =    1.875*V999+    1.000 D1
                       .899
                      2.085
ABILITY2    = F2 =     .895*F1    +   3.628*V999  +  1.000 D2
                       .052           .480
                     17.145          7.558
```

Since the Control's V999 → F1 path is set to zero, the Experimental's comparable path shows that Experimental subjects were significantly higher in the verbal ability factor F1 at pretest ($\underline{z}$ = 2.085). Thus there is some reason to doubt that the two groups were initially equal in ability (the intercept for F1 is the mean, since there are no indirect paths from V999 to F1). Given that they may have been higher in ability, nonetheless, the experimental training on the verbal materials improved that group's subsequent performance, when compared to the controls. This can be seen in the intercept for F2, which is significantly greater than zero, thus reflecting the observed mean differences between the groups on V3 and V4. Overall, the model is also acceptable, with χ^2 = 3.952, based on 5 df, having an associated probability of .556.

An obvious question is how this model might perform when the intercepts for F1 are forced to be equal for Controls and Experimentals. Such a specification would be consistent with a randomized assignment of subjects to conditions. Rerunning the above model with the path V999 → F1 set to zero in both groups, the following results occur. While the model is statistically acceptable by the χ^2 goodness-of-fit test, the LM test shows a definite problem.

```
CHI-SQUARE =          8.234 BASED ON      6 DEGREES OF FREEDOM
PROBABILITY VALUE FOR THE CHI-SQUARE STATISTIC IS      .22144


LAGRANGE MULTIPLIER TEST (FOR RELEASING CONSTRAINTS)
CONSTRAINTS TO BE RELEASED ARE:
!SEE LINES 55-61 IN THE INPUT FILE

         UNIVARIATE TEST STATISTICS:

  NO      CONSTRAINT CHI-SQUARE        PROBABILITY

   1      CONSTR:  1   5.198          .023  !FOR (1,V1,V999) = (2,V1,V999);
   2      CONSTR:  2   1.210          .271
   3      CONSTR:  3    .003          .954
   4      CONSTR:  4    .003          .954
   5      CONSTR:  5    .168          .682
   6      CONSTR:  6    .077          .782
   7      CONSTR:  7   1.125          .289
```

It is apparent that the constraint of equal intercepts for V1 across the two groups may be implausible. Consequently a final model will be considered in which this constraint is released. Note particularly that, as a result, the basic level of V1 across groups is not forced to be the same. This final model shows the following results.

```
MEASUREMENT EQUATIONS WITH STANDARD ERRORS AND TEST STATISTICS   !CONTROLS

SYNONYM1    = V1 =    1.000 F1   +   18.738*V999  +  1.000 E1
                                         .541
                                       34.637
OPPOSIT1    = V2 =     .888*F1   +   20.651*V999  +  1.000 E2
                        .051             .442
                      17.353           46.736
SYNONYM2    = V3 =    1.000 F2   +   20.768*V999  +  1.000 E3
                                         .465
                                       44.659
OPPOSIT2    = V4 =     .891*F2   +   21.607*V999  +  1.000 E4
                        .055             .461
                      16.307           46.880


CONSTRUCT EQUATIONS WITH STANDARD ERRORS AND TEST STATISTICS

ABILITY1    = F1 =    1.000 D1
ABILITY2    = F2 =     .906*F1   +    1.000 D2
                        .053
                      17.165


MEASUREMENT EQUATIONS WITH STANDARD ERRORS AND TEST STATISTICS  !EXPERIMENTAL

SYNONYM1    = V1 =    1.000 F1   +   20.002*V999  +  1.000 E1
                                         .515
                                       38.811
OPPOSIT1    = V2 =     .888*F1   +   20.651*V999  +  1.000 E2
                        .051             .442
                      17.353           46.736
SYNONYM2    = V3 =    1.000 F2   +   20.768*V999  +  1.000 E3
                                         .465
                                       44.659
OPPOSIT2    = V4 =     .891*F2   +   21.607*V999  +  1.000 E4
                        .055             .461
                      16.307           46.880


CONSTRUCT EQUATIONS WITH STANDARD ERRORS AND TEST STATISTICS

ABILITY1    = F1 =    1.000 D1
ABILITY2    = F2 =     .906*F1   +    4.342*V999  +  1.000 D2
                        .053             .538
                      17.165            8.075


CHI-SQUARE =          2.962 BASED ON      5 DEGREES OF FREEDOM
PROBABILITY VALUE FOR THE CHI-SQUARE STATISTIC IS        .70590

   BENTLER-BONETT NORMED     FIT INDEX      = .996
   BENTLER-BONETT NONNORMED  FIT INDEX      = 1.007
   COMPARATIVE FIT INDEX                    = 1.000
```

The equal intercepts for F1 in this model across groups suggests that the children in the two groups may well have been equal in mean verbal ability at pretest, but that, for reasons that cannot be ascertained from within the analysis, the Controls had a lower mean on V1 as well as lower variance on D1, and hence, on verbal ability F1 (variances not shown above). While the model fits even better than the model proposed by Sörbom, ideally, a further understanding of the experimental procedure would be called for to explain the pre-test imbalances between conditions. Nonequivalence of groups should occur relatively rarely by chance alone under random assignment at the given sample sizes (e.g., Hsu, 1989).

MISSING DATA MODELS

Traditional approaches to analysis of data with missing values involve the use of so-called listwise deletion, in which a case is eliminated completely if data are missing, or pairwise deletion, in which a case is eliminated in the computation of summary statistics such as means or correlations if the corresponding data is unavailable. These procedures are practical, but problematic. Both are inefficient, that is, do not produce the best possible or least variance estimates. Listwise deletion is inefficient in the obvious way: it throws away a substantial amount of potentially useful data. Pairwise deletion sometimes yields correlation matrices that have inappropriate properties (specifically, they may not be positive definite).

In recent years some rather general approaches to missing data have been developed. One can distinguish between several interrelated concepts in this literature, going back to Rubin (1976). "Data are missing at random [MAR] if the probability of obtaining the particular pattern of missing data found in the sample does not depend on the values of the data that are missing. It may, however, depend on the values of the data that are observed. Data are observed at random [OAR] if the probability of obtaining the missing data pattern found in the sample does not depend on the data that are observed; however, it may depend on the data that are missing" (Allison, 1987, p. 76). If both of these conditions MAR and OAR are satisfied, the data are said to missing completely at random (MCAR). Listwise and pairwise deletion can be fully justified only when the data are MCAR, which is a very strong assumption that may not be met in practice.

Allison (1987) and Muthén, Kaplan, and Hollis (1987) suggested that structural modeling provides a useful implementation of these ideas in some situations. In particular, if the data contains a few predominant patterns of missing data (e.g., some subjects have data only from waves 1 and 2; all others have complete data from waves 1, 2, and 3), modeling is an attractive approach. Allison and Muthén et al. have shown that data do not need to be MCAR for structural modeling to yield consistent estimates of the parameters, appropriate standard error estimates, and by some manipulation, appropriate χ^2 tests. In particular, when the data is only missing at random (MAR), but not necessarily observed at random (OAR), under mild conditions the procedure produces appropriate inferences. However, even the weaker assumption that the data are MAR may be violated in longitudinal research, since attrition may depend on the values of the variables that would have been observed in later waves. Nonetheless, it appears that the structural modeling approach will more likely yield appropriate (less biased) inferences than listwise or pairwise deletion even when MAR does not hold.

A structural modeling approach to missing data creates groups or samples of subjects in accord with their pattern of missing data. This can be done conveniently using BMDP's AM program, for example. If there are three patterns of missing data, three sets of data are created and a 3-group structural model is used. If there are dozens of patterns of missing data, with only a few subjects showing a given pattern of missing data, the modeling approach is useless because some of these samples may be too small to yield stable results (or a positive definite covariance matrix for observed data), and the method may be too computationally demanding to work with so many samples. Allison (1987) and Muthén et al. (1987) use dummy variables and factors in the groups with missing data, with pseudo-values replacing the missing means and covariances. Equality constraints across groups are used to assure that the same parameters (means and covariances, or structural modeling parameters) are estimated in both groups when these parameters would be identified if the data were complete (they may not be identified in any single sample), and the process is carried out so that the pseudo-values are fitted exactly. Both means and covariances must be modeled.

An example of the structural modeling approach to missing data is given in the job setup shown below. The data and model are taken from Allison (1987), who used the LISREL program to estimate and test the model; this required using a number of "tricks", such as using dummy variables and parameters, and adjusting the degrees of freedom, to yield the correct missing-data results. These tricks are unnecessary to the theory involved, and serve to confuse the simplicity of the ideas. They are also not necessary in EQS, in which the model setup is essentially the same as in any multisample analysis with structured means. The critical point in such a setup is that *the samples with missing data can contain specifications of equations, intercepts, variances and covariances only for variables that are actually observed, as well as for hypothesized factors and residual variables relevant to those variables.*

```
 1   /TITLE
 2   INCOMPLETE DATA FACTOR MODEL (ALLISON, 1987)
 3   COMPLETE DATA SUBSAMPLE
 4   /SPECIFICATIONS
 5   VAR = 4; CASES = 348; ANAL = MOM; GROUPS = 2;
 6   /EQUATIONS
 7   V1 = 17*V999 +    F1       + E1;
 8   V2 = 17*V999 + 1*F1        + E2;
 9   V3 =  7*V999        +  F2 + E3;
10   V4 =  7*V999        +1*F2 + E4;
11   /VARIANCES
12   F1 = 117*; F2 = 14*;
13   E1 = 94*; E2 = 47*; E3 = 2*; E4 = 1*;
14   /COVARIANCES
15   F1,F2 = 25*;
16   /MATRIX
17   180.90
18   126.77 217.56
19    23.96  30.20 16.24
20    22.86  30.47 14.36   15.13
21   /MEANS
22    16.62  17.39  6.65    6.75
23   /END
24   /TITLE
25   INCOMPLETE DATA SUBSAMPLE
26   /SPECIFICATIONS
27   VAR = 4; CASES = 1672; ANAL = MOM;
28   /EQUATIONS
29   V1 = 17*V999 +    F1       + E1;
30   V3 =  7*V999        +  F2 + E3;
31   /VARIANCES
32   F1 = 117*; F2 = 14*;
33   E1 = 94*; E3 = 2*;
```

```
34   /COVARIANCES
35   F1,F2 = 25*;
36   /MATRIX
37   217.27
38      0        1
39    25.57      0      16.16
40      0        0       0       1
41   /MEANS
42    16.98      0      6.83      0
43   /CONSTRAINTS
44   (1,V1,V999) = (2,V1,V999);
45   (1,V3,V999) = (2,V3,V999);
46     (1,F1,F1) = (2,F1,F1);
47     (1,F2,F2) = (2,F2,F2);
48     (1,F1,F2) = (2,F1,F2);
49     (1,E1,E1) = (2,E1,E1);
50     (1,E3,E3) = (2,E3,E3);
51   /LMTEST
52   /PRINT
53    COVARIANCE =YES;
54   /END
```

The model described above is a two group model in which one sample has complete information on all variables, and the other sample contains a particular pattern of missing data, and thus contains observed data on a subset of the variables. The data originally came from Bielby, Hauser and Featherman (1977), and the specific meaning of the variables in the example can be found in Allison (1987). What is relevant here is that the model is essentially that shown in Figure 9.2, except that 1) the paths from V999 to F1 and F2 are removed from the model, so that the Fs are independent variables and there are no Ds; 2) the path from F1 to F2 is replaced by a two way arrow, a covariance; and 3) there is no error covariance E2,E4. Thus, a two-group model similar to Figure 9.2 is being evaluated. In fact, as seen in lines 6 − 15 above, the model is a simple two factor model with intercepts for the measured variables (paths from V999 to the measured variables). The data from this sample, based on 348 cases, is complete, that is, all variances and covariances among V1 − V4, as well as the means of these variables, are available for analysis, as shown in lines 16 − 22. Thus in this first group the model is a rather standard factor analysis model, except that the variable intercepts (which are means in this example) are also being estimated. If this sample were the only one being analyzed, these intercepts would be estimated at the sample means.

The second, much larger, sample, based on 1672 cases, contains incomplete data. Allison states that the data are missing at random. As can be seen in lines 36 − 42 above, data are available only on variables V1 and V3, i.e., no data exists for V2 and V4. The covariance matrix and means shown in the input file is of the same dimension as in the complete data sample, that is, with 4 variables, in order to keep the notation V1 and V3 for the available data (rather than V1 and V2 for two variables, which is what EQS otherwise would assume for two input variables; see p. 21). The entries corresponding to V2 and V4 are completely arbitrary and have no meaning; in fact, by the model setup, EQS will not even read these entries, and only the data corresponding to V1 and V3 will be read in by the program and analyzed. The model for these variables is given in lines 28 − 35 above. Since only V1 and V3 have data, equations for only these variables are provided. Variances and covariances are specified for factors and errors given in these equations. The final critical part of the setup lies in the cross-group constraints, which specify that every free parameter in the incomplete data sample is to be estimated at the same value as in the complete data sample.

The model was estimated with EQS, yielding $\chi^2_{(6)} = 7.69$, an acceptable model with probability p = .26. Note that there were 19 sample covariances and means to be analyzed, 20 free parameters in the model setup, and 7 cross-group constraints, yielding $19 - 20 + 7 = 6$ degrees of freedom. The final parameter estimates, not shown here, make optimal use of all available data. In addition, the usual output, such as a standard error for each estimate, is available for further analysis. In this example, the Lagrange Multiplier test (specified in input line 51) indicated that the constraint of equal variances of E1 across samples may not be consistent with the data ($\chi^2_{(1)} = 4.08$, p = .04). The equality of residual variances across these samples may not be an important model feature, so the model was reestimated after removing line 49 (above). The resulting model yielded an excellent fit ($\chi^2_{(5)} = 3.21$, p = .67), with a comparative fit index (Bentler, 1988a) of 1.00.

If there are several experimental and control samples, the total number of groups that must be analyzed is the total number of missing data patterns across all samples. Thus the structural modeling approach is impractical if the number of missing data patterns is very large. Then, as in the usual approach, it may be necessary to discard those patterns of missing data that only a few subjects exhibit, in order to bring the problem down to a managable size. Minimal bias will result if this loss of data does not include much selectivity bias.

10. SOME TECHNICAL ASPECTS OF EQS

This chapter reviews some technical material related to the internal operations performed by EQS and to the results produced in the program output. Most of the concepts have been described in the published literature cited in Chapter 1, but a few are original, are based on technical reports, or are implemented in a way that deserves mention.

THE BENTLER-WEEKS MODEL

The model specification used in EQS is translated by the computer program into the matrices of the Bentler-Weeks model that are used to provide a representation system for the particular structure under investigation. As noted in Chapter 2, a key concept of this system involves the designation of each and every variable in a model as either an independent or a dependent variable. Dependent variables can be expressed as a structural regression function of other variables; independent variables are never structurally regressed on other variables. Dependent variables are collected in the column vector variable η, while independent variables are collected in the vector variable ξ. There are thus as many elements in η as there are dependent variables and as many elements in ξ as there are independent variables. The structural matrix equation that relates these variables is given by

$$\eta = \beta\eta + \gamma\xi, \tag{10.1}$$

where β contains the coefficients for the regression of η variables on each other and γ contains the coefficients for the regression of η variables on ξ variables. Only independent variables have variances and covariances as parameters of the model. Assuming that all variables are in deviation from mean form for simplicity,

$$\Phi = \mathcal{E}(\xi\xi') \tag{10.2}$$

represents the covariance matrix of the independent variables. Thus the parameter matrices of the model are β, γ, and Φ.

EQS translates the input specifications and parameter estimates into the three parameter matrices. The program uses the logic of ordering each of the vectors of dependent and independent variables in accord with the sequence V, F, E, and D, using ascending order within each type of variable. These vectors and parameter matrices will now be illustrated for some of the models considered in Chapter 2. Although the reader need not have studied Chapter 2, the cited figures and model specifications should be consulted.

Regression Model

The model of Figure 2.2 has one dependent and three independent variables.

Dependent variables: $V4 = \eta_1$

Independent variables: $V2 = \xi_1$; $V5 = \xi_2$; $E4 = \xi_3$.

It follows that the vector η is a 1×1 number, the vector ξ is a 3×1 vector, that β is a number, γ is a 1×3 vector, and Φ is a 3×3 matrix. The input on p. 19 can be translated as follows. First, $\beta = 0$ since there is no regression of η_1 on η_1 (i.e., V4 on V4). Since V4 is $1*V2 - 1*V5 + E4$; $\eta_1 = 1*\xi_1 - 1*\xi_2 + 1 \cdot \xi_3$. These coefficients describe the regression of η_1 on some ξ variables, i.e., they are all found in γ. In particular, (10.1) becomes

$$\eta_1 = 0 \cdot \eta_1 + [1^* \quad -1^* \quad 1] \begin{bmatrix} \xi_1 \\ \xi_2 \\ \xi_3 \end{bmatrix},$$

so $\gamma = [1 \ -1 \ 1]$. The stars are simply a reminder that some parameters of the model are free, and hence will be changed during the iterations, while others are fixed. The covariance matrix Φ of the independent variables contains the following variables and elements:

$$V2=\xi_1 \ V5=\xi_2 \ E4=\xi_3$$

$$\begin{matrix} V2=\xi_1 \\ V5=\xi_2 \\ E4=\xi_3 \end{matrix} \begin{bmatrix} 9^* & -4^* & 0 \\ -4^* & 9^* & 0 \\ 0 & 0 & 2^* \end{bmatrix}$$

The elements of Φ are taken from the VARIANCE and COVARIANCE sections of the input. Information on whether an element is a fixed or free element is of course not stored inside Φ, but it is included above to identify which elements will be updated during the iterations and which elements will stay the same. Notice that zero covariances are assumed if nothing is specified in COV. The matrix Φ is symmetric. Henceforth, the symmetric redundant elements will not be noted.

Path Analysis Model

The path analysis model shown in Figure 2.3 is translated into the Bentler-Weeks vectors and equations as follows:

Dependent variables: $V3 = \eta_1$; $V4 = \eta_2$

Independent variables: $V1 = \xi_1$; $V2 = \xi_2$; $E3 = \xi_3$; $E4 = \xi_4$.

Thus η is of order 2×1, ξ is 4×1, β is 2×2, γ is 2×4, and Φ is 4×4. The input of p. 24 has the equations $\eta_1 = 1*\xi_1 + 1*\xi_2 + 1 \cdot \xi_3$ and $\eta_2 = 1*\xi_1 + 1*\xi_2 + 1 \cdot \xi_4$. Thus,

$$\begin{bmatrix} \eta_1 \\ \eta_2 \end{bmatrix} = \begin{bmatrix} 0 & 0 \\ 0 & 0 \end{bmatrix} \begin{bmatrix} \eta_1 \\ \eta_2 \end{bmatrix} + \begin{bmatrix} 1^* & 1^* & 1 & 0 \\ 1^* & 1^* & 0 & 1 \end{bmatrix} \begin{bmatrix} \xi_1 \\ \xi_2 \\ \xi_3 \\ \xi_4 \end{bmatrix}$$

$$\eta \quad = \quad \beta \quad \quad \eta \quad + \quad \gamma \quad \quad \xi \quad .$$

Note that β and γ have two rows, which is the number of equations. The first equation can be completely generated by the first row of these matrices, and the second equation by the second row. Using elementary rules of matrix multiplication,

$$\eta_1 = 0 \cdot \eta_1 + 0 \cdot \eta_2 + 1^*\xi_1 + 1^*\xi_2 + 1 \cdot \xi_3 + 0 \cdot \xi_4$$

and

$$\eta_2 = 0 \cdot \eta_1 + 0 \cdot \eta_2 + 1^*\xi_1 + 1^*\xi_2 + 0 \cdot \xi_3 + 1 \cdot \xi_4.$$

The zeros in the matrices are necessary to give a particular variable a zero weight, i.e., to eliminate it from the equation. The stars are shown as a reminder of which parameters are free (and hence, which are fixed), but this information is carried elsewhere in EQS; the same practice will be followed henceforth without further comment. It should be noted that the model of Figure 2.3 does not include any paths that represent the regression of dependent variables on each other. If such paths had existed, the coefficients would have been shown in the matrix β.

The coefficients of equations are not the only parameters of a model. The variances and covariances of the independent variables are also parameters. In this case the input can be used to generate

$$
\Phi =
\begin{array}{c}
\\
\xi_1 \\
\xi_2 \\
\xi_3 \\
\xi_4
\end{array}
\begin{array}{cccc}
\xi_1 & \xi_2 & \xi_3 & \xi_4 \\
\end{array}
\left[
\begin{array}{cccc}
10^* & & & \\
7^* & 10^* & & \\
0 & 0 & 2^* & \\
0 & 0 & 0 & 2^*
\end{array}
\right].
$$

Factor Analysis Model

The model of Figure 2.7 is translated into the Bentler-Weeks representation as follows:

Dependent variables: $V1 = \eta_1$; $V2 = \eta_2$; $V3 = \eta_3$; $V4 = \eta_4$

Independent variables: $F1 = \xi_1$; $F2 = \xi_2$; $E1 = \xi_3$; $E2 = \xi_4$; $E3 = \xi_5$; $E4 = \xi_6$.

Thus, η is of order 4×1, ξ is 6×1, β is 4×4, γ is 4×6; and Φ is 6×6. The input on p. 29 generates the following matrices:

$$
\beta =
\begin{array}{c}
\\
\eta_1 \\
\eta_2 \\
\eta_3 \\
\eta_4
\end{array}
\begin{array}{cccc}
\eta_1 & \eta_2 & \eta_3 & \eta_4 \\
\end{array}
\left[
\begin{array}{cccc}
0 & 0 & 0 & 0 \\
0 & 0 & 0 & 0 \\
0 & 0 & 0 & 0 \\
0 & 0 & 0 & 0
\end{array}
\right]
\qquad
\gamma =
\begin{array}{c}
\\
\eta_1 \\
\eta_2 \\
\eta_3 \\
\eta_4
\end{array}
\begin{array}{cccccc}
\xi_1 & \xi_2 & \xi_3 & \xi_4 & \xi_5 & \xi_6 \\
\end{array}
\left[
\begin{array}{cccccc}
2^* & 0 & 1 & 0 & 0 & 0 \\
2^* & 0 & 0 & 1 & 0 & 0 \\
0 & 2^* & 0 & 0 & 1 & 0 \\
0 & 2^* & 0 & 0 & 0 & 1
\end{array}
\right]
$$

The number of equations (four) is evidently given by the number of dependent variables. Each equation has only two predictor variables in it, since each row of $[\beta, \gamma]$ has only two nonzero numbers. Each equation has only one unknown parameter given the estimated value two. The covariance matrix of the independent variables is the following:

$$\Phi = \begin{array}{c} \\ \xi_1 \\ \xi_2 \\ \xi_3 \\ \xi_4 \\ \xi_5 \\ \xi_6 \end{array} \begin{array}{cccccc} \xi_1 & \xi_2 & \xi_3 & \xi_4 & \xi_5 & \xi_6 \\ \left[\begin{array}{cccccc} 1.0 & & & & & \\ .3^* & 1.0 & & & & \\ 0 & 0 & 3.0^* & & & \\ 0 & 0 & 0 & 3.0^* & & \\ 0 & 0 & 0 & 0 & 3.0^* & \\ 0 & 0 & 0 & 0 & 0 & 3.0^* \end{array} \right] \end{array}$$

It is apparent that the model has a total of nine free parameters.

Complete Latent Variable Model

The model in Figure 2.8, shown on p. 34 and specified in the input on p. 36 has the following characteristics:

Dependent variables: $V1 = \eta_1$; $V2 = \eta_2$; $V3 = \eta_3$; $V4 = \eta_4$; $V5 = \eta_5$; $V6 = \eta_6$; $F1 = \eta_7$; $F2 = \eta_8$.

Independent variables: $F3 = \xi_1$; $E1 = \xi_2$; $E2 = \xi_3$; $E3 = \xi_4$; $E4 = \xi_5$; $E5 = \xi_6$; $E6 = \xi_7$; $D1 = \xi_8$; $D2 = \xi_9$.

Evidently, η is of order 8×1, ξ is 9×1, β is 8×8, γ is 8×9, and Φ is 9×9. Rather than writing out the complete β and γ matrices, only the nonzero elements of these matrices will be defined. These are obtained from the input and the indexing above. Consider row 1 of β and γ, corresponding to the first equation $V1 = F1 + E1$. This equation is

$$\eta_1 = 1 \cdot \eta_7 + 1 \cdot \xi_2.$$

Thus, β_{17}, which connects η_1 and η_7, is given by $\beta_{17} = 1$. Similarly, $\gamma_{12} = 1$ based on the connection of η_1 and ξ_2.

The remaining equations show

β_{27}	$= .833,$	γ_{23}	$= 1.0;$
β_{38}	$= 1.0,$	γ_{34}	$= 1.0;$
β_{48}	$= .833,$	γ_{45}	$= 1.0;$
γ_{51}	$= 1.0,$	γ_{56}	$= 1.0;$
γ_{61}	$= .5^*,$	γ_{67}	$= 1.0;$
γ_{71}	$= -.5^*,$	γ_{78}	$= 1.0;$
β_{87}	$= .5^*,$	γ_{81}	$= -5^*, \quad \gamma_{89} = 1.0.$

In this example, dependent variables are regressed on other dependent variables; the relevant coefficients are given in β. The diagonal elements of Φ contain the variances

$$\Phi_{11} = 6^*; \; \Phi_{22} = 3^*; \; \Phi_{33} = 3^*; \; \Phi_{44} = 3^*;$$
$$\Phi_{55} = 3^*; \; \Phi_{66} = 3^*; \; \Phi_{77} = 3^*; \; \Phi_{88} = 4^*; \; \Phi_{99} = 4^*.$$

The covariances E3,E1 and E4,E2 are given as follows: $\Phi_{42} = .2^*; \; \Phi_{53} = .2^*$. The matrices do not contain the information on equality constraints among parameters, which is stored elsewhere in EQS.

It will be apparent from this last example that the matrices β, γ, and Φ can be quite large, but that most of their elements are zero. EQS makes use of this fact in its storage and multiplication routines. Actually, the matrices themselves are not in general kept in EQS. Only the nonzero elements, and their locations and values, are stored. During matrix manipulations, sparse matrix procedures are used to multiply only the relevant nonzero numbers, and, as much as possible, complete matrices are used only when needed. The matrix manipulations that are required come from the covariance structure.

Covariance Structure

Some matrix algebra is needed to develop the covariance structure of the Bentler-Weeks model (thinking of the matrices as numbers will work quite well for the nontechnical reader). The basic structural equation (10.1) is first rewritten so as to yield the so-called reduced form:

$$(I - \beta)\eta = \gamma\xi$$

$$\eta = (I - \beta)^{-1}\gamma\xi.$$

On the necessary assumption of invertability of $(I - \beta)$, it is thus possible to express the dependent variables as a linear combination of the independent variables. As a consequence, any covariances involving dependent variables can be expressed in terms of the parameters of the model, which are the regression coefficient matrices β and γ, and the covariance matrix Φ of the independent variables. In particular, the covariances between dependent and independent variables are given in matrix form as

$$\mathcal{E}(\eta\xi') = \mathcal{E}(I - \beta)^{-1}\gamma\xi\xi' = (I - \beta)^{-1}\gamma\Phi, \tag{10.3}$$

where Φ is defined in (10.2). The covariances among dependent variables are then given by the matrix expression

$$\mathcal{E}(\eta\eta') = \mathcal{E}(I - \beta)^{-1}\gamma\xi\xi'\gamma'(I - \beta)^{-1'}$$
$$= (I - \beta)^{-1}\gamma\Phi\gamma'(I - \beta)^{-1'}. \tag{10.4}$$

Thus, along with Φ, the covariance matrix of the independent variables, the remaining covariance matrices have been specified in terms of the parameter matrices β, γ, Φ of the model.

It is apparent from the examples that the measured variables are a subset of the dependent and independent variables. Consequently, the covariance matrix of the observed variables is found among the elements of (10.2), (10.3), and (10.4). Symbolically, Bentler and Weeks (1980) use the selection matrices G_y and G_x to search out the measured dependent variables y from η, and the measured independent variables x from ξ. In the complete latent variable example above, the first six of the eight dependent variables are measured variables, so that y (6 × 1) $= G_y\eta$ simply selects these variables. G_y is a 6 × 8 partitioned matrix containing $(I,0)$, where I is a 6 × 6 identity matrix and 0 is a 6 × 2 null matrix. The elements of G_y are known 1's and 0's designed to do this selection; G_y does not contain unknown parameters. This example does not contain any independent V's; since x is null and $x = G_x\xi$, G_x is a 0 × 9 (nonexistent) vector. In the path analysis model, G_y is a 2 × 2 identity matrix, since each of the two η_i is a measured variable; G_x is a 2 × 4 matrix containing $(I,0)$, and $x = G_x\xi$ selects the two measured variables from the four independent variables. It follows immediately that the covariance matrices for the measured variables can be represented as

$$\Sigma_{yy} = G_y(I - \beta)^{-1}\gamma\Phi\gamma'(I - \beta)^{-1'}G_y'$$

$$\Sigma_{yx} = G_y(I - \beta)^{-1}\gamma\Phi G_x' \tag{10.5}$$

$$\Sigma_{xx} = G_x\Phi G_x',$$

since G_y and G_x simply represent a way of selecting the appropriate elements out of (10.4), (10.3), and (10.2), respectively. Notice that in a complete latent variable model, as in the example, there are no x variables, so that Σ_{yx} and Σ_{xx} are null and the entire structure is given by Σ_{yy}. In general, (10.5) can be written more compactly as

$$\Sigma = G(I - B)^{-1}\Gamma\Phi\Gamma'(I - B)^{-1'}G', \tag{10.6}$$

where G is a partitioned supermatrix containing rows $(G_y,0)$ and $(0,G_x)$, B is a partitioned supermatrix containing rows $(\beta,0)$ and $(0,0)$, and Γ is a partitioned matrix defined by $\Gamma' = (\gamma',I)$. It can be shown that (10.6) is the covariance matrix of the measured variables $z = (y',x')'$, with $z = G\nu$, $\nu = (\eta',\xi')'$, and where

$$\nu = B\nu + \Gamma\xi \tag{10.7}$$

is an alternative representation of (10.1).

Moment Structure

General linear statistical models can be concerned with more than only the covariance structure of the variables. The means and higher-order moments are also of interest.

It follows from (10.7) that $z = A\xi$, where $A = G(I - B)^{-1}\Gamma$. Then the mean of z is given by

$$\mathcal{E}(z) = \mu = \Sigma_{(1)} = A\mathcal{E}(\xi) = A\mu_\xi = A\Phi_1, \tag{10.8}$$

where Φ_1 is the mean of the independent variables ξ. The means μ of the observed variables are thus structured in terms of the parameter matrices β and γ used in the covariance structure, as well as the new parameter vector $\mu_\xi = \Phi_1$ representing the means of the independent variables. The structure (10.8) provides the mathematical basis for mean structures. As described in Chapter 8, structured means models are set up in practice so that ν in (10.7) contains a constant unit "variable" that is an independent variable having a mean of 1.0, zero variance, and zero covariances with other independent variables, with coefficients for regression on the constant yielding the intercepts of the dependent variables.

The higher product moments about the mean $\mathcal{E}(z - \mu) \otimes (z - \mu) \otimes \cdots$ are given by

$$\text{Vec}(\Sigma_{(2)}) = (A \otimes A)\text{Vec}(\Phi_2)$$
$$\text{Vec}(\Sigma_{(3)}) = (A \otimes A \otimes A)\text{Vec}(\Phi_3) \qquad (10.9)$$
$$\text{Vec}(\Sigma_{(4)}) = (A \otimes A \otimes A \otimes A)\text{Vec}(\Phi_4)$$

etc., where the subscript level indicates the order, $(A \otimes A)$ represents the right Kronecker product of matrices, and Vec is the operator that takes rows of a matrix and strings them into a single column. It can be shown that $\Sigma_{(2)}$ represents the covariance structure of the Bentler-Weeks model, given in (10.6) as Σ, while Φ_2 is the covariance matrix Φ. Thus the covariance structure (10.6) of Σ is the same whether or not the means of the observed variables are further decomposed into parameters, as in (10.8), and the assumption that $\mu_\xi = 0$, made in association with (10.2), is not a necessary assumption. However, the first-order moments $\Sigma_{(1)}$ and Φ_1 are not used in standard covariance structure analysis, while they are an important part of the analysis of mean and covariance structure models.

$\Sigma_{(3)}$ provides information on skewness of the measured variables based on skewness of the generating variables, and $\Sigma_{(4)}$ provides comparable information on kurtosis. In this extension of the Bentler-Weeks model (Bentler, 1983a), the moments of the measured variables are expressed in terms of the moments of the independent variables ξ. With arbitrarily distributed nonnormal data, Φ_3 and Φ_4 are new parameter matrices that need to be estimated. These matrices are currently ignored in EQS since the sample moments $S_{(3)}$ and $S_{(4)}$, corresponding to $\Sigma_{(3)}$ and $\Sigma_{(4)}$, are not analyzed structurally. Consequently, the arbitrary distribution estimators in EQS are not fully efficient, since they are based on covariance information alone. The structure given in (10.9) for $\Sigma_{(4)}$ has proven to be a key element in the analysis of models to determine whether normal theory statistics are liable to be robust to violation of the normality assumption. See Chapter 1.

FUNCTIONS, ESTIMATORS, AND TESTS

In covariance structure analysis, the statistical problem addressed by EQS is one of estimating the free parameters in β, γ, and Φ so that when these estimates are placed into $\hat{\beta}$, $\hat{\gamma}$, and $\hat{\Phi}$, the resulting covariance matrix $\hat{\Sigma}$ obtained from (10.5) − (10.6) closely reproduces the p × p sample covariance matrix S obtained from sample of N subjects. This estimation is done in an iterative fashion in the program, using the initial estimates provided by the user and improving the estimates iteratively using the Gauss-Newton algorithm defined in a later section to minimize

$$Q = (s - \sigma(\theta))'W(s - \sigma(\theta)) \qquad\qquad (10.10)$$

as noted in Chapter 1. In (10.10), s is the vector of $p^* = p(p + 1)/2$ elements obtained by stringing out the lower triangular elements of the unbiased sample covariance matrix S, σ is the corresponding vector obtained from Σ, and θ is the vector of free parameters of β, γ, and Φ. The notation $\sigma(\theta)$ simply is a reminder that Σ arises from β, γ, and Φ in accord with (10.6). If $s = \sigma(\theta)$, the model fits perfectly. In practice, even the optimal choice of $\hat{\theta}$ leading to a $\hat{\sigma} = \sigma(\hat{\theta})$ designed to make Q as small as possible will lead to a nonzero $\hat{Q} = Q(\hat{\theta})$. The minimum modified chi-square or generalized least squares (GLS) method of estimation that is used in EQS is based on defining W to be a matrix such that a constant times $\hat{Q}$ in large samples converges to a χ^2 variate, so that the adequacy of the model $\hat{\Sigma}$ can be evaluated probabilistically. The multiplier needed to make $\hat{Q}$ behave as an asymptotic χ^2 variate under optimal choice of W is some constant depending on sample size N, since as N $\rightarrow$ ∞, so does (N $-$ k) for some fixed k. In practice in covariance structure analysis in a single population, typically W is defined so that $n\hat{Q}$ is asymptotically χ^2, where n = (N $-$ 1). This convention usually accompanies use of S as the unbiased sample covariance matrix, and is the convention that will be followed in this section on covariance structure analysis. An alternative convention would be to use the biased sample covariance and replace n in the equations below with the sample size N. In either case, the definition of W depends on the distribution theory assumed for the observed variables, but, in general, elements of $V = W^{-1}$ are related to the variances and covariances of the empirical data points in (10.10), the s_{ij} and s_{kl} elements of S.

The statistical development of estimation under minimization of Q is provided by such authors as Browne (1982, 1984) and Shapiro (1983) for covariance structures, by Bentler, Lee, and Weng (1987) for multiple population covariance structure analysis under arbitrary distributions, and by Bentler and Dijkstra (1985), Shapiro (1986) and Satorra (1989). The results of the latter authors are sufficiently general to include structured means and multiple population models. As presented below, the following results are based on Bentler and Dijkstra, who provide the necessary regularity conditions, details, proofs, extensions, and applications. Assume that $s \xrightarrow{p} s_+$ and p(lim) $W = W_+$. It can be shown that if the q-vector $\hat{\theta}$ minimizes Q, $\hat{\theta} \xrightarrow{p} \theta_+$, the unique minimum point of $Q_+ = (s_+ - \sigma(\theta))'W_+ (s_+ - \sigma(\theta))$ under the $r \le q$ constraints $c(\theta_+) = 0$. Furthermore, let W be a random matrix and assume that

$$\sqrt{n} \begin{bmatrix} s - s_+ \\ \mathrm{Vec}(W - W_+) \end{bmatrix} \xrightarrow{\mathcal{L}} \mathcal{N} \left(\begin{bmatrix} 0 \\ 0 \end{bmatrix}, \begin{bmatrix} V_{ss} & V_{sw} \\ V_{ws} & V_{ww} \end{bmatrix} \right) ,$$

where $\xrightarrow{\mathcal{L}}$ refers to convergence in distribution (see e.g., White, 1984).

The notation is that any set of functions partially differentiated with respect to (w.r.t.) a vector is shown by a dot above the function e.g., $\dot{c}(\theta) = \partial c / \partial \theta'$. Derivatives without arguments will refer to derivatives w.r.t. θ, e.g., $\dot{c} = \dot{c}(\theta)$, and when evaluated at θ_+, will be written as c_+. The notation $[\cdot]_+$ indicates that the matrix in brackets has all random elements evaluated at their probability limits. Argument matrices are sometimes not used when the meaning is unambiguous, e.g., $\sigma = \sigma(\theta)$.

Suppose that

$$\sqrt{n}(s - \sigma(\theta_+)) \xrightarrow{\mathcal{L}} \mathcal{N}(\delta, V_{ss}) \qquad (10.11)$$

with $c(\theta_+) = 0$, that δ is a vector of appropriate order, and that $\hat{\lambda}$ is the Lagrangian multiplier associated with $c(\hat{\theta})$. Then

$$\sqrt{n} \begin{bmatrix} \hat{\theta} - \theta_+ \\ \hat{\lambda} \end{bmatrix} \xrightarrow{\mathcal{L}} \mathcal{N} \left(J_+^{-1} \begin{bmatrix} (\dot{\sigma}'W)_+\delta \\ 0 \end{bmatrix}, J_+^{-1} \begin{bmatrix} \dot{\sigma}'WV_{ss}W\dot{\sigma} & 0 \\ 0 & 0 \end{bmatrix}_+ J_+^{-1} \right), \qquad (10.12)$$

where

$$J_+ = \begin{bmatrix} \dot{\sigma}'W\dot{\sigma} & \dot{c}' \\ \dot{c} & 0 \end{bmatrix}_+ .$$

The covariance matrix of (10.12) can be written as

$$\begin{bmatrix} M\dot{\sigma}'WV_{ss}W\dot{\sigma}M & M\dot{\sigma}'WV_{ss}W\dot{\sigma}D \\ D'\dot{\sigma}'WV_{ss}W\dot{\sigma}M & D'\dot{\sigma}'WV_{ss}W\dot{\sigma}D \end{bmatrix}_+ , \qquad (10.13)$$

with $M = \Delta - \Delta\dot{c}'(\dot{c}\Delta\dot{c}')^{-1}\dot{c}\Delta$ and $D = \Delta\dot{c}'(\dot{c}\Delta\dot{c}')^{-1}$. The asymptotic bias of $\hat{\theta}$ is given by

$$\sqrt{n}^{-1}[(\Delta - \Delta\dot{c}'(\dot{c}\Delta\dot{c}')^{-1}\dot{c}\Delta)\dot{\sigma}'W\delta]_+ ,$$

where $\Delta \equiv (\dot{\sigma}'W\dot{\sigma})^{-1}$. When $\delta = 0$, so that the model is correct, $\hat{\theta}$ is asymptotically unbiased. If $s_+ = \sigma(\theta_+)$ but $c(\theta_+) = \delta^*(\sqrt{n}^{-1})$, the result remains valid except that the expressions for the bias change. For $\hat{\theta}$ one now gets $\sqrt{n}^{-1}D_+\delta^*$. If no constraints are imposed, the formulae simplify.

Under the model, the covariance matrix (10.13) is correct asymptotically even if the weight matrix W chosen in the function (10.10) is not optimal. In a typical application, W may be chosen to be correctly specified for a normal distribution, but, in fact, the variables may be nonnormal. Then (10.13) gives the correct standard errors. When evaluated at $\hat{\theta}$ with consistent estimates substituting the population quantities in (10.13), n^{-1} times the matrix (10.13) is called the *robust* covariance matrix of the estimator in EQS; robust standard errors are given by the square root of the diagonal elements.

In most applications one hopes that the model and its constraints are correct. Let $s_+ = \sigma(\theta_+)$ with $c(\theta_+) = 0$. The behavior of $\hat{\theta}$ obviously depends on W. A basic result can be deduced from Q in (10.10). Q can be rewritten as $[W^{1/2}(s - \sigma(\theta))]'[W^{1/2}(s - \sigma(\theta))]$ so that Q is just the sum of squares of the bracketed term. Since χ^2 variates are generated from sums of squares of independent normal variates, the optimal W should be of a form that allows Q to be so interpreted. Thus it is easy to see that W should tend in probability to V_{ss}^{-1}. Under such an optimal choice,

$$\sqrt{n}(\hat{\theta} - \theta_+) \xrightarrow{\mathcal{L}} \mathcal{N}(0, [\Delta_s - \Delta_s\dot{c}'(\dot{c}\Delta_s\dot{c}')^{-1}\dot{c}\Delta_s]_+) \qquad (10.14)$$

where

$$\Delta_s = (\dot{\sigma}' V_{ss}^{-1} \dot{\sigma})^{-1}. \tag{10.15}$$

The imposition of constraints leads to a singular covariance matrix, as is well known. Clearly, incorporation of correct constraints leads to a gain in efficiency, since the covariance matrix in (10.14) simplifies to (10.15) when no constraints are imposed.

Under each of the three distribution theories (normal, elliptical, arbitrary) EQS uses an estimator V of V_{ss} such that, assuming a correct model with appropriate restrictions, and the appropriate distributional assumption, the asymptotic covariance matrix of the estimator is given by (10.14). The estimator is asymptotically efficient. As noted earlier, in principle under arbitrary distributions, estimators that can make use of higher-order sample information would have still smaller variance, but these are not available in EQS or any similar program at this time.

The distribution of $n\hat{Q}$, where $\hat{Q} = Q(\hat{\theta})$ at the minimum of (10.10) is, in general, a mixture of 1-df χ^2 variates (Bentler & Dijkstra, 1985; Satorra & Bentler, 1986, 1988, 1990, 1994). See (10.46) below. This general result specializes down to the goodness-of-fit χ^2 statistic used in practice. Under an appropriate choice of W, and under the hypothesis $\sigma = \sigma(\theta)$ and the constraints $c(\theta) = 0$, in large samples

$$n\hat{Q} \xrightarrow{\mathcal{L}} \chi^2_{(p*-q+r)}, \tag{10.16}$$

i.e., $n\hat{Q}$ is distributed as a central χ^2 variate with $(p* - q + r)$ df. Under small model misspecifications, the distribution of (10.16) is noncentral rather than central χ^2 (see Chapter 5, or Satorra, 1989). This fact is used to create the comparative fit index printed out in EQS, which assesses model noncentrality relative to the noncentrality of the model of uncorrelated variables.

The typical standard errors produced in EQS are based on the assumption of a correct model and distribution. Specifically, in GLS, EGLS, ML, and ERLS estimation, $\hat{\theta}$-based sample estimates of $[\cdot]_+/n$ in (10.14) are used to provide an empirical estimate of the variability of $\hat{\theta}$. In LS and ELS estimation, standard errors are based on (10.13) with V_{ss} replaced by estimators of the corresponding normal theory or elliptical matrix (see 10.41 and (10.26) below). As a consequence, the standard errors are not, in general, robust to violation of the distributional assumption. Formula (10.13), the *robust* covariance matrix, should be used when the distributional assumption is suspect.

Linearized Generalized Least Squares

Linearization is currently used in EQS so as to provide inexpensive elliptical theory and arbitrary distribution theory estimators. These estimators depend upon having an appropriate initial estimator. Assume that there exists a random vector θ_1, not necessarily asymptotically normal, having the property that $\theta_1 = \theta_+ + O_p(\sqrt{n}^{-1})$. In EQS, any of the normal and elliptical theory estimators meet this condition.

The structural model as well as the constraint functions are linearized. The vector $\sigma(\theta)$ is replaced by $\sigma(\theta_1) + \dot{\sigma}(\theta_1)(\theta - \theta_1)$, which will be written as $\sigma_1 + \dot{\sigma}_1(\theta - \theta_1)$. Similarly, $c(\theta)$ is replaced by $c(\theta_1) + \dot{c}(\theta_1)(\theta - \theta_1)$, which will be written as $c_1 + \dot{c}_1(\theta - \theta_1)$. The linearized generalized least squares (LGLS) function is defined as

$$Q_L = (s - (\sigma_1 + \dot{\sigma}_1(\theta - \theta_1)))'W(s - (\sigma_1 + \dot{\sigma}_1(\theta - \theta_1))). \tag{10.17}$$

This function is minimized with respect to θ, subject to the side conditions $c_1 + \dot{c}_1(\theta - \theta_1) = 0$. An explicit solution for the optimal estimator $\bar{\theta}$ is given by

$$\bar{\theta} = \theta_1 + [\Delta - \Delta\dot{c}'(\dot{c}\Delta\dot{c}')^{-1}\dot{c}\Delta]_1\dot{\sigma}'_1 W(s - \sigma_1)$$
$$- \Delta_1\dot{c}'_1(\dot{c}\Delta\dot{c}')_1^{-1}c_1, \tag{10.18}$$

where $\Delta_1 = (\dot{\sigma}'_1 W\dot{\sigma}_1)^{-1}$. It will be noted that the linearized estimator $\bar{\theta}$ can be calculated by the explicit matrix expression (10.18) based on information that is available from the initial estimators.

Under an optimal choice of W, as noted above, Bentler and Dijkstra show that the LGLS estimators are asymptotically equivalent to GLS estimators and that they are asymptotically efficient. From the asymptotic equivalence, it follows that if plim $W = V_{ss}^{-1}$,

$$\sqrt{n}(\bar{\theta} - \theta_+) \xrightarrow{\mathcal{L}} \mathcal{N}(0,[\Delta - \Delta\dot{c}'(\dot{c}\Delta\dot{c}')^{-1}\dot{c}\Delta]_+) \tag{10.19}$$

where $\Delta = (\dot{\sigma}'V_{ss}^{-1}\dot{\sigma})^{-1}$. It is apparent that (10.19) is of the form (10.14), but now the covariance matrix of $\bar{\theta}$ is consistently estimated at $[\cdot]_1/n$. Furthermore, with the use of an optimal weight matrix, under the correct model and restrictions,

$$n\hat{Q}_L = n(s - \sigma(\bar{\theta}))'W(s - \sigma(\bar{\theta})) \xrightarrow{\mathcal{L}} \chi^2_{(p*-q+r)}. \tag{10.20}$$

Thus (10.16) and (10.20) have the same distributions in large samples.

EQS uses linearization for elliptical and arbitrary distribution estimators. The initial estimate θ_1 for elliptical theory can be based on any of the normal theory LS, GLS, or ML estimates, and W is based on an appropriate elliptical estimator. Under arbitrary distribution theory, the initial estimate θ_1 can be any of the normal theory estimates or the comparable elliptical ELS, EGLS, or ERLS estimates, and the weight matrix is optimal for arbitrarily distributed variables. The linearized estimators LELS, LEGLS, LERLS and LAGLS are produced by default, but the default can be overridden to produce fully iterated estimators if desired. Tanaka and Bentler (1984) and Huba and Bentler (1983) found the LAGLS estimator to provide results comparable to the AGLS estimator, but additional empirical performance of the estimators and tests would be desirable.

Arbitrary Distribution Theory

Implementation of AGLS estimation with a sample data vector s containing second-moment covariance information requires the use of fourth-moment information to optimally estimate the weight matrix W in the functions Q and Q_L. The population elements of the optimal V_{ss} are given by

$$[V_{ss}]_{ij,kl} = \sigma_{ijkl} - \sigma_{ij}\sigma_{kl}, \tag{10.21}$$

which can be consistently estimated by the matrix V having elements

$$v_{ij,kl} = s_{ijkl} \; - \; s_{ij}s_{kl},$$

(10.22)

where s_{ij} and s_{kl} are biased sample covariances, and where

$$s_{ijkl} = N^{-1}\Sigma_1^N(z_{it} \; - \; \overline{z}_i)(z_{jt} \; - \; \overline{z}_j)(z_{kt} \; - \; \overline{z}_k)(z_{lt} \; - \; \overline{z}_l)$$

(10.23)

is a fourth-order multivariate product moment of variables z_i about their means $\overline{z}_i$. In covariance structure analysis, EQS uses (10.22) to compute V to generate $W = V^{-1}$, in accord with the results of Browne (1982, 1984), Chamberlain (1982), Dijkstra (1981), Hsu (1949), and others. Browne also provides a formula for an unbiased estimator of V_{ss} that is not currently used in EQS.

In order to discourage the use of AGLS estimation in small samples, EQS rejects this method of estimation when N < p*. When N $\geq$ p*, V will almost surely be invertible, as is necessary to obtain W. Although Bentler and Dijkstra have shown that V may be invertible in samples with approximately symmetric distribution with small kurtosis for sample sizes as low as p + 1, EQS does not currently allow for an evaluation of this possibility.

In accord with the theory of Bentler (1983a), the elements σ_{ijkl} of $\Sigma_{(4)}$ are a function of the model parameters, as shown in (10.9). ARLS estimation thus considers $W = W(\theta)$ and substitutes model-based estimates of V_{ss} in (10.21) in the calculation of the inverse weight matrix. However, ARLS estimation is not yet implemented in EQS. Tanaka (1984) and Mooijaart and Bentler (1985) have argued that model-based estimation of W should lead to greater stability in the solution and less biased estimation of parameters.

Elliptical Distribution Theory

When the multivariate distribution of the variables z has a mean vector μ and a covariance matrix Σ, and can be described by a density of the form

$$k_1 \det(\Sigma)^{-1/2}g(k_2(z \; - \; \mu)'\Sigma^{-1}(z \; - \; \mu))$$

where k_1 and k_2 are constants and g is a nonnegative function, contours of constant probability are ellipsoids and the variables have a common kurtosis parameter

$$\kappa = \sigma_{iiii}/3\sigma_{ii}^2 \; - \; 1.$$

(10.24)

This parameter describes the heaviness or lightness of the tails of the distribution relative to those of the multinormal distribution. More generally (Bentler, 1983a) the expected values of the fourth order multivariate product moments are related to κ by

$$\sigma_{ijkl} = (\kappa + 1)(\sigma_{ij}\sigma_{kl} + \sigma_{ik}\sigma_{jl} + \sigma_{il}\sigma_{jk}).$$

(10.25)

The multivariate normal distribution is a special case of the multivariate elliptical class of distributions, having $\kappa = 0$. The parameter κ is one of a series that characterizes elliptical distributions (Berkane & Bentler, 1986, 1987a).

As shown by Browne (1984) and Bentler (1983a) (see also Tyler, 1982, 1983), and as can be developed by substituting (10.25) in (10.21), in covariance structure analysis the optimal inverse weight matrix V_{ss} can be simplified to

$$V_{ss} = K_p'[2(\kappa + 1)(\Sigma \otimes \Sigma) + \kappa \text{Vec}(\Sigma)\text{Vec}(\Sigma)']K_p, \qquad (10.26)$$

where K_p' reduces the $p^2 \times p^2$ matrix in brackets to appropriate p^* order, i.e., the effects of redundancy caused by symmetry in S are eliminated (see Browne, 1974). As a consequence, Q in (10.10) takes on the form

$$Q_E = 2^{-1}(\kappa + 1)^{-1}\text{tr}[(S - \Sigma)W_2]^2 - \delta[\text{tr}(S - \Sigma)W_2]^2, \qquad (10.27)$$

where W_2 is any consistent estimator of Σ^{-1} and $\delta = \kappa/[4(\kappa + 1)^2 + 2p\kappa(\kappa + 1)]$ (Browne, 1984; Bentler, 1983a). Under elliptical theory, with $W_2 = \Sigma^{-1}$, $Q \equiv Q_E$, but if Q_E is minimized when the distribution is not elliptical or if W_2 is not a consistent estimator of Σ^{-1}, minimizing Q_E instead of Q would yield estimators that are not asymptotically efficient and $n\hat{Q}_E$ based on $\hat{\Sigma} = \Sigma(\hat{\theta})$ at the minimum of (10.27) would not necessarily be interpretable as an asymptotic χ^2 variate. As shown by Bentler and Dijkstra (1985) the unconstrained estimator that results from minimizing (10.27) has an asymptotically normal distribution

$$\sqrt{n}(\hat{\theta} - \theta) \xrightarrow{\mathcal{L}} \mathcal{N}(0,[\Delta\dot{\sigma}'\bar{W}\text{Cov}(s,s')\bar{W}\dot{\sigma}\Delta]_+), \qquad (10.28)$$

where $\bar{W} = K_p^-[(\kappa + 1)^{-1}(W_2 \otimes W_2) - 2\delta\text{Vec}(W_2)\text{Vec}(W_2)']K_p^{-'}$, $\dot{\sigma}$ was defined previously, and $\Delta = [\dot{\sigma}'\bar{W}\dot{\sigma}]_+^{-1}$. If W_2 is optimally estimated so that $\bar{W}_+ = V_{ss}^{-1}$ and $\text{Cov}(s,s')$ is given by (10.26), then the covariance matrix in (10.28) is equivalent to (10.15). It is also asymptotically efficient, and the estimated covariance matrix of the unconstrained estimator is more simply given by $2n^{-1}$ times the inverse of the matrix having elements

$$(\kappa + 1)^{-1}\text{tr}W_2\dot{\Sigma}_iW_2\dot{\Sigma}_j - 2\delta\text{tr}(W_2\dot{\Sigma}_i)\text{tr}(W_2\dot{\Sigma}_j), \qquad (10.29)$$

as shown by Browne (1982, 1984) and Bentler (1983a). Here $\dot{\Sigma}_i$ is the symmetric matrix $\partial\Sigma/\partial\theta_i$. The advantage of using (10.29) over (10.15) and their appropriately constrained counterparts (see 10.14), as well as (10.27) instead of (10.10) for the function, is that under correct specifications small $p \times p$ weight matrices W_2 are needed rather than the larger $p^* \times p^*$ matrices W.

EQS defines three special cases of Q_E in (10.27) with the associated derivatives, expected Hessian matrices, and computations:

$W_2 = I$ gives elliptical least squares (ELS)
$W_2 = S^{-1}$ (fixed) gives elliptical generalized least squares (EGLS)
$W_2 = \hat{\Sigma}^{-1}$ (iteratively updated) gives elliptical reweighted least squares (ERLS).

EGLS and ERLS yield χ^2 statistics via $n\hat{Q}_E$ and standard errors via (10.29). ELS yields a χ^2 statistic via (10.45), see below, and standard errors based on an estimator of (10.13) with V_{ss} estimated by (10.26) using W_2 based on ERLS and the estimate $\hat{\kappa}$ specified in the analysis.

Browne (1982, 1984) and Tyler (1983) have concentrated on models that are invariant with respect to a constant scaling. In such models functions $f = f(\Sigma)$ have the property that for all $\alpha > 0$, $f(\Sigma) = f(\alpha\Sigma)$ (Tyler, 1983), or, for any θ there exists a $\theta*$ such that $\Sigma(\theta*) = \alpha\Sigma(\theta)$ (Browne, 1982, 1984). In these models the normal theory maximum likelihood estimator is asymptotically efficient, the second term in (10.27) drops out at $\hat{Q}_E$, and the ML χ^2 based on (10.41) below can be corrected by the multiplier $(\kappa + 1)^{-1}$. EQS does not print out this corrected ML chi-square statistic since its appropriate use depends on verifying the scale-invariance of the model (the correction can be easily hand-computed). When the model does possess this property, ERLS and LERLS based on an initial normal ML solution automatically yield Browne's estimator, covariance matrix, and the quadratic form test statistic. However, EGLS and ERLS and their linearized counterparts starting from any of the normal theory estimators yield asymptotically efficient statistics regardless of whether scale invariance holds.

The implementation of elliptical theory requires an estimate of κ. As a default when raw data are available, EQS uses the Mardia-based coefficient

$$\hat{\kappa}_1 = g_{2,p}/p(p + 2) \tag{10.30}$$

recommended by Browne (1982, 1984), Steiger and Browne (1984), and Shapiro and Browne (1987), where

$$g_{2,p} = N^{-1}\Sigma_1^N[(z_t - \bar{z})'S^{-1}(z_t - \bar{z})]^2 - p(p + 2) \tag{10.31}$$

is the deviation from expectation variant of Mardia's (1970, 1974) multivariate kurtosis coefficient. Vectors z_t and $\bar{z}$ are individual case score and mean vectors. The normalized estimate

$$g_{2,p}/(8p(p + 2)/N)^{1/2} \tag{10.32}$$

behaves, in very large samples, like a unit normal variate. It can be used to test the null hypothesis of multinormality. The hypothesis would be rejected for both large and small values of (10.32).

EQS also computes a number of other elliptical kurtosis estimators and prints them out. The user can choose one of these coefficients or any other coefficient instead of (10.30) by specifying it in the input. Univariate g_2 kurtosis estimates are computed for the ith variable as

$$g_{2(i)} = N\Sigma_1^N(z_{it} - \bar{z}_i)^4/[\Sigma_1^N(z_{it} - \bar{z}_i)^2]^2 - 3. \tag{10.33}$$

Since $3^{-1}g_{2(i)}$ for each i should estimate (10.24), a reasonable estimate of κ is given by the mean of the scaled univariate kurtosis estimates

$$\hat{\kappa}_2 = (3p)^{-1}\Sigma_1^p g_{2(i)}. \tag{10.34}$$

Note that $g_{2(i)}$ values should be homogeneous if the variables are truly elliptically distributed. Bentler and Berkane (1985; Berkane & Bentler, 1987b) describe a test for homogeneity of kurtoses, but it is not yet implemented in EQS.

It is implicit in the work of Tyler (1982, 1983) that $\kappa \geq -2/(p + 2)$. Bentler and Berkane (1986) have proven that the inequality must be strict, that is, $\kappa > -2(p + 2)$. The estimates $\hat{\kappa}_1$ and $\hat{\kappa}_2$ do not necessarily respect this bound. If $\hat{\kappa}_1$ is inadmissible, EQS substitutes $\hat{\kappa}_2$. If $\hat{\kappa}_2$ is inadmissible, EQS uses the adjusted mean scaled univariate kurtosis estimate

$$\hat{\kappa}_3 = (3p)^{-1}\Sigma_1^p g_{2(i)}^*, \tag{10.35}$$

where $g_{2(i)}^* = g_{2(i)}$ if $g_{2(i)}/3 > -2/(p + 2)$ and $g_{2(i)}^* = -6/(p + 2)$ otherwise. Thus, (10.35) is the mean of univariate coefficients whose inadmissible values have been adjusted to meet the admissibility constraint.

It is apparent that (10.25) represents another key relation under elliptical theory. The sample counterpart to (10.25) is given by the approximation

$$s_{ijkl} \simeq (\kappa + 1)(s_{ij}s_{kl} + s_{ik}s_{jl} + s_{il}s_{jk}). \tag{10.36}$$

Simple manipulation of (10.36) shows that for every multivariate product moment,

$$\hat{\kappa}_{ijkl} = s_{ijkl}/(s_{ij}s_{kl} + s_{ik}s_{jl} + s_{il}s_{jk}) - 1 \tag{10.37}$$

provides an estimate of κ. When AGLS estimation is requested, EQS computes the mean of the set of estimates (10.37) and prints it out as the multivariate mean kappa. Based on the $a = p(p + 1)(p + 2)(p + 3)/24$ different terms (10.37), this is given as

$$\hat{\kappa}_4 = \Sigma_1^a \hat{\kappa}_{ijkl}/a. \tag{10.38}$$

Finally, if s_4 is the vector of left-side elements of (10.36) and s_2 is the vector of the parenthesized far right side, the multivariate least squares kappa suggested by Bentler (1983a) is printed out as

$$\hat{\kappa}_5 = s_2's_4/s_2's_2 - 1. \tag{10.39}$$

The relative merit of alternative estimators of κ has not yet been established. In nonelliptical populations these estimators do not converge on the same value. EQS uses the Mardia-based estimator as a default because of its ease of computation, its potential role in the identification of outliers as discussed subsequently, and its asymptotic expectation and variance. Bentler and Berkane (1985) proved that asymptotically, under elliptical distributions,

$$E(\hat{\kappa}_1) = \kappa. \tag{10.40}$$

They also did two Monte Carlo studies of elliptical populations and found that $\hat{\kappa}_1$ tended to have the smallest variance of the estimators considered. A similar result with nonelliptical populations was obtained by Harlow (1985). Shapiro and Browne (1987) recommend $\hat{\kappa}_1$. Use of $\hat{\kappa}_4$ is generally not recommended because of a tendency for large outlying values to occur, no doubt as a result of the division in (10.37). While robustified versions of (10.38) are being explored, including those that pull in inadmissible values or trim (10.37), empirical results show $\hat{\kappa}_4$ to have unacceptably large variance. All of the estimators appear to be downward biased in small to intermediate-sized samples (Bentler & Berkane, 1985; Harlow, 1985).

The user should be aware that the application of elliptical distributions to structural modeling is based on theoretical considerations. There is as yet little experience that can be used to provide guidance on how to avoid breakdowns in the method, e.g., misleading test statistics. It may be proposed that potential failures of elliptical estimation and testing would be associated with poor estimation of κ and, based on the work of Tyler (1983), poor estimation of the sample covariance matrix. Since from one point of view elliptical theory represents a correction to normal theory to incorporate kurtosis, it may be that elliptical methods can be off the mark when normal theory methods work well (see e.g. Harlow, 1985). Satorra and Bentler (1988a, 1988b) found that estimation of κ by $\hat{\kappa}_1$ can yield results that are not robust to violation of the assumption of elliptical data, i.e., use of elliptical theory can be surprisingly misleading. They present another estimator of κ that avoids this serious problem. Their estimator is automatically implemented when the Satorra-Bentler scaled χ^2 statistic, see (10.49) below, is implemented.

Multivariate Normal Distribution Theory

EQS automatically generates estimates and test statistics for structural models based on multinormal theory whenever elliptical estimates are requested. As a consequence, both types of estimates can be compared. EQS generates only multinormal estimates when these alone are requested. The computations are a special case of elliptical computations, since multinormal theory formulas are generated when $\kappa = 0$ above.

It follows from (10.26) that the optimal GLS inverse weight matrix is

$$V_{ss} = 2K'_p(\Sigma \otimes \Sigma)K_p. \tag{10.41}$$

As a consequence, Q in (10.10) takes on the form

$$Q_N = 2^{-1}\text{tr}[(S - \Sigma)W_2]^2, \tag{10.42}$$

as will be obvious from (10.27). This is the GLS function studied by Browne (1974). If the assumption of multivariate normality is correct, estimation by minimizing Q_N rather than Q will have no drawbacks, only virtues. In particular, under the correct choice of an optimal weight matrix W_2 that is a consistent estimator of Σ^{-1}, $n\hat{Q}_N$ evaluated at the minimum of (10.42) under $\hat{\Sigma} = \Sigma(\hat{\theta})$ is an asymptotic χ^2 variate, and the covariance matrix of the estimator obtained via the relevant estimate of (10.29) with $\kappa = 0$ yields the minimum variance Cramér-Rao bound. As before, EQS defines three special cases of Q_N that can be optimized iteratively:

$W_2 = I$ gives normal theory least squares (LS)
$W_2 = S^{-1}$ gives normal theory generalized least squares (GLS)
$W_2 = \hat{\Sigma}^{-1}$ gives normal theory reweighted least squares (RLS) (= ML).

With the LS method, EQS uses (10.44), see below, as the χ^2 statistic, and estimators of (10.13) with V_{ss} estimated via (10.41) using W_2 based on ML, to compute standard error estimates. The LS estimates will typically not be efficient. The GLS and RLS methods use an estimate of the optimal weight matrix and thus yield asymptotically efficient estimates as well as the relevant χ^2 statistics. Furthermore, Lee and Jennrich (1979) showed that RLS estimation in which the weight matrix is iteratively updated in accord with the current model $\Sigma(\hat{\theta})$ leads to normal theory maximum likelihood estimates (ML). Thus, the estimates that result when using the RLS method are simultaneously RLS and ML estimates. As a consequence, an evaluation of the goodness-of-fit of a model can be based on either the RLS χ^2 or the likelihood ratio χ^2.

Since most users of EQS will desire to see the ML function rather than the RLS function, EQS prints out the values of the ML function

$$F = \ln \det(\Sigma) + \mathrm{tr}S\Sigma^{-1} - \ln \det(S) - p \qquad (10.43)$$

during the iterations. The ML χ^2 statistic is given by $n\hat{F}$, where $\hat{F} = F(\hat{\theta})$ at the minimum of (10.43). EQS gives the probability value associated with this statistic. It also prints the RLS χ^2 obtained as $n\hat{Q}_N$. Since the two chi-square statistics are asymptotically equivalent, in large samples model acceptance or rejection based on these statistics will usually agree, as was found empirically by Harlow (1985). In small samples and some borderline model fits, they may on occasion disagree by more than a trivial amount. Results of Satorra and Saris (1985) or Matsueda and Bielby (1986) can be used to estimate the power of these statistics.

Chi-square Tests for LS and ELS

The tests (10.16) and (10.20) for model adequacy are not appropriate when a misspecified weight matrix W is used, e.g., when $W = I$ but $V_{ss} \neq I$. In least-squares estimation with elliptical or normal theory, $n\hat{Q}_E$ and $n\hat{Q}_N$ in the ELS and LS methods do not have χ^2 distributions even when the model is correct. Browne (1982, 1984) developed a test based on residuals that was further studied and extended by Satorra and Bentler (1988a,b). This test in its general form is very similar to the linearized test statistic in Bentler (1983b), holding for any distribution of the variables. A variant of the test is used in EQS to reduce the computational burden and the need for very large sample sizes. In this variant, the distribution of the measured variables is assumed to be known, specifically, as normal under LS estimation, and elliptical under ELS estimation.

Let $\hat{\theta}$ be the LS estimator, obtained by minimizing Q_N under the model; $\hat{F}_{ML}$ be F in (10.43) evaluated at $\hat{\theta}$; and $\hat{g}_{ML} = \partial F/\partial \theta$ be the gradient and $\hat{H}_{ML}$ be the covariance matrix in (10.14), based on (10.41), all evaluated at $\hat{\theta}$. Then

$$T_{LS} = n(\hat{F}_{ML} - \hat{g}'_{ML}\hat{H}^-_{ML}\hat{g}_{ML}) \qquad (10.44)$$

is the statistic computed for the LS solution. Similarly, if $\hat{\theta}$ is the ELS estimator obtained by minimizing Q_E; $\hat{Q}_{ERLS}$ is (10.27) evaluated at $\hat{\theta}$ with $\hat{\kappa}$ and $W_2 = \hat{\Sigma}^{-1}$; $\hat{g}_{ERLS} = \partial Q_E/\partial \theta$ is the gradient and $\hat{H}^-_{ERLS}$ is the covariance matrix in (10.14), based on (10.26), all evaluated at $\hat{\theta}$ with the chosen estimate $\hat{\kappa}$; then

$$T_{ELS} = n(\hat{Q}_{ERLS} - \hat{g}'_{ERLS}\hat{H}^-_{ERLS}\hat{g}_{ERLS}) \qquad (10.45)$$

is the statistic computed for the ELS solution. The goodness-of-fit test statistics (10.44) and (10.45) are evaluated using the χ^2 distribution with $(p^* - q + r)$ df.

Satorra-Bentler Scaled Chi-square Test

In most estimation methods except the AGLS method, an assumption underlying the goodness-of-fit χ^2 test is that the variables have some particular multivariate distribution, in

EQS, elliptical or normal. If this assumption is false, the test statistic T that is computed, e.g., (10.16) based on some distributional assumption, may not have the expected χ^2 distribution. Hence, it may be desirable to use another test statistic that may behave better under distributional misspecification. The most obvious alternative is the AGLS statistic or its linearized counterpart, but in large models these may be difficult or impossible to compute, and in smaller samples there may be a question as to whether the AGLS estimator, standard errors, or test statistics behave as expected (e.g., Harlow, 1985; Hu, Bentler, & Kano, 1992; Muthén & Kaplan, 1992; Tanaka, 1984).

Satorra and Bentler (1988, 1994) developed modifications of the standard goodness-of-fit test T to yield distributional behavior that should more closely approximate χ^2. One of these, the scaled test statistic, is available in EQS. The concept behind the scaled statistic is very old, going back to Bartlett (1937). The idea is to scale the given test statistic with a simple multiplier to yield a new statistic whose mean is closer to that of the reference χ^2 distribution. In particular, Satorra and Bentler (1986) note that the general distribution of T is in fact not χ^2, but rather

$$T \xrightarrow{\mathcal{L}} \Sigma_1^{df} \alpha_i T_i, \tag{10.46}$$

where α_i is one of the df $= (p^* - q + r)$ nonnull eigenvalues of the matrix UV_{ss}, T_i is one of the df independent $1 - df \chi^2$ variates, and

$$U = W - W\dot{\sigma}M\dot{\sigma}'W \tag{10.47}$$

is the residual weight matrix under the model, the constraints, and the weight matrix W used in the estimation method. In (10.47), $\dot{\sigma}$ and M are the matrices defined in association with (10.13). The mean of the asymptotic distribution of T is given by trace(UV_{ss}). Now, defining the estimate

$$k = \text{trace}(\hat{U}\hat{V}_{ss})/df, \tag{10.48}$$

where $\hat{U}$ is a consistent estimator of (10.47) based on the estimate $\hat{\theta}$, and $\hat{V}_{ss}$ is based on (10.22), the scaled test statistic is given by

$$\overline{T} = T/k. \tag{10.49}$$

The Satorra-Bentler statistic (10.49) is referred to a χ^2 distribution with df degrees of freedom. It seems to be the best-performing test statistic at this time (Hu et al., 1992).

When all the eigenvalues α_i are equal to one, T is in fact χ^2 distributed and the correction (10.48) has no effect asymptotically; thus, the scaled statistic (10.49) will behave appropriately. When the variables are elliptically distributed, the α_i are all equal to a constant, and (10.48) can be used to provide an estimate of κ. Specifically, (10.49) will behave appropriately when the variables are elliptical. When the α_i have a high dispersion, the scaled statistic $\overline{T}$ will be only approximately χ^2 distributed. Satorra and Bentler provide a more accurate adjustment to the statistic T to cover this circumstance, but this adjustment is not currently available in EQS.

Lagrange Multiplier (LM) Test

When minimizing Q in (10.10) subject to the constraints $c(\theta) = 0$, a Lagrangian Multiplier λ_i corresponding to each of the r constraints $c_i(\theta) = 0$ is created. The vector λ of these constraints is defined by the equation

$$g + \dot{c}'\lambda = 0, \tag{10.50}$$

where g is $\partial Q/\partial\theta = -\dot{\sigma}'W(s - \sigma(\theta))$ and the other terms have already been defined. A similar expression arises when minimizing other functions subject to constraints. Given an estimator $\hat{\theta}$ that minimizes Q and meets the constraint, the sample vector $\hat{\lambda}$ must meet (10.50), evaluated at $\hat{\theta}$. An explicit expression for $\hat{\lambda}$ is

$$\hat{\lambda} = (\dot{c}\Delta\dot{c}')^{-1}\dot{c}\Delta\dot{\sigma}'W(s - \sigma(\hat{\theta})), \tag{10.51}$$

all evaluated at $\hat{\theta}$. The asymptotic distribution of $\hat{\lambda}$ was given in (10.12) – (10.13). Using the usual definition of a χ^2 variate in terms of quadratic forms, it follows that

$$LM = n\hat{\lambda}'(D'\dot{\sigma}'WV_{ss}W\dot{\sigma}D)^{-1}\hat{\lambda} \overset{\mathcal{L}}{\rightarrow} \chi^2_{(r)}. \tag{10.52}$$

In practice, the matrix in parentheses is evaluated at $\hat{\theta}$. This test statistic, which follows directly from Bentler and Dijkstra (1985), is the Lagrange Multiplier or LM test that evaluates the statistical necessity of the r constraints. Satorra (1989) calls it the generalized score (or LM) test. It is not the classical test statistic discussed, say, by Rao (1948) and Aitchison and Silvey (1958), and introduced into structural modeling by Lee and Bentler (1980), because it can be applied under misspecification of the distribution of the variables, i.e., even when W is not the optimal weight matrix for the distribution involved. For example, it can be applied under LS estimation with $W = I$ when the distribution of the variables is normal and V_{ss} is given by (10.41). When W is a consistent estimator of V_{ss}^{-1}, in particular, when the correct distribution of variables is specified, the covariance matrix of $\hat{\lambda}$ simplifies, and (10.52) simplifies to

$$LM = n\hat{\lambda}'(\dot{c}\Delta\dot{c}')\hat{\lambda}, \tag{10.53}$$

where, in practice, $(\dot{c}\Delta\dot{c}')$ is evaluated at $\hat{\theta}$. This is the form of the LM test that is currently available in EQS. This statistic, developed by Lee and Bentler (1980) for covariance structure analysis under normality assumptions, is available in EQS for all distributional assumptions, including arbitrary distributions and linearized estimation, as well as for evaluating cross-group equality constraints in multisample models. Appropriate substitution of the relevant estimator $\hat{\theta}$ and the associated Lagrange Multiplier $\hat{\lambda}$ into the equations above produces the correct statistic, and more details need not be given here. See, e.g., Bentler and Dijkstra (1985, Eq. 2.1.8) for the linearized LM test.

Bentler and Chou (1986; Bentler, 1986a) developed a procedure to partition the multivariate LM test into a sequence of 1-df hierarchical and forward stepwise tests, to help separate the statistically important constraints from the statistically unnecessary constraints, as well as a procedure for conducting restricted tests for subsets of constraints, given that other constraints are accepted. This methodology is described in Chapter 6. See (10.12) and Satorra (1989) for explicit expressions for the noncentrality parameters involved when the null hypothesis $c(\theta) = 0$ is minimally false. Satorra's discussion of LM tests in relation to other test procedures for structural modeling is highly recommended reading, though technical in nature.

Simple univariate tests that are not part of a sequence of tests, typically known as modification indexes, are sometimes also of interest. The LM test for a single constraint, say, the ith constraint (often the simple constraint that a given parameter equals zero), is a special case of the multivariate test. The ith test corresponding to (10.52) is

$$\text{LM}_i = n\hat{\lambda}_i^2/[D'\dot{\sigma}'WV_{ss}W\dot{\sigma}D]_{ii} \xrightarrow{\mathcal{L}} \chi_{(1)}^2, \tag{10.54}$$

where the matrix in brackets is evaluated at $\hat{\theta}$. The corresponding test for (10.53) is

$$\text{LM}_i = n\hat{\lambda}_i^2/[(\dot{c}\Delta\dot{c}')^{-1}]_{ii} \xrightarrow{\mathcal{L}} \chi_{(1)}^2, \tag{10.55}$$

evaluated at $\hat{\theta}$. This is the univariate LM test currently printed out by EQS. In practice, large numbers of univariate LM_i tests may be scanned to suggest constraints to release, especially, to locate fixed parameters that may best be freed. In such a case the $\chi_{(1)}^2$ distribution may not describe the behavior of LM_i tests.

It is sometimes helpful to estimate the value that a parameter, fixed at a known value such as zero, might take if estimated freely. Conceptually, this problem is approached by considering the fixed parameter as in fact a free parameter, subject to the simple constraint that its value is a known constant, and asking what would happen if the constraint were released. Bentler and Dijkstra's development of linearized estimation provides an answer. Let $\hat{\theta}$ be the estimator obtained under the restricted model with $c(\hat{\theta}) = 0$, where the constraints guarantee that some elements of $\hat{\theta}$ are fixed at a known value. For consistency with the previous discussion on linearized estimation, we take $\hat{\theta} = \theta_1$ as an initial consistent estimator. Applying linearized GLS (10.17) without the constraint, the improvement (10.18) simplifies to

$$\overline{\pi} = \overline{\theta} - \theta_1 = \Delta_1\dot{\sigma}_1'W(s - \sigma_1), \tag{10.56}$$

where the subscript indicates evaluating at the constrained estimate (see Bentler & Dijkstra, 1985, Eq. 2.1.10). While all parameters may change when the constraints are released, the main interest will focus on those fixed parameters for which the corresponding element of θ_1 is known a priori. The relevant element of (10.56) then gives the parameter value to be expected when freeing the parameter. The effects of the multivariate parameter change $\overline{\pi}$ can also be evaluated on all of the constraint equations, to suggest which constraints $c(\theta)$ might be worth releasing. Multiplying (10.56) by the derivatives of the constraint function $\dot{c}_1$ yields $\dot{c}_1(\overline{\theta} - \theta_1) = \dot{c}_1\overline{\pi}$. But, according to Bentler and Dijkstra (1985, p. 25), asymptotically $c(\overline{\theta}) = c(\theta_1) + \dot{c}_1(\overline{\theta} - \theta_1)$. In this application, $c(\theta_1) = 0$, so that

$$c(\overline{\theta}) = \dot{c}_1\overline{\pi}. \tag{10.57}$$

This gives the expected change for all constraint functions, and, as a consequence, the relative size of this multivariate constraint change can give a clue as to which constraints might be fruitful to release. This information can supplement the LM χ^2 test on the corresponding constraint. The multivariate constraint change $c(\overline{\theta})$ was developed independently by Satorra (1989), though not through the steps given above. It will be noted that when the constraints being evaluated involve fixing a set of parameters to a constant, $\dot{c}_1$ can be permuted to the form $(I, 0)$, so that for these fixed parameters (10.56) yields the same result as (10.57). The multivariate parameter change and constraint change statistics are not printed out in EQS. Only the constraint change statistic is computed, applied in univariate fashion to constraints that involve fixed parameters. In this instance, the constraint change and parameter change are identical, that is,

$$\overline{\pi}_i = c(\overline{\theta})_i = \hat{\lambda}_i/[(\dot{c}\Delta\dot{c}')^{-1}]_{ii}, \tag{10.58}$$

where, as usual all elements are evaluated at the restricted solution.

It will be apparent that $LM_i = n\hat{\lambda}_i c(\overline{\theta})_i$, and, more generally, that $LM = n\hat{\lambda}' c(\overline{\theta})$. These expressions make clear that constraints associated with small changes (in absolute value), or small Lagrange Multipiers, do not contribute to a large LM test statistic. Stated differently, in the multivariate test constraints associated with products $\hat{\lambda}_i c_i(\overline{\theta})$ that are large will have a big impact on the LM test. The relative size of these products provide an indication of the importance of the constraints. Saris, Satorra, and Sörbom (1987) emphasized studying the size of elements in $c(\overline{\theta})$ (in a univariate version) to detect model misspecifications. See also Kaplan (1988) and Luijben, Boomsma, and Molenaar (1988). The current analysis makes clear that the size of a Lagrange Multipliers $\hat{\lambda}_i$ is just as important as the size of the constraint change in determining the statistical importance of misspecifications.

Wald (W) Test

Let $\hat{\theta}$ be an estimator for a model, and assume that the constraints $c(\theta) = 0$ have *not* been imposed during the estimation. In practice, this means that $c(\hat{\theta}) \neq 0$, and it may be desirable to test the hypothesis that $c(\theta) = 0$. In the simplest case, where the constraint functions simply select given parameters, this hypothesis evaluates whether the selected parameters are zero in the population. From Bentler and Dijkstra (1985, p. 24 last line), correcting a misprint, and the asymptotic equivalence of linearized and fully iterated estimators,

$$\sqrt{n}c(\hat{\theta}) = \dot{c}_+\sqrt{n}(\hat{\theta} - \theta_+) + o_p(1), \tag{10.59}$$

so that, under the null hypothesis, in view of (10.12) − (10.13), the large sample distribution of (10.59) is given by

$$\sqrt{n}c(\hat{\theta}) \xrightarrow{\mathcal{L}} \mathcal{N}(0, [\dot{c}M\dot{\sigma}'WV_{ss}W\dot{\sigma}M\dot{c}']_+). \tag{10.60}$$

It follows that a quadratic form based on (10.60) can be used to test the constraints. Specifically, letting $c(\hat{\theta}) = \hat{c}$, the Wald statistic is given by

$$W = n\hat{c}'(\dot{c}M\dot{\sigma}'WV_{ss}W\dot{\sigma}M\dot{c}')^{-1}\hat{c} \xrightarrow{\mathcal{L}} \chi^2_{(r)}, \tag{10.61}$$

where the matrix in parentheses is evaluated at $\hat{\theta}$. In principle, the W test given in (10.61) does not depend on the distribution of variables when V_{ss} is estimated in a distribution-free way. The test is called the generalized Wald test by Satorra (1989), who provides the noncentrality parameter when the null hypothesis is minimally false. In EQS, (10.61) is computed with least squares estimation when a normal or elliptical distribution is assumed, that is, with LS or ELS estimation. It is not computed for other estimators.

When the weight matrix W is chosen optimally, $W = V_{ss}^{-1}$ in the typical case asymptotically, and the covariance matrix in (10.60) simplifies. As a result

$$W = n\hat{c}'(\dot{c}\Delta\dot{c}')^{-1}\hat{c} \xrightarrow{\mathcal{L}} \chi^2_{(r)}, \tag{10.62}$$

where, in practice, the matrix in parentheses is evaluated at the unrestricted estimate $\hat{\theta}$. This test is also used when $\hat{\theta}$ is based on linearized estimation, see Bentler and Dijkstra (Eq. 2.2.3). See also Lee (1985a), and Satorra (1989). The Wtest printed out in EQS for all distributional methods except LS and ELS is given by (10.62).

Bentler and Chou (1986; Bentler, 1986a) developed a procedure to partition the multivariate Wtest into a sequence of 1-df hierarchical and backward stepwise tests, to help determine which constraints might be added to a model without significant loss of overall fit. This methodology is described in Chapter 6.

The W test also exists in a univariate version. The W test for a single constraint, say, the ith constraint, is given by

$$W_i = n\hat{c}_i^2/[\dot{c}M\dot{\sigma}'WV_{ss}W\dot{\sigma}M\dot{c}']_{ii} \xrightarrow{\mathcal{L}} \chi^2_{(1)}, \tag{10.63}$$

and

$$W_i = n\hat{c}_i^2/[\dot{c}\Delta\dot{c}']_{ii} \xrightarrow{\mathcal{L}} \chi^2_{(1)}, \tag{10.64}$$

depending on the variant of (10.61) or (10.62) desired. As usual, the matrices in brackets are evaluated at the unconstrained estimate $\hat{\theta}$, and the $\chi^2_{(1)}$ distribution is appropriate if the tests are a priori. The W_i tests simplify if the constraint is a simple test on whether a free parameter is zero in the population. In that case, (10.64) becomes $n\hat{\theta}_i^2/\Delta_{ii}$, i.e., the square of an asymptotic z-test for evaluating the significance of a single parameter.

MULTISAMPLE COVARIANCE STRUCTURE ANALYSIS

A general approach to multisample covariance structure analysis was given by Bentler, Lee, and Weng (1987), covering the case where there are m sample covariance matrices S_g (with nonredundant elements in the vector s_g) and m corresponding model matrices Σ_g (with vector of nonredundant elements σ_g), one for each of g groups. The statistical problem is one of estimating all the parameters $\theta = (\theta_1', \theta_2', ..., \theta_m')'$ of the separate models $\sigma_g = \sigma_g(\theta)$ subject to within-sample and between-sample constraints $c(\theta) = 0$, obtaining standard error estimates, and testing goodness of fit of the models to the data. This approach generalizes the distribution-free work of Browne (1982, 1984) and Chamberlain (1982) to multiple groups, and permits use of specific distributions, e.g., normal or elliptical, in each of the samples. The theory summarized here is relevant to the EQS models and procedures given in Chapter 7.

In m samples, there are m discrepancy functions $(s_g - \sigma_g)'W_g(s_g - \sigma_g)$. A combination of these functions, weighted by sample size N_g, is minimized. Let $n_g = (N_g - 1)$, $N = \Sigma_1^m N_g$, and $n = N - m$. Then EQS finds $\hat{\theta}$ to minimize

$$T = \Sigma_1^m n_g T_g, \tag{10.65}$$

where T_g is any of the fitting functions (10.10), (10.17), (10.27), (10.42), or (10.43) defined for each group. As a GLS problem of the form (10.10), (10.65) can be written as

$$T = \Sigma_1^m n_g(s_g - \sigma_g)'W_g(s_g - \sigma_g), \tag{10.66}$$

using an appropriate choice of model, constraints, and weight matrices W_g. If the matrices W_g are chosen correctly in accord with the distribution of variables in each sample, at the minimum (10.65) or (10.66) are asymptotically χ^2 distributed with degrees of freedom $(p^* - q + r)$, where p^* is the total number of nonredundant sample covariances across all groups, and q and r are the corresponding total number of free parameters and constraints. Note that when m = 1, (10.66) evaluated at $\hat{\theta}$ is just (10.16) if W is a consistent estimator of V_{ss}^{-1}.

If the variables in each group are multivariate normal, V_{ss} for each group, V_{ssg}, is given by (10.41) with Σ_g replacing Σ. Note that the covariance matrices Σ_g need not be the same in the various groups. If the variables in each group are elliptical, V_{ssg} is given by (10.26) with Σ_g replacing Σ and κ_g, one for each group, replacing κ. If the variables are arbitrarily distributed, V_{ssg} is of the form (10.21) for each group. In practice, different groups may have different distributions, and W_g would be chosen, if possible, to consistently estimate V_{ssg}^{-1}. Computations would be easiest if the most restrictive distributional assumption possible, specifically, normality, were true in all m groups.

The function to be optimized in multisample analysis can be written in the form (10.10). The advantage of such an approach is that all the statistical theory developed above for the single-group situation carries over directly to the multisample situation. Let $s = (s_1',...,s_m')'$, $\sigma = (\sigma_1',...,\sigma_m')'$, and W be the block-diagonal matrix containing diagonal blocks $(n_g/n)W_g$. Then, EQS finds $\hat{\theta}$ to minimize Q in (10.10) under the constraint $c(\theta) = 0$ and the various choices of W_g depending on the distribution involved. As usual, $n\hat{Q} = nQ(\hat{\theta})$ has the χ^2 distribution (10.16) if all W_g are correctly specified and the models $\sigma_g(\theta)$ and constraints $c(\theta) = 0$ are correct, and $n\hat{Q} = T$ in (10.65) and (10.66). Lee and Jennrich's (1979) results on RLS extend immediately to the multiple group case, and, at the minimum $\hat{Q}$, (10.65) with T_g given by (10.43) for each groups yields the maximum likelihood test statistic, and $\hat{\theta}$ is the ML estimator. Of course, the generality afforded by minimizing (10.65) permits ML estimators in some groups, and other estimators in other groups.

Other results described for the single group carry over immediately to multisample analysis. When estimated under constraints, (10.12) − (10.13) give the distribution of $\hat{\theta}$ and the Lagrange Multiplier $\hat{\lambda}$. The covariance matrix of $\hat{\theta}$ is obtained from (10.14) when W_g are optimally chosen. Linearized estimation by minimizing (10.17), estimating with (10.18), and computing statistics with (10.19) − (10.20) carry over immediately. The specialization of W to yield different forms for the fit functions in the various groups, and other corresponding formulas, also follow. Although the Satorra-Bentler scaled χ^2 test also follows, it is not computed in EQS in the multisample context. Lagrange Multiplier and Wald theory follows immediately, although EQS currently only evaluates cross-group equality constraints with the LM test and prints no W test in this situation.

MEAN AND COVARIANCE STRUCTURES

Consider the covariance/mean sample and model matrices

$$\begin{bmatrix} S & \bar{z} \\ \bar{z}' & 1 \end{bmatrix} \quad \text{and} \quad \begin{bmatrix} \Sigma & \mu \\ \mu' & 1 \end{bmatrix}, \tag{10.67}$$

in which S and $\bar{z}$ are sample covariance matrices and mean vectors, and $\Sigma = \Sigma(\theta)$ and $\mu = \mu(\theta)$, i.e., in which both covariances and means are functions of the basic parameter vector θ, here, the parameters of the Bentler-Weeks model. The data to be modeled are s_2, the vector of lower triangular elements of S, and $s_1 = \bar{z}$. The subscripts indicate the order of moments involved, s_2 referring to 2nd moments about the mean, and s_1 referring to 1st-order moments, while the constant 1 in (10.67) is irrelevant to both data and model. The matrices given in (10.67) are used in EQS for models involving intercepts and means, as well as covariances. Let $s = (s_1' \; s_2')'$, and $\sigma = (\sigma_1' \; \sigma_2')'$ be the corresponding model vectors. Then, $\sigma = \sigma(\theta)$ as usual, and the general statistical theory summarized above still applies for estimating parameters, testing goodness of fit, and so on. The number of data points to be modeled, the sample elements of s, are now redefined as $p^* = p(p + 1)/2 + p$, but q and r can still describe the number of free parameters and restrictions $c(\theta) = 0$, respectively, as before. The theory specializes, depending on the sampling covariance of s_1 and s_2.

Dependence of Sample Covariances and Means

The asymptotic distribution of $\sqrt{n}(s_2 - \sigma_2)$ has already been described abstractly in (10.11), in the distribution-free case in (10.21), and in specialized cases in (10.26) and (10.41). Redefining V_{ss} in these equations as V_{22}, the distribution of sample covariances in (10.11) becomes, in the new notation,

$$\sqrt{n}(s_2 - \sigma_2(\theta_+)) \xrightarrow{\mathcal{L}} \mathcal{N}(\delta_2, V_{22}). \tag{10.68}$$

Typically, one assumes that $s_{2+} = \sigma_2(\theta_+)$, and $\delta_2 = 0$. It is well-known that, without any distributional assumptions, $E(s_1) = s_{1+}$ and $s_1 \xrightarrow{p} s_{1+}$, with an asymptotic distribution

$$\sqrt{N}(s_1 - \sigma_1(\theta_+)) \xrightarrow{\mathcal{L}} \mathcal{N}(\delta_1, \Sigma), \tag{10.69}$$

where $\delta_1 = 0$ with no misspecification and $s_{1+} = \sigma_1(\theta_+)$ under the model. The constant $\sqrt{N}$ in (10.69) does not appear to match $\sqrt{n}$ in (10.68), but (10.68) would hold if n were replaced by N, and/or if s_2 were the vector of biased rather than unbiased sample covariances. As another way to match the constants, for consistency with previous sections, we multiply the variable in (10.69) by $\sqrt{a_n} = \sqrt{n}/\sqrt{N}$, yielding

$$\sqrt{n}(s_1 - \sigma_1(\theta_+)) \overset{\mathcal{L}}{\to} \mathcal{N}(\sqrt{a_n}\delta_1, V_{11}) \tag{10.70}$$

where

$$V_{11} = a_n\Sigma, \ a_n = n/N. \tag{10.71}$$

Of course, since the distribution in (10.70) depends upon N $\to$ ∞, it follows that $a_n \to 1.0$, i.e., that $V_{11} = \Sigma$. So (10.69) or (10.70) can be used interchangeably. Letting $\delta = (a_n\delta_1', \delta_2')'$, the joint vectors in (10.68) and (10.70) are in fact jointly asymptotically normally distributed (Kendall & Stuart, 1969)

$$\sqrt{n}(s - \sigma(\theta_+)) \overset{\mathcal{L}}{\to} \mathcal{N}(\delta, V_{ss}), \tag{10.72}$$

where V_{ss} is the supermatrix

$$\begin{bmatrix} V_{11} & V_{12} \\ V_{21} & V_{22} \end{bmatrix} \tag{10.73}$$

whose elements V_{11} and V_{22} have been given in (10.70) and (10.21), and where

$$[V_{12}]_{ijk} = \sqrt{a_n} \ \mathcal{E}(z_i - \mu_i)(z_j - \mu_j)(z_k - \mu_k) = \sqrt{a_n}\sigma_{ijk} \tag{10.74}$$

describes the covariance of a sample covariance and a sample mean. Of course, as n $\to$ ∞, $\sqrt{a_n} \to 1.0$, so the constant $\sqrt{a_n}$ is essentially irrelevant. A consistent estimator of σ_{ijk} is

$$s_{ijk} = N^{-1}\Sigma_1^N(z_{it} - \bar{z}_i)(z_{jt} - \bar{z}_j)(z_{kt} - \bar{z}_k).$$

The asymptotic distributions given here specialize to yield Browne's (1982, 1984) and Chamberlain's (1982) distribution-free covariance structure analysis with $\sigma_1 = \sigma(\theta_1)$ with $\mu = \theta_1$ and $\sigma_2 = \sigma(\theta_2)$. However, $\bar{z}$ may not be the optimal estimator of σ_1, as is implicitly assumed in their approach. When both means and covariances are structured in terms of some of the same parameters in the vector θ, (10.72) must be based on both s_1 and s_2. It is clear from the set-up, however, that (10.10) is an appropriate function to minimize, (10.12) gives the distribution of the resulting estimator, (10.16) gives the χ^2 statistic under appropriate choice of W, that linearized estimation has the same properties as before, and that Lagrange Multiplier and Wald theory described above is directly relevant.

In models where the means and covariances are functions of a common set of parameters, such as factor loadings, estimators of these common parameters have smaller sampling variances than when these parameters are estimated in covariance structure models alone. This gain in efficiency can be appreciable (Bentler & Chou, 1989). The same phenomenon occurs, of course, in a multisample context.

Independence of Sample Covariances and Means

If $\sigma_{ijk} = 0$ in (10.74), then V_{ss} is a block diagonal matrix since

$$V_{12} = 0. \tag{10.75}$$

As a consequence, one may take W in (10.10) to be block diagonal with blocks W_{11} and W_{22}. Then (10.10) specializes to

$$Q = (s_1 - \sigma_1)'W_{11}(s_1 - \sigma_1) + (s_2 - \sigma_2)'W_{22}(s_2 - \sigma_2). \tag{10.76}$$

Thus if W_{11} consistently estimates V_{11}^{-1} in (10.71), and W_{22} is consistent for V_{22}^{-1} based on (10.21), a distribution-free mean/covariance structure analysis remains, and the general statistical theory summarized above holds. Of course V_{22} may have a still more specialized structure, as was given with elliptical and normal distributions above.

Suppose that the variables z are multinormally distributed. Then V_{22} is given by (10.41), and (10.76) can be specialized further to

$$Q = (s_1 - \sigma_1)'W_{11}(s_1 - \sigma_1) + Q_N, \tag{10.77}$$

where Q_N was given in (10.42). (Under a more general elliptical assumption one would use Q_E in place of Q_N in (10.77)). A complete LS analysis results when $W_{11} = I$, and $W_2 = I$ in (10.42). Optimal choices for W_{11} are more meaningful, especially V_{11}^{-1} as obtained by (10.71). Combined with optimal choices for W_2 in (10.42) as $W_2 = S^{-1}$ for GLS or $W_2 = \hat{\Sigma}^{-1}$ for RLS or ML, one obtains in the notation surrounding (10.42)

$$Q = a_n^{-1}(s_1 - \sigma_1)'W_2(s_1 - \sigma_1) + Q_N. \tag{10.78}$$

If $W_2 = S^{-1}$ one obtains a GLS generalization of Browne's (1974) covariance structure function, namely

$$Q_{N(GLS)} = a_n^{-1}(s_1 - \sigma_1)'S^{-1}(s_1 - \sigma_1) + 2^{-1}\mathrm{tr}[(S - \Sigma)S^{-1}]^2 \tag{10.79}$$

while if $W_2 = \hat{\Sigma}^{-1}$, iteratively updated, one obtains

$$Q_{N(RLS)} = a_n^{-1}(s_1 - \sigma_1)'\hat{\Sigma}^{-1}(s_1 - \sigma_1) + 2^{-1}\mathrm{tr}[(S - \Sigma)\hat{\Sigma}^{-1}]^2. \tag{10.80}$$

Of course, asymptotically, $a_n \rightarrow 1.0$, so a_n can be ignored in (10.78) − (10.80). Standard errors, χ^2 tests, tests on restrictions $c(\theta) = 0$ and related statistical results follow immediately from the general theory above. For example, at the minimum of (10.80), $n\hat{Q}_{N(RLS)} \xrightarrow{\mathcal{L}}$ $\chi^2_{(p*-q+r)}$. The work of Lee and Jennrich (1979) can be extended directly to show that $\hat{\theta}$ based on minimizing (10.80) gives the ML estimator, and minor adjustments to Lee and Bentler's (1980) work can verify that GLS and ML estimators, standard errors, and test statistics are asymptotically equal. Of course, (10.78) permits mixed LS/GLS/RLS estimation as well, where different estimators for W_2 are used in the two parts of the overall function.

In ML estimation, the log likelihood for given model, aside from a constant, is

$$L = -2^{-1}N[\ln|\Sigma| + \mathrm{tr}S\Sigma^{-1} + (s_1 - \sigma_1)'\Sigma^{-1}(s_1 - \sigma_1)]$$

while the corresponding likelihood for a saturated model is

$$L_s = -2^{-1}N[\ln|S| + p].$$

Consequently, maximizing L under choice of estimator $\hat{\theta}$ permits forming the likelihood ratio statistic $LR = 2(\hat{L}_s - \hat{L})$, given by

$$LR = N[\ln|\hat{\Sigma}| + tr S\hat{\Sigma}^{-1} + (s_1 - \hat{\sigma}_1)'\hat{\Sigma}^{-1}(s_1 - \hat{\sigma}_1) - \ln|S| - p]$$

$$= N[\hat{F} + (s_1 - \hat{\sigma}_1)'\hat{\Sigma}^{-1}(s_1 - \hat{\sigma}_1)], \tag{10.81}$$

where F was given in (10.43). It is apparent that the ML estimator minimizes (10.81), which is the ML asymptotic χ^2 goodness of fit test. In standard ML applications, S in (10.81) is based on the biased sample covariance matrix. However, typical applications of structural modeling use the unbiased sample covariance matrix in (10.81), and give the test statistic as

$$a_n LR \xrightarrow{\mathcal{L}} \chi^2_{(p*-q+r)}. \tag{10.82}$$

It is apparent that these adjustments vanish as $N \rightarrow \infty$. In structured means models EQS uses (10.82) as the ML χ^2 statistic, and the matrix $[\cdot]$ in (10.19), based on (10.68) − (10.72) under normal theory (e.g., under (10.75)), evaluated at $\hat{\theta}$, with $[\cdot]/n$ as the estimated covariance matrix of $\hat{\theta}$. Compatible formulas for other statistics given in previous sections apply directly, e.g., to evaluate restrictions.

The current version of EQS limits covariance/mean structure models to situations in which the assumption of multivariate normality is appropriate. Only ML estimators and statistics are provided. Where structured means models are implemented in multisample analysis, the theory summarized in the current and previous section is combined to yield the appropriate ML analysis. For example, (10.82) is taken as the function T_g given in (10.65).

EVALUATION OF NORMALITY

Mardia's measure of multivariate kurtosis can be used to test for multivariate normality, as was noted in the discussion surrounding the normalized estimate (10.32) above. Normality would be rejected if the variables are either too light- or heavy-tailed compared with the distribution expected under normal theory. If multinormality is not a reasonable description of the distribution of variables, then GLS or RLS (ML) estimation may not yield appropriate statistical statements. The estimates that result from LS, GLS, and ML estimation will no doubt be reasonable (see Tanaka, 1984), but the standard errors and chi-square tests may be incorrect. In such a case, fit indices (e.g., Bentler & Bonett, 1980; Bentler, 1988a; Bollen, 1989b) become a better guide as to the adequacy of a model.

There are two problems with evaluating (10.32) as a standard unit-normal variate and drawing a conclusion about multivariate normality based on this test. In the first place, the distribution of the coefficient is somewhat skewed for intermediate size samples. Mardia (1974) provides a correction to (10.32) that has not been built into EQS, primarily because of the second problem. In particular, testing for statistically significant departures from normality is not equivalent to testing for practically significant departures. In large samples, even small deviations from normality are liable to be statistically significant, but it is possible that the distortion in structural modeling statistics may be relatively trivial as well, so that little might be lost in retaining the assumption of normality. There is currently little empirical or theoretical guidance available as to when a statistically significant variation from normality becomes large enough to affect structural modeling conclusions. If the deviation from normality is in the direction of excess or lowered but homogeneous kurtosis, then elliptical estimation provides a generally available alternative to normal theory estimation. If the elliptical distribution is unreasonable (EQS provides no test; see Beran, 1979), arbitrary distribution estimation would be needed. However, Harlow (1985) found a substantial robustness to normal theory methods under moderate violations of distributional assumptions, and recent theory (see references in Chapter 1) suggests that under a wide variety of conditions some non-robust standard errors may be correct and the χ^2 goodness-of-fit test asymptotically robust. Nonetheless, conditions for robustness are not yet easy to check, and robustness should not be automatically assumed.

The hypothesis of multivariate normality can also be tested in part by an evaluation of the marginal kurtoses and skewnesses of the variables. In particular, the univariate kurtoses computed in (10.33) that are printed in the program can be scanned for gross deviations from expectations under normality. Under normality, the $g_{2(i)}$ coefficients in very large samples (say, $N > 1000$) are distributed normally with a standard error that can be estimated as $(24/N)^{1/2}$. If the variables have significant nonzero univariate kurtosis they will, of course, not be multivariate normally distributed. The program also computes the univariate skewness coefficients of the variables as

$$g_{1(i)} = N^{1/2}\Sigma_1^N(z_{it} - \bar{z}_i)^3/[\Sigma_1^N(z_{it} - \bar{z}_i)^2]^{3/2}. \tag{10.83}$$

In intermediate size samples (say, $N > 200$), under normality (10.83) has a standard error that can be estimated as $(6/N)^{1/2}$. This can be used to evaluate the statistical significance of skewness. If the variables are significantly positively or negatively skewed, neither the normal or elliptical distribution would in general be correct to use as a basis for structural modeling. The distribution-free methods are then more appropriate. However, sample size may need to be very large for these methods to perform well in large models (Hu, Bentler, & Kano, 1992; Muthén & Kaplan, 1992).

DETECTION OF OUTLIERS

In some situations the vector of scores for an individual case may represent gross recording errors or some other anomaly that make the scores quite unrepresentative of the population being studied. Such a case can distort an otherwise appropriate analysis (e.g., Bollen, 1987b). In such a situation it may be prudent to use robust estimates of variance and covariance (see Devlin, Gnanadesikan, & Kettenring, 1981; Huber, 1981) instead of the standard estimator S provided in EQS. EQS does not currently provide any facility for computing a robust covariance matrix. However, it does provide an indicator of the general tendency of a case to be an outlier in multidimensional space, so that the user can eliminate the case if necessary in subsequent computer runs. Based on Bentler (1985), EQS prints out the five case numbers that make the largest contribution to the normalized multivariate kurtosis measure in (10.32). In particular, the estimate (10.32) is the mean across all cases of these case contributions. Thus if a case is an outlier, its contribution will be very large relative to the other cases, which should be noticeable in the printout. Eliminating such a case should have the effect of reducing the normalized multivariate kurtosis measure. However, the exact effect is somewhat difficult to predict because the mean and covariance matrix that form a basis of the statistic are themselves altered by the elimination of a deviant case. A model-based approach to detection and deletion of outliers (e.g., Berkane & Bentler, 1988) has not yet been implemented in EQS.

Cases may be eliminated from the input by using a DELETE statement in the /SPECIFICATION section of the program. Up to 20 cases can be eliminated. The score vectors of the cases to be deleted are simply ignored in the computations. The data remain intact in the input file.

ITERATIVE COMPUTATIONS

The user of EQS provides detailed information on the structural model to be tested in the input. As was noted in the first section of this chapter, EQS translates the user's specifications into the parametric structure of the Bentler-Weeks model. As it does this, it keeps track of which parameters are zero, which are fixed nonzero, and which parameters are free parameters. Equality and inequality constraints are also noted. The statistical theory reviewed above requires that the initial estimates of the free parameters provided by the user be modified systematically until an optimal set of estimates is obtained, in particular, the set that minimizes (10.10) or its special cases. EQS uses a modified Gauss-Newton method (see Jennrich & Sampson, 1968; Kennedy & Gentle, 1980) to minimize (10.10).

The essence of the algorithm is given in the following equations that relate unknown parameters on iteration (k) to those on (k + 1):

$$H^{(k)}d^{(k)} = -g^{(k)}, \text{ and} \tag{10.84}$$

$$\theta^{(k+1)} = \theta^{(k)} + \alpha d^{(k)}, \tag{10.85}$$

where $g^{(k)} = -\dot{\sigma}'W(s - \sigma(\theta))$ and $H^{(k)} = \dot{\sigma}'W\dot{\sigma}$ are evaluated at $\theta = \theta^{(k)}$. Specific formulas for g and H under the various distribution theories were given previously, and by Browne (1982, 1984), Chamberlain (1982), Bentler (1983a), and Bentler and Weeks (1980). At iteration (k), $\theta^{(k)}$ is known and hence $g^{(k)}$ and $H^{(k)}$ can be computed. The system of linear equations (10.84) must be solved for $d^{(k)}$. Then, upon choosing the line search parameter α, (10.85) yields the updated parameter vector.

A solution for $d^{(k)}$ in (10.84) is, in the simple unconstrained case, given by $d^{(k)} = -H^{(k)-1}g^{(k)}$. However under equality and inequality constraints the solution is somewhat more complex. These constraints are handled in practice by forming the augmented matrix J shown in association with (10.12), bordered with the gradient and modified constants of the constraint equation. (The constraints on parameters are translated into constraints on $d^{(k)}$.) A stepwise regression version of the Gauss-Jordan algorithm for matrix inversion is used to sweep on the diagonal elements of the augmented matrix, as used in algorithms in BMDP's 3R and PAR programs (Dixon, 1985). Sweeping is accomplished so that the tolerance limit is not violated and so that the direction of the new estimate is constrained to be along the boundaries of some active constraints if necessary.

Once $d^{(k)}$ is known, step (10.85) is taken with $\alpha = 1.0$, unless, for k > 3, the program notes that the function Q has on the average not decreased during the previous three iterations. In that case, α is cut in half successively up to a total of five times until the program notes a function decrease. Then $\theta^{(k+1)}$ becomes the new $\theta^{(k)}$ and the process (10.84) − (10.85) is repeated. The default convergence criterion currently implemented in EQS is that the elements of the parameter change vector $d^{(k)}$ have an average absolute value less than .001.

No claim is made that the modified Gauss-Newton algorithm implemented in EQS is the best possible one. It is known, for example, that the Gauss-Newton algorithm may fail if the model of the data is very bad, i.e., when the residual vector $(s - \hat{\sigma})$ is large. Similarly, the algorithm may fail if the problem is very nonlinear, since the "information matrix" $H^{(k)}$ ignores second derivative information. Thus, the speed of convergence decreases as the relative nonlinearity and residual size increases, and in fact, in very difficult problems the method may not converge at all. In this way the method may be similar to other popular programs for structural modeling that can have problems with convergence, especially when sample size is small. If the initial start values are very poor, it is possible that the initial $\hat{\Sigma}$ is not positive definite. In such a case, the message IN ITERATION #n, MATRIX W_CFUNT MAY NOT BE POSITIVE DEFINITE will be printed. This is not a problem unless the program cannot find improved estimates that will lead to convergence. Then new and better start values must be provided, e.g. higher residual covariances. In general, if a convergence failure is encountered in practice, the user is urged to attempt to start the algorithm from some quite different start values. The user also can control the maximum number of iterations, and may need to raise this limit if it appears that further iterations may lead to successful minimization of Q.

In spite of the known problems with the Gauss-Newton algorithm, the algorithm does have some virtues in the context of structural modeling. The algorithm is relatively easy to implement, and is asymptotically stable and convergent under the model (cf. Jennrich, 1969; Bentler & Dijkstra, 1985). In addition, as noted by Lee and Jennrich (1979) and Browne (1982), the algorithm readily yields the estimated covariance matrix of the parameter estimates. The algorithm also provides information on the linear dependence among parameters that can provide a hint as to parameter underidentification (see McDonald & Krane, 1979; Shapiro & Browne, 1983).

REFERENCES

Abbey, A., & Andrews, F. (1985). Modeling psychological determinants of life quality. Social Indicators Research, 16, 1-34.

Acito, F., & Anderson, R. D. (1984). On simulation methods for investigating structural modeling. Journal of Marketing Research, 21, 107-112.

Acock, A., & Fuller, T. D. (1986). Standardized solutions using LISREL on multiple populations. Sociological Methods & Research, 13, 551-557.

Aigner, D. J., & Goldberger, A. S. (1977). Latent variables in socioeconomic models. Amsterdam: North-Holland.

Aigner, D. J., Hsiao, C., Kapteyn, A., & Wansbeek, T. (1984). Latent variable models in econometrics. In Z. Griliches & M. D. Intriligator (Eds.), Handbook of econometrics, Vol. 2 (pp. 1321-1393). Amsterdam: North-Holland.

Aitchison, J., & Silvey, D. C. (1958). Maximum likelihood estimation of parameters subject to restraints. Annals of Mathematical Statistics, 29, 813-828.

Akaike, H. (1987). Factor analysis and AIC. Psychometrika, 52, 317-332.

Allen, H. M., Bentler, P. M., & Gutek, B. A. (1985). Probing theories of individual well being: A comparison of quality-of-life models assessing neighborhood satisfaction. Basic and Applied Social Psychology, 6, 181-203.

Allison, P. D. (1987). Estimation of linear models with incomplete data. In C. Clogg (Ed.), Sociological Methodology 1987 (pp. 71-103). San Francisco: Jossey Bass.

Alwin, D. F., & Hauser, R. M. (1975). The decomposition of effects in path analysis. American Sociological Review, 40, 37-47.

Alwin, D. F., & Jackson, D. J. (1981). Applications of simultaneous factor analysis to issues of factorial invariance. In D. Jackson & E. Borgatta (Eds.), Factor analysis and measurement in sociological research: A multi-dimensional perspective. Beverly Hills: Sage.

Amemiya, Y. (1985a). On the goodness-of-fit tests for linear statistical relationships. Technical Report No. 10, Econometric Workshop, Stanford University.

Amemiya, Y. (1985b). Instrumental variable estimator for the nonlinear errors-in-variables model. Journal of Econometrics, 28, 273-289.

Amemiya, Y., & Anderson, T. W. (1985). Asymptotic chi-square tests for a large class of factor analysis models. Technical Report No. 13, Econometric Workshop, Stanford University. Annals of Statistics, (1990), 18, 1453-1463.

Amemiya, Y., Fuller, W. A., & Pantula, S. G. (1987). The asymptotic distributions of some estimators for a factor analysis model. Journal of Multivariate Analysis, 22, 51-64.

Anderson, J. C. (1985). A measurement model to assess measure-specific factors in multiple informant research. Journal of Marketing Research, 22, 86-92.

Anderson, J. C., & Gerbing, D. W. (1984). The effect of sampling error on convergence, improper solutions, and goodness-of-fit indices for maximum likelihood confirmatory factor analyses. Psychometrika, 49, 155-173.

Anderson, J. C., & Gerbing, D. W. (1988). Structural equation modeling in practice: A review and recommended two-step approach. Psychological Bulletin, 103, 411-423.

Anderson, J. C., Gerbing, D. W., & Hunter, J. E. (1987). On the assessment of unidimensional measurement: Internal and external consistency and overall consistency criteria. Journal of Marketing Research, 24, 432-437.

Anderson, J. G. (1987). Structural equation models in the social and behavioral sciences: Model building. Child Development, 58, 49-64.

Anderson, T. W. (1988). Multivariate linear relations. In T. Pukkila & S. Tuntanen (Eds.) Proceedings of the Second International Conference on Statistics. Tampere, Finland.

Anderson, T. W. (1990). Linear latent variable models and covariance structures. Journal of Econometrics, 41, 91-119.

Anderson, T. W., & Amemiya, Y. (1988). The asymptotic normal distribution of estimators in factor analysis under general conditions. The Annals of Statistics, 16, 759-771.

Arminger, G. (1986). Linear stochastic differential equation models for panel data with unobserved variables. In N. Tuma (Ed.), Sociological Methodology 1986, (pp. 187-212). San Francisco: Jossey-Bass.

Arminger, G. (1987). Misspecification, asymptotic stability, and ordinal variables in the analysis of panel data. Sociological Methods & Research, 15, 336-348.

Asher, H. B. (1983). Causal modeling (2nd ed.). Beverly Hills: Sage.

Atkinson, L. (1988). The measurement-statistics controversy: Factor analysis and subinterval data. Bulletin of the Psychonomic Society, 26, 361-364.

Babakus, E., Ferguson, C. E. Jr., & Jöreskog, K. G. (1987). The sensitivity of confirmatory maximum likelihood factor analysis to violations of measurement scale and distributional assumptions. Journal of Marketing Research, 24, 222-228.

Bagozzi, R. P. (1980). Causal models in marketing. New York: Wiley.

Bagozzi, R. P., & Burnkrant, R. E. (1985). Attitude organization and the attitude-behavior relation: A reply to Dillon and Kumar. Journal of Personality and Social Psychology, 49, 47-57.

Bagozzi, R. P., & Yi, Y. (1988). On the evaluation of structural equation models. Journal of the Academy of Marketing Science, 16, 74-94.

Balderjahn, I. (1985). The robustness of LISREL unweighted least squares estimation against small sample size in confirmatory factor analysis models. In W. Gaul & M. Schader (Eds.), Classification as a tool of research (pp. 3-10). Amsterdam: Elsevier Science Publishers.

Balderjahn, I. (1988). A note to Bollen's alternative fit measure. Psychometrika, 53, 283-285.

Bank, L., Dishion, T., Skinner, M., & Patterson, G. R. (1990). Method variance in structural equation modeling: Living with "glop." In G. R. Patterson (Ed.), Aggression and depression in family interactions (pp. 247-279). Hillsdale, NJ: Erlbaum.

Bartholomew, D. J. (1984). The foundations of factor analysis. Biometrika, 71, 221-232.

Bartholomew, D. J. (1987). Latent variable models and factor analysis. Oxford, U.K.: Oxford University Press.

Bartholomew, D. J. (1988). The sensitivity of latent trait analysis to choice of prior distribution. British Journal of Mathematical and Statistical Psychology, 41, 101-107.

Bartlett, M. S. (1937). Properties of sufficiency and statistical tests. Proceedings of the Royal Society A, 160, 268-282.

Bearden, W. O., Sharma, S., & Teel, J. E. (1982). Sample size effects on chi-square and other statistics used in evaluating causal models. Journal of Marketing Research, 19, 425-430.

Bekker, P. A. (1986). Essays on identification in linear models with latent variables. Ph.D. Dissertation, Catholic University of Tilburg, Holland.

Bentler, P. M. (1976). Multistructural statistical model applied to factor analysis. Multivariate Behavioral Research, 11, 3-25.

Bentler, P. M. (1980). Multivariate analysis with latent variables: Causal modeling. Annual Review of Psychology, 31, 419-456.

Bentler, P. M. (1982). Linear systems with multiple levels and types of latent variables. In K. G. Jöreskog & H. Wold (Eds.), Systems under indirect observation: Causality, structure, prediction. Part I (pp. 101-130). Amsterdam: North-Holland.

Bentler, P. M. (1983a). Some contributions to efficient statistics for structural models: Specification and estimation of moment structures. Psychometrika, 48, 493-517.

Bentler, P. M. (1983b). Simultaneous equations as moment structure models: With an introduction to latent variable models. Journal of Econometrics, 22, 13-42.

Bentler, P. M. (1985). Theory and implementation of EQS, A structural equations program. Los Angeles: BMDP Statistical Software.

Bentler, P. M. (1986a). Lagrange Multiplier and Wald tests for EQS and EQS/PC. Los Angeles: BMDP Statistical Software.

Bentler, P. M. (1986b). Structural modeling and Psychometrika: An historical perspective on growth and achievements. Psychometrika, 51, 35-51.

Bentler, P. M. (1986c). EQS - Ein Ansatz zur Analyse von Strukturgleichungs modellen für normal-bzw.nichtnormal verteilte quantitativen Variablen. In C. Möbus & W. Schneider (Eds.), Strukturmodelle fur Langschnittdaten und Zeitreihen (pp. 27-56). Bern: Verlag Hans Huber.

Bentler, P. M. (1987a). Structural modeling and the scientific method: Comments on Freedman's critique. Journal of Educational Statistics, 12, 151-157.

Bentler, P. M. (1987b). Drug use and personality in adolescence and young adulthood: Structural models with nonnormal variables. Child Development, 58, 65-79.

Bentler, P. M. (1988a). Comparative fit indexes in structural models. Psychological Bulletin, (1990), 107, 238-246.

Bentler, P. M. (1988b). Bentler critiques structural equation modeling. The Score, 11, 3, 6.

Bentler, P. M. (1988c). Causal modeling via structural equation systems. In J. R. Nesselroade & R. B. Cattell (Eds.), Handbook of multivariate experimental psychology, 2nd Ed. (pp. 317-335). New York: Plenum.

Bentler, P. M. (1989). Latent variable structural models for separating specific from general effects. In L. Sechrest, J. Bunker, & E. Perrin (Eds.), Improving methods in non-experimental research. Newbury Park, CA: Sage.

Bentler, P. M., & Berkane, M. (1985). Developments in the elliptical theory generalization of normal multivariate analysis. Proceedings of the Social Statistics Section, American Statistical Association, 291-295.

Bentler, P. M., & Berkane, M. (1986). The greatest lower bound to the elliptical theory kurtosis parameter. Biometrika, 73, 240-241.

Bentler, P. M., & Bonett, D. G. (1980). Significance tests and goodness of fit in the analysis of covariance structures. Psychological Bulletin, 88, 588-606.

Bentler, P. M., & Bonett, D. G. (1987). This week's citation classic (comments on Bentler & Bonett, 1980). Current Contents A & H, 9 (#37), 16.

Bentler, P. M., & Chou, C.-P. (1986, April). Statistics for parameter expansion and contraction in structural models. Paper presented at American Educational Research Association meeting, San Francisco, CA.

Bentler, P. M., & Chou, C.-P. (1987). Practical issues in structural modeling. Sociological Methods and Research, 16, 78-117.

Bentler, P. M., & Chou, C.-P. (1989, July). Mean and covariance structure models: A distribution-free approach. Paper presented at Psychometric Society meetings, Los Angeles.

Bentler, P. M., Chou, C.-P., & Lee, S.-Y. (1987, June). Evaluating the distribution of latent variables. Paper presented at Psychometric Society meeting, Montreal, Canada.

Bentler, P. M., & Dijkstra, T. (1985). Efficient estimation via linearization in structural models. In P. R. Krishnaiah (Ed.), Multivariate analysis VI (pp. 9-42). Amsterdam: North-Holland.

Bentler, P. M., & Lee, S.-Y. (1983). Covariance structures under polynomial constraints: Applications to correlation and alpha-type structural models. Journal of Educational Statistics, 8, 207-222, 315-317.

Bentler, P. M., Lee, S.-Y., & Weng, L.-J. (1987). Multiple population covariance structure analysis under arbitrary distribution theory. Communications in Statistics - Theory, 16, 1951-1964.

Bentler, P. M., & Mooijaart, A. (1989). Choice of structural model via parsimony. Psychological Bulletin, 106, 315-317.

Bentler, P. M., & Newcomb, M. D. (1986). Personality, sexual behavior, and drug use revealed through latent variable methods. Clinical Psychology Review, 6, 363-385.

Bentler, P. M., Poon, W.-Y., & Lee, S.-Y. (1988). Generalized multimode latent variable models: Implementation by standard programs. Computational Statistics & Data Analysis, 7, 107-118.

Bentler, P. M., Poon, W.-Y., & Lee, S.-Y. (1989). Goodness of fit statistics for categorical variable models with computationally efficient estimators. Under editorial review.

Bentler, P. M., & Speckart, G. (1981). Attitudes "cause" behaviors: A structural equation analysis. Journal of Personality and Social Psychology, 40, 226-238.

Bentler, P. M., & Weeks, D. G. (1979). Interrelations among models for the analysis of moment structures. Multivariate Behavioral Research, 14, 169-185.

Bentler, P. M., & Weeks, D. G. (1980). Linear structural equations with latent variables. Psychometrika, 45, 289-308.

Bentler, P. M., & Weeks, D. G. (1982). Multivariate analysis with latent variables. In P. R. Krishnaiah & L. Kanal (Eds.), Handbook of statistics, Vol. 2 (pp. 747-771). Amsterdam: North-Holland.

Bentler, P. M., & Weeks, D. G. (1985). Some comments on structural equation models. British Journal of Mathematical and Statistical Psychology, 38, 120-121.

Bentler, P. M., & Woodward, J. A. (1978). A head start reevaluation: Positive effects are not yet demonstrable. Evaluation Quarterly, 2, 493-510.

Beran, R. (1979). Testing for ellipsoidal symmetry of a multivariate density. The Annals of Statistics, 7, 150-162.

Berkane, M., & Bentler, P. M. (1986). Moments of elliptically distributed random variates. Statistics & Probability Letters, 4, 333-335.

Berkane, M., & Bentler, P. M. (1987a). Characterizing parameters of multivariate elliptical distributions. Communications in Statistics-Simulation, 16, 193-198.

Berkane, M., & Bentler, P. M. (1987b). Distribution of kurtoses, with estimators and tests of homogeneity of kurtosis. Statistics & Probability Letters, 5, 201-207.

Berkane, M., & Bentler, P. M. (1988). Estimation of contamination parameters and identification of outliers in multivariate data. Sociological Methods & Research, 17, 55-64.

Berkson, J. (1980). Minimum chi-square, not maximum likelihood! The Annals of Statistics, 8, 457-487.

Berry, W. D. (1984). Nonrecursive causal models. Beverly Hills: Sage.

Biddle, B. J., & Marlin, M. M. (1987). Causality, confirmation, credulity, and structural equation modeling. Child Development, 58, 4-17.

Bielby, D. V., & Bielby, W. T. (1984). Work commitment, sex-role attitudes, and women's employment. American Sociological Review, 49, 234-247.

Bielby, W. T. (1986). Arbitrary metrics in multiple-indicator models of latent variables. Sociological Methods & Research, 15, 3-23, 62-63.

Bielby, W. T., & Hauser, R. M. (1977). Structural equation models. Annual Review of Sociology, 3, 137-161.

Bielby, W. T., Hauser, R. M., and Featherman, D. L. (1977). Response errors of black and nonblack males in models of the intergenerational transmission of socioeconomic status. American Journal of Sociology, 82, 1242-1288.

Blalock, H. M., Jr., (Ed.) (1985a). Causal models in panel and experimental designs. New York: Aldine.

Blalock, H. M., Jr., (Ed.) (1985b). Causal models in the social sciences. Second Edition. New York: Aldine.

Bock, R. D., Gibbons, R., & Muraki, E. (1988). Full-information item factor analysis. Applied Psychological Measurement, 12, 261-280.

Bohrnstedt, G. W., & Borgatta, E. F. (Eds.) (1981). Social measurement: Current issues. Beverly Hills: Sage.

Bollen, K. A. (1986). Sample size and Bentler and Bonett's nonnormed fit index. Psychometrika, 51, 375-377.

Bollen, K. A. (1987a). Total, direct, and indirect effects in structural equation models. In C. Clogg (Ed.), Sociological Methodology 1987 (pp. 37-69). San Francisco: Jossey Bass.

Bollen, K. A. (1987b). Outliers and improper solutions: A confirmatory factor analysis example. Sociological Methods & Research, 15, 375-384.

Bollen, K. A. (1989a). Structural equations with latent variables. New York: Wiley.

Bollen, K. A. (1989b). A new incremental fit index for general structural equation models. Sociological Methods & Research, 17, 303-316.

Bollen, K. A., & Jöreskog, K. G. (1985). Uniqueness does not imply identification. A note on confirmatory factor analysis. Sociological Methods & Research, 14, 155-163.

Bollen, K. A., & Liang, J. (1988). Some properties of Hoelter's CN. Sociological Methods & Research, 16, 492-503.

Boomsma, A. (1983). On the robustness of LISREL (maximum likelihood estimation) against small sample size and nonnormality. Ph.D. Thesis, University of Groningen.

Boomsma, A. (1985). Nonconvergence, improper solutions, and starting values in LISREL maximum likelihood estimation. Psychometrika, 50, 229-242.

Boomsma, A. (1986). On the use of bootstrap and jackknife in covariance structure analysis. COMPSTAT, 7, 205-210.

Boomsma, D. I., & Molenaar, P. C. M. (1986). Using LISREL to analyze genetic and environmental covariance structure. Behavior Genetics, 16, 237-250.

Botha, J. D., Shapiro, A., & Steiger, J. H. (1988). Uniform indices-of-fit for factor analysis models. Multivariate Behavioral Research, 23, 443-450.

Bozdogan, H. (1987). Model selection and Akaike's information criteria (AIC): The general theory and its analytical extensions. Psychometrika, 52, 345-370.

Brecht, M. L., Bentler, P. M., & Tanaka, J. S. (1986). A case study in evaluating statistical computer programs: Comparison of three programs for specifying and testing structural equation models. Journal of Educational Technology Systems, 14, 217-227.

Brown, R. L. (1986). A comparison of the LISREL and EQS programs for obtaining parameter estimates in confirmatory factor analysis studies. Behavior Research Methods, Instruments, and Computers, 18, 382-388.

Browne, M. W. (1974). Generalized least squares estimators in the analysis of covariance structures. South African Statistical Journal, 8, 1-24.

Browne, M. W. (1982). Covariance structures. In D. M. Hawkins (Ed.), Topics in applied multivariate analysis (pp. 72-141). London: Cambridge University Press.

Browne, M. W. (1984). Asymptotically distribution-free methods for the analysis of covariance structures. British Journal of Mathematical and Statistical Psychology, 37, 62-83.

Browne, M. W. (1987). Robustness of statistical inference in factor analysis and related models. Biometrika, 74, 375-384.

Browne, M. W., & Shapiro, A. (1988). Robustness of normal theory methods in the analysis of linear latent variate models. British Journal of Mathematical and Statistical Psychology, 41, 193-208.

Buhrmester, D., Furman, W., Wittenberg, M. T., & Reis, H. T. (1988). Five domains of interpersonal competence in peer relationships. Journal of Personality and Social Psychology, 55, 991-1008.

Buse, A. (1982). The likelihood ratio, Wald and Lagrange multiplier tests: An expository note. The American Statistician, 36, 153-157.

Busemeyer, J. R., & Jones, L. E. (1983). Analysis of multiplicative combination rules when causal variables are measured with error. Psychological Bulletin, 93, 549-562.

Bye, B. V., Gallicchio, S. J., & Dykacz, J. M. (1985). Multiple-indicator, multiple-cause models for a single latent variable with ordinal indicators. Sociological Methods & Research, 13, 487-509.

Bynner, J. (1988). Factor analysis and the construct-indicator relationship. Human Relations, 41, 389-405.

Bynner, J. M., & Romney, D. M. (1986). Intelligence, fact or artifact: Alternative structures for cognitive abilities. British Journal of Educational Psychology, 56, 13-23.

Byrne, B. M. (1988). Measuring adolescent self-concept: Factorial validity and equivalency of the SDQ III across gender. Multivariate Behavioral Research, 23, 361-375.

Cambanis, S., Huang, S., & Simons, G. (1981). On the theory of elliptically contoured distributions. Journal of Multivariate Analysis, 11, 368-385.

Carmines, E. G. (1986). The analysis of covariance structure models. In W. Berry & M. Lewis-Beck (Eds.), New tools for social scientists: Advances and applications in research methods (pp. 23-55). Beverly Hills: Sage.

Chamberlain, G. (1982). Multivariate regression models for panel data. Journal of Econometrics, 18, 5-46.

Chen, H.-T. (1983). Flowgraph analysis of effect decomposition: Use in recursive and nonrecursive models. Sociological Methods & Research, 12, 3-29.

Chen, M.-S., & Land, K. C. (1986). Testing the health belief model: LISREL analysis of alternative models of causal relationships between health beliefs and preventive dental behavior. Social Psychology Quarterly, 49, 45-60.

Chou, C.-P., & Bentler, P. M. (1987, April). Model modification in covariance structure modeling: A comparison among likelihood ratio, Lagrange Multiplier, and Wald tests. Paper presented at American Educational Research Association meetings, Washington, DC.

Chou, C.-P., & Bentler, P. M. (1988, June). Estimation of AIC with the Wald and Lagrange Multiplier statistics: Model modification in covariance structure analysis. Paper presented at Psychometric Society meetings, Los Angeles, CA.

Chou, C.-P., Bentler, P. M., & Satorra, A. (1991). Scaled test statistics and robust standard errors for nonnormal data in covariance structure analysis: A Monte Carlo study. British Journal of Mathematical and Statistical Psychology, 44, 347-357.

Clément, R., & Kruidenier, B. G. (1985). Aptitude, attitude and motivation in second language proficiency: A test of Clément's model. Journal of Language and Social Psychology, 4, 21-37.

Cliff, N. (1983). Some cautions concerning the application of causal modeling methods. Multivariate Behavioral Research, 18, 115-126.

Cochran, S. D., & Hammen, C. L. (1985). Perceptions of stressful life events and depression: A test of attribution models. Journal of Personality and Social Psychology, 48, 1561-1571.

Cohen, J., & Cohen, P. (1983). Applied multiple regression/correlation analysis for the behavioral sciences, 2nd ed. Hillsdale, NJ: Erlbaum.

Cole, D. A. (1987). Utility of confirmatory factor analysis in test validation research. Journal of Consulting and Clinical Psychology, 55, 584-594.

Cole, D. A., & Maxwell, S. E. (1985). Multitrait-multimethod comparisons across populations: A confirmatory factor analytic approach. Multivariate Behavioral Research, 20, 389-417.

Comrey, A. L. (1985). A method for removing outliers to improve factor analytic results. Multivariate Behavioral Research, 20, 273-281.

Collins, L. M., Cliff, N., McCormick, D. J., & Zatkin, J. L. (1986). Factor recovery via binary data sets: A simulation. Multivariate Behavioral Research, 21, 377-391.

Cooper, M. L., Russell, M., & George, W. H. (1988). Coping, expectancies, and alcohol abuse: A test of social learning formulations. Journal of Abnormal Psychology, 97, 218-230.

Crano, W. D., & Mendoza, J. L. (1987). Maternal factors that influence children's positive behaviour: Demonstration of a structural equation analysis of selected data from the Berkeley growth study. Child Development, 58, 38-48.

Cudeck, R. (1988). Multiplicative models and MTMM matrices. Journal of Educational Statistics, 13, 131-147.

Cudeck, R. (1989). Analysis of correlation matrices using covariance structure models. Psychological Bulletin, 105, 317-327.

Cudeck, R., & Browne, M. W. (1983). Cross-validation of covariance structures. Multivariate Behavioral Research, 18, 147-157.

Cutrona, C., & Russell, D. (1987). The provisions of social relationship and adaptations to stress. In W. Jones & D. Perlman (Eds.), Advances in personal relationships, Vol. 1 (pp. 37-67). Greenwich, CT: Jai Press.

Cuttance, P., & Ecob, R. (1987). Structural modelling by example: Applications in Educational, Behavioral, and Social Research. Cambridge, U.K.: Cambridge University Press.

De Leeuw, J. (1983). Models and methods for the analysis of correlation coefficients. Journal of Econometrics, 22, 113-137.

De Leeuw, J. (1988a). Multivariate analysis with linearizable regressions. Psychometrika, 53, 437-454.

De Leeuw, J. (1988b). Model selection in multinomial experiments. In T. K. Dijkstra (Ed.), On model uncertainty and its statistical implications (pp. 118-138). New York: Springer-Verlag.

Devlin, S. J., Gnanadesikan, G., & Kettenring, J. R. (1981). Robust estimation of dispersion matrices and principal components. Journal of the American Statistical Association, 76, 354-362.

Dillon, W. R., & Goldstein, M. (1984). Multivariate analysis: Methods and applications. New York: Wiley.

Dillon, W. R., & Kumar, A. (1985). Attitude organization and the attitude-behavior relation: A critique of Bagozzi and Burnkrant's reanalysis of Fishbein and Ajzen. Journal of Personality and Social Psychology, 49, 33-46.

Dillon W. R., Kumar, A., & Mulani, N. (1987). Offending estimates in covariance structure analysis: Comments on the causes of and solutions to Heywood cases. Psychological Bulletin, 101, 126-135.

Dijkstra, T. (1981). Latent variables in linear stochastic models. Ph.D. Thesis, University of Groningen.

Dijkstra, T. (1983). Some comments on maximum likelihood and partial least squares methods. Journal of Econometrics, 22, 67-90.

Dixon, W. J. (Ed.) (1988). BMDP statistical software manual, Vols. 1 & 2. Berkeley, CA: University of California Press.

Duncan, O. D. (1975). Introduction to structural equation models. New York: Academic.

Dwyer, J. H. (1983). Statistical models for the social and behavioral sciences. New York: Oxford.

Dwyer, J. H. (1992). Differential equation models for longitudinal data. In J. H. Dwyer, M. Feinlieb, P. Lippert, & H. Hoffmeister (Eds.), Statistical models for longitudinal studies of health (pp. 71-98). New York: Oxford.

Ecob, R. (1987). Applications of structural equation modeling to longitudinal educational data. In P. Cuttance & R. Ecob (Eds.), Structural modeling by example (pp. 138-159). New York: Cambridge.

Efron, B. (1982). The jackknife, bootstrap and other resampling plans. Philadelphia: SIAM.

Engle, R. F. (1984). Wald, likelihood ratio, and Lagrange Multiplier tests in econometrics. In A. Griliches & M. D. Intriligator (Eds.), Handbook of econometrics (pp. 776-826). Amsterdam: North-Holland.

Epstein, R. J. (1987). A history of econometrics. Amsterdam: North-Holland.

Etezadi-Amoli, A., & McDonald, R. P. (1983). A second generation of nonlinear factor analysis. Psychometrika, 48, 315-342.

Ethington, C. A., & Wolfle, L. M. (1986). A structural model of mathematics achievement for men and women. American Educational Research Journal, 23, 65-75.

Everitt, B. S. (1984). An introduction to latent variable models. London: Chapman & Hall.

Farley, J. U., & Reddy, S. K. (1987). A factorial evaluation of effects of model specification and error on parameter estimation in a structural equation model. Multivariate Behavioral Research, 22, 71-90.

Fassinger, R. E. (1985). A causal model of college women's career choice. Journal of Vocational Behavior, 27, 123-153.

Fassinger, R. E. (1987). Use of structural equation modeling in counseling psychology research. Journal of Counseling Psychology, 34, 425-436.

Faulbaum, F. (1987). Intergroup comparisons of latent means across waves. Sociological Methods & Research, 15, 317-335.

Ferguson, T. S. (1958). A method of generating best asymptotically normal estimates with application to the estimation of bacterial densities. Annals of Mathematical Statistics, 29, 1046-1062.

Fink, E. L., & Monge, P. R. (1986). An exploration of confirmatory factor analysis. In B. Dervin & M. J. Voigt (Eds.), Progress in communication sciences (pp. 167-197). Norwood, NJ: Ablex.

Fleishman, A. I. (1978). A method of simulating non-normal distributions. Psychometrika, 43, 521-532.

Forgatch, M. S., Patterson, G. R., & Skinner, M. L. (1988). A mediational model for the effect of divorce on antisocial behavior in boys. In E. M. Hetherington & J. D. Aresteh (Eds.), Impact of divorce, single parenting, and step-parenting on children (pp. 135-154). Hillsdale, NJ: Erlbaum.

Fornell, C. (Ed.) (1982). A second generation of multivariate analysis. New York: Praeger.

Fornell, C. (1983). Issues in the application of covariance structure analysis: A comment. Journal of Consumer Research, 9, 443-448.

Fornell, C., & Larcker, D. F. (1984). Misapplications of simulations in structural equation models. Reply to Acito and Anderson. Journal of Marketing Research, 21, 113-117.

Fox, J. (1980). Effect analysis in structural equation models: Extensions and simplified methods of computation. Sociological Methods & Research, 9, 3-28.

Fox, J. (1985). Effect analysis in structural-equation models II: Calculation of specific indirect effects. Sociological Methods & Research, 14, 81-95.

Frane, J. W. (1977). A note on checking tolerance in matrix inversion and regression. Technometrics, 19, 513-514.

Fredricks, A. J., & Dossett, D. L. (1983). Attitude-behavior relations: A comparison of the Fishbein-Ajzen and Bentler-Speckart models. Journal of Personality and Social Psychology, 45, 501-512.

Freedman, D. A. (1987). As others see us: A case study in path analysis. Journal of Educational Statistics, 12, 101-128. (With discussion)

Fritz, W. (1986). The Lisrel-approach of causal analysis as an instrument of critical theory comparison within management science. In W. Gaul & M. Schader (Eds.), Classification as a tool of research (pp. 145-152). Amsterdam: Elsevier Science.

Fuller, W. A. (1987). Measurement error models. New York: Wiley.

Gallant, A. R. (1987). Nonlinear statistical models, New York: Wiley.

Gallini, J. K., & Casteel, J. F. (1987). An inquiry into the effects of outliers on estimates of a structural equation model of basic skills assessment. In P. Cuttance & R. Ecob (Eds.), Structural modeling by example (pp. 189-201). New York: Cambridge.

Gallini, J. K., & Mandeville, G. K. (1984). An investigation of the effect of sample size and specification error on the fit of structural equation models. Journal of Experimental Education, 53, 9-19.

Gerbing, D. W., & Anderson J. C. (1985). The effects of sampling error and model characteristics on parameter estimation for maximum likelihood confirmatory factor analysis. Multivariate Behavioral Research, 20, 255-271.

Gerbing, D. W., & Anderson, J. C. (1987). Improper solutions in the analysis of covariance structures: Their interpretability and a comparison of alternate respecifications. Psychometrika, 52, 99-111.

Geweke, J. F., & Singleton, K. J. (1980). Interpreting the likelihood ratio statistic in factor models when the sample size is small. Journal of the American Statistical Association, 75, 133-137.

Glymour, C., Scheines, R., & Spirtes, P. (1988). Exploring causal structures with the TETRAD program. In C. C. Clogg (Ed.), Sociological methodology 1988 (pp. 411-448). Washington, DC: American Sociological Association.

Glymour, C., Scheines, R., Spirtes, P., & Kelly, K. (1987). Discovering causal structure. Orlando: Harcourt, Brace, Jovanovich.

Goldberger, A. S., & Duncan, O. D. (Eds.) (1973). Structural equation models in the social sciences. New York: Seminar.

Gollob, H. F., & Reichardt, C. S. (1987). Taking account of time lags in causal models. Child Development, 58, 80-92.

Gorsuch, R. L. (1983). Factor analysis. Hillsdale, NJ: Erlbaum.

Graff, J., & Schmidt, P. (1982). A general model for decomposition of effects. In K. G. Jöreskog & H. Wold (Eds.), Systems under indirect observation, Part I (pp. 131-148). Amsterdam: North-Holland.

Greenland, S., Schesselman, J. J., & Criqui, M. H. (1986). The fallacy of employing standardized regression coefficients and correlations as measures of effect. American Journal of Epidemiology, 123, 203-208.

Greene, V. L. (1977). An algorithm for total and indirect causal effects. Political Methodology, 44, 369-381.

Hansen, C. P. (1989). A causal model of the relationship among accidents, biodata, personality, and cognitive factors. Journal of Applied Psychology, 74, 81-90.

Harlow, L. L. (1985). Behavior of some elliptical theory estimators with nonnormal data in a covariance structures framework: A Monte Carlo study, Ph.D. Thesis, University of California, Los Angeles.

Harlow, L. L., Newcomb, M. D., & Bentler, P. M. (1986). Depression, self-derogation, substance use, and suicide ideation: Lack of purpose in life as a mediational factor. Journal of Clinical Psychology, 42, 5-21.

Hattie, J., & Fraser, C. (1988). The constraining of parameters in restricted factor analysis. Applied Psychological Measurement, 12, 155-162.

Hauser, R. M., & Mossel, P. A. (1985). Fraternal resemblance in educational attainment and occupational status. American Journal of Sociology, 91, 650-673.

Hauser, R. M., Tsai, S.-L., & Sewell, W. H. (1983). A model of stratification with response error in social and psychological variables. Sociology of Education, 56, 20-46.

Hayduk, L. A. (1987). Structural equation modelling with LISREL: Essentials and advances. Baltimore: The Johns Hopkins University Press.

Hays, R. D., Widaman, K. F., DiMatteo, M. R., & Stacy, A. W. (1987). Structural equation models of current drug use: Are appropriate models so simple(x)? Journal of Personality and Social Psychology, 52, 134-144.

Heise, D. R. (1975). Causal analysis. New York: Wiley.

Heise, D. R. (1986). Estimating nonlinear models: Correcting for measurement error. Sociological Methods & Research, 14, 447-472.

Henry, N. W. (1986). On "arbitrary metrics" and "normalization" issues. Sociological Methods & Research, 15, 59-61.

Herting, J. R., & Costner, H. L. (1985). Respecification in multiple indicator models. In H. M. Blalock (Ed.), Causal models in the social sciences (pp. 321-393). New York: Aldine.

Hertzog, C., & Nesselroade, J. R. (1987). Beyond autoregressive models: Some implications of the trait-state distinction for the structural modeling of developmental change. Child Development, 58, 93-109.

Hill, P. W. (1987). Modeling the hierarchical structure of learning. In P. Cuttance & R. Ecob (Eds.), Structural modeling by example (pp. 65-85). New York: Cambridge.

Hoelter, J. W. (1983). Factorial invariance and self-esteem: Reassessing race and sex differences. Social Faces, 61, 834-846.

Hogan, E. A., & Martell, D. A. (1987). A confirmatory structural equations analysis of the job characteristics model. Organizational Behavior and Human Decision Processes, 39, 242-263.

Holland, P. W. (1986). Statistics and causal inference. Journal of the American Statistical Association, 81, 945-970.

Holland, P. W. (1988). Causal inference, path analysis, and recursive structural equations models. In C. C. Clogg (Ed.), Sociological methodology 1988 (pp. 449-484). Washington, DC: American Sociological Association.

Homer, P. M., & Kahle, L. R. (1988). A structural equation test of the value-attitude-behavior hierarchy. Journal of Personality and Social Psychology, 54, 638-646.

Hsu, L. M. (1989). Random sampling, randomization, and equivalence of contrasted groups in psychotherapy outcome research. Journal of Consulting and Clinical Psychology, 57, 131-137.

Hsu, P. L. (1949). The limiting distribution of functions of sample means and applications to testing hypotheses. Proceedings of the First Berkeley Symposium in Mathematical Statistics and Probability. Pp. 359-402. Reprinted in Collected Papers, New York: Springer-Verlag, 1983.

Hu, L., Bentler, P. M., & Kano, Y. (1992). Can test statistics in covariance structure analysis be trusted? Psychological Bulletin, 112, 351-362.

Huba, G. J., & Bentler, P. M. (1983). Test of a drug use causal model using asymptotically distribution free methods. Journal of Drug Education, 13, 3-14.

Huba, G. J., & Harlow, L. L. (1987). Robust structural equation models: Implications for developmental psychology. Child Development, 58, 147-166.

Huba, G. J., & Palisoc, A. L. (1983). Computerized path diagrams on a line printer. Computational Statistics & Data Analysis, 1, 137-140.

Huber, P. J. (1981). Robust statistics. New York: Wiley.

Hughes, M. A., Price, R. L., & Marrs, D. W. (1986). Linking theory construction and theory testing: Models with multiple indicators of latent variables. Academy of Management Review, 11, 128-144.

Irzik, G., & Meyer, E. (1987). Causal modelling: New directions for statistical explanation. Philosophy of Science, 54, 495-514.

Jaccard, J., & Turrisi, R. (1987). Cognitive processes and individual differences in judgments relevant to drunk driving. Journal of Personality and Social Psychology, 53, 135-145.

Jackson, D. N., & Chan, D. W. (1980). Maximum-likelihood estimation in common factor analysis: A cautionary note. Psychological Bulletin, 88, 502-508.

Jaech, J. L. (1985). Statistical analysis of measurement errors. New York: Wiley.

Jagodzinski, W., & Kühnel, S. M. (1987). Estimation of reliability and stability in single-indicator multiple-wave models. Sociological Methods & Research, 15, 219-258.

James, L. R., Mulaik, S. A., & Brett, J. M. (1982). Causal analysis: Assumptions, models, and data. Beverly Hills: Sage.

James, L. R., & Tetrick, L. (1986). Confirmatory analytic tests of three causal models relating job perceptions to job satisfaction. Journal of Applied Psychology, 71, 77-82.

Jennrich, R. I. (1969). Asymptotic properties of nonlinear least squares estimators. Annals of Mathematical Statistics, 40, 633-643.

Jennrich, R. I., & Sampson, P. F. (1968). Application of stepwise regression to nonlinear estimation. Technometrics, 10, 63-72.

Johnson, D. R., & Creech, J. C. (1983). Ordinal measures in multiple indicator models: A simulation study of categorization errors. American Sociological Review, 48, 398-407.

Jöreskog, K. G. (1969). A general approach to confirmatory maximum likelihood factor analysis. Psychometrika, 34, 183-202.

Jöreskog, K. G. (1971). Simultaneous factor analysis in several populations. Psychometrika, 57, 409-426.

Jöreskog, K. G. (1973). A general method for estimating a linear structural equation system. In A. S. Goldberger & O. D. Duncan (Eds.), Structural equation models in the social sciences (pp. 85-112). New York: Seminar.

Jöreskog, K. G. (1977). Structural equation models in the social sciences: Specification, estimation and testing. In P. R. Krishnaiah (Ed.), Applications of statistics (pp. 265-287). Amsterdam: North-Holland.

Jöreskog, K. G. (1978). Structural analysis of covariance and correlation matrices. Psychometrika, 43, 443-477.

Jöreskog, K. G., & Sörbom, D. (1988). LISREL 7, A guide to the program and applications. Chicago: SPSS.

Jöreskog, K. G., & Wold, H. (Eds.) (1982). Systems under indirect observation: Causality, structure, prediction. Amsterdam: North-Holland.

Judd, C. M., Jessor, R., & Donovan, J. E. (1986). Structural equation models and personality research. Journal of Personality, 54, 149-198.

Judd, C. M., & Kenny, D. A. (1981). Process analysis: Estimating mediation in treatment evaluations. Evaluation Review, 5, 602-619.

Kano, Y. (1989). A new estimation procedure using g-inverse matrix in factor analysis. Mathematica Japonica, 34, 43-52.

Kano, Y. (1990). Non-iterative estimation and the choice of the number of factors in exploratory factor analysis. Psychometrika, 55, 277-291.

Kano, Y., & Shapiro, A. (1987). On asymptotic variances of uniqueness estimators in factor analysis. South African Statistical Journal, 21, 131-139.

Kaplan, D. (1989). Model modification in covariance structure analysis: Application of the expected parameter change statistic. Multivariate Behavioral Research, 24, 285-305.

Kaplan, D. (1989). A study of the sampling variability and z-values of parameter estimates from misspecified structural equation models. Multivariate Behavioral Research, 24, 41-57.

Kaplan, H. B., Johnson, R. J., & Bailey, C. A. (1987). Deviant peers and deviant behavior: Further elaboration of a model. Social Psychology Quarterly, 50, 277-284.

Kaplan, H. B., Johnson, R. J., & Bailey, C. A. (1988). Explaining adolescent drug use: An elaborations strategy for structural equations modeling. Psychiatry, 51, 142-163.

Kendall, M. G., & Stuart, A. (1969). The advanced theory of statistics, Vol. 1. London: Griffin.

Kennedy, W. J. Jr., & Gentle, J. E. (1980). Statistical computing. New York: Marcel Dekker.

Kenny, D. A. (1979). Correlation and causality. New York: Wiley.

Kenny, D. A., & Judd, C. M. (1984). Estimating the nonlinear and interactive effects of latent variables. Psychological Bulletin, 96, 201-210.

Kessler, R. C., & Greenberg, D. F. (1981). Linear panel analysis: Models of quantitative change. New York: Academic.

Kiiveri, H. T. (1987). An incomplete data approach to the analysis of covariance structures. Psychometrika, 52, 539-554.

Kroonenberg, P. M., & Lewis, C. (1982). Methodological issues in the search for a factor model: Exploration through confirmation. Journal of Educational Statistics, 7, 69-89.

Kumar, A., & Dillon, W. R. (1987). Some further remarks on measurement-structural interaction and the unidimensionality of constructs. Journal of Marketing Research, 24, 438-444.

Kühnel, S. M. (1988). Testing MANOVA designs in LISREL. Sociological Methods & Research, 16, 504-523.

Küsters, U. (1987). Hierarchische Mittelwert-und Kovarianzstruktur modelle mit nichtmetrischen endogenen Variablen. Heidelberg: Physica-Verlag.

LaDu, T. J., & Tanaka, J. S. (1989). The influence of sample size, estimation method, and model specification on goodness-of-fit assessments in structural equation models. Journal of Applied Psychology, 74, 625-635.

Lance, C. E. (1989). Disturbance term regression tests: A note on the computation of standard errors. Multivariate Behavioral Research, 24, 135-141.

Lance, C. E., Cornwell, J. M., & Mulaik, S. A. (1988). Limited information parameter estimates for latent or mixed manifest and latent variable models. Multivariate Behavioral Research, 23, 171-187.

Laumann, E. O., Knoke, D., & Kim, Y.-H. (1985). An organizational approach to state policy formation: A comparative study of energy and health domains. American Sociological Review, 50, 1-19.

Lauritzen, S. L., & Wermuth, N. (1989). Graphical models for associations between variables, some of which are qualitative and some quantitative. The Annals of Statistics, 17, 31-57.

Leamer, E. E. (1988). Discussion. In C. C. Clogg (Ed.), Sociological methodology 1988 (pp. 485-493). Washington, DC: American Sociological Association.

Lee, S.-Y. (1985a). On testing functional constraints in structural equation models. Biometrika, 72, 125-131.

Lee, S.-Y. (1985b). Analysis of covariance and correlation structures. Computational Statistics & Data Analysis, 2, 279-295.

Lee, S.-Y. (1986). Estimation for structural equation models with missing data. Psychometrika, 51, 93-99.

Lee, S.-Y., & Bentler, P. M. (1980). Some asymptotic properties of constrained generalized least squares estimation in covariance structure models. South African Statistical Journal, 14, 121-136.

Lee, S.-Y., & Jennrich, R. I. (1979). A study of algorithms for covariance structure analysis with specific comparisons using factor analysis. Psychometrika, 44, 99-113.

Lee, S.-Y., & Poon, W.-Y. (1985). Further developments on constrained estimation in the analysis of covariance structures. The Statistician, 34, 305-316.

Lee, S.-Y., Poon, W.-Y., & Bentler, P. M. (1989). Simultaneous analysis of multivariate polytomous variates in several groups. Psychometrika, 54, 63-73.

Lee, S.-Y., Poon, W.-Y., & Bentler, P. M. (1990 a). A three-stage estimation procedure for structural equation models with polytomous variables. Psychometrika, 55, 45-51.

Lee, S.-Y., Poon, W.-Y., & Bentler, P. M. (1990 b). Full maximum likelihood analysis of structural equation models with polytomous variables. Statistics & Probability Letters, 9, 91-97.

Lee, S.-Y., & Tsui, K. L. (1982). Covariance structure analysis in several populations. Psychometrika, 47, 297-308.

Lehmann, E. L. (1983). Theory of point estimation. New York: Wiley.

Levin, J. (1988). Multiple group factor analysis of multitrait-multimethod matrices. Multivariate Behavioral Research, 23, 469-479.

Lewis, P. A. W., & Orav, E. J. (1989). Simulation methodology for statisticians, operations analysts, and engineers. Pacific Grove, CA: Wadsworth.

Li, C. C. (1975). Path analysis: A primer. Pacific Grove: Boxwood.

Loehlin, J. C. (1987). Latent variable models: An introduction to factor, path, and structural analysis. Hillsdale, NJ: Erlbaum.

Lomax, R. G. (1983). A guide to multiple-sample structural equation modeling. Behavior Research Methods and Instrumentation, 15, 580-584.

Long, J. S. (1983a). Confirmatory factor analysis. Beverly Hills: Sage.

Long, J. S. (1983b). Covariance structure models: An introduction to LISREL. Beverly Hills: Sage.

Lorence, J., & Mortimer, J. T. (1985). Job involvement through the life course: A panel study of three age groups. American Sociological Review, 50, 618-638.

Luijben, T. C., Boomsma, A., & Molenaar, I. W. (1988). Modification of factor analysis models in covariance structure analysis, A Monte Carlo study. In T. K. Dijkstra (Ed.), On model uncertainty and its statistical implications (pp. 70-101). New York: Springer-Verlag.

Lunneborg, C. E., & Abbott, R. D. (1983). Elementary multivariate analysis for the behavioral sciences. Amsterdam: North-Holland.

MacCallum, R. (1986). Specification searches in covariance structure modeling. Psychological Bulletin, 100, 107-120.

Mardia, K. V. (1970). Measures of multivariate skewness and kurtosis with applications. Biometrika, 57, 519-530.

Mardia, K. V. (1974). Applications of some measures of multivariate skewness and kurtosis in testing normality and robustness studies. Sankhya, B36, 115-128.

Marini, M. M., & Singer, B. (1988). Causality in the social sciences. In C. C. Clogg (Ed.), Sociological methodology 1988 (pp. 347-409). Washington, DC: American Sociological Association.

Marsh, H. W., Balla, J. R., & McDonald, R. P. (1988). Goodness-of-fit indexes in confirmatory factor analysis: The effect of sample size. Psychological Bulletin, 103, 391-410.

Marsh, H. W., & Hocevar, D. (1985). Application of confirmatory factor analysis to the study of self-concept: First- and higher-order factor models and their invariance across groups. Psychological Bulletin, 97, 562-582.

Marsh, H. W., & Richards, G. E. (1988). Tennessee self concept scale: Reliability, internal structure, and construct validity. Journal of Personality and Social Psychology, 55, 612-624.

Martin, J. A. (1987). Structural equation modeling: A guide for the perplexed. Child Development, 58, 33-37.

Matsueda, R. L., & Bielby, W. T. (1986). Statistical power in covariance structure models. In N. B. Tuma (Ed.), Sociological Methodology 1986 (pp. 120-158). San Francisco: Jossey Bass.

McArdle, J. J. (1986). Latent variable growth within behavior genetic models. Behavior Genetics, 16, 163-200.

McArdle, J. J., & Epstein, D. (1987). Latent growth curves within developmental structural equation models. Child Development, 58, 110-133.

McArdle, J. J., & McDonald, R. P. (1984). Some algebraic properties of the reticular action model for moment structures. British Journal of Mathematical and Statistical Psychology, 37, 234-251.

McCarthy, J. D., & Hoge, D. R. (1984). The dynamics of self-esteem and delinquency. American Journal of Sociology, 90, 396-410.

McDonald, R. P. (1980). A simple comprehensive model for the analysis of covariance structures: Some remarks on applications. British Journal of Mathematical and Statistical Psychology, 33, 161-183.

McDonald, R. P. (1985). Factor analysis and related methods. Hillsdale, NJ: Erlbaum.

McDonald, R. P., & Krane, W. R. (1979). A Monte Carlo study of local identifiability and degrees of freedom in the asymptotic likelihood ratio test. British Journal of Mathematical and Statistical Psychology, 32, 121-132.

McFadden, D. L. (1984). Econometric analysis of qualitative response models. In Z. Griliches & M. D. Intriligator (Eds.), Handbook of econometrics, Vol. 2 (pp. 1396-1457). Amsterdam: North-Holland.

McFatter, R. F. (1987). Use of latent variable models for detecting discrimination in salaries. Psychological Bulletin, 101, 120-125.

McGaw, B., & Jöreskog, K. G. (1971). Factorial invariance of ability measures in groups differing in intelligence and socio-economic status. British Journal of Mathematical and Statistical Psychology, 24, 154-168.

McGaw, B., Sörbom, D., & Cumming, J. (1986). Analysis of linear structural relations. International Journal of Educational Research, 10, 173-181.

Micceri, T. (1989). The unicorn, the normal curve, and other improbable creatures. Psychological Bulletin, 105, 156-166.

Miller, K. A., Kohn, M. L., & Schooler, C. (1985). Educational self-direction and the cognitive functioning of students. Social Forces, 63, 923-944.

Mislevy, R. (1986). Recent developments in the factor analysis of categorical variables. Journal of Educational Statistics, 11, 3-31.

Möbus, C., & Schneider, W. (1986). Structurmodelle für Längsschnittdaten und Zeitreihen. Bern: Hans Huber.

Molenaar, P. C. M. (1985). A dynamic factor model for the analysis of multivariate time series. Psychometrika, 50, 181-202.

Mooijaart, A. (1985). Factor analysis for non-normal variables. Psychometrika, 50, 323-342.

Mooijaart, A., & Bentler, P. M. (1985). The weight matrix in asymptotic distribution-free methods. British Journal of Mathematical and Statistical Psychology, 38, 190-196.

Mooijaart, A., & Bentler, P. M. (1986). Random polynomial factor analysis. In E. Diday et al. (Eds.), Data analysis and informatics IV (pp. 241-250). Amsterdam: Elsevier Science.

Mooijaart, A., & Bentler, P. M. (1987, July). <u>Robustness of normal theory statistics in structural equation models.</u> Paper presented at European meeting, Psychometric Society, Enschede.

Mooijaart, A., & Bentler, P. M. (1989). Robustness of normal theory statistics in structural equation models. <u>Statistica Neerlandica,</u> 1991, <u>45,</u> 159-171.

Muirhead, R. J. (1982). <u>Aspects of multivariate statistical theory.</u> New York: Wiley.

Mulaik, S. A. (1987). Toward a conception of causality applicable to experimentation and causal modeling. <u>Child Development, 58,</u> 18-32.

Mulaik, S. A., James, L. R., Van Alstine, J., Bennett, N., Lind, S., & Stillwell, C. D. (1989). Evaluation of goodness-of-fit indices for structural equation models. <u>Psychological Bulletin, 105,</u> 430-445.

Muthén, B. (1984). A general structural equation model with dichotomous, ordered categorical, and continuous latent variable indicators. <u>Psychometrika, 49,</u> 115-132.

Muthén, B. O. (1987). Response to Freedman's critique of path analysis: Improve credibility by better methodological training. <u>Journal of Educational Statistics, 12,</u> 178-184.

Muthén, B., & Hofacker, C. (1988). Testing the assumptions underlying tetrachoric correlations. <u>Psychometrika, 53,</u> 563-578.

Muthén, B., & Kaplan, D. (1985). A comparison of some methodologies for the factor analysis of non-normal Likert variables. <u>British Journal of Mathematical and Statistical Psychology, 38,</u> 171-189.

Muthén, B., & Kaplan, D. (1992). A comparison of some methodologies for the factor analysis of non-normal Likert variables: A note on the size of the model. <u>British Journal of Mathematical and Statistical Psychology, 45,</u> 19-30.

Muthén, B., Kaplan, D., & Hollis, M. (1987). On structural equation modeling with data that are not missing completely at random. <u>Psychometrika, 52,</u> 431-462.

Neale, M. C., & Stevenson, J. (1989). Ratio bias in the EASI Temperament Scales: A twin study. <u>Journal of Personality and Social Psychology, 56,</u> 446-455.

Nelson, F. H., Lomax, R. G., & Perlman, R. (1984). A structural equation model of second language acquisition for adult learners. <u>Journal of Experimental Education, 53,</u> 29-39.

Newcomb, M. D. (1986). Nuclear attitudes and reactions: Associations with depression, drug use, and quality of life. <u>Journal of Personality and Social Psychology, 50,</u> 906-920.

Newcomb, M. D. (1988). Nuclear anxiety and psychosocial functioning among young adults. <u>Basic and Applied Psychology, 9,</u> 107-134.

Newcomb, M. D. (1988). <u>Drug use in the workplace.</u> Dover, MA: Auburn House.

Newcomb, M. D., & Bentler, P. M. (1983). Dimensions of subjective female orgasmic responsiveness. <u>Journal of Personality and Social Psychology, 44,</u> 862-873.

Newcomb, M. D., & Bentler, P. M. (1986). Loneliness and social support: A confirmatory hierarchical analysis. <u>Personality and Social Psychology Bulletin, 12,</u> 520-535.

Newcomb, M. D., & Bentler, P. M. (1987). The impact of late adolescent substance use on young adult health status and utilization of health services: A structural equation model over four years. <u>Social Science and Medicine, 24,</u> 71-82.

Newcomb, M. D., & Bentler, P. M. (1988). <u>Consequences of adolescent drug use: Impact on the lives of young adults.</u> Beverly Hills: Sage Publications.

Newcomb, M. D., & Chou, C.-P. (1989). Social support among young adults: Latent-variable models of quantity and satisfaction within six life areas. <u>Multivariate Behavioral Research, 24,</u> 233-256.

Newcomb, M. D., Huba, G. J., & Bentler, P. M. (1986). Determinants of sexual and dating behaviors among adolescents. <u>Journal of Personality and Social Psychology, 50,</u> 428-438.

O'Grady, K. E. (1989). Factor structure of the WISC-R. <u>Multivariate Behavioral Research, 24,</u> 177-193.

Olsson, U. (1979). On the robustness of factor analysis against crude classification of the observations. Multivariate Behavioral Research, 14, 485-500.

Olsson, U., Drasgow, F., & Dorans, N. J. (1982). The polyserial correlation coefficient. Psychometrika, 47, 337-347.

Parkerson, J. A., Lomax, R. G., Schiller, D. P., & Walberg, H. J. (1984). Exploring causal models of educational achievement. Journal of Educational Psychology, 76, 638-646.

Parkes, K. R. (1987). Field dependence and the differentiation of neurotic syndromes. In P. Cuttance & R. Ecob (Eds.), Structural modeling by example (pp. 24-50). New York: Cambridge.

Patterson, G. R., & Bank, L. (1989). Some amplifying mechanisms for pathologic processes in families. In M. R. Gunnar & E. Thelen (Eds.), Systems and development: The Minnesota symposium on child psychology, Vol. 22 (pp. 167-209). Hillsdale, NJ: Erlbaum.

Patterson, G. R., & Chamberlain (1988). Treatment process: A problem at three levels. In L. C. Wynne (Ed.), The state of the art in family therapy research: Controversies and recommendations (pp. 189-223). New York: Family Process Press.

Pedhazur, E. (1982). Multiple regression in behavioral research. New York: Holt.

Pfanzagl, J. (1982). Contributions to a general asymptotic statistical theory. New York: Springer.

Pfeifer, A., & Schmidt, P. (1987). LISREL: Die Analyse komplexer strukturgleichungsmodelle. Stuttgart, Germany: Gustav Fischer Verlag.

Piliavin, I., Thornton, C., Gartner, R., & Matsueda, R. (1986). Crime, deterrence and rational choice. American Sociological Review, 51, 101-119.

Plewis, I. (1985). Analyzing change: Measurement and explanation using longitudinal data. Chichester: Wiley.

Poon, W.-Y., & Lee, S.-Y. (1987). Maximum likelihood estimation of multivariate polyserial and polychoric correlation coefficients. Psychometrika, 52, 409-430.

Poon, W.-Y., Lee, S.-Y., Afifi, A. A., & Bentler, P. M. (1989). Analysis of multivariate polytomous variates in several groups via the partition maximum likelihood approach. Computational Statistics & Data Analysis, (1990), 10, 17-27.

Porst, R., Schmidt, P., & Zeifang, K. (1987). Comparisons of subgroups by models with multiple indicators. Sociological Methods & Research, 15, 303-315.

Pratt, J. W., & Schlaifer, R. (1984). On the nature and discovery of structure. Journal of the American Statistical Association, 79, 9-21.

Prochaska, J. O., Velicer, W. F., DiClemente, C. C., & Fava, J. (1988). Measuring process of change: Applications to the cessation of smoking. Journal of Personality and Social Psychology, 56, 520-528.

Punj, G. N., & Staelin, R. (1983). A model of consumer information search behavior for new automobiles. Journal of Consumer Research, 9, 366-380.

Raaijmakers, J. G. W., & Pieters, J. P. M. (1987). Measurement error and ancova: Functional and structural relationship approaches. Psychometrika, 52, 521-538.

Raffalovich, L. E., & Bohrnstedt, G. W. (1987). Common, specific, and error variance components of factor models: Estimation with longitudinal data. Sociological Methods & Research, 15, 385-405.

Rao, C. R. (1948). Large sample tests of statistical hypotheses concerning several parameters with application to problems of estimation. Proceedings of the Cambridge Philosophical Society, 44, 50-57.

Rasmussen, J. L. (1988). Evaluating outlier identification tests: Mahalanobis D squared and Comrey Dk. Multivariate Behavioral Research, 23, 189-202.

Reddy, S. K., & LaBarbera, P. A. (1985). Hierarchical models of attitude. Multivariate Behavioral Research, 20, 451-471.

Reichardt, C. S., & Gollob, H. F. (1986). Satisfying the constraints of causal modeling. In W. M. K. Trochim (Ed.), Advances in quasi-experimental design and analysis (pp. 91-107). San Francisco: Jossey-Bass.

Rice, T., Fulker, D. W., & DeFries, J. C. (1986). Multivariate path analysis of specific cognitive abilities in the Colorado adoption project. Behavior Genetics, 16, 107-125.

Rindskopf, D. (1983). Parameterizing inequality constraints on unique variances in linear structural models. Psychometrika, 48, 73-83.

Rindskopf, D. (1984a). Structural equation models: Empirical identification, Heywood cases, and related problems. Sociological Methods & Research, 13, 109-119.

Rindskopf, D. (1984b). Using phantom and imaginary latent variables to parameterize constraints in linear structural models. Psychometrika, 49, 37- 47.

Rindskopf, D. (1984c). Latent variable models: Applications in education. Contemporary Educational Psychology, 9, 104-121.

Rindskopf, D., & Rose, T. (1988). Some theory and applications of confirmatory second-order factor analysis. Multivariate Behavioral Research, 23, 51-67.

Rubin, D. B. (1976). Inference and missing data. Biometrika, 63, 581-592.

Russell, D. W., McAuley, E., & Tarico, V. (1987). Measuring causal attributions for success and failure: A comparison of methodologies for assessing causal dimensions. Journal of Personality and Social Psychology, 52, 1248-1257.

Saris, W. E., den Ronden, J., & Satorra, A. (1987). Testing structural equation models. In P. Cuttance & R. Ecob (Eds.), Structural modeling by example (pp. 202-220). New York: Cambridge.

Saris, W. E., Satorra, A., & Sörbom, D. (1987). The detection and correction of specification errors in structural equation models. In C. Clogg (Ed.), Sociological Methodology 1987 (pp. 105-129). San Francisco: Jossey Bass.

Saris, W. E., & Stronkhurst, L. H. (1984). Causal modelling in nonexperimental research. Amsterdam: Sociometric Research Foundation.

Saris, W. E., & Van den Putte, B. (1988). True score or factor models, A secondary analysis of the ALLBUS-test-retest data. Sociological Methods & Research, 17, 123-157.

Sato, M. (1987). Pragmatic treatment of improper solutions in factor analysis. Annals of the Institute of Statistical Mathematics, 39, 443-455.

Satorra, A. (1989). Alternative test criteria in covariance structure analysis: A unified approach. Psychometrika, 54, 131-151.

Satorra, A., & Bentler, P. M. (1986). Some robustness properties of goodness of fit statistics in covariance structure analysis. American Statistical Association: Proceedings of the Business & Economic Statistics Section, 549-554.

Satorra, A., & Bentler, P. M. (1988). Scaling corrections for chi-square statistics in covariance structure analysis. Proceedings of the American Statistical Association, 308-313.

Satorra, A., & Bentler, P. M. (1990). Model conditions for asymptotic robustness in the analysis of linear relations. Computational Statistics & Data Analysis, 10, 235-249.

Satorra, A., & Bentler, P. M. (1994). Corrections to test statistics and standard errors in covariance structure analysis. In A. von Eye & C. C. Clogg (Eds.), Latent variables analysis: Applications for developmental research (pp. 399-419). Thousand Oaks, CA: Sage.

Satorra, A., & Saris, W. E. (1985). Power of the likelihood ratio test in covariance structure analysis. Psychometrika, 50, 83-90.

Saxena, K. M. L., & Alam, K. (1982). Estimation of the non-centrality parameter of a chi-squared distribution. The Annals of Statistics, 10, 1012-1016.

Schmitt, N., & Stults, D. M. (1986). Methodology review: Analysis of multitrait-multimethod matrices. Applied Psychological Measurement, 10, 1-22.

Schoenberg, R. (1982). Multiple indicator models: Estimation of unconstrained construct means and their standard errors. Sociological Methods & Research, 10, 421-433.

Sekuler, R., Wilson, H. R., & Owsley, C. (1984). Structural modeling of spatial vision. Vision Research, 24, 689-700.

Shapiro, A. (1983). Asymptotic distribution theory in the analysis of covariance structures. South African Statistical Journal, 17, 33-81.

Shapiro, A. (1985a). Asymptotic equivalence of minimum discrepancy function estimators to GLS estimators. South African Statistical Journal, 19, 73-81.

Shapiro, A. (1985b). Asymptotic distribution of test statistics in the analysis of moment structures under inequality constraints. Biometrika, 72, 133-144.

Shapiro, A. (1986). Asymptotic theory of overparameterized structural models. Journal of the American Statistical Association, 81, 142-149.

Shapiro, A. (1987). Robustness properties of the MDF analysis of moment structures. South African Journal, 21, 39-62.

Shapiro, A., & Browne, M. W. (1983). On the investigation of local identifiability: A counterexample. Psychometrika, 48, 303-304.

Shapiro, A., & Browne, M. W. (1987). Analysis of covariance structures under elliptical distributions. Journal of the American Statistical Association, 82, 1092-1097.

Sidanius, J. (1988). Political sophistication and political deviance: A structural equation examination of context theory. Journal of Personality and Social Psychology, 55, 37-51.

Silverman, R. A., & Kennedy, L. W. (1985). Loneliness, satisfaction and fear of crime: A test for nonrecursive effects. Canadian Journal of Criminology, 27, 1-12.

Silvia, E. S. M., & MacCallum, R. C. (1988). Some factors affecting the success of specification searches in covariance structure modeling. Multivariate Behavioral Research, 23, 297-326.

Smith, D. A., & Patterson, E. B. (1984). Applications and generalization of MIMIC models to criminological research. Journal of Research in Crime and Delinquency, 21, 333-352.

Sobel, M. E. (1982). Asymptotic confidence intervals for indirect effects in structural equation models. In S. Leinhardt (Ed.), Sociological Methodology 1982 (pp. 290-312). San Francisco: Jossey Bass.

Sobel, M. E. (1986). Some new results on indirect effects and their standard errors in covariance structure models. In N. B. Tuma (Ed.), Sociological Methodology 1986 (pp. 159-186). Washington, DC: American Sociological Association.

Sobel, M. E. (1987). Direct and indirect effects in linear structural equation models. Sociological Methods & Research, 16, 155-176.

Sobel, M. E., & Arminger, G. (1986). Platonic and operational true scores in covariance structure analysis. Sociological Methods & Research, 15, 44-58.

Sobel, M. E., & Bohrnstedt, G. W. (1985). Use of null models in evaluating the fit of covariance structure models. In N. B. Tuma (Ed.), Sociological Methodology 1985 (pp. 152-178). San Francisco: Jossey Bass.

Sörbom, D. (1974). A general method for studying differences in factor means and factor structures between groups. British Journal of Mathematical and Statistical Psychology, 27, 229-239.

Sörbom, D. (1978). An alternative to the methodology for analysis of covariance. Psychometrika, 43, 381-396.

Sörbom, D. (1982). Structural equation models with structured means. In K. G. Jöreskog & H. Wold (Eds.), Systems under indirect observation: Causality, structure, prediction. I (pp. 183-195). Amsterdam: North-Holland.

Speckart, G., & Bentler, P. M. (1982). Application of attitude-behavior models to varied content domains. Academic Psychology Bulletin, 4, 453-466.

Spirtes, P., Scheines, R., & Glymour, C. (1990). Simulation studies of the reliability of computer-aided model specification using the TETRAD II, EQS, and LISREL programs. Sociological Methods & Research, 19, 3-66. (With discussion)

Stanislaw, H., & Brain, P. F. (1983). The systemic response of male mice to differential housing: A path-analytic approach. Behavioural Processes, 8, 165-175.

Steiger, J. H. (1988). Aspects of person-machine communication in structural modelling of correlations and covariances. Multivariate Behavioral Research, 23, 281-290.

Steiger, J. H., & Browne, M. W. (1984). The comparison of interdependent correlations between optional linear composites. Psychometrika, 49, 11-24.

Steiger, J. H., Shapiro, A., & Browne, M. W. (1985). On the multivariate asymptotic distribution of sequential chi-square statistics. Psychometrika, 50, 253-264.

Stein, J. A., Newcomb, M. D., & Bentler, P. M. (1988). Structure of drug use behaviors and consequences among young adults: Multitrait-multimethod assessment of frequency, quantity, work site, and problem substance use. Journal of Applied Psychology, 73, 595-605.

Stelzl, I. (1986). Changing a causal hypothesis without changing the fit: Some rules for generating equivalent path models. Multivariate Behavioral Research, 21, 309-331.

Stone, C. A. (1985). CINDESE: Computing indirect effects and their standard errors. Educational and Psychological Measurement, 45, 601-606.

Sullivan, J. L., & Feldman, S. (1979). Multiple indicators: An introduction. Beverly Hills: Sage.

Tanaka, J. S. (1984). Some results on the estimation of covariance structure models. Ph.D. Thesis, University of California, Los Angeles.

Tanaka, J. S. (1987). "How big is enough?": Sample size and goodness of fit in structural equation models with latent variables. Child Development, 58, 134-146.

Tanaka, J. S., & Bentler, P. M. (1983). Factorial invariance of premorbid social competence across multiple populations of schizophrenics. Multivariate Behavioral Research, 18, 135-146.

Tanaka, J. S., & Bentler, P. M. (1985). Quasi-likelihood estimation in asymptotically efficient covariance structure models. American Statistical Association: 1984 Proceedings of the Social Statistics Section (pp. 658-662).

Tanaka, J. S., & Huba, G. J. (1985). A fit index for covariance structure models under arbitrary GLS estimation. British Journal of Mathematical and Statistical Psychology, 38, 197-201.

Tanaka, J. S., & Huba, G. J. (1987). Assessing the stability of depression in college students. Multivariate Behavioral Research, 22, 5-19.

Tanaka, J. S., Panter, A. T., Winborne, W. C., & Huba, G. J. (1990). Theory testing in personality and social psychology with structural equation models: A primer in 20 questions. Review of Personality and Social Psychology, Vol. 11.

Ten Houten, W. D., Walter, D. A., Hoppe, K. D., & Bogen, J. E. (1987). Alexithymia and the split brain. Psychotherapy and Psychosomatics, 47, 1-10.

Thornton, A., Alwin, D. F., & Camburn, D. (1983). Causes and consequences of sex-role attitudes and attitude change. American Sociological Review, 48, 211-227.

Tucker, L. R, & Lewis, C. (1973). A reliability coefficient for maximum likelihood factor analysis. Psychometrika, 38, 1-10.

Tyler, D. E. (1982). Radial estimates and the test for sphericity. Biometrika, 69, 429-436.

Tyler, D. E. (1983). Robustness and efficiency properties of scatter matrices. Biometrika, 70, 411-420.

Vale, C. D., & Maurelli, V. A. (1983). Simulating multivariate nonnormal distributions. Psychometrika, 48, 465-471.

Van Montfort, K. (1989). Estimating in structural models with non-normal distributed variables: Some alternative approaches. Ph.D. Thesis, University of Leiden, Leiden.

Van Praag, B. M. S., de Leeuw, J., & Kloeck, T. (1986). The population-sample decomposition approach to multivariate estimation methods. Applied Stochastic Models and Data Analysis, 2, 99-119.

Van Praag, B. M. S., Dijkstra, T. K., & Van Velzen, J. (1985). Least-squares theory based on general distributional assumptions with an application to the incomplete observations problem. Psychometrika, 50, 25-36.

Wald, A. (1943). Tests of statistical hypotheses concerning several parameters when the number of observations is large. Transactions of the American Mathematical Society, 54, 426-482.

Waternaux, C. M. (1984). Principal components in the nonnormal case: The test of equality of q roots. Journal of Multivariate Analysis, 14, 323-335.

Weng, L.-J., & Bentler, P. M. (1987). Linear structural equation modeling with dependent observations. Proceedings of the Social Statistics Section, American Statistical Association, 498-500.

Werts, C. E., Rock, D. A., & Grandy, J. (1979). Confirmatory factor analysis applications: Missing data problems and comparison of path models between populations. Multivariate Behavioral Research, 14, 199-213.

Wesselman, A. M. (1987). The population-sample decomposition method: A distribution-free estimation technique for minimum distance parameters. Ph.D. thesis, Erasmus University, Rotterdam.

Wheaton, B. (1987). Assessment of fit in overidentified models with latent variables. Sociological Methods & Research, 16, 118-154.

Wheaton, B., Muthén, B., Alwin, D. F., & Summers, G. F. (1977). Assessing reliability and stability in panel models. In D. R. Heise (Ed.), Sociological methodology 1977 (pp. 84-136). San Francisco: Jossey Bass.

White, H. (1984). Asymptotic theory for econometricians. Orlando: Academic.

Widaman, K. F. (1985). Hierarchically nested covariance structure models for multitrait-multimethod data. Applied Psychological Measurement, 9, 1-26.

Wiley, D. E. (1973). The identification problem for structural equation models with unmeasured variables. In A. S. Goldberger & O. D. Duncan (Eds.), Structural equation models in the social sciences (pp. 69-83). New York: Seminar.

Williams, L. J., & Hazer, J. T. (1986). Antecedents and consequences of satisfaction and commitment in turnover models: A reanalysis using latent variable structural equation models. Journal of Applied Psychology, 71, 219-231.

Williams, R., & Thomson, E. (1986). Normalization issues in latent variable modeling. Sociological Methods & Research, 15, 24-43, 64-68.

Windle, M., Barnes, G. M., & Welte, J. (1989). Causal models of adolescent substance use: An examination of gender differences using distribution-free estimators. Journal of Personality and Social Psychology, 56, 132-142.

Wolfle, L. M., & Ethington C. A. (1985). SEINE: Standard errors of indirect effects. Educational and Psychological Measurement, 45, 161-166.

Wood, R., & Bandura, A. (1989). Impact of conceptions of ability on self-regulatory mechanisms and complex decision making. Journal of Personality and Social Psychology, 56, 407-415.

Wong, S.-K., & Long, J. S. (1987). Parameterizing nonlinear constraints in models with latent variables. Unpublished manuscript, Washington State University.

Wothke, W., & Browne, M. W. (1990). The direct product model for the MTMM matrix parameterized as a second order factor analysis model. Psychometrika, 55, 255-262.

Zantra, A. J., Guarnaccia, C. A., & Reich, J. W. (1988). Factor structure of mental health measures for older adults. Journal of Consulting and Clinical Psychology, 56, 514-519.

INDEX

APPENDIX I

NEW BLOCK FEATURE OF THE LM TEST

The LM test, or Lagrange Multiplier test, is a test designed to evaluate the statistical necessity of one or more restrictions on a model. The evaluated restrictions tend to be: whether a parameter that has been fixed to a given value is appropriately fixed or might better be left free to estimate; and whether an equality restriction is appropriate, given the data. A discussion of the LM test, and how to use it in EQS, is given in Chapter 6. This appendix documents a new feature of the LM test that has been implemented in the Windows, EM-386, Unix, and Mac versions of EQS.

Variables used in structural modeling often can be ordered implicitly or explicitly along a time dimension. For example, data may be gathered in three annual waves. In such a case one can make a strong *a priori* assumption that any causal processes to be specified among the variables should also be ordered in time. This means that no "backward in time" causal paths should be permitted. If the waves of measurement occur at T_1, T_2, and T_3, then only paths of the type $T_1 \rightarrow T_2$, $T_2 \rightarrow T_3$, and $T_1 \rightarrow T_3$ would be appropriate. A backward path of the type $T_2 \rightarrow T_1$ would not be appropriate.

The BLOCK feature of the LM test is designed to assure that backward paths are eliminated from the LM test. As a result, nonsense paths are avoided, and much larger sets of restrictions can be evaluated at the same time. When there are 3 periods of measurement, we say that the variables can be grouped into 3 blocks.

To implement this feature, three commands must also be used at the same time in the /LMTEST section of the program setup: SET, BLOCK, and LAG.

1.   SET.   This is the standard command of the LM test. It specifies submatrices of parameter matrices to be investigated by the LM test. In simple applications of the LM test, you can leave it out so that default matrices are chosen for the LM test. When SET is used with the BLOCK feature, however, no default submatrices will be chosen, and those matrices desired for analysis must be stated. For example, SET = GVF; refers to the VF subpart of the Gamma matrix, i.e. regression coefficients for dependent Vs on independent Fs. Please see p. 135 for more detail on the SET specification.

2.   BLOCK. The BLOCK command permits you to group variables into blocks. It also partitions the matrices specified in SET into smaller submatrices for analysis, then specifies the direction of possible paths. In addition, it specifies possible covariance linkages among variables to be included or eliminated.

Only V and F types of variables can be listed; the program will search for E and D types of variables and group them appropriately based on their correspondence to V and F variables. BLOCK will group together into a single block all of the V and F variables that are listed in a statement, whether the variables are listed individually or included in a sequence via a TO convention. When listed separately, each variable must be separated from other variables by a comma. Each block must be identified by a pair of parentheses ( ).

If there are to be several blocks of variables, each set must be surrounded by parentheses and a comma must separate the blocks. So, for example: BLOCK = (V1,V2,V3,F1), (V4,V5,V6,F2), (V7 TO V9, F3); creates three blocks of variables corresponding, for example, to three measurement times. V1-V3 and F1 are in the first block. V4-V6 and F2 are in the second block. V7-V9 and F3 are in the third block. The listing sequence of the blocks indicates the directional sequence in which paths are permitted to be evaluated, i.e., only forward paths or covariances will be analyzed. (If you want to shift the direction of the paths, you must reverse the sequence listing of the blocks.) Still greater control is made possible by the LAG command.

3. **LAG.** The LAG specification defines the "time" lag desired for paths between variables in the LM test. Possible values are LAG = 0; up to LAG = *b-1*, where *b* is the number of blocks created by the block statement. LAG = 0 means that only variables within the same block will be selected; with 3 blocks, there would be 3 possible sets of within-block paths or covariances to evaluate. With LAG = 1; only paths or covariances across adjacent blocks would be evaluated, for example, from T_1 to T_2 and from T_2 to T_3. If you wanted to study the cross-block effects from T_1 to T_3, you would write LAG = 2;. In typical practice, one might consider only LAG = 0; in one analysis, LAG = 1; in another analysis, and so on. However, several lags can also be specified simultaneously, for example, LAG = 1,2,4;. When LAG is not specified, a default is implemented, which is ALL, i.e. 0,1, up to *b-1*.

Examples of the directional blocking feature are as follows:

/LMTEST
      BLOCK = (V1,V7,V9,F1), (V2,V3), (F2,V4,V5,V6), (F3,V10 TO V15);
      SET = BFF, BVV;
      LAG = 1;

In this example, there are 4 blocks, and only paths between adjacent blocks will be evaluated. Paths are to be of the type involving regression of dependent Vs on other dependent Vs, and dependent Fs on other dependent Fs.

/LMTEST
      BLOCK = (V1 TO V5), (V6 TO V10), (V11 TO V15);
      SET = PEE;
      LAG = 0;

In this example, correlated errors are evaluated, but only covariances within blocks are to be searched. If LAG = 1; had been used instead, only cross-time covariances with lag one would have been evaluated.

APPENDIX II

NEW RETEST FEATURE

The most recent versions of EQS (Windows, EM-386, Unix, and Mac) have incorporated a new feature that can be very practical in saving computer time and aiding program convergence of multiple job runs. This feature is implemented in the /PRINT section of the job file.

When specified, RETEST takes the final parameter estimates from a completed EQS run and inserts these into a new file that can be submitted, with only minor modifications, for another EQS run. Specifically, new /EQUATION, /VARIANCE, and /COVARIANCE sections are created that contain the optimal parameter estimates from the just-completed run. These sections can be used in a new run. If a previous run took many iterations to converge, and each iteration takes a lot of computing time, the next run that can be made with this feature will almost certainly converge much more rapidly than the previous run, even if a reasonable number of model adjustments (e.g. dropping parameters or adding parameters) are made. On big jobs, the savings in computational time can be substantial.

RETEST is implemented by a statement in the PRINT section as follows:

/PRINT
       RETEST = 'output.eqs';

where "output.eqs" is the name of a new file that is to be used in the future as an input file to the EQS run. When such a specification is given, EQS does the following:

1.   Puts the file that was used as the input file for the current run at the beginning section of output.eqs.

2.   Puts new /EQUATION, /VARIANCE, and /COVARIANCES sections, based on final optimal parameter estimates, into output.eqs, following the current input file.

The newly created output.eqs must then be edited to delete parts of the file that are obsolete, and to update the model in the desired way. For example, the /TITLE may need to be changed. The /SPECIFICATION section may be perfectly all right, or may need to be modified. The old /EQU, /VAR, and /COV sections and the /END commands, and some intermediate lines created where the new output joins the old output file, must typically be completely removed. This is usually easily done with the block-delete feature of an editor. Other sections, such as /LMTEST, may also need to be modified to be appropriate to the current run. *If RETEST was used in the previous run, the file name that was used must be updated, or the old file will be written over.* As usual, the file to be submitted for an EQS run must end with /END.

AUTOMATIC MODEL MODIFICATION IN RETEST FILE

The Windows, Unix and Mac versions of EQS permit RETEST to be implemented in such a way that model modifications suggested in the previous run are automatically included in the new model file created by RETEST. If the LM test and W test have yielded meaningful information in the previous run, then incorporating their test results into the new model will be meaningful. However, if the LM test and W test have yielded some nonsense information, then the model setup created by RETEST must be edited to eliminate this nonsense. *It is the user's responsibility to assure that this advanced option is used with great care.*

Automatic model modification will make sense when the parameters tested by the LM test and/or the W test are theoretically meaningful, and their inclusion or deletion from the model can be well-justified from a substantive point of view. In that case, results based on the LM test will suggest parameters to add to a model that are both theoretically meaningful and statistically necessary, and it is entirely appropriate that such parameters be added to the model. Similarly, results based on the W test will suggest parameters that, although theoretically interesting, can be trimmed from the model due to lack of their statistical necessity. If these tests are thus performed on meaningful parameters, carrying forward the results to the new model automatically can save a substantial amount of model setup time.

The LM test results can be carried forward to the new model by adding two statements to the /PRINT section as illustrated next.

/PRINT
        RETEST = 'output.eqs'; LMTEST = YES;

The LMTEST option must accompany the RETEST specification. The default LMTEST = NO; is assumed without the above statement. The resulting action is that all of the parameters that were found to be statistically significant in the multivariate LM test will be added in the appropriate sections of the model setup created by RETEST. That is, variances, covariance, or predictor terms in equations may be added automatically. *The newly added parameters can be recognized in the file because only these parameters will have no start value.* RETEST uses the previous run's final estimates as start values in the new file; but newly added parameters will not have such start values. They will appear with only a "*". Thus all of the newly added parameters can be easily scanned. *They must be scanned for meaningfulness.*

If the LM test is used primarily for exploration of potential missing parameters, where many of the parameters may be uninterpretable (e.g., a coefficient that represents a causal path going backward in time), these uninterpretable parameters also will get incorporated into the new model setup if they were statistically significant. Obviously, it is imperative that such nonsense parameters be edited out of the newly-created file.

The W test results will get carried forward in a similar manner in the /PRINT section, as follows.

/PRINT
        RETEST = 'output.eqs'; WTEST = YES;

WTEST in the /PRINT section must be accompanied by a RETEST statement. A consequence of use of this specification is that parameters found to be nonsignificant by the W test will be eliminated from the new model setup, in the following sense. *The newly dropped parameters do appear in the file, but they can be located in the model setup as follows: 1) there is no "*" next to the parameter, and 2) the fixed start value of the parameter is 0.* Parameters that have a fixed zero weight, of course, do not contribute to the model. If desired, they can be edited out of the file, but this is not necessary. In the absence of WTEST =YES; the assumption is that "NO" is intended.

A danger in automatically dropping parameters is that variances of residual variables (Es, Ds) may be nonsignificant and hence may be suggested to be dropped. In general, it does not make sense to remove such parameters, even if the variances vanish. For example, variances may not vanish in other, similar models. It is suggested that the NOFIX option in the W test be used to avoid dropping of residual variances or any other parameters that are considered crucial to be left free. If a parameter is mistakenly suggested to be dropped, all that needs to be done is that a "*", perhaps with a start value, be added to the parameter in the new file.

OPTIONAL /WTEST SETUP IN RETEST FILE

There are times when it is desirable to have a complete listing of the free parameters in a model run. This can be accomplished with the new WPAR print feature. *This feature must be used with the RETEST option.* WPAR refers to Wald (test) parameters. The parameters are listed in the output file created under RETEST using the double label convention of the EQS program (see p. 60). If desired, the value of the final parameter estimates, as computed in the run, can also be obtained. When both the parameter names and the estimates are required, the option is specified as

/PRINT
    RETEST = 'output.eqs'; WPAR = YES;

This produces the double-label listing of the parameters, as well as the associated estimated values, in the last section of the designated RETEST file. Each parameter is printed after the headings /WTEST and APRIORI in the illustrative format (V1,F1): 0.8925, giving the double label followed by the estimate.

At least two purposes can be envisioned for the use of the WPAR option. First, the resulting listing and estimates can be moved from the file into a word processing program for use in a report or a table. Second, a complete /WTEST setup is created that can be used as is, if desired, or modified in some way to provide a desired W test in the next run. See Appendix III for a discussion of the use of nonzero constants in the /WTEST.

If the final estimates are not desired, /PRINT can be activated with WPAR = NO;. Then, if RETEST is active, the double-label parameter names are printed in the file created by RETEST, and the optimal estimates are omitted.

APPENDIX III

NEW /PRINT AND /WTEST FEATURES

The Windows, EM-386, Unix, and Mac versions of EQS contain several new print control features as well as two extensions of the W test.

/PRINT

The default line length in an EQS output file has 132 columns. In new releases of EQS, jobs that are run interactively have a default line length of 80 columns, and those that are run as batch jobs have a default line size of 132 columns. These defaults, which hold for the screen and printed page, can be modified. Output in an 80 column format for a batch run can be obtained as follows.

/PRINT
    LINESIZE = 80;

An 80 column output format may be desirable for scanning output on a printed page. Similarly, LINESIZE = 132; creates 132 column output.

/WTEST

As described in Chapter 6, the W test can evaluate whether free parameters are significantly different from zero. The /WTEST feature of the program has now been extended to permit evaluating whether or not parameters are equal to prespecified constants. The specific parameters involved in such hypotheses must be given: hence, this feature is available only under the APRIORI and HAPRIORI implementations of the W test. The format is as follows:

/WTEST
    APRIORI = (V5,F1): 0.98, (E2,E3): .33, (F2,F2): 1.0;

where the parenthesized expressions represent free parameter names in the usual double-label convention, and the colon ":" indicates that the number which follows represents the hypothesized value of the parameter. Commas separate the various parameters, and a semicolon completes the statement. Note that if a constant is not specified after the double-label parameter name, the W test will be based on a hypothesized constant of zero, as before. Thus if ": 0.98" is not specified for (V5,F1), then (V5,F1) would be tested against 0.0. This implementation works with both HAPRIORI and APRIORI variants of the Wald test. Results from the W test are printed in the usual way, under the heading "WALD TEST ON ** USER SPECIFIED PARAMETER CONSTANTS". In addition, two correlational statistics are reported.

When parameter constants are specified, EQS computes two correlation coefficients to summarize the degree of similarity, across all free parameters, between the hypothesized constants and the final parameter estimates in the current run. These are printed out under the heading "CORRELATION BETWEEN A PRIORI CONSTANTS AND FINAL ESTIMATES IS **" and "RANK CORRELATION BETWEEN A PRIORI CONSTANTS AND FINAL ESTIMATES IS **". The first correlation reported is a standard product-moment correlation; the second is the Spearman rank-order correlation. The rank-order correlation may be preferred for interpretation because it is based on weaker assumptions. Obviously, both of these correlations will be 1.0 if each estimate is exactly equal to its corresponding constant, and will be somewhat less otherwise.

The correlations between constants and current estimates can be used as indicators of similarity between two sets of estimates when the constants in the W test represent previously estimated free parameters. That is, the list of fixed constants given in /WTEST can be based on the final estimates from the previous run's results. These final estimates can be obtained from the new WPAR=YES; feature in /PRINT, used with RETEST, as described in Appendix II. Suppose, for example, that the current model being estimated is identical to the previous model, except that it contains additional parameters. Then the free parameters from the previous model are also free parameters in the current model, and the correlation coefficients summarize the degree of similarity of the final estimates from the two runs. If the correlations are high, the estimates of the common parameters are very similar even if the overall models differ substantially otherwise. Such a result implies that the added parameters in the new model did not distort the pattern of results from the previous model. On the other hand, if the correlations are intermediate to low, substantial changes in estimates have occurred.

It is also possible to use the backward-stepping feature of the W test with constants to locate those free parameters that remain stable under change in model, and those that change substantially. The earliest steps in the W test will be associated with parameter estimates that change little or not at all, while the last steps that reflect significant increments in the W test will be associated with parameters whose estimates change substantially due to model change. In contrast to the correlational index of parameter estimate similarity, the W test uses the estimated sampling variabilities and covariances of the estimates to help gauge the extent of change, and it helps to locate where nontrivial changes in estimates have occurred.

These types of analysis also can be used in comparing results from different samples. Furthermore, specified constants in the W test can be useful to evaluating the power of the model against a specified alternative. Bollen's text (1989, pp. 338-349) provides a good discussion of power, based on the work of Satorra and Saris (1985), and Matsueda and Bielby (1986).

New **PRIORITY** feature. While the HAPRIORI feature of the W test permits tests on the parameters to be sequenced, there are times where one may not be able to provide a logical sequencing of all parameters. Of course, APRIORI accomplishes a test based only on the empirical sequencing of least significant increments to the χ^2 test. Something intermediate, akin to the SEQUENTIAL option in the LM test, is sometimes useful. PRIORITY provides such an option; *it must be used with the APRIORI or HAPRIORI specification*, since it indicates which of two types of parameters in a specified list are to be given priority in the test. One option is that tests based on the null hypothesis that a parameter is zero are to be performed before tests based on the null hypothesis that a parameter is equal to some fixed nonzero value. The reverse priority is also possible. Implementation is as follows.

/WTEST
    PRIORITY = ZERO; APRIORI = (F2,F1):0, (V6,F2):1.0,(E3,E2):0;

indicates to the program to first select from the APRIORI list all parameters that are to be evaluated against the fixed value of zero, perform the W test on these parameters as a group in the specified APRIORI way, and thereafter select from the list the remaining parameters to be tested as a group in the specified way. Thus, (F2,F1) and (E3,E2) would be tested first in the example, and (V6,F2) would only be tested subsequently. Within each group of such parameters, the test will be conducted in the usual APRIORI or HAPRIORI way, in accord with the given specification. In the example, either (F2,F1) or (E3,E2) would enter first, depending on their univariate χ^2 values. If HAPRIORI had been specified, of course (F2,F1) would be entered first.

PRIORITY = NONZERO; is the other alternative. In this case, the W test would give priority to the fixed nonzero constants in the APRIORI or HAPRIORI list of parameters. The parameters associated with nonzero constants would thus be tested first as a group. The parameters associated with zero constants would then be tested subsequently.

The output from this procedure is printed under the usual heading WALD TEST (FOR DROPPING PARAMETERS) in the output file. The additional sentence WALD TEST IS IMPLEMENTED WITH PRIORITY FOR ZERO (or NONZERO) PARAMETERS is printed subsequently. Then, there are two parts to the W test printout. The first part would correspond to the hypotheses given priority; and the second part, to the hypotheses that remain.

The PRIORITY procedure is intended to provide a more useful way to partition the overall χ^2 into components. The final cumulative multivariate χ^2 statistic is, of course, the same no matter what sequence of parameters is chosen for the W test. However, PRIORITY permits evaluating the contribution to the total χ^2 of the tests associated with zero parameters, as well as those associated with nonzero parameters.

APPENDIX IV

NEW CATEGORICAL DATA FEATURE

All versions of EQS now permit the analysis of models that have categorical as well as continuous measured variables, based on theory developed by Drs. Sik-Yum Lee and Wai-Yin Poon, with some assistance by Bentler. The procedures to accomplish this are described in this appendix.

THEORY

It is assumed that any categorical variables that you plan to model are categorized versions of variables that are truly continuous, as well as multivariate normally distributed. This assumption is the same as that made by others in the literature, and it is a strong assumption that may not be appropriate in certain contexts. If it is not an assumption that you wish to make, you should not use this method. At present, there are no good diagnostics available for evaluating this assumption empirically.

When this assumption is true, then the correlations between the underlying variables can be estimated by coefficients known as polychoric and polyserial correlations. The correlation between the underlying variables yielding two categorical variables is known as the polychoric correlation. The correlation between the underlying variables that generate a categorical and a continuous variable is the polyserial correlation.

Structural modeling with such variables proceeds in two major stages.

     1. These correlations are estimated without any concern for the structural model under consideration.
     2. This correlation matrix is then considered to be a function of more basic parameters.

In this program, these parameters are the parameters of the Bentler-Weeks model. A generalized least squares procedure is used to estimate these model parameters, yielding the goodness of fit chi-square test and standard error estimates for the free parameters.

The literature contains several approaches to the estimation of polychoric and polyserial correlations. The statistics used in this program were developed by Lee, S. -Y., Poon, W. -Y., & Bentler, P. M. (1994). Covariance and correlation structure analyses with continuous and polytomous variables. In T. W. Anderson, K. -T. Fang, & I. Olkin (Eds.), *Multivariate analysis and its applications: Vol. 24* (pp. 347-358). Hayward CA: Institute of Mathematical Statistics; and Lee, S. -Y., Poon, W. -Y., & Bentler, P. M. (in press). A two stage estimation of structural equation models with continuous and polytomous variables. *British Journal of Mathematical and Statistical Psychology*. This work is based on prior work of Poon, W. -Y., & Lee, S. -Y. (1987). Maximum likelihood estimation of multivariate polyserial and polychoric correlation coefficients. *Psychometrika, 52,* 409-430, and Lee, S. -Y., Poon, W. -Y., & Bentler, P. M. (1992). Structural equation models with continuous and polytomous variables. *Psychometrika, 57,* 89-105. Technical details cannot be developed in this appendix.

A modification to the Lee-Poon-Bentler approach is used in this program. In their approach, as with related approaches implemented in other programs, a correlation matrix is used as input.

When considering standard models with additive error or unique variances, such as factor analysis or standard latent variable models, the usual approach to setting up models is not appropriate for correlation matrices. The parameters of a correlation structure require nonlinear constraints so that the diagonals of the correlation matrix, all 1, are reproduced exactly. This is difficult to do, so other researchers, as well as Lee-Poon-Bentler, consider the additive unique variances not as free parameters, but rather as functions of the remaining parameters in the model.

This method is convenient computationally, but has the difficulty that one cannot impose standard constraints, such as equality constraints, on the unique variances. Also, it is possible for these variances to be estimated as negative.

In EQS, we use the usual parameterization of standard models. As a result, the typical parameters are free parameters. We impose nonlinear constraints on the parameters so that the resulting matrix is in fact a correlation matrix.

The theory for these constraints was given, for example, in Bentler, P. M., & Lee, S. -Y. (1983). Covariance structures under polynomial constraints: Applications to correlation and alpha-type structural models. *Journal of Educational Statistics, 8*, 207-222, 315-317, and Jamshidian, M., & Bentler, P. M. (1993). A modified Newton method for constrained estimation in covariance structure analysis. *Computational Statistics & Data Analysis, 15*, 133-146.

Of course, the specific application is different from that considered in these previous discussions. You can evaluate whether the constraints have been imposed by checking the diagonal of the residual covariance matrix. If the constraints are not precisely imposed, the chi-square goodness of fit statistic will be too large by the sum of squares of the diagonal residual entries.

IMPLEMENTATION

There are several requirements to run a model with categorical data. First, raw data must be analysed. Second, those variables that are categorical must not have too many categories (in practice, about 5-7 or so maximum, but more are allowed). Third, a reasonably large sample size is highly recommended. A reason for these requirements is that all categorical data methods require the cross-tabulation tables of the categorical variables. These tables will be very sparse if there are too few subjects or too many categories, and hence the computational procedures can easily break down.

To specify a categorical data model, in the /SPECIFICATION section, you must:

1. Indicate which variables are categorical, using a statement such as

CATEGORY = V2,V5;

The abbreviation CAT is sufficient. The program will figure out the scoring of your variables.

2. Indicate the base method that would be used with continuous variables. ME=ML; is recommended. Whenever categorical data models are run, a standard method is first run.

3. Specify that MATRIX = RAW; and point to the external data file using the DATA statement.

As usual, create the model file in accord with the EQS formatting requirements given elsewhere in this **Manual**. Below we shall illustrate this method with a data file called poon.ess that is distributed with the **EQS for Windows** and **EQS for Macintosh** programs. These data represent the scores of 200 subjects on eight variables, and will be modeled by a two factor confirmatory factor analysis model with variables 1-4 being indicators of factor 1, and variables 5-8 being indicators of factor 2. The factor variances are fixed, and the factors can correlate. The key part of the model file should look as follows.

```
/SPECIFICATIONS
!DATA=' C:\EQS\POON.ESS'; VARIABLES=  8; CASES=  200;!Windows already
 METHODS=ML;                                        !knows the data
 CATEGORY=V7,V8;                                    !file
 MATRIX=RAW;
/LABELS
V1=V1; V2=V2; V3=V3; V4=V4; V5=V5;
V6=V6; V7=V7; V8=V8;
/EQUATIONS
V1 =  + *F1  + E1;
V2 =  + *F1  + E2;
V3 =  + *F1  + E3;
V4 =  + *F1  + E4;
V5 =  + *F2  + E5;
V6 =  + *F2  + E6;
V7 =  + *F2  + E7;
V8 =  + *F2  + E8;
/VARIANCES
F1 = 1;
F2 = 1;
E1 = *;
E2 = *;
E3 = *;
E4 = *;
E5 = *;
E6 = *;
E7 = *;
E8 = *;
/COVARIANCES
F2 , F1 = *;
```

Notice that there is nothing remarkable about this setup except for the line CATEGORY = V7,V8; in the /SPECIFICATIONS section. This identifies the variables as categorical variables.

Note: There is one limitation to the current implementation. Consistent with the statistical theory, all measured variables in models with categorical variables must be dependent variables. However, we can trick the theory. If you want to use a measured variable as an independent variable, you can create a dummy factor to represent it. For example, if you want to include V7 in your model as an independent variable, create an equation like V7=F7; and use F7 in the model as if it were V7. Research will be needed to evaluate this procedure.

OUTPUT

By and large, the output from an EQS run with categorical variables follows the output from a run with AGLS. The normal theory method is run first, then the analysis based on categorical variables follows. There are, however some additional sections of output. These come immediately after the listing of the model file in the output.

```
YOUR MODEL HAS SPECIFIED CATEGORICAL VARIABLES
        TOTAL NUMBER OF VARIABLES ARE          8
        NUMBER OF CONTINUOUS VARIABLES ARE     6
        NUMBER OF DISCRETE    VARIABLES ARE    2

        INFORMATION ON DISCRETE VARIABLES
        V7  WITH    3 CATEGORIES
        V8  WITH    3 CATEGORIES
```

The program informs you that it has figured out how many categories your variables have. The category information is used in the computations. Information on the polyserial correlations is presented first, for each of the variables in turn. The estimated thresholds are given first, followed by the covariance and correlation estimates. Standard error estimates also are provided.

RESULTS OF POLYSERIAL PARTITION USING V7 --   3 CATEGORIES

THRESHOLDS

ESTIMATES	STD. ERR
-0.5113	0.0745
0.4319	0.0788

VARIABLE	COVARIANCE	ESTIMATES STD. ERR	CORRELATION	STD. ERR
V 1	0.4161	0.0521	0.4151	0.0520
V 2	0.4451	0.0508	0.4440	0.0507
V 3	0.4967	0.0494	0.4955	0.0493
V 4	0.4290	0.0519	0.4279	0.0517
V 5	0.6192	0.0443	0.6177	0.0442
V 6	0.6369	0.0436	0.6353	0.0435

RESULTS OF POLYSERIAL PARTITION USING V 8 --   3 CATEGORIES

THRESHOLDS

ESTIMATES	STD. ERR
-0.4567	0.0750
0.4988	0.0805

VARIABLE	COVARIANCE	ESTIMATES STD. ERR	CORRELATION	STD. ERR
V 1	0.3818	0.0533	0.3808	0.0532
V 2	0.2660	0.0554	0.2653	0.0553
V 3	0.3563	0.0540	0.3554	0.0538

V 4	0.4397	0.0506	0.4386	0.0504
V 5	0.6228	0.0421	0.6213	0.0420
V 6	0.6737	0.0409	0.6720	0.0408

Information on polychoric correlations is presented next. Again, thresholds are computed and then the polychoric correlation estimates are given.

```
RESULTS OF POLYCHORIC PARTITION
                        AVERAGE THRESHOLDS
            V 7  -0.5044   0.4327
            V 8  -0.4581   0.4855
```

```
POLYCHORIC CORRELATION MATRIX BETWEEN DISCRETE VARIABLES
            V 7       V 8
    V  7   1.000
    V  8   0.583     1.000
```

Following this output, the constructed correlation matrix to be analyzed is presented. Then, the usual normal theory statistics are given in the standard EQS format. While normal theory estimates may be useful, the statistics in the normal theory output cannot be trusted. That is, the chi-square goodness of fit values and z-statistics are in fact not distributed as chi-square and z, respectively.

In the subsequent section, the output for the polychoric/polyserial model are presented. This is titled

GENERALIZED LEAST SQUARES SOLUTION (LEE, POON, AND BENTLER THEORY)

because the statistics implement the theory developed by these authors. The format for the output is exactly that of the AGLS method in EQS, which this **Manual** describes in some detail.